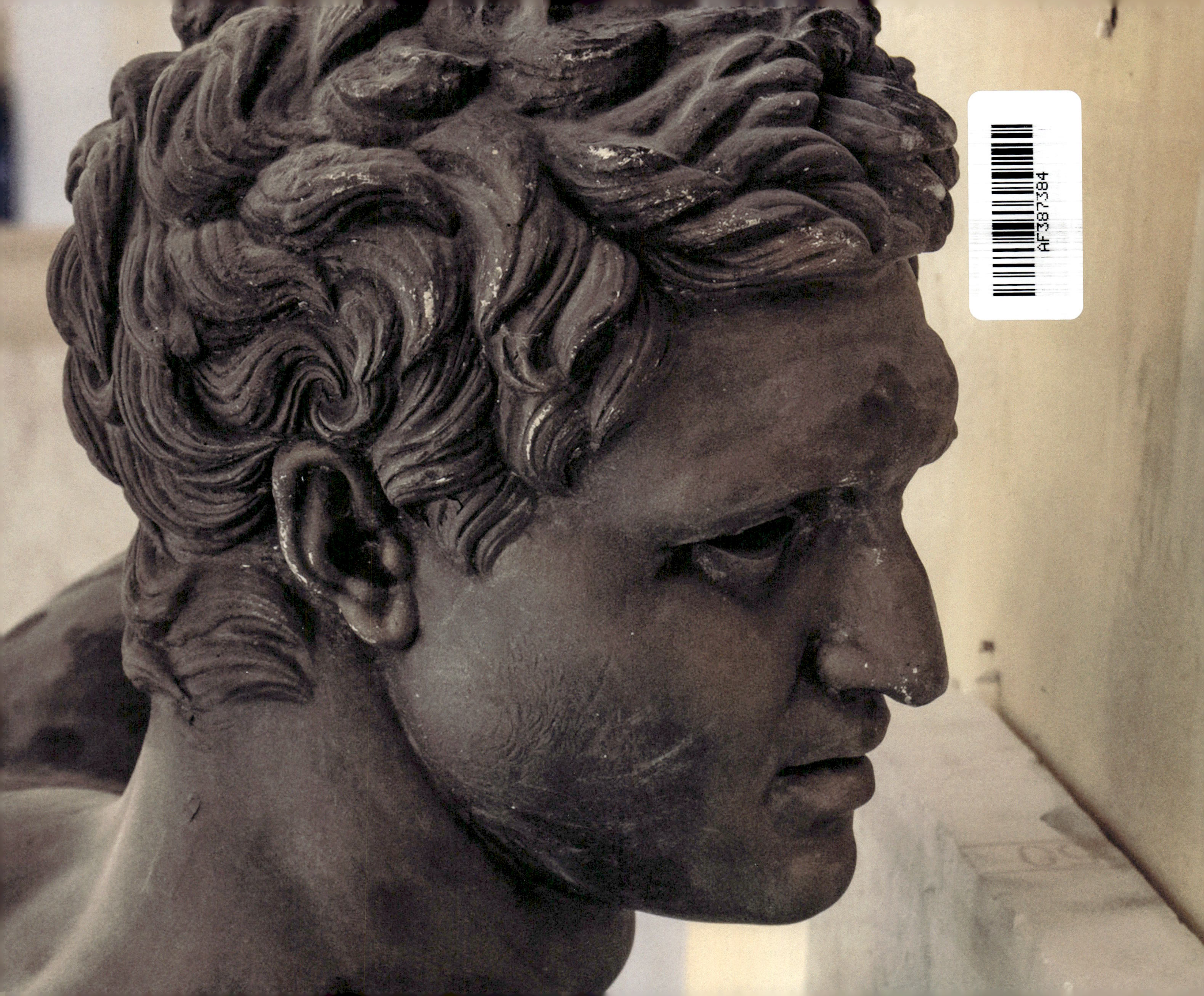
AF387384

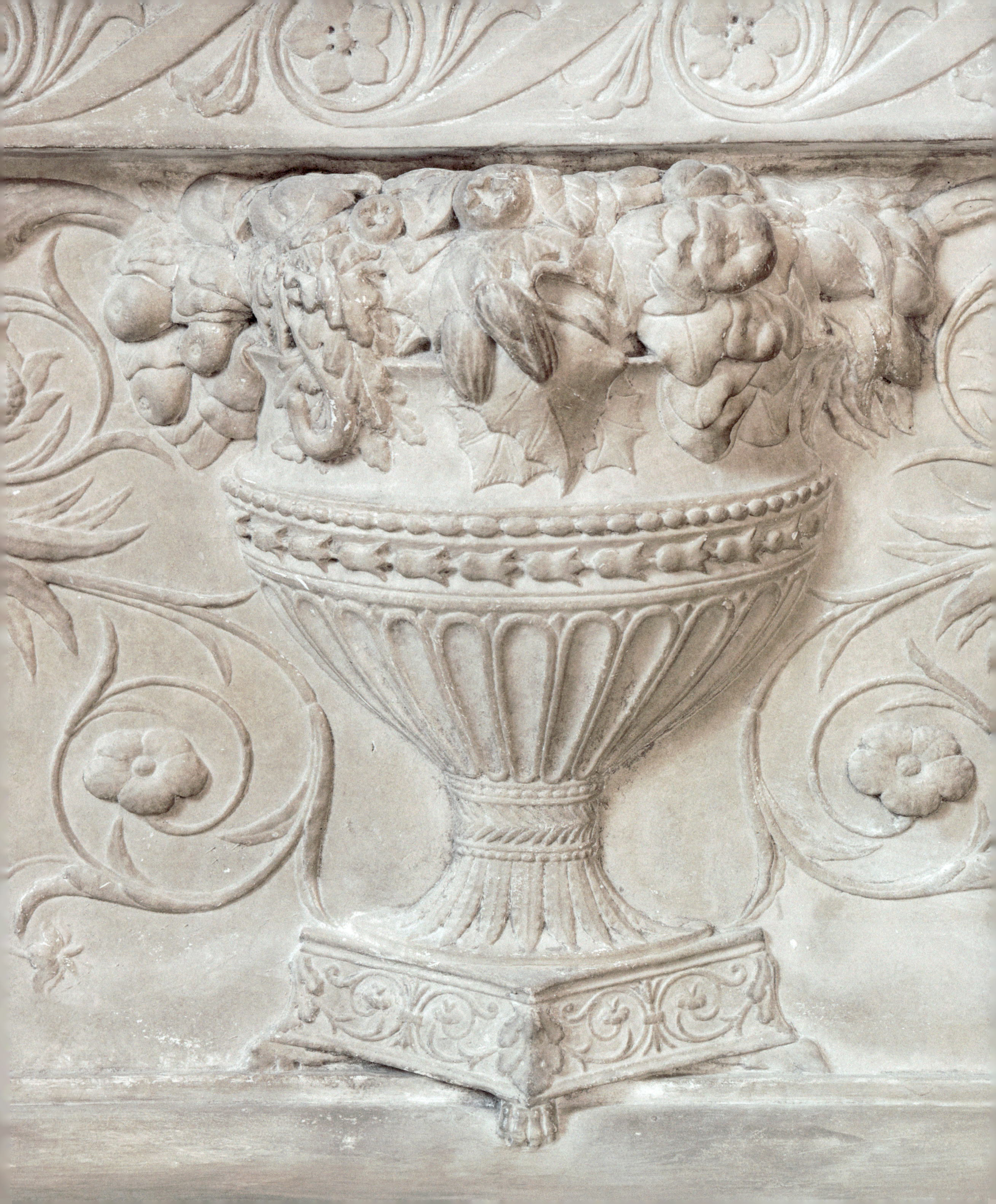

Casting a New Light

Plaster Casts & Cast Collections in Europe and Beyond

Edited by

Miriam Szőcs and Márton Tóth

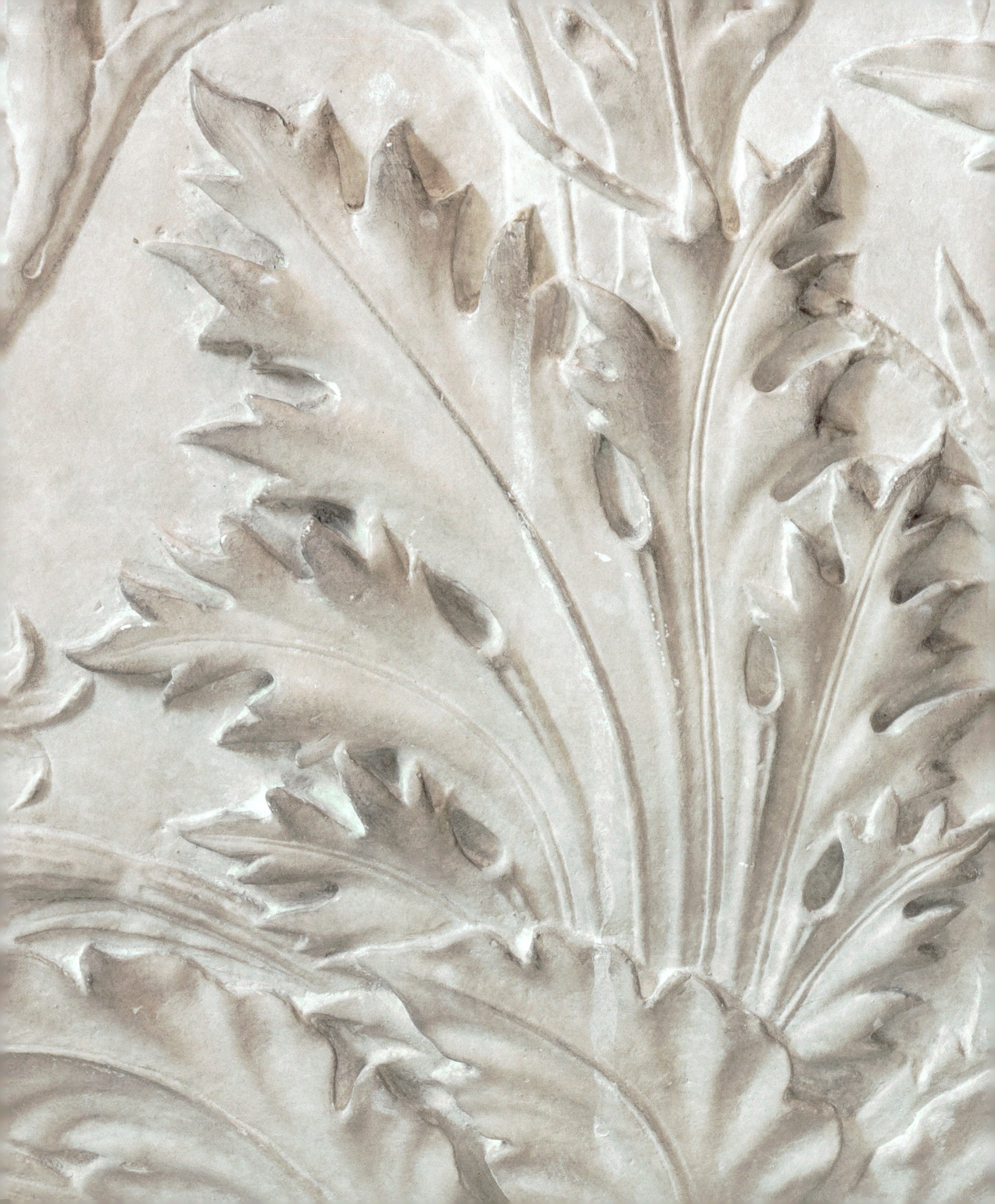

Casting a New Light
Plaster Casts & Cast Collections in Europe and Beyond

The editors would like to dedicate this volume to the memory of Rune Frederiksen (1971–2023).

The volume publishes the papers of the conference *Plaster Casts & Cast Collections across Europe. History and Future* held in the Museum of Fine Arts, Budapest in 24 May 2022. The conference was organised on the occasion of the refurbishment of the plaster cast collection of the Museum of Fine Arts, Budapest, and its exhibition in the Star Fortress in Komárom, opened in the autumn of 2021, and in the visible storage in the newly built National Museum Conservation and Storage Centre in Budapest, the installation of which was finished in 2022.

Editors: Miriam Szőcs, Márton Tóth
Assistant to the editors: Zsófia Vargyas
Copy editor: Noémi Böröczki
Proofreading: Steve Kane
Translation of Lorenz Winkler-Horaček's paper: Sasha Agins
Image processing: Szabolcs Mezei
Photographic credits: Virág Hegyi
Graphic design and pre-press: Szabolcs Mezei
Special thanks to Gellért Áment, László Baán, Enikő Cser, Blanka Cserépy, Marianna Dági, Áron Harasztos, László Nagy, Ágnes Megyeri, Ádám Tarcsi and Annamária Vígh, for their assistance in the realisation of this book.

Publisher: Dr. László Baán General Director
Museum of Fine Arts, Budapest, 2024
ISBN 978-615-6595-23-2
Printed by: EPC Nyomda, Budaörs

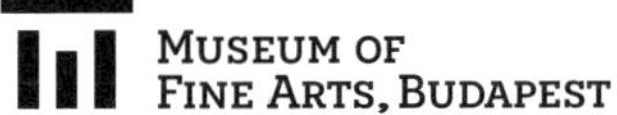

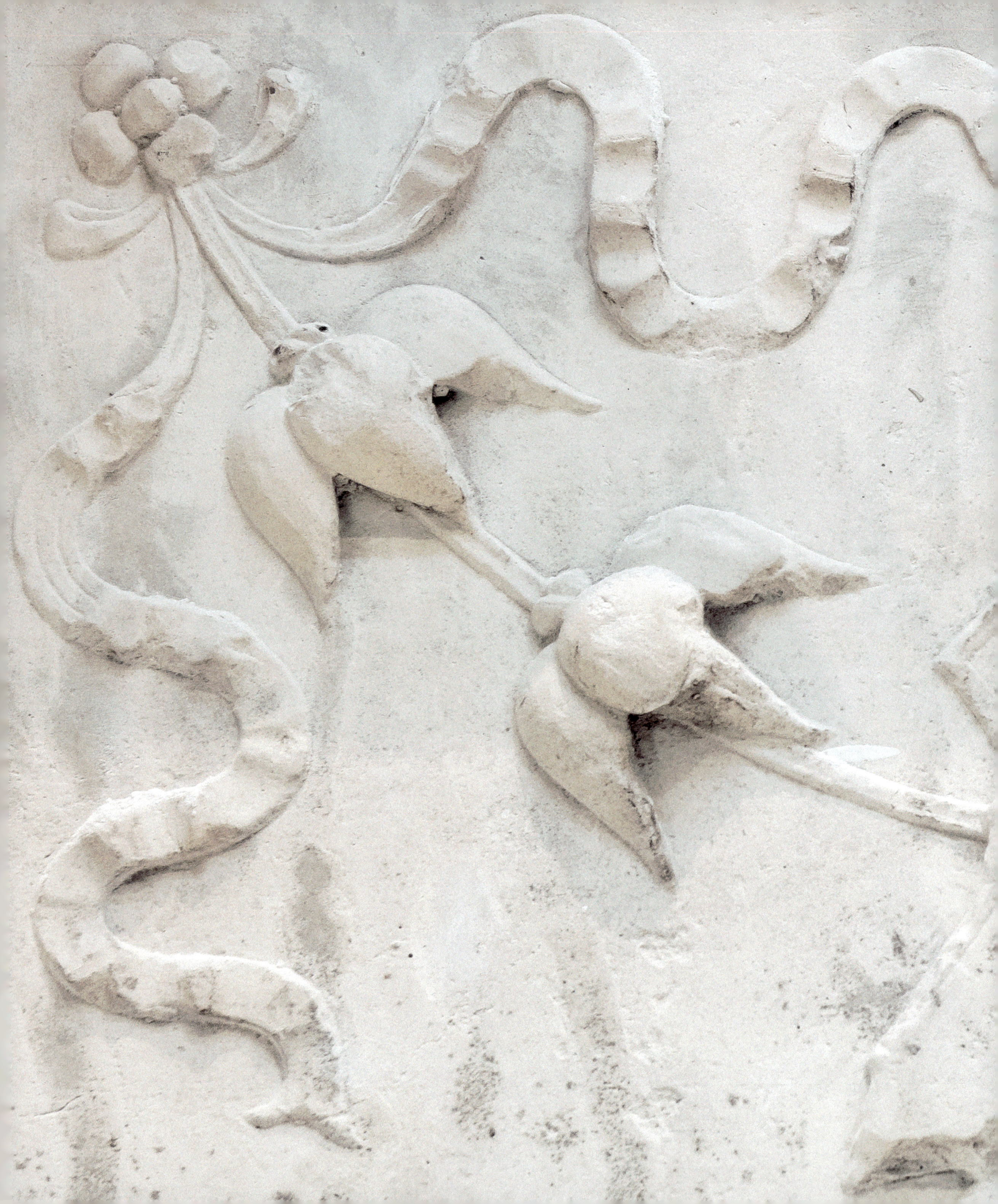

Contents

Foreword   9

Introduction   10

Eckart Marchand
"The best laid schemes …":
The Politics of the Universal Museum and the Vicissitudes of their Plaster Cast Collections
at the Turn of the Twentieth Century   12

Miriam Szőcs
The *Colleoni Monument* and the *Medici Tombs*:
Monumental Renaissance Casts in the Museum of Fine Arts in Budapest   26

Flavia Berizzi
From Northern Italy to Hungary:
Medieval and Renaissance Monumental Casts from the Museo Campi Carlo in Milan
to the Museum of Fine Arts in Budapest   40

Jean-Marc Hofman
Generation and Regeneration of the Cast Collections of the Musée de Sculpture Comparée, Paris   58

Géza Andó and Eszter Süvegh
The Ways of the Casts:
Plaster Casts of Antiquities in Budapest and Kolozsvár (today Cluj-Napoca, Romania)   74

Eszter Hajós-Baku and Beáta Szűts
A Brief History of the Plaster Cast Collection of the Department of Graphics, Form, and Design
at the Budapest University of Technology and Economics   88

Júlia Katona
Nineteenth-Century Constructions and Monument Reconstruction in Hungary
in the Context of Educational Plaster Cast Collections:
A Case Study with Special Focus on the Romanesque Hall of the Museum of Fine Arts, Budapest   106

Rune Frederiksen
The Role of Ancient Plaster Casts in Ancient Art:
The Written Evidence   118

Lorenz Winkler-Horaček
Appreciation and Rejection:
Plaster Casts in the Discourse of Copy and Original. With an Excursus on the *Sleeping Ariadne*
in the Berlin Cast Collection   130

Marjorie (Holly) Trusted
The Making and Meaning of Plaster Casts in the Nineteenth Century:
Their Future in the Twenty-First Century   144

About the Authors   156

Bibliography   158

Abbreviations   174

Illustration Credits   174

Index of Names   176

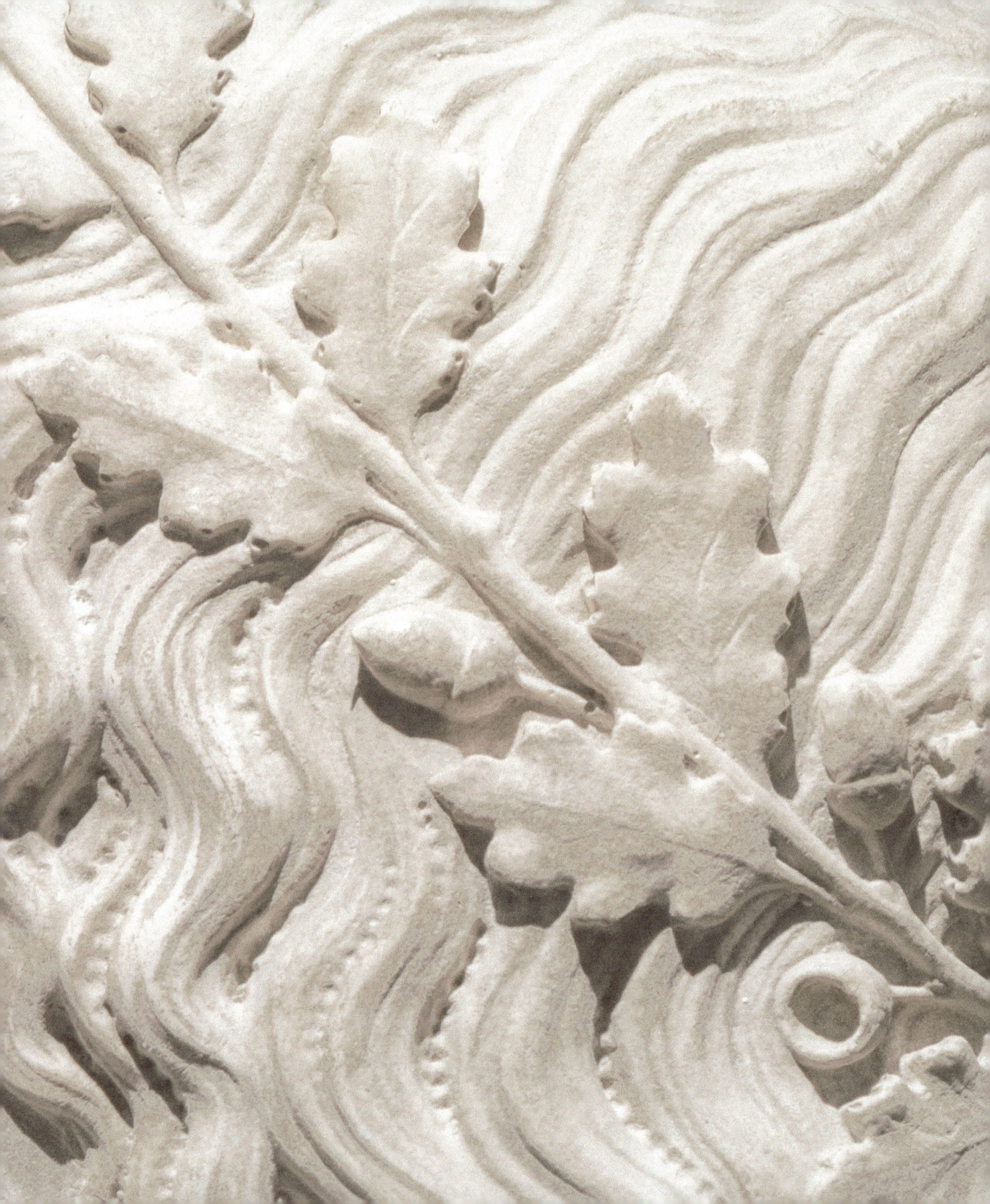

Foreword

In the autumn of 2021, we opened a large plaster cast exhibition in Komárom, a regional city one hundred kilometres northwest of Budapest, presenting a selection of replicas of some of the most renowned sculptures from Classical Antiquity, the Middle Ages, and the Renaissance. The ensemble shown here once formed part of the large plaster cast collection of the Museum of Fine Arts, Budapest, assembled during the first period of the museum's history in the late nineteenth and early twentieth centuries. In line with the European tendencies of the time, the museum's founding leaders decided to present the history of sculpture through copies made of plaster. These plaster casts were originally exhibited in the first decades of the twentieth century in most of the ground floor halls of the museum in Budapest, where they were on display until World War II. Subsequently, the collection of casts in Budapest shared a similar fate to the majority of European and American plaster cast assemblages, in that they suffered decades of neglect. By 2014, our plaster casts, many in a severely damaged state, were kept in storage in the Romanesque Hall of the museum and in Fort Igmánd in Komárom. We then launched a major initiative, carried out as part of the Liget Budapest Project – one of the largest urban cultural developments in Europe – to refurbish our cast collection and to exhibit it as completely as possible. The venue chosen for the redisplay of the cast collection was the Star Fortress, a disused fortification in Komárom. This building formed part of a military complex constructed around the city on both banks of the Danube in the nineteenth century, with four further locations on the Hungarian and the Slovakian sides.

Built between 1850 and 1870 on the site of a fort dating back to the sixteenth century, the Star Fortress was abandoned sometime after World War II, and its condition progressively deteriorated. Before the plaster casts could be installed in this fortification, the historic monument itself had to be renovated. Reconstruction of the Star Fortress also involved adding new spaces to house the exhibits and cater for visitor needs. The casts, meanwhile, were conserved and installed between 2014 and 2021. The result is an outstanding accomplishment in terms of both reconstructing the fortress as a historic monument and rehabilitating the long-ignored collection. The exhibition was also highly significant to the field of art history and museology. Shortly after the project was completed in 2022, the Museum of Fine Arts celebrated this exhibition with an international conference. Held that May, the conference was honoured with the presence of many important scholars invited from Hungary and across Europe. This volume, dedicated to the lecturers at the conference, is intended to express our gratitude to all those who accepted our invitation to share their thoughts, both at the conference and in this publication. We hope that this book will help sustain dialogue about the vital topic of the purpose and future of plaster cast collections, and moreover, that it will lead to further research about this significant segment of art history. The restoration of the plaster cast collection was deeply related to the museum's history, and a heartfelt achievement of the museum itself and of the Liget Budapest Project, and we therefore consider it equally important to support the conversation about casts in the form of a scholarly publication.

Dr. László Baán

General Director of the Museum of Fine Arts, Budapest

Introduction

Refurbishing an entire plaster cast collection after decades of neglect and redisplaying it in completely new sites is a unique opportunity and an immense honour in the life of a curator. The project included not only the restoration of the casts but also a complete reimagining of the arrangement of the works within new exhibition spaces, making it a challenging but also rewarding endeavour. We began the initial planning process at the end of 2013, and we opened the new exhibition of casts in the Star Fortress in Komárom in the autumn of 2021. A smaller part of the museum's historic cast collection

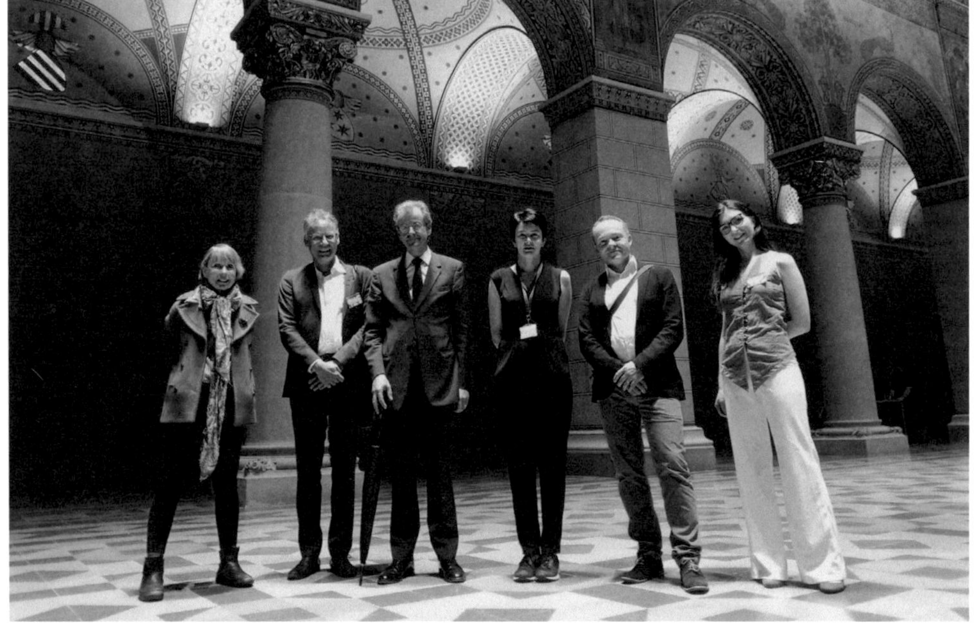

has been re-installed in visible storage in the newly built National Museum Conservation and Storage Centre in Budapest; the installation was completed a year later in 2022. The last period of our work coincided with the Covid-19 pandemic, which also meant that we were working in relative isolation.

The conference initiated and organised in 2022 by the Museum of Fine Arts, Budapest – shortly after finishing the installation in Komárom – gave us the opportunity to start a dialogue with other scholars and curators from Hungary and abroad on this intriguing subject, which has been attracting ever greater interest in recent times. As these plaster casts already have a long history, some of them being unique replicas, several questions inevitably arose, such as how to treat, use and reuse the casts, as well as the legitimate question of whether we should consider them as artworks in their own right. From the moment we first made contact with the possible participants in the conference, we received only warm and positive feedback. Also bearing in mind the funding possibilities of the conference, we decided to invite scholars whose work in this field we already knew and esteemed, and whose publications on this subject we used extensively during our own work on the exhibition and on the catalogue. We were and continue to be deeply grateful to all the scholars who accepted our invitation. The first day of the conference was dedicated to the lectures, while the second day included a trip to Komárom to visit the new exhibition in the Star Fortress. The two days of the event not only offered the possibility to discuss issues related to the plaster casts, but we also had the chance to get to know the participants better. By the second day of the conference, the idea of publishing the conference papers in a volume had been outlined. The enthusiasm shown by the participants guided us throughout our editing work.

Sadly, we must remember Rune Frederiksen, whose passion and interest gave us great motivation from the very beginning, and we never anticipated that we would dedicate this volume to him and to his memory. The devastating news about his unexpected and untimely death reached us while we were still working on this volume, in August 2023. We initially knew him from his publications, such as the volume he co-edited with his friend Eckart Marchand, titled *Plaster Casts: Making, Collecting and Displaying from Classical Antiquity to the Present* (2010), which we used as a handbook. The catalogue of the Ashmolean Museum's cast gallery (Frederiksen and Smith 2013) was also very valuable for our project.

By getting to know him better, we gained a broader view of his diverse interests and scholarly activity. He was Head of Collections at the Ny Carlsberg Glyptotek. Earlier, he had taken part in several archaeological field projects in Denmark, Italy, Greece, Jordan and Cyprus, being intensively involved as Danish director of the excavations at Calydon in Aitolia, Greece (2011–2014) and subsequently as Danish director at the investigations at pre-Hellenistic Sicyon, Greece (2015). During his stay in Budapest, and while working with him on this publication, we were also able to get to know him better personally, experiencing such friendliness and kindness that we will certainly never forget. We hope that with this publication, we will be able to keep his memory in our hearts and minds, and we will integrate at least partially in our own perspectives the zeal he showed towards the different aspects of history, art history, and architecture.

Last but not least, we would like to express our gratitude to the many individuals whose invaluable contributions made this publication possible. First and foremost, we are indebted to the leaders of the Museum of Fine Arts for their generous support both for the conference and for the present volume, especially to General Director László Baán, who fully endorsed the conference from the very first initiative, and to Deputy Director Annamária Vígh and Finance Director Enikő Cser, for their kind assistance with the organisational and financial arrangements.

We also wish to acknowledge the hard work of the team behind the scenes: copy editor Noémi Böröczki; proofreader Steve Kane; Virág Hegyi, manager of the reproduction rights; and Szabolcs Mezei, graphic designer of the book. During our work on this publication, we have benefitted greatly from the assistance of László Nagy, chief archivist of the museum. Furthermore, we are deeply grateful to several staff members of the museum for their help, particularly to Zsófia Vargyas, Blanka Cserépy, Áron Harasztos and Gellért Áment.

It goes without saying that our deepest gratitude extends to each of our authors for their scholarly contributions to the conference and for their supportive acknowledgement of our rehabilitation project. We hope that they are as pleased with the results of this publication as we are.

The Editors

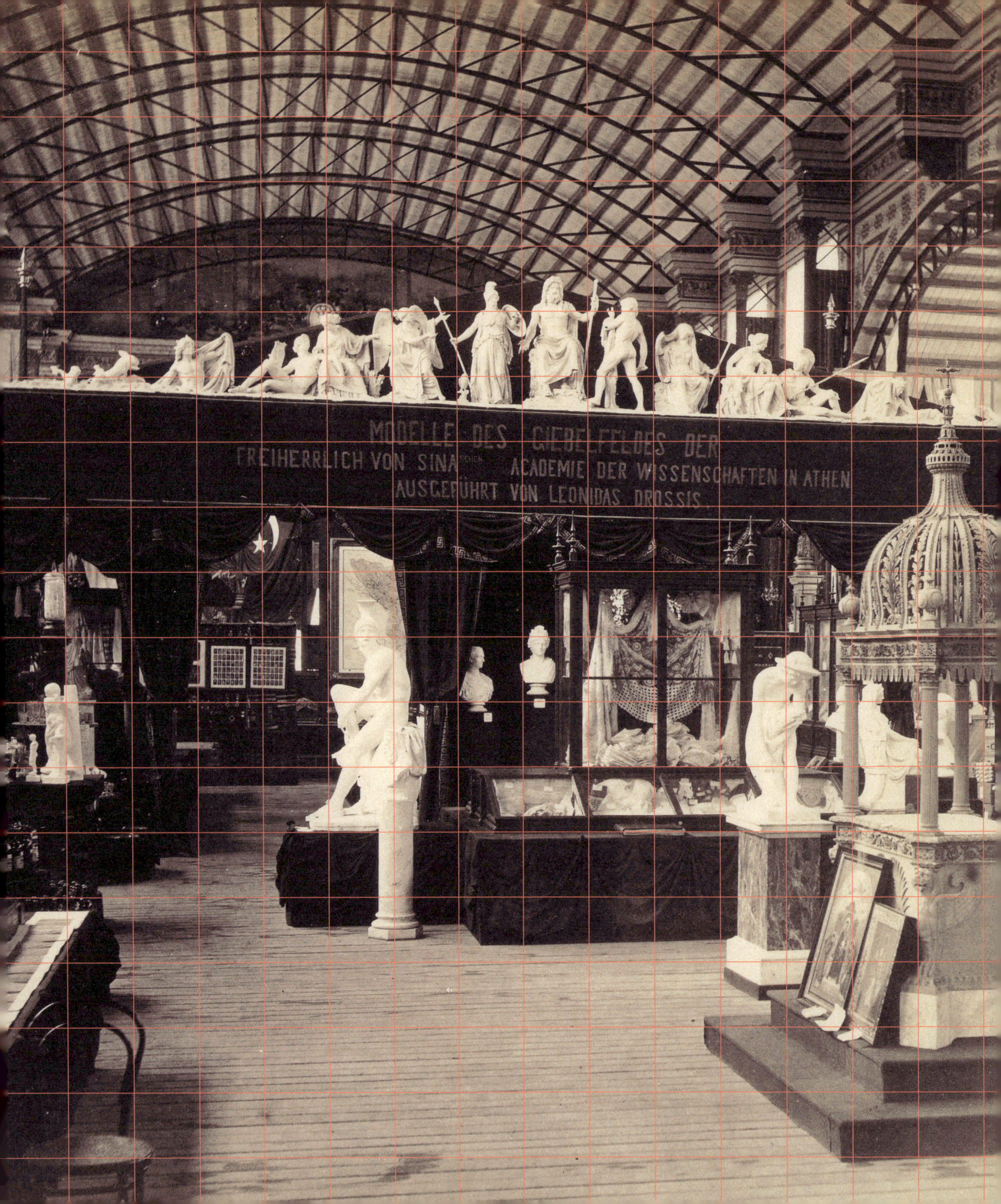
MODELLE DES GIEBELFELDES DER
FREIHERRLICH VON SINA'schen ACADEMIE DER WISSENSCHAFTEN IN ATHEN
AUSGEFÜHRT VON LEONIDAS DROSSIS

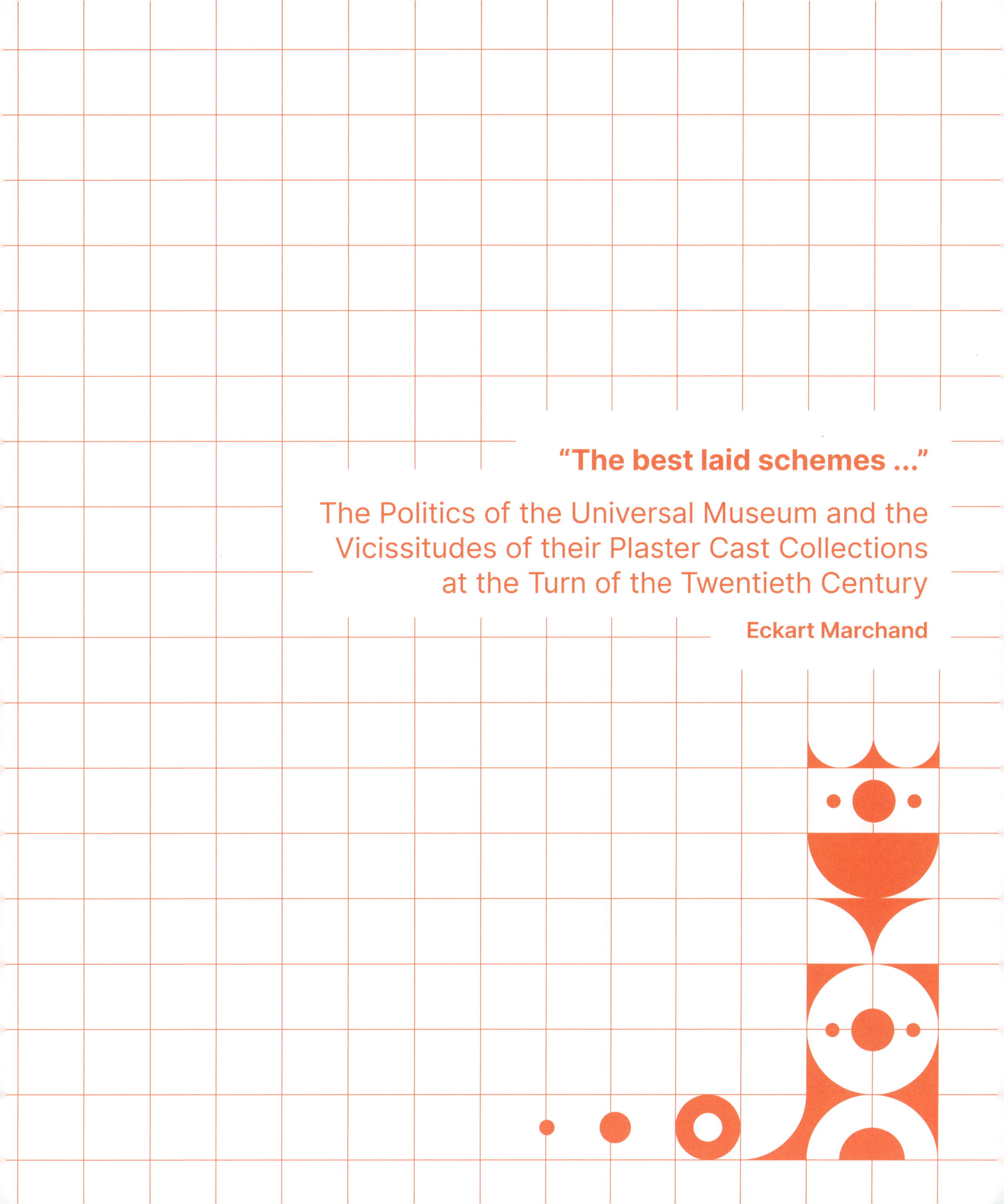

"The best laid schemes ..."

The Politics of the Universal Museum and the Vicissitudes of their Plaster Cast Collections at the Turn of the Twentieth Century

Eckart Marchand

"The best laid schemes …"

The Politics of the Universal Museum and the Vicissitudes of their Plaster Cast Collections at the Turn of the Twentieth Century*

Eckart Marchand

On 17 February 1881, a few weeks before the scheduled opening of the Museo de Reproducciones Artísticas in Madrid, its assistant director, Juan Facundo Riaño, wrote the following words in a letter to the British archaeologist and diplomat Sir Austen Henry Layard: "I hope the new change of government may not affect the interests of the museum. So much money has already been spent upon decorating it that they hardly will think of making use of the building for any other purpose. [U]nfortunately it has not yet been opened and the first thing the architect has done has been to send away almost all the workmen, who were busy painting the pedestals, etc. I am happy to say I have nothing to do with the building itself which saves me from many worries."[1]

The passage illustrates the precariousness of many projects of museums of plaster casts and other copies at a time which is commonly seen as the heyday of such collections. From the 1870s to 1910, across Europe and the Americas, a number of cast collections were conceived as crucial parts of what were referred to as "Universal Museums".[2] These museums varied considerably, but what they all had in common was the aim to teach the history of art, if not "western civilization", through the representation of what were believed to be the most important works of the most important periods in art history. To do so, many Universal Museums relied in part, or entirely, on copies.

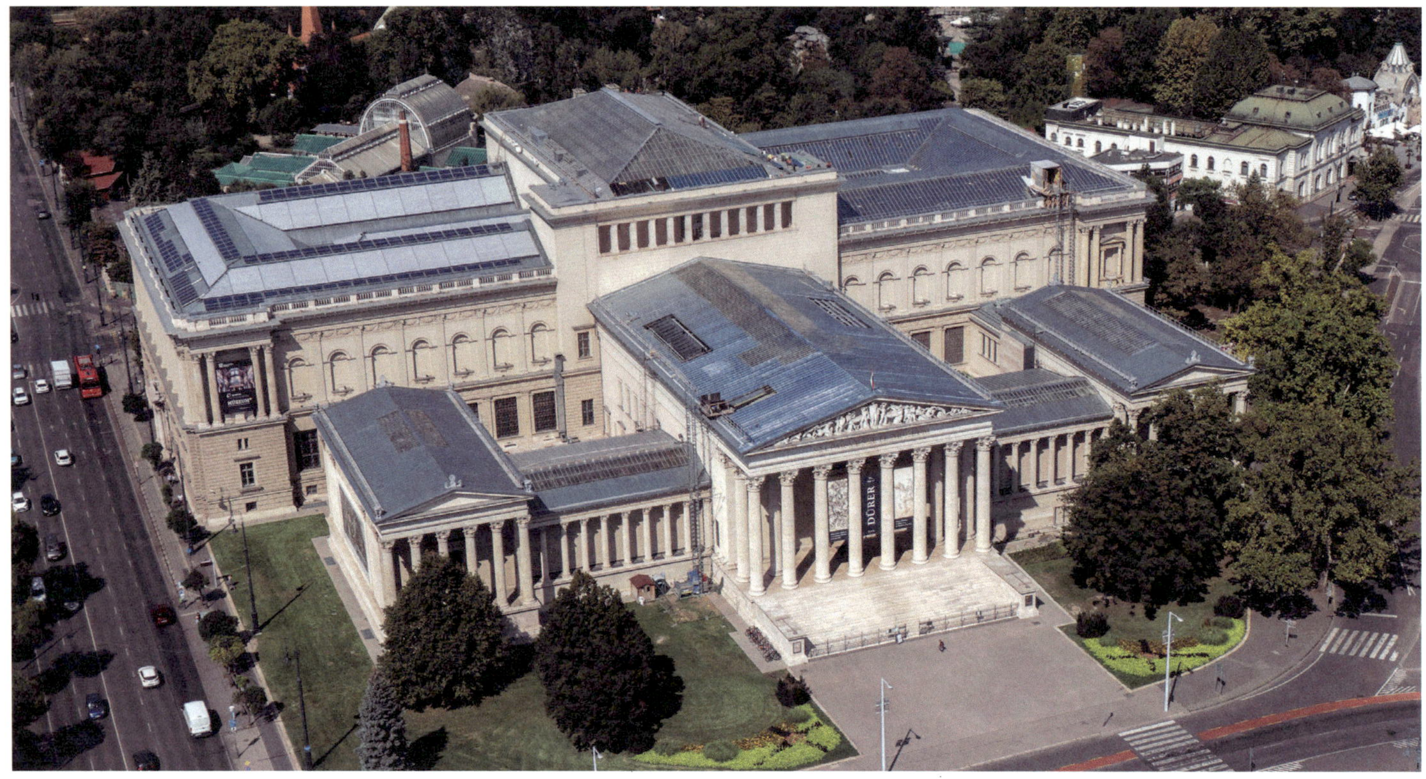

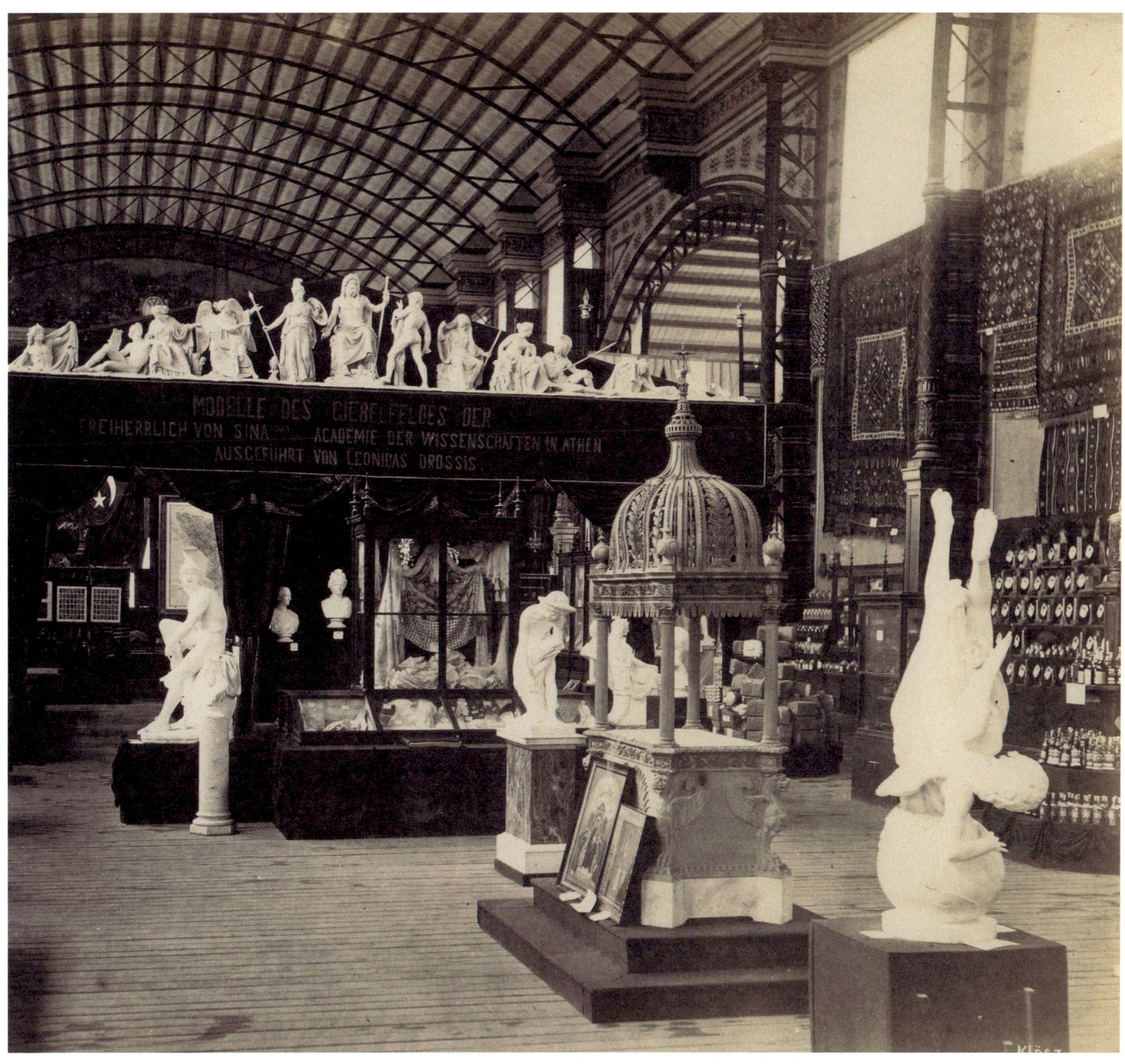

Fig. 1 | previous page

Aerial view of the building of the Museum of Fine Arts, Budapest

Fig. 2

Vienna, World exhibition, Greek Gallery, 1873

Production techniques for such copies had evolved dramatically during the nineteenth century and featured regularly at world exhibitions, where they were presented both as technological achievements and as a means to represent the world's civilisations from a colonial, Euro-centric perspective (fig. 2). The Universal Museum, with its display of copies of masterpieces from all over the world, was only possible because of these technical achievements, and it was conceptually linked to the world exhibitions, sharing, as I shall point out, their colonialist dimension.[3]

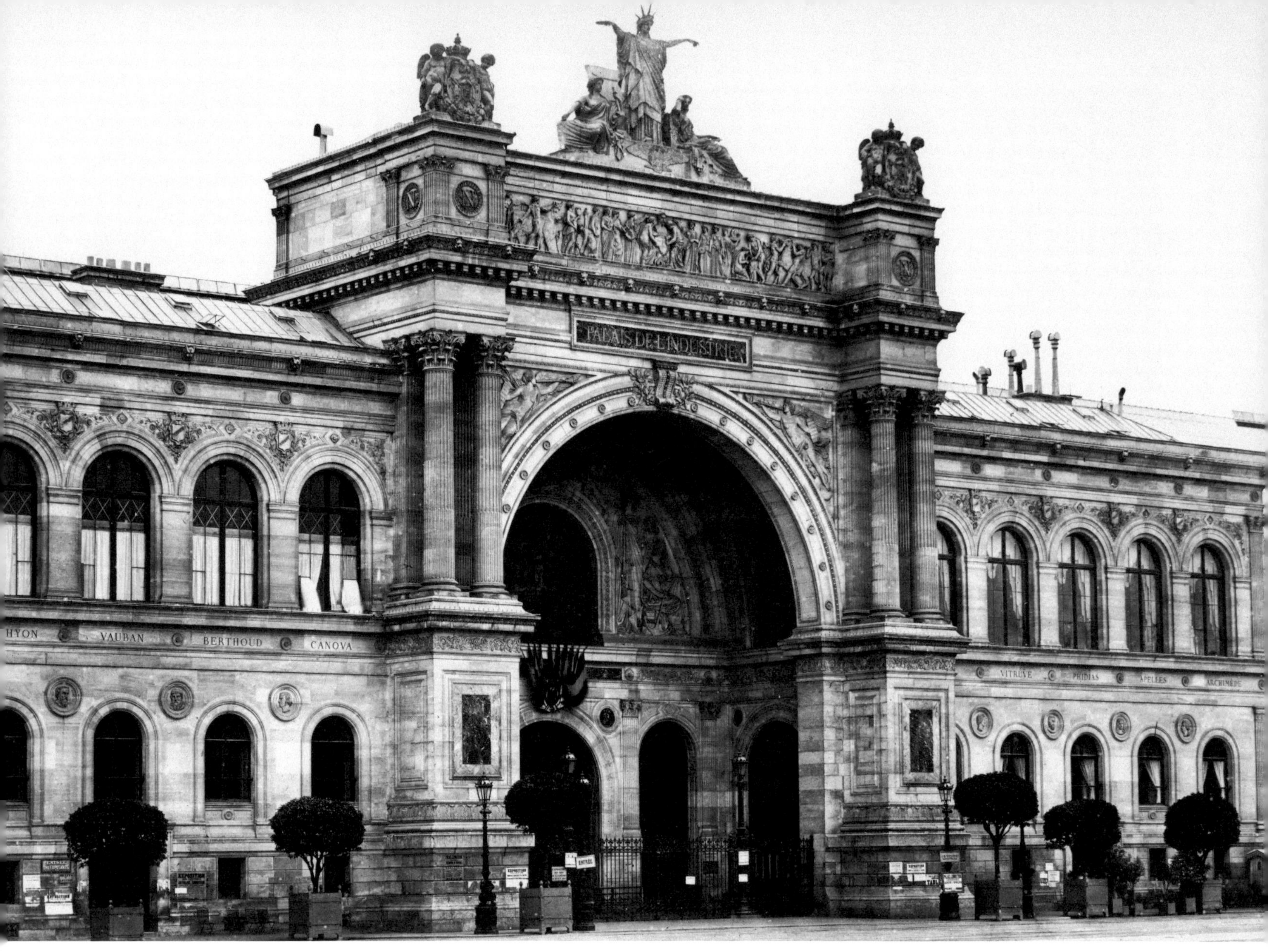

Many plans for collections of copies that were devised along the lines of the Universal Museum were less successful in their implementation than the cast collection at the Museum of Fine Arts in Budapest. Across Europe and the Americas, projects of this kind suffered defeat at various stages; some never made it beyond the planning stage, others only opened, to be quickly dismantled and absorbed into other collections, while yet others expanded impressively but were expelled from the museums they had formed part of, as soon as they were perceived as something of their own. As for the Museo de Reproducciones Artísticas in Madrid, the change in the Spanish government in 1881 seems indeed to have impacted on its history, albeit simply by delaying its official opening, which, according to Garcia-Ventura and Vidal, occurred only in 1897, sixteen years later than planned.[4] In the following, I shall look at the early moments of several of these collections to draw out some of their characteristics. Their didactic ambitions, I shall point out, were regularly informed by highly political motives. I shall argue that it was these underlying political agendas that made the Universal Museum with its collections of copies so vulnerable to changes in government.

The museum in Budapest was conceived as a Universal Museum of Fine Arts and designed to include three departments: sculpture and architecture, painting, and prints and drawings (fig. 1).[5] Within this framework, the acquisition of copies was limited to the department of sculpture and architecture, whose collection was to consist almost exclusively of plaster casts. Copies of paintings were arguably not needed, as the museum was to include, in a distinct and physically elevated part of the building, the impressive collection of the former National Picture Gallery, comprising works by Dürer, Raphael, Giorgione, van Dyck, Velázquez, etc.[6]

In Paris in the early 1870s, Charles Blanc[7] also envisaged a Universal Museum of Fine Arts that was to include copies of sculpture and painting. As a first step, in spring 1873 Blanc opened the Musée Européen des Copies, with 166 painted copies after works from the Renaissance onwards, in the Palais de l'Industrie on the Champs-Elysées (fig. 3). This was an interim location, available for one year only, but Blanc expressed plans for a purpose-built accommodation for the more broadly conceived *musée universel*.[8]

The start of the project, with copies of paintings only, related to Blanc's focus on artists and the established role of copying in French academic training, especially at the Académie de France in Rome, where members regularly had to provide copies after Roman masterpieces. Blanc argued that his museum was to give new scope to this practice as well as providing French artists with urgently needed employment.[9] While theoretically this did include sculptors, in practice, sculptural reproductions for such a museum would have been mostly plaster casts, which were made by *mouleurs*, or cast makers, not sculptors.

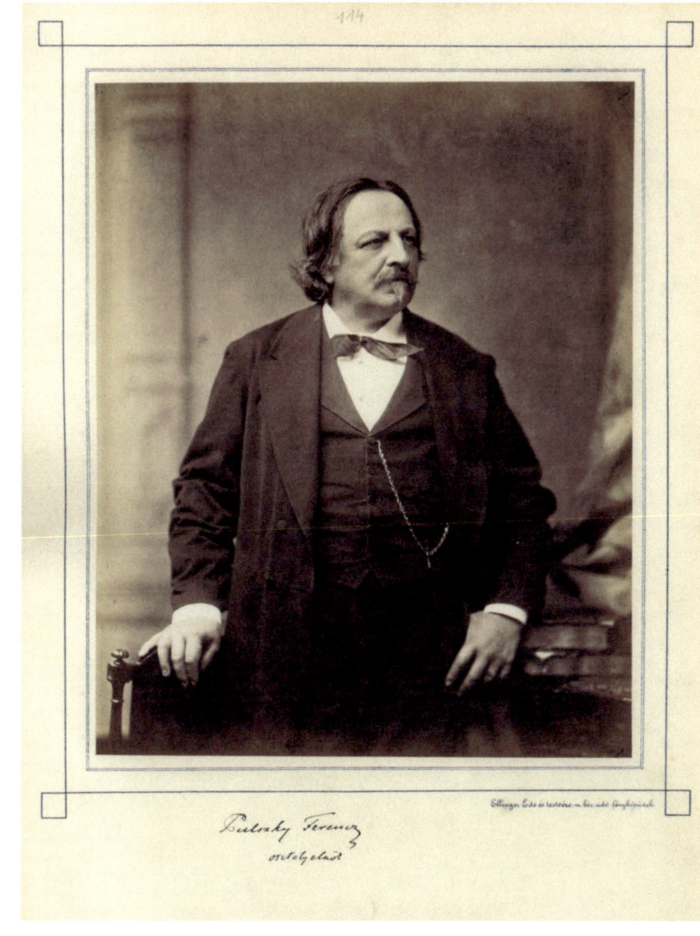

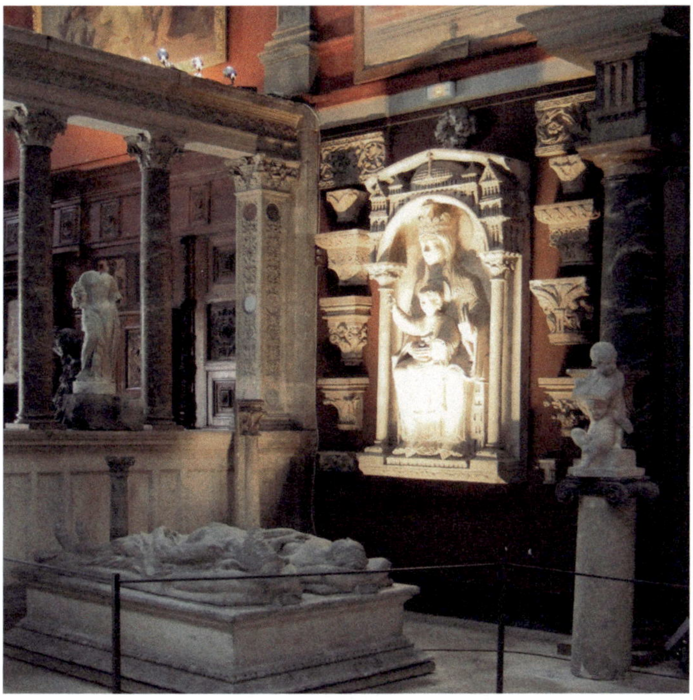

The museum was to present in one place the canon of European art to everybody, especially those unable to travel. As a collection of copies after masterpieces it was complementary to the Musée du Louvre with its collection of originals of varying quality. Elisa Rodríguez Castresana has convincingly argued that it was deliberately conceived as a didactic pendant to the connoisseurial Louvre.[10] During the administration of Adolphe Thiers, first president of the French Third Republic and a trained art historian, the project enjoyed strong political support from the president himself, even if Thiers's minister for culture voiced concerns about Blanc's

Fig. 3 | previous page

Palais de l'Industrie, Paris, ca. 1860

Fig. 4 | at left
École nationale superieure des Beaux-Arts, Paris, Chapelle des Petits Augustins with plaster casts and copies of European paintings

Fig. 5 | above
Portrait of Ferenc Pulszky, 1881

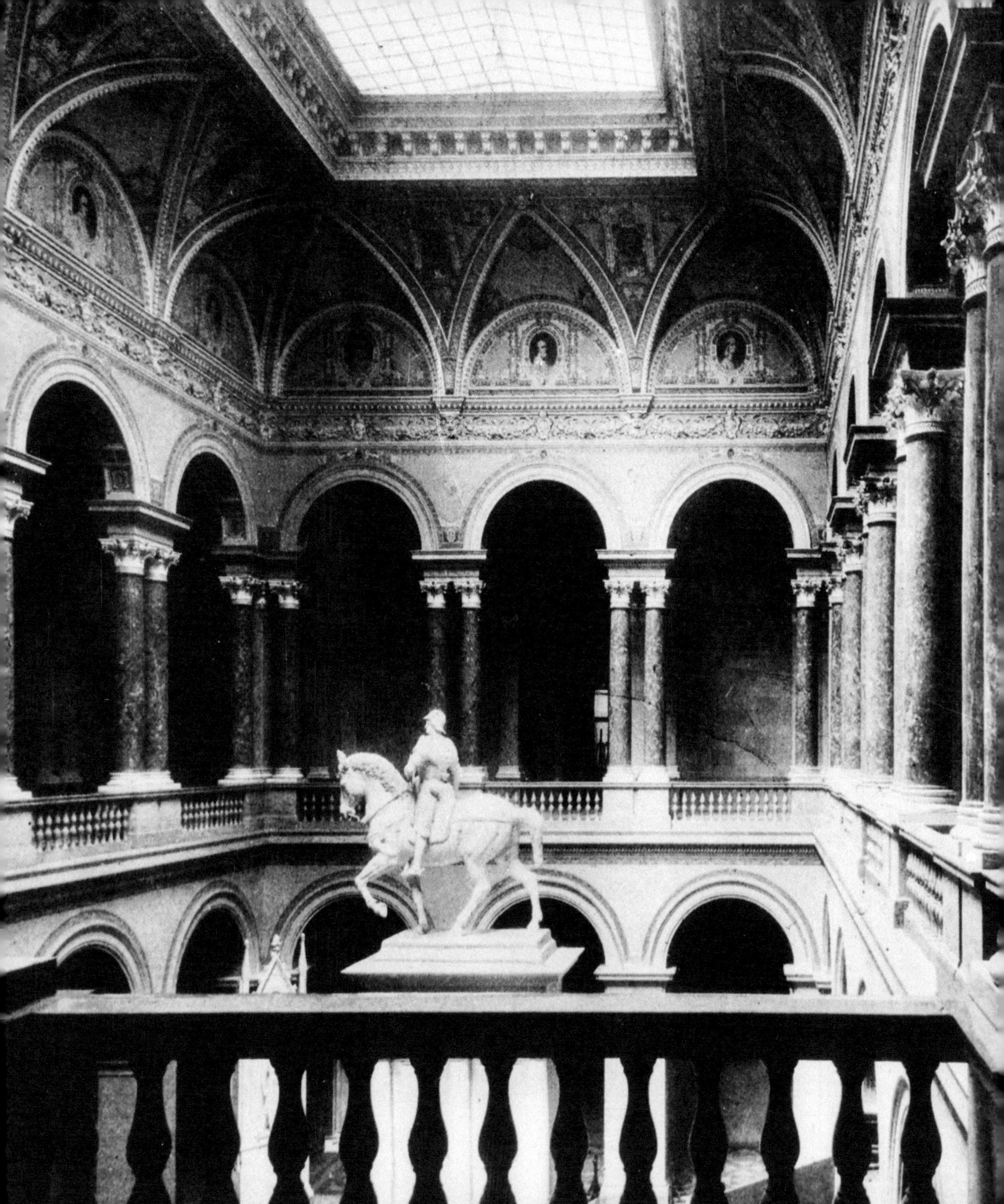

extravagant spending.[11] It seems in fact that the museum was rushed into existence in recognition of the threat to its very idea by the monarchist majority in parliament. When in May 1873 the republican Thiers had to resign and a new monarchist government came to power, the situation grew more precarious and in December Blanc lost his post. The new director, Marquis Charles-Philippe de Chennevières-Pointel, was a monarchist, who tellingly criticised Blanc for being more interested in theory than in works of art.[12] Within days, Chennevières issued a report on the museum, arguing for its immediate closure. This occurred by the end of the year, and many of the copies were transferred to the teaching collections of the École des Beaux-Arts, where they survive still today (fig. 4).[13]

In Vienna, a vast museum of plaster casts was proposed in 1885. There were already three plaster cast collections in the city, attached to the Academy of Fine Arts and the Imperial and Royal Museum of Art and Industry, as well as to the Institute of Classical Archaeology at the University of Vienna. In a lecture on 5 February 1885, Carl von Lützow,[14] Head of Collections at the Academy of Fine Arts, outlined the planned fourth collection.[15] While Charles Blanc in Paris had been acting on his own with the highest government support, von Lützow was speaking for a broad committee; the elaborate plans he presented had developed out of a parliamentary initiative and had been fleshed out for over a year by a committee of artists, scholars and other members of the cultural establishment, under the leadership of the director of the Museum of Art and Industry where von Lützow gave his lecture.[16] Von Lützow was keen to highlight the strengths of the existing cast collections, but he pointed out that they were specialised and that their institutional functions would always discourage the wider public from visiting. Therefore, he argued, a fourth collection was required, one that was more ambitious in its scope.[17] It was to serve the general public, not the professionals, nor the elites who visited the grand museums on the Ringstrasse. The planned museum had to represent everything: all periods and all styles, through their most characteristic and artistically most important works. He listed oriental and classical antiquity, the art of Egypt, ancient Asia, Greece, and Rome, early Christian and Medieval art, the Renaissance with its various branches pertaining to the artistic peoples of Europe, and finally, modern art. And, of course, there would be an Austrian department that would give the museum its local and patriotic imprint, displaying, among other objects, portrait busts, casts after important works, as well as reduced models of Austrian monuments and buildings.[18] The aim to educate the general public, in contrast to the more established museums, struck a similar chord to Blanc's project, while the addition of a local, national section became a standard feature of Universal Museums in most countries.[19]

Charles Blanc had envisaged for his *musée universel* a large, cathedral-like edifice with lateral chapels, the church analogy arguably signalling the transcendental values of the museum.[20] Von Lützow, by contrast, outlined a simple, undecorated building of brick and mortar, one storey high in order to accommodate top-lit rooms. As for the location, the committee had chosen the Prater, that is the Volkspark, "People's Park", to meet their target audiences where they tended to frequent.[21] Such aspects were echoed some fifteen years later in Gyula Wlassics's[22] 1899 report to the Hungarian parliament, in which he recounted his quest for a suitable location for the Museum of Fine Arts in Budapest, in planning since 1894.[23] Here, too, when looking for the ideal site for the proposed vast building with its top-lit halls, the first choice was that part of the local City Park which was called the Népliget, "People's Park", but that proved unobtainable. Wlassics then outlined the advantages of the plot that was ultimately chosen (where the Museum of Fine Arts stands today), in particular its proximity to the Millennium Monument and the Műcsarnok (Kunsthalle) exhibition hall. This, he pointed out, was already a popular spot on the tourist trail, well connected by public transport.[24]

In Budapest, the cultural establishment was closely knit and marked by an astonishing continuity of personnel and ideas, with strong connections between museum administrations and the political sphere. As early as the 1850s, while in exile in London, Ferenc Pulszky (fig. 5) had developed the notion of an educational Universal Museum. After his return in the 1860s, he soon became director of the Hungarian National Museum, where he started acquiring a cast collection of ancient sculpture that was to form the nucleus of the present one. Pulszky was a politician, repeatedly a member of the Hungarian Diet in the 1840s, and again, after his return from exile, of the then-reformed Diet. The first keeper of Coins and Antiquities in the National Museum, József Hampel, became his son-in-law in 1883, and Pulszky's son Károly was the first keeper of the Museum of Applied Arts before being appointed the first director of the Museum of Fine Arts.In 1896 the above-mentioned Gyula Wlassics, Minister of Culture and Religion, had to dismiss Károly Pulszky over irregularities in acquisitions for the museum, especially regarding the

Fig. 6 | previous page

The Renaissance Hall of the Museum of Fine Arts, Budapest with the plaster cast of the *Colleoni Monument,* ca. 1920

Fig. 7 | next page

View of the interior of the Museo Nacional de Bellas Artes at Santiago, Chile, 1914

purchase of a painting thought to be by Raphael. After this, he himself took on the task of planning the museum, and it was only in 1901 that Wlassics appointed Ernő Kammerer, another elected member of parliament, as the new director, with the art historian Gábor Térey as curator. This was a tightly interrelated community with direct links to government.[25]

However, this local establishment was also internationally connected. In his 1899 report, Wlassics regularly emphasised the involvement of international specialists, which was borne out in practice by the appointment of an international jury for the architectural competition, extensive fact-finding missions to European collections, and close liaising with Wilhelm von Bode in Berlin and Georg Treu in Dresden, whose museums and cast collections served as important models.[26]

The Hungarian government never spent the full amount allocated to the cast collection, and the absence, for example, of the equestrian monument to Marcus Aurelius, included in Wlassics's plan and an obvious precursor and pendant to the two Renaissance monuments in the collection, indicates that expenditure cuts took place.[27] However, the museum itself, with its plaster cast collection covering most of the raised ground floor, was eventually completed, and the extravagant commission of a cast of the original plinth of the *Colleoni Monument* in 1907, even after the museum's official opening in 1906, attests to ongoing government support for the casts collection (fig. 6).[28]

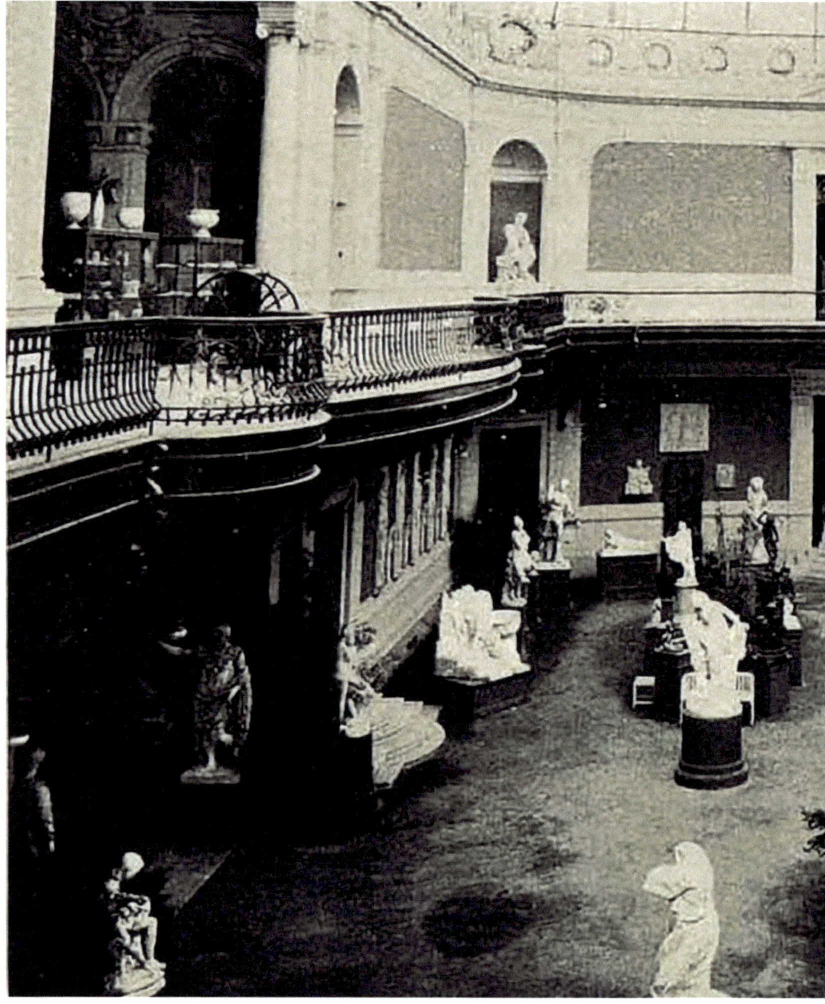

By contrast, across the border in Austria, nothing came of the plans presented by von Lützow. Sources at the time and modern art historians point towards the reshaping and rationalisation of the three existing cast collections that took place instead, which may be seen as a move away from the idea of the Universal Museum.[29] A more important consideration seems to be the fact that, as part of the Ringstrasse development, construction had begun on the Kunsthistorisches Museum, which would eventually house the vast imperial Habsburg collections of originals. With von Lützow's project serving the sole purpose of educating the general public, without simultaneously fulfilling functions of national representation or providing direct connections to teaching institutions, the future of the Plastisches Museum must have been very vulnerable indeed.

When arguing for the acquisition of casts, Wlassics made the point that the country was unlikely ever to have the opportunities or funds to acquire significant ancient originals on which to base the reputation of a major national collection.[30] Here, the contrast between originals and copies functions as a common rhetorical device:[31] the slow and persistent accumulation of a collection of originals was never an alternative to the *ad hoc* acquisition of a collection of plaster casts. Such a collection of copies could tell an apparently "complete" narrative and act as a coherent, impressive ensemble. With the knowledge of what was available in cast-makers' workshops across Europe, it was perfectly possible to plan an entire collection and its layout, and to achieve this in a relatively short period. This facilitated the creation of spectacular displays in which specific works played clearly defined roles, both educational and representational.[32] Like the great cast collections in North American museums such as Boston, New York or Chicago, the Budapest collection was conceived and presented as both an educational project and as one of national self-representation.[33]

Nationalist ideas pervade all these projects. In 1866, Ferenc Pulszky discussed the concept of the Universal Museum as an indicator of national ambition, contrasting it with the inward-looking provincial museums by "nations with more

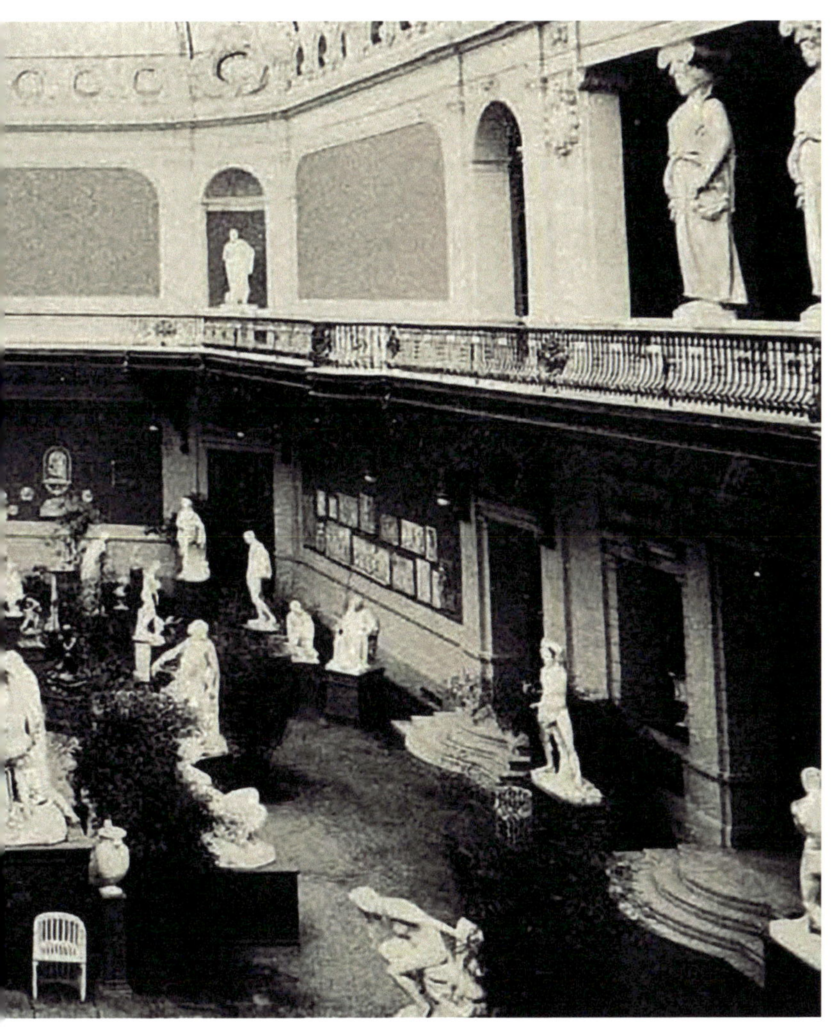

thus underpinned in terms of Austria's standing among the European colonial powers.[35] Plaster casts had other direct roles in colonialism. European powers took casts of pre-colonial monuments they were unable to remove, asserting their assumed rights over the colonies' heritage as owners, guardians, and interpreters.[36]

Then there was the traffic of casts in the other direction, that is, from the colonising countries to their colonies. An early example is that of a set of casts dispatched in 1791 from Madrid to the Academia de San Carlos in Mexico City. This academy had been founded ten years earlier under the auspices of the viceroy of Nueva Espagna.[37] Most other Latin American countries founded their academies or art schools after gaining independence, still following European models, often that of the French École des Beaux-Arts. An early instance was the Academia de Pintura in Chile in 1849, followed in 1891 by the Academia de Cuenca in Ecuador and in 1897 the Escuela Nacional de Bellas Artes in Costa Rica. All of these institutions swiftly began to accumulate cast collections.[38]

In Chile, in addition to the academy's cast collection, plans for a Universal Museum consisting solely of copies were conceived as early as 1869, and eventually one such museum was established in 1911; thus, these events developed roughly parallel to those in Hungary and elsewhere in Europe.[39] In 1869 Daniel Barros Grez, a scientist, engineer, major literary figure, and active politician, proposed the erection of a national Universal Museum, humbler, but broader in scope than Pulszky's or Blanc's Universal Museums of Fine Arts.[40]

limited standards" that were "trying to compensate for the self-esteem great nations have".[34] Von Lützow, in his lecture, went one step further and explicitly addressed the colonial dimension. In Vienna in 1885 this was a sensitive issue, as Austria was experiencing the waning of its imperial power and the dramatic rise of the recently founded German Empire next door.

Von Lützow directly addresses the fierce competition between European nations. Each of them, he states, wanted to establish itself in faraway countries to assert its authority. Soon, every corner of the non-European world would be dominated by one of the European nations. This colonial expansion he puts into a domestic cultural context. The most powerful nations, Britain, Germany, and France, he says, also invested substantially in their own culture, something he contrasts with the woefully small spending on art in Austria. As a result, Austrian artists and art students were leaving Vienna. Local Austrian talent no longer reached the requisite level to make it into Viennese museums. The call for a Universal Museum was

He envisaged painted copies and plaster casts, as well as photographic and print reproductions of paintings and sculptures. Beyond this, his museum was to include historical collections of agricultural tools, specimens of local industrial production, and representations of national customs.[41] Barros Grez's museum was intended as a didactic tool for the country's wider public, "the people", designed to train their skills in observation and judgement, and to shape and improve "good taste".[42] Showing how the arts, agriculture and forms of life had evolved, the museum was to teach a notion of progression towards modern civilisation. This was to stimulate the visitors' confidence in their own ability to develop further.[43]

The idea of a museum of copies resurfaced in 1899 in a speech by Alberto Mackenna Subercaseaux, who also came from an established Chilean family and was engaged in politics and the arts. In the 1920s he would become mayor of Santiago and later director of the Museo Nacional de Bellas Artes.[44] His plans were less wide ranging than Barros Grez's and entirely Euro-centric. In addition to a canonical cast collection, his Museo de Copias was to include a department of applied arts consisting of imported copies of French furniture. Attached to this, Mackenna envisioned a design school offering evening courses to the working classes. In 1900, the Chilean government placed 30,000 dollars at the disposal of the project, and 135 copies, mainly plaster casts, were acquired in Paris, Naples, Florence, and Rome, with Mackenna directly involved.[45]

Early in 1901, writing from Florence, Mackenna published an open letter to the Chilean Minister of Public Instruction in the newspaper *La Libertad Electoral,* in which he insisted on an appropriate building for the collection.[46] This was finally inaugurated in 1911 when the Museo de Copias opened in the Palacio de Bellas Artes (fig. 7), erected a year earlier originally to house the Exposición Internacional del Centenario, an international exhibition to mark a hundred years since the beginning of the Chilean War of Independence.[47] Back in 1901, in his open letter, Mackenna outlined the collection that was on its way to Chile, referencing in particular the masterpieces of the Florentine Renaissance, and asking what these proud guests would think finding themselves exhibited in the dark and uninviting premises of the existing academy and art museum.[48] He then argued that for a general public, alien to fine arts, like that of Chile, it was important that a museum was well lit and inviting. Describing European casts museums, he evoked in particular the efforts of the German and British governments. All the civilised nations of the world invested in museums as a means to cultivate and educate their populations.[49] Mackenna declared this a task of patriotism, stating that it was impossible for all

the European nations to be mistaken on this issue.[50] We find here, in a post-colonial context, the very argument for the Universal Museum that von Lützow had employed against the background of Austria's sidelined position in the colonial race of the European powers. Where von Lützow had referred to colonialism and the assertion of imperial power, for Mackenna and Barros Grez, this was Chile's patriotic pursuit of civilisation. Entirely Euro-centric, this notion of civilisation enabled members of the leading classes, many of whom, like Mackenna and Barros Grez, were descended from the former colonisers, to assert their social dominance as civilisers in what was perceived to be a peripheral country.[51] Mackenna was caricatured at his time as a man with a mission, fighting with an almost religious zeal.[52] However – in contrast to Charles Blanc's plans – Mackenna's ideas seem to have had a strong enough basis in Chile's establishment to resonate and materialise.

In the long term, the notion of the Universal Museum did not survive, and neither did the juxtaposition of casts and originals. If the collection of the Museum of Fine Arts in Budapest was successfully realised and managed to survive until World War II, then, I would argue, this was to a great extent because of the absence of competing collections of originals, and the largely distinct and hierarchically differentiated presentation of copies and originals. The most important factor, however, was the continuous support in government and society for Ferenc Pulszky's ideas of the Universal Museum as an educational institution that also served the country's self-representation among competing European nations.

Notes

* The quote is an English rendering of a passage from Robert Burns's Scottish poem *To a Mouse,* from 1786. The sentence runs in full: "The best laid schemes of mice and men go often askew, and leave us nothing but grief and pain, for promised joy!" ("The best-laid schemes o' mice an' men gang aft agley, an' lea'e us nought but grief an' pain, for promis'd joy!").

I should like to thank Miriam Szőcs and Márton Tóth for the invitation to speak at their conference.

1 For a discussion of the letter and the early history of the Museo de Reproducciones Artísticas, see Garcia-Ventura and Vidal 2020. The letter is cited in full length in ibid., 486–87. Juan Facundo Riaño was an art historian and Arabist, politician and advisor to London's South Kensington Museum and Austen Henry Layard. Cf. Trusted 2006.

2 Charlotte Schreiter speaks in this context of a second wave of cast collections, the first including prominently those in Berlin and Dresden, which also function as models for those discussed here; Schreiter 2014, esp. 42; see also Burg 2010.

3 Falser 2019, esp. vol. 1; Schreiter 2014.

4 Garcia-Ventura and Vidal 2020, 482–83.

5 Andó 2021, esp. 95–101.

6 Nagy 2006, esp. 217–18; see also Andó 2021, 98–99. An important study of the museum's history is Bacher 1956, esp. 27–32. I am grateful to Miriam Szőcs for this reference but have been unable to profit from the Hungarian text.

7 Charles Blanc (1813–1822) was a French art critic.

8 Boime 1964; Vaisse 1976 (see page 61 for Blanc's wider plans and page 65, note 77 for designs by other parties to establish plaster cast collections complementary to Blanc's museum); Rodríguez Castresana 2017.

9 Boime 1964, 240–41.

10 Rodríguez Castresana 2017, 4–6. A similar relationship between the didactic collections of casts at Crystal Palace, Sydenham and the collections of the British Museum is discussed by Schreiter 2014, 38.

11 Vaisse 1976, 55–56, note 14.

12 Ibid., 54–55.

13 Ibid., 58.

14 Carl von Lützow (1832–1897) was a German art historian, Head of Collections at the Academy of Fine Arts, Vienna.

15 Lützow 1885.

16 Ibid., 474–75; Stiassny 1910, esp. 1.

17 Lützow 1885, 475–77.

18 Ibid., 477.

19 See, e.g., Wlassics 1900, 10–11. [The report is dated 31 December 1899 on page 29]. I am indebted to Zsuzsanna van Ruyven-Zeman for the translation of large sections of this report and for summaries of others. In the context of an earlier tradition of Universal Museums, and the Musée du Louvre in particular, the nationalist dimension of the Universal Museum is discussed by McClellan 1999, 81–82.

20 Vaisse 1976, 61, note 54.

21 Lützow 1885, 479–80, 503.

22 Gyula Wlassics (1852–1937), lawyer, politician, minister of religion and education from 1895 to 1903, later president of the Administrative Court.

23 Wlassics 1900, 1–2. On this report see Andó 2021, 100.

24 Ibid., 1–2. On the exhibition hall see Tóth F. 2016, esp. 202.

25 For a general outline of the early history of the Museum of Fine Arts and the main players involved, see Andó 2021, 95–101, as well as Nagy 2006, 217; see also Szentesi 2006A; Bacher 1956, 8–34. On Ferenc Pulszky and his exile in London in particular, see Wilson 2010, esp. 273–74. Károly Pulszky and his dismissal by Wlassics is more extensively discussed by Tóth F. 2007, 233–58 [English summary on 257–58]; see also Fehér 2010–2012, esp. 335. On Gábor Térey, see Radványi 2006, esp. 15–28, in the English summary on 167–85, esp. 169–71. I am indebted to Miriam Szőcs for pointing me towards this text.

26 Wlassics 1900, 2, 26–27. On the international connections of the Budapest Museum elites, see also, e.g., Szentesi 2006A. Térey visited sixty-five European museums in 1897 while planning the display; Rózsavölgyi 2021, esp. 137–38. For the role of the museums in Dresden and Berlin as models, see Andó 2021, 94–102; see also Platz-Horster 2011; on the Berlin cast collections see Winkler-Horaček 2022A, esp. 349–55 with additional bibliography. I am grateful to Annetta Alexandridis for bringing this recent publication to my immediate attention.

27 For the reference to the monument of Marcus Aurelius: Wlassics 1900, 6, 26–29. Wlassics refers extensively to financial issues.

28 The museum was opened by Franz Joseph, Emperor of Austria and King of Hungary, on 1 December 1906; Andó 2021, 101; see also Nagy 2006, 220.

29 Stiassny 1910, 1; Bauer 2012, esp. 288.

30 A similar point was made by von Lützow in his lecture in 1885, see Lützow 1885, 474. The argument was questioned by art critic Artúr Elek, who in 1923 pointed towards the collections of The Metropolitan Museum of Art, New York, the Boston Museum of Fine Arts, and the Ny Carlsberg Glyptotek in Copenhagen as three world-class antiquity collections that were built up during this period. Árpád Nagy also argues that it was rather the lack of competent archaeologists than funding or opportunities that for so long prevented the museum from building up a substantial collection. Elek 1923, 597, cited in Nagy 2006, 218–29.

31 Recently, this false dichotomy of originals and copies has often been employed in arguments against plaster casts, e.g., by the former Director of the Statens Museum for Kunst, Copenhagen, Allis Helleland, who in the context of the dramatic reduction of funds for the museum's cast collection argued that in difficult financial circumstances choices had to be made and that originals had to be prioritised, Helleland 2005, esp. 28, see English summary on 191–92.

32 Both the reports by Wlassics and Térey demonstrate the confidence with which museum planners at the time could envisage the shape of their future collections. See Wlassics 1900 and *Dr Térey Gábor jelentése a Szépművészeti Muzeum olasz renaissance plasztikai osztálya számára megszerendő gypsöntvények tárgyában, az öntvények jegyzékével* [Report of Dr Gábor Térey in the case of the plaster casts to be acquired for the Italian Renaissance sculpture department of the Museum of Fine Arts, with a list of the casts], compiled 15 May 1901, Archives MFAB, 232/1901. I should like to thank Márton Tóth for translating this document for me.

33 On American cast collections see Wallach 1998; Dyson 2010. On the collections in Boston see also Cambareri 2011, esp. 95–106.

34 Pulszky 1875, cited here in English translation after Andó 2021, 96. The colonial and other political implications of the cast collection of the Museum of Fine Arts throughout its existence are addressed poignantly by Tali 2021 and by this publication in general, and the 2017 exhibition project it documents. This artistic project focused on the interrelated histories of the Budapest cast collection and the former synagogue in Tata, where large parts of the collection were stored and displayed between 1977 and its recent transferral to Komárom.

35 Lützow 1885, 505–6. On cast museums and international exhibitions, see also Schreiter 2014.

36 See, e.g., the recent publication by Falser 2019, esp. vol. 1; for an example of how central and South American indigenous artists engage with these colonial casts in the postcolonial context, see Reynolds-Kaye 2019. A wider assessment of plaster cast collections (and of plaster casts in general) in colonial contexts and discourses has only just begun. See Alexandridis 2022, esp. 497–502; Holm 2022, esp. 42–44 and Berlin 2019A, esp. the section "Zu nah am Leben", 60–95.

37 Fuentes Rojas 2010, esp. 230–31; see also Báez Macías 2019, esp. 21–36. In Rio de Janeiro the Imperial Academy of Fine Arts of Brazil was founded in 1820, during the last two years of Portuguese rule in the country; Cardoso Denis 2000, esp. 55.

38 Raabe Cercone 2012, esp. 95; on the academy in Chile and its collection, see Gallardo Saint-Jean 2015A, 19–21.

39 In the following I am largely drawing on the anthology about these projects, Gallardo Saint-Jean 2015A. The publication includes a substantial introductory essay: Gallardo Saint-Jean 2015B, 9–52. See also Keller 2022.

40 Barros Grez 1869; reprinted in Gallardo Saint-Jean 2015A, 55–59.

41 Ibid., 58.

42 Ibid., 55.

43 Ibid., 59.

44 On Mackenna Subercaseaux, see Gallardo Saint-Jean 2015A, 16. The speech was only published in 1915. Mackenna Subercaseaux 1915, reprinted in Gallardo Saint-Jean 2015A, 75–81.

45 Gallardo Saint-Jean 2015B, 17–18; for the government approval, see in particular page 17, note 31. Apart from plaster casts, which formed the majority of the works acquired, there were also copies in terracotta, marble, and bronze. Ibid., 18, note 33; see also Keller 2022, 55–61.

46 Mackenna Subercaseaux 1901; reprinted in Gallardo Saint-Jean 2015A, 85–88.

47 In 1910, Alberto Mackenna Subercaseaux was also the Comisario General of the international exhibition; see Gallardo Saint-Jean 2015A, 31 and 115; for Mackenna's speech in 1911, see ibid., 117–20.

48 Mackenna Subercaseaux 1901, 1. Reprinted in Gallardo Saint-Jean 2015A, 86.

49 Ibid. Reprinted in Gallardo Saint-Jean 2015A, 87.

50 Mackenna Subercaseaux 1901, 1. Reprinted in Gallardo Saint-Jean 2015A, 88.

51 Discussing post-colonial academies in Latin America, Rafael Cardoso Denis points out that the experience of colonialism and post-colonialism in the Americas was very different from that in, e.g., India, with the United States arguably developing a self- image as a colonising power in its own right, while in a phrase that brings to mind Mackenna Subercaseaux's words, he refers to the "mantle of European civilisation, worn proudly by Latin American elites of the past"; Cardoso Denis 2000, 53. Mackenna Subercaseaux's invocation of European civilisation is similar to that found in Ferenc Pulszky's London speech of 1850, as cited in Wilson 2010, 273.

Discussing Mackenna Subercaseaux, Gallardo Saint-Jean 2015B, 11, note 10, makes the convincing point that the conception of a *Museo de Copias* in Chile was not a delayed anachronistic phenomenon but in step with its time for a peripheral country; the author refers to the term "modernidades perifericas", coined by Laura Malosetti Costa in Malosetti Costa 2001, 23. Keller 2022, 53 discusses also Mackenna Subercaseaux's older cousin Ramòn Subercaseaux Vicuña as an advocate of the model function of European culture in Chile.

52 Gallardo Saint-Jean discusses and reproduces a caricature originally published in the journal *Revista Pluma y Lápiz* 1901, introduced, reprinted and reproduced in Gallardo Saint-Jean 2015A, 103–7; see also Gallardo Saint-Jean 2015B, 29–30. The cartoon in *Pluma y Lápiz* depicts Mackenna with a truck full of figures of ancient heroes and gods, trailing various institutions in vain before he is beaten to death by his "guests". The final sketch shows his memorial, inscribed "to the redeemer". In the 1920s, Mackenna found himself again caricatured when zealously (and ultimately ineffectively) arguing for the first public park in Santiago; see Hecht 2019.

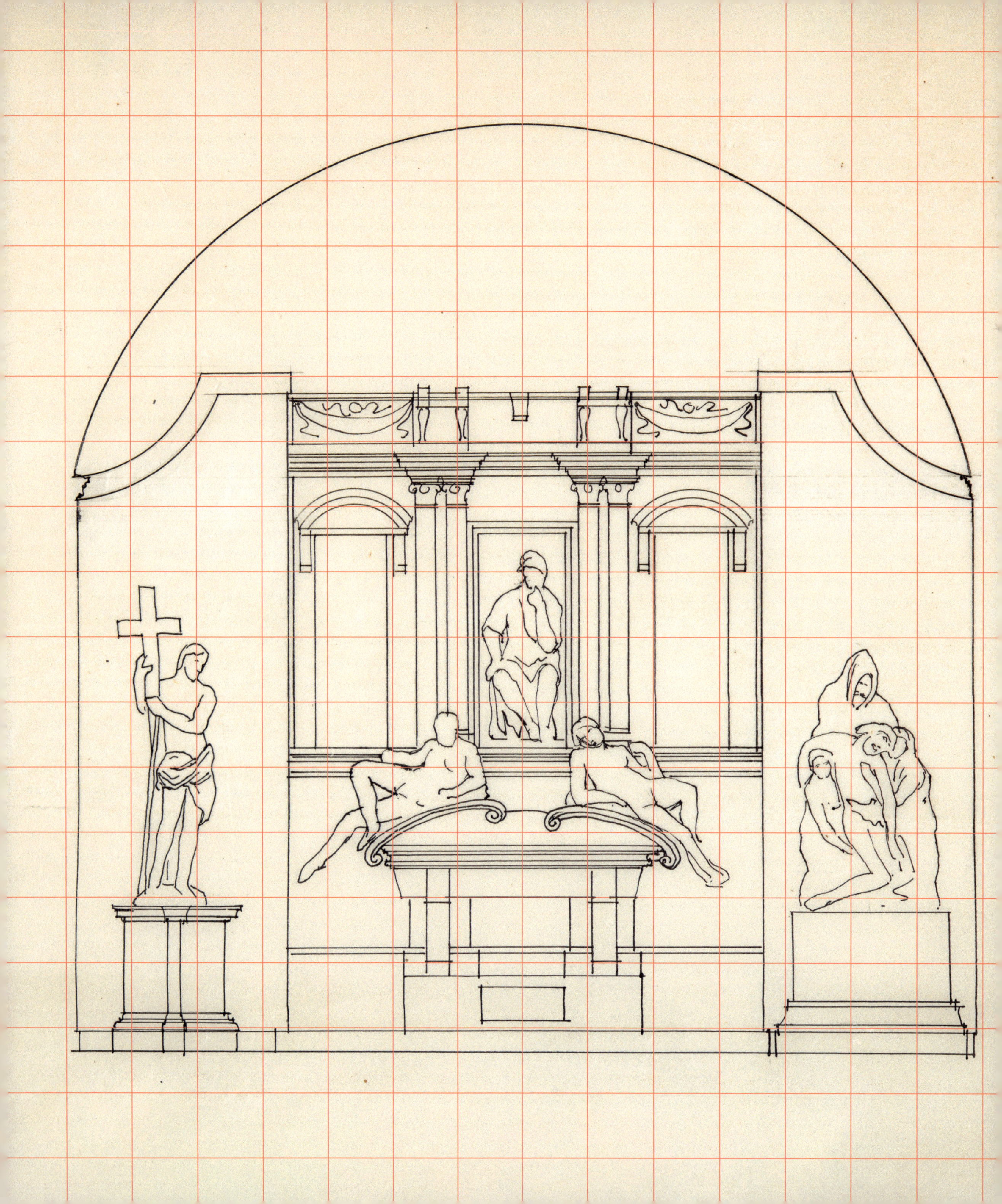

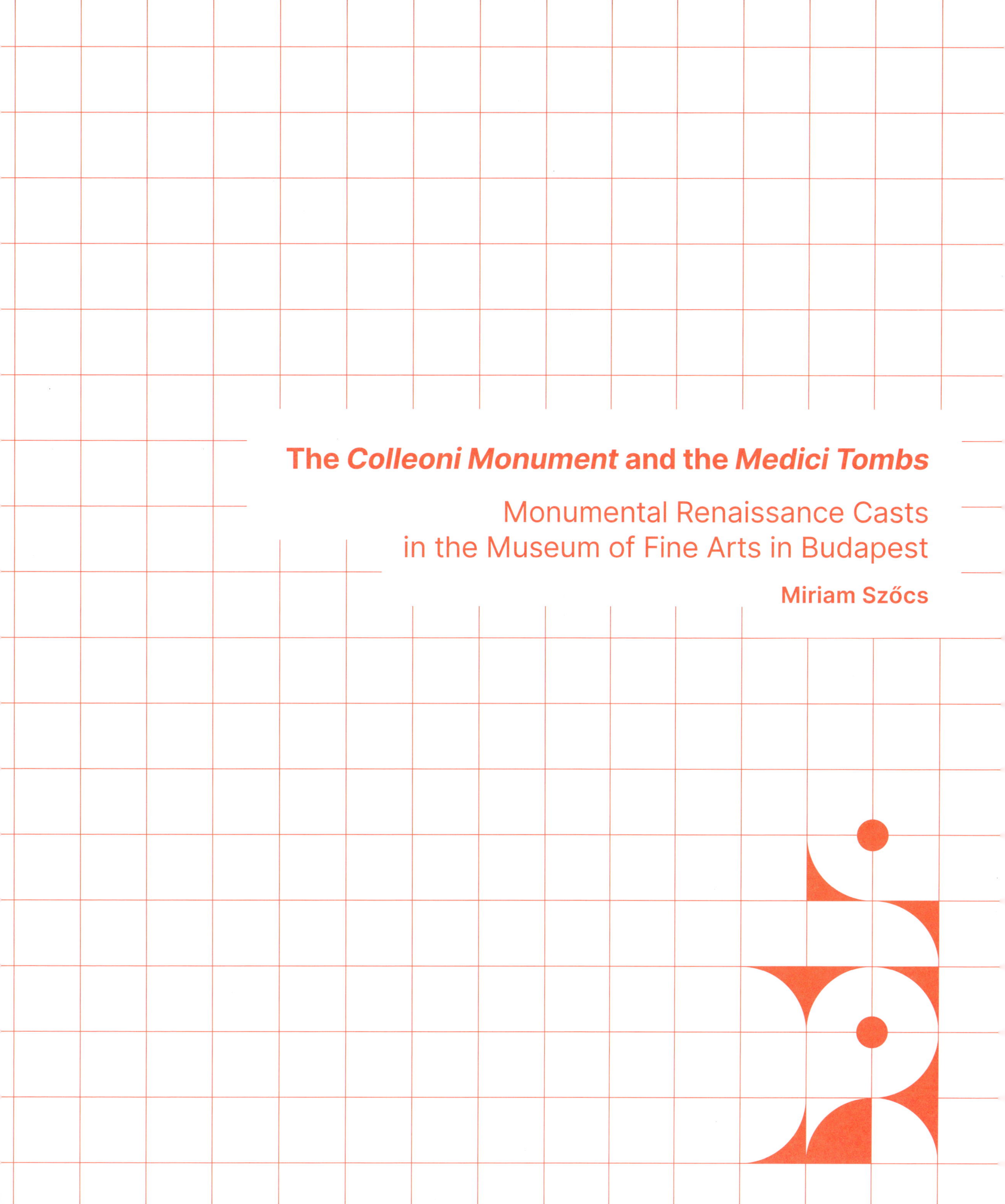

The *Colleoni Monument* and the *Medici Tombs*

Monumental Renaissance Casts in the Museum of Fine Arts in Budapest

Miriam Szőcs

The *Colleoni Monument* and the *Medici Tombs*

Monumental Renaissance Casts in the Museum of Fine Arts in Budapest

Miriam Szőcs

The plaster cast collection of Classical Antiquities, medieval and Renaissance sculptures of the Museum of Fine Arts, Budapest was formed following the foundation of the museum in 1896. The newly created museum inherited the casts previously held by the Hungarian National Museum: those of Classical Antiquities commissioned from 1870 onwards, and those of Hungarian artworks ordered from the 1880s. After 1902, further casts were commissioned for the Museum of Fine Arts, which was still under construction at that time.[1]

In my study I will focus on the history of three monumental Renaissance casts of the museum which are in many aspects unique in the collection, and also are exceptional when compared with other cast collections in Europe and America. In the case of all three artworks, copies of the entire monument were purchased by the Museum. The cast of the *Colleoni Horseman* was ordered together with that of its pedestal, on which the sculpture still stands today in Venice.[2] No other life-size plaster cast is known of the pedestal of this monument, with other cast collections having acquired copies only of the horse and horseman.[3] The casts of Michelangelo's *Tombs of Lorenzo and Giuliano de' Medici* arrived in the museum with copies of the architectural parts of the monuments. Cast collections usually only purchased copies of the main figures from the *Medici Tombs:* the sarcophagi with the reclining figures of *Night* and *Day,* and *Dawn* and *Dusk,* respectively, and the two main figures, Giuliano and Lorenzo de' Medici. In my paper, I will present the ideas that led the Museum of Fine Arts in Budapest to acquire the entire monuments when obtaining copies of these three artworks.

The initiative in Hungary to purchase a copy of Andrea del Verrocchio's *Equestrian Monument of Bartolomeo Colleoni* first appeared as early as the 1880s. In 1885 the Hungarian minister of religion and public education,

Ágost Trefort (1817–1888), through his secretary Imre Szalay (1846–1917), proposed acquiring the cast of the *Colleoni Horseman* from Berlin for the Hungarian National Museum in Budapest. The director of the National Museum, Ferenc Pulszky (1814–1897), replied that although the copy would be useful and valuable, due to its enormous size it would be impossible to install it inside the museum building, and so should not be ordered unless the minister could provide a proper place for such a monumental cast, where copies of works by Donatello or Michelangelo could also be exhibited.[4] By this time, plans to construct a separate building dedicated to a fine art collection had already been put forward, and in his response, Pulszky also argued in favour of such a new museum.[5]

Two decades later, in the newly established and specially constructed Museum of Fine Arts, the *Colleoni Monument* and the Michelangelo casts occupied a prominent position among medieval and Renaissance copies. In the museum, built between 1900 and 1906, the Colleoni cast, installed in 1908, soon became the main attraction in the Renaissance Hall, one of the large ground floor halls of the Museum. To house the casts of Michelangelo's works, a separate gallery was designed, named after the great Renaissance master.

The first copies to be purchased for the medieval and Renaissance part of the collection were specified in the collecting concept of the Museum of Fine Arts published in 1900 under the auspices of Gyula Wlassics (1852–1937), then minister for religion and public education. In this document, the idea can be traced that the museum aimed to present not only the history of fine arts, but also that of architecture. This effort is also reflected in the design of the building, completed a few years later with several different historical architectural styles represented in its interior. The same document clearly indicates that in the case of sculptures related to architecture or serving as part of the decoration of a building, the casts of the architectural elements of the artworks should also be acquired. Besides the examples of the Romanesque and Gothic portals, the *Medici Tombs* are especially worth mentioning. At this stage of planning, the Michelangelo casts were to be included in the exhibition of Renaissance casts in the Renaissance Hall, and the idea of a separate gallery for them was only conceived later. This document also refers to the *Colleoni Monument* as a cast to be ordered.[6]

The first detailed list specifying which sculptures should be purchased in copies was drawn up one year later by Gábor Térey (1864–1927). Térey studied in Basel as a student of Jacob Burckhardt (1818–1897), and afterwards he taught at Freiburg University. He was recalled to Budapest in 1896 specifically to work in the Museum of Fine Arts.[7] Térey was tasked with writing the detailed concept and the lists of works for the plaster cast

collection. Originally, the artworks related to the "Christian age" were to encompass the period between the first and the eighteenth centuries. He probably wrote several lists and concepts, but only the proposal containing the Italian Renaissance artworks has survived.

Echoing the earlier report of minister Gyula Wlassics, in the document dated 15 May 1901 Térey reiterates the importance of obtaining sculptures together with their architectural elements, giving as an example Lorenzo Ghiberti's *Gates of Paradise*, which was to be ordered complete with its architectural frame. Accordingly, a few years later, the copy of the *Gates of Paradise* arrived in the museum with its frame, and the complete cast was assembled in the Renaissance Hall in 1908.[8] Térey also noted that a large hall would be needed to house the Italian Renaissance casts, which resulted in the Renaissance Hall, while a specially dedicated gallery should be reserved for the Michelangelo casts, a requirement that later led to the creation of the Michelangelo Gallery.[9] By this time, construction had begun on the museum's building in Heroes' Square. Térey's notes reflect that he was making his plans with a knowledge of the layout of the museum, and he commented that the gallery for the

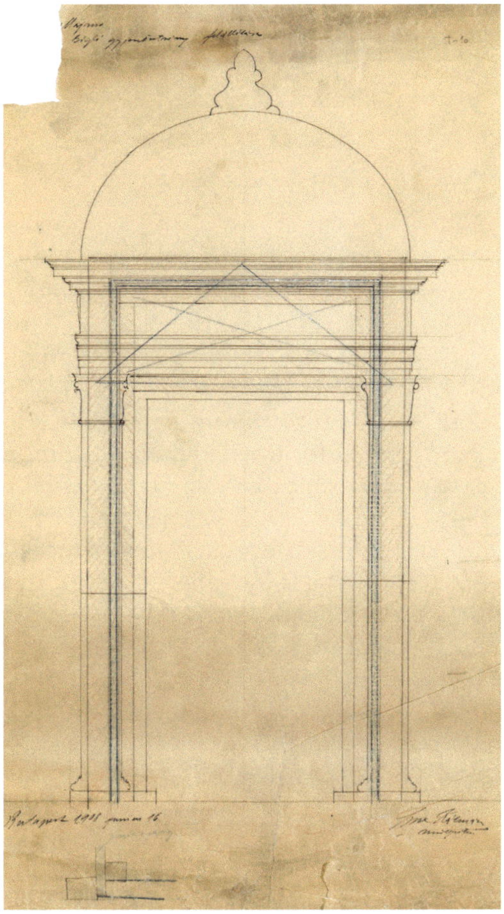

Fig. 1

Layout for the installation of the cast of Benedetto da Maiano's door of the *Sala dei Gigli,* ca. 1906

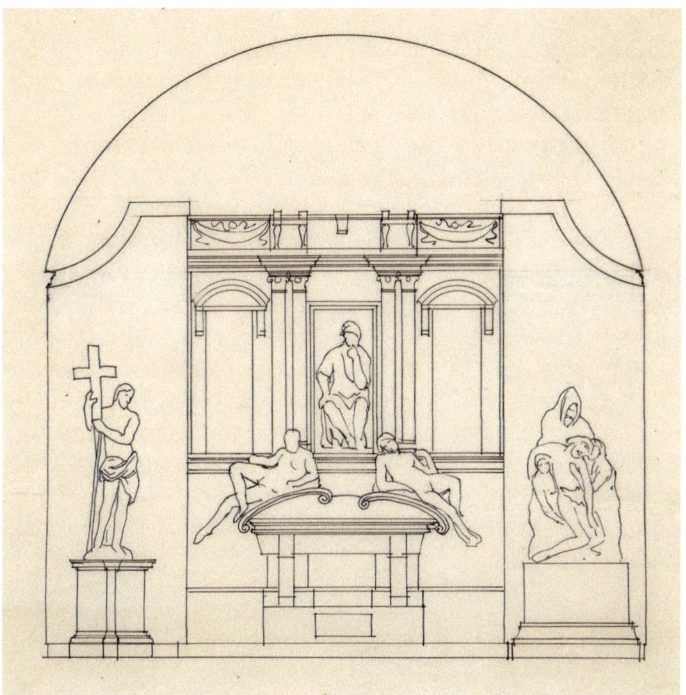

Fig. 2

Layout for the installation of the copy of the *Tomb of Lorenzo de' Medici* with the casts of the Risen Christ and Florentine Pietà, ca. 1905–1906

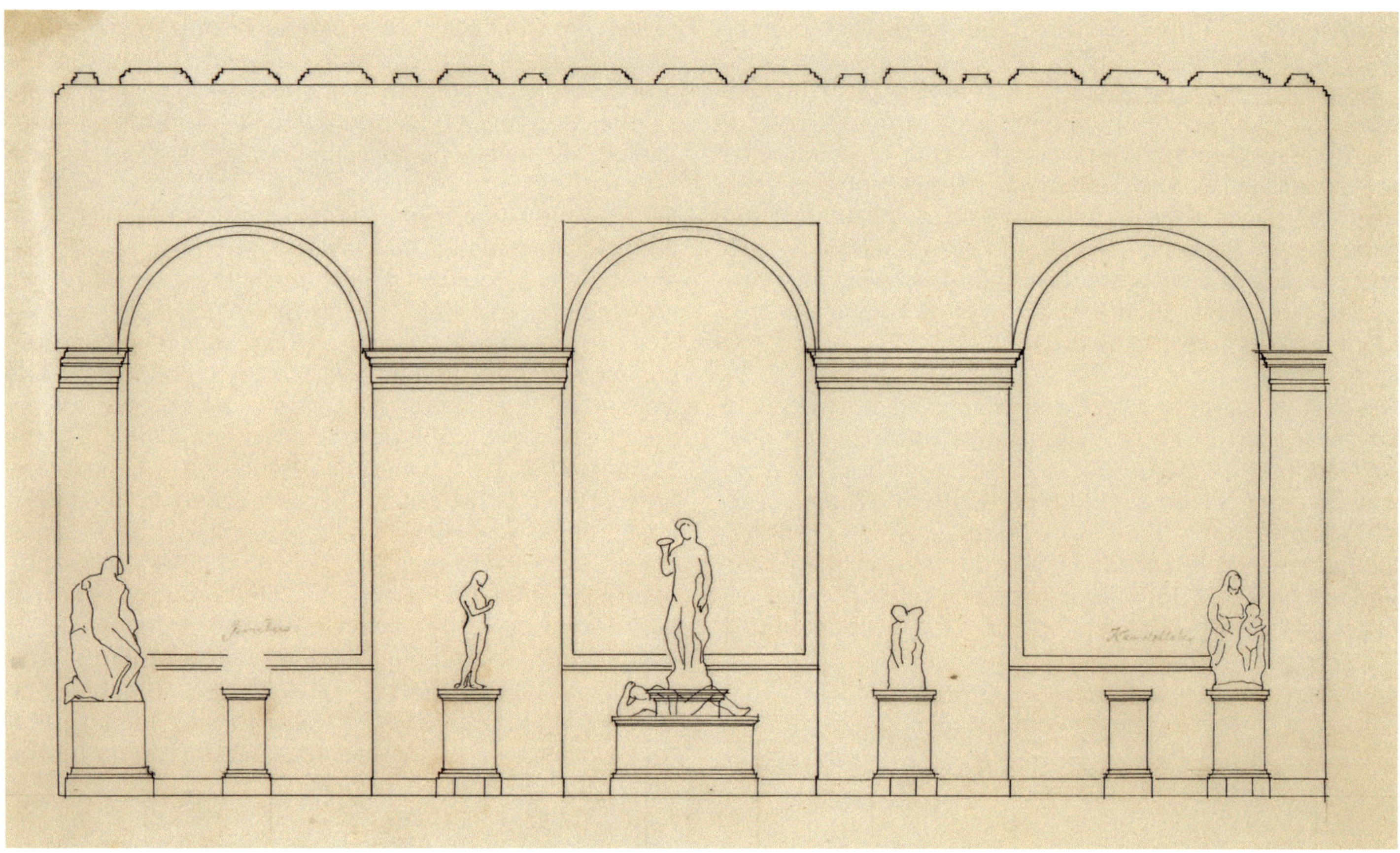

Michelangelo casts would be easily accessible from the Renaissance Hall, as is still the case in the museum's arrangement today. He also specified that the frame of the entrance to the Michelangelo Gallery should be a copy of the door of the *Sala dei Gigli* (original in the Palazzo Vecchio, Florence) by Benedetto da Maiano. The museum ordered the cast of this latter door frame too, and the sketches made for the installation of this cast do not exclude the possibility that the copy was ultimately installed as the entrance to the Michelangelo Gallery (fig. 1).[10] In the next decades, almost all of the Michelangelo works enumerated by Térey entered the museum as plaster casts, including the *Medici Tombs*.[11] Among the artworks listed by Térey, the *Colleoni Equestrian Monument* also appears, and the history of this unusual acquisition forms the subject of the second part of this paper.

The first architectural designs for the building of the Museum of Fine Arts were made in 1899 when an architectural competition was announced for the new museum. The detailed plans were finalised in 1900 by the winning architects Albert Schickedanz (1846–1915) and Fülöp Herzog (1860–1925). The layouts were published in early 1901 in a specialist journal for the Hungarian building industry, featuring the Michelangelo Gallery, albeit without its purpose being specified.[12] In the minutes of the committee meeting on the construction of the museum held in 1902, the gallery is already referred to as the "Michelangelo room".[13] The committee for the construction of the museum was formed as soon as the design by Schickedanz and Herzog was approved, and in addition to artists and architects, Gábor Térey, as the museum's curator, was also a permanent member of the board supervising the construction process.[14]

Between 1899 and 1900, at the request of the ministry for religion and public education, the chief architects slightly modified the design and layout to fulfil the exhibition demands of the museum. By the end of 1900, all the plans were finalised, and the exhibition gallery for the Michelangelo casts was also most likely designed by this time.

Fig. 3

Layout of one of the long walls of the Michelangelo Gallery of the Museum of Fine Arts, Budapest with the plaster casts of Michelangelo's works, ca. 1905–1906

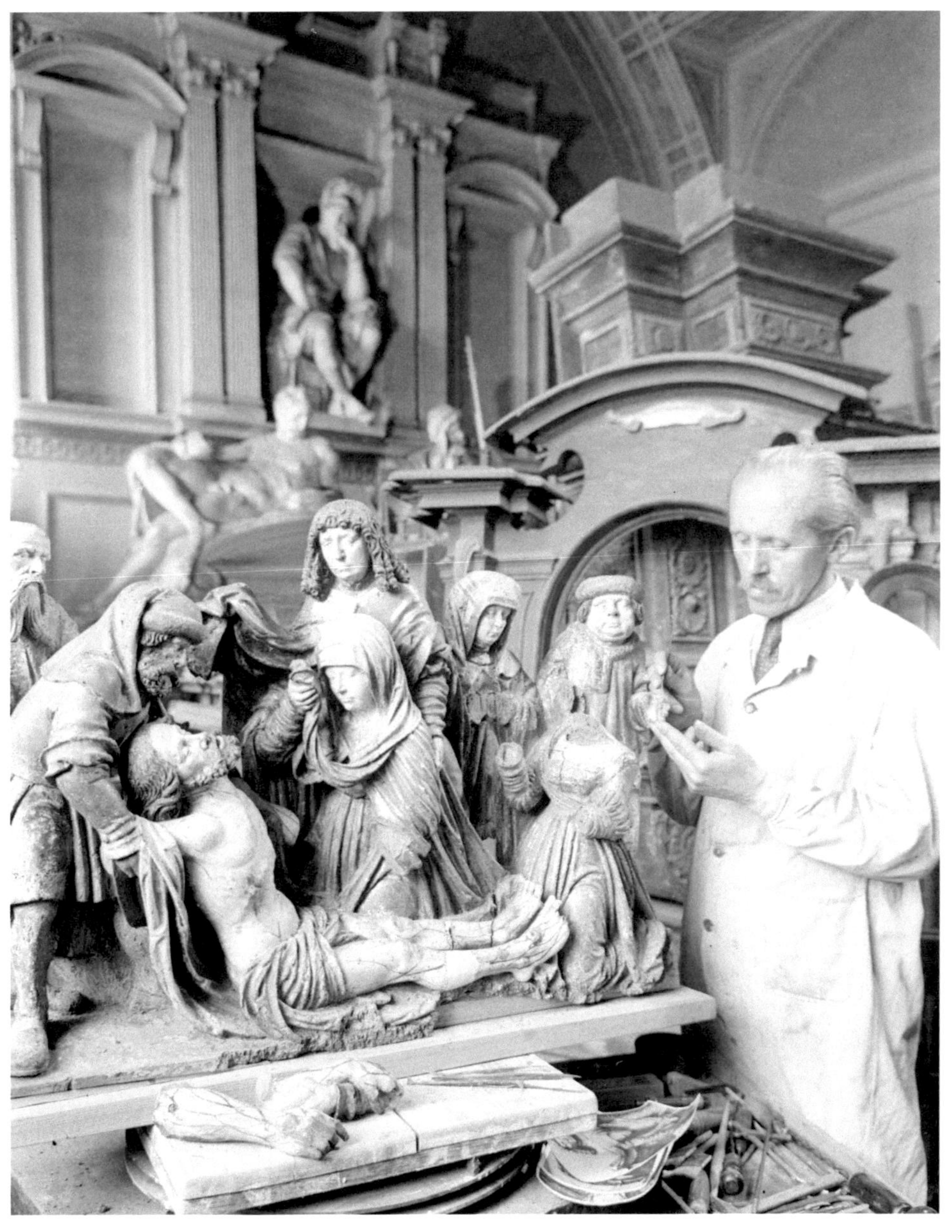

not only enumerates the copies, but also states the intention of the museum to arrange the Michelangelo Gallery similarly to the Medici Chapel in Florence, where the original tombs are preserved. Besides showing the *Medici Tombs*, the aim was for this gallery to present Michelangelo's sculptural oeuvre as completely as possible: together with the two tombs from Cologne they ordered copies of the *Moses* statue, the *David* bust, the *Bruges Madonna*, the *Medici Madonna*, and the Roman *Pietà*.[16] Although the initial concepts had focused on the importance of purchasing artworks together with their architectural elements, with this requirement also specified in the case of the *Medici Tombs*, from this first correspondence it seems that only the main figures and the sarcophagi were ordered at that time. As some of the documents are missing, it is only from the correspondence between the museum and August Gerber in June 1906 that we know the architectural parts of the tombs were also ordered in the meantime. In a letter from 23 June, Gerber informs the museum that, to the best of his knowledge, no other institution had previously commissioned the *Medici Tombs* in their entirety.[17] The museum also exchanged letters concerning the layer of paint to be applied to the casts. Gerber suggested coating the raw casts in situ after the works were installed in the museum, as the joints would anyway have to be covered after the copies were assembled. This recommendation was accepted by the museum and had a major effect on how plaster casts in general were displayed in Budapest. Most of the casts ordered after this time were delivered as raw casts, and after installation they were covered with a thin layer of paint, imitating the surface of the original artworks, by the decorative painters who also worked on the building's interior. Consequently, most of the casts of the museum are still preserved today with this painted layer.[18]

Although the lists of casts to be acquired had been drawn up in 1901, most of the commissions were not initiated until 1905 and 1906, when the building was almost finished, so that the ordered copies could be installed.[15] This was also the case with the *Medici Tombs*. Most of the documents on this commission have fortunately survived, which not only allows the history of the acquisition to be reconstructed, but also provides valuable information about the casts themselves and about the museum's intentions. The first contact with August Gerber, the cast maker from Cologne, was probably made at the end of 1905, although the related document is untraced; the earliest extant letter in this correspondence dates from 16 January 1906, and includes a list of the ordered works. The letter, signed by Ernő Kammerer (1856–1920), then director of the museum,

Fig. 4

The conservator of the Museum of Fine Arts
with the copy of the *Tomb of Giuliano de' Medici*
in the background, Budapest, 12 July 1961

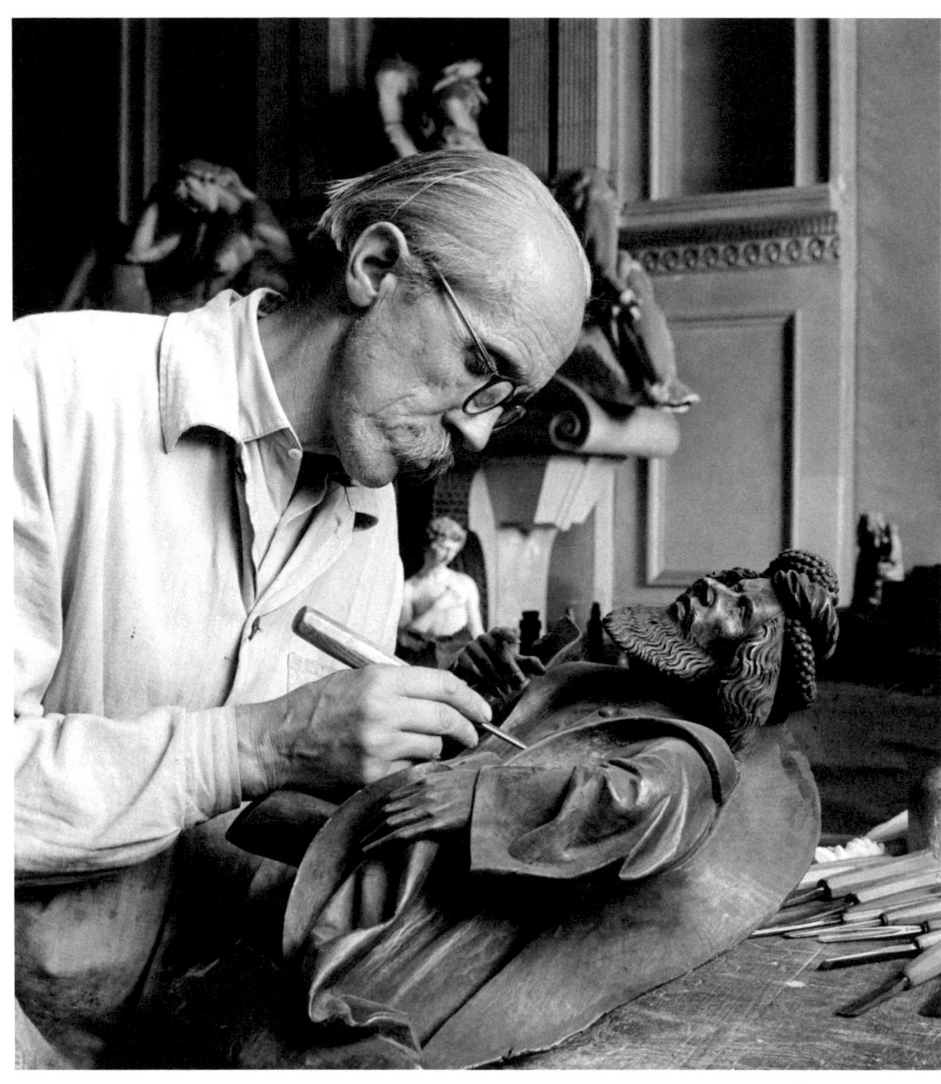

Fig. 5

The conservator of the Museum of Fine Arts
with the copy of the *Tomb of Lorenzo de' Medici*
in the background, Budapest, 16 March 1954

The first series of casts – the *Moses*, the *David* bust,
the *Bruges Madonna*, the *Medici Madonna*, the Roman
Pietà, the figural parts of the *Medici Tombs* and the sarcophagi, as well as a few newly ordered antique pieces
– arrived in Budapest from Gerber's workshop in October 1906. The original plan was to send the architectural parts one month later, but this schedule could not be
kept, partly due to the unexpected death of the workshop leader August Gerber, but also because the work
was more complicated than the cast makers had initially
supposed.[19] In a letter of 11 January 1907, the workshop
informed the museum that, for the sake of some details,
a new visit to Florence was required.[20] The lower parts of
the architectural background were finally transported to
Budapest in April 1907, with the upper parts and the final
casts following in August.[21] The installation of the casts
started in 1907 and was concluded in 1908.[22]

Several layouts and sketches have survived with the
planned arrangement of the Michelangelo Gallery. The
Medici Tombs were placed at either end of the room
(fig. 2), while other casts of Michelangelo's works were
installed along the walls (fig. 3).

Although work on assembling most of the casts in the
Michelangelo room began in 1908 and in 1909, the gallery was not opened to the public until 1913. Unfortunately no archive photograph is known today of how the
installed gallery looked before World War II. The only
pictures which partially record the original appearance
of the gallery date from the 1950s and 1960s, when
the room was used as conservation workshop, and
photos were taken of the work carried out there (fig. 4).
In the background, the copy of the *Tomb of Giuliano
and Lorenzo de' Medici* is visible (fig. 5).

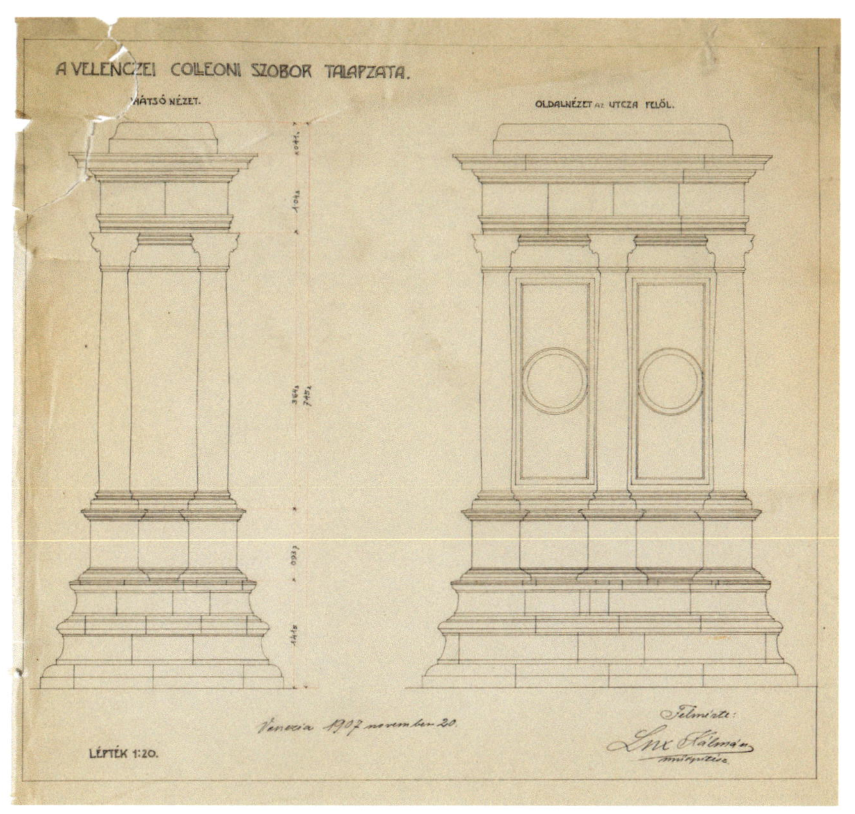

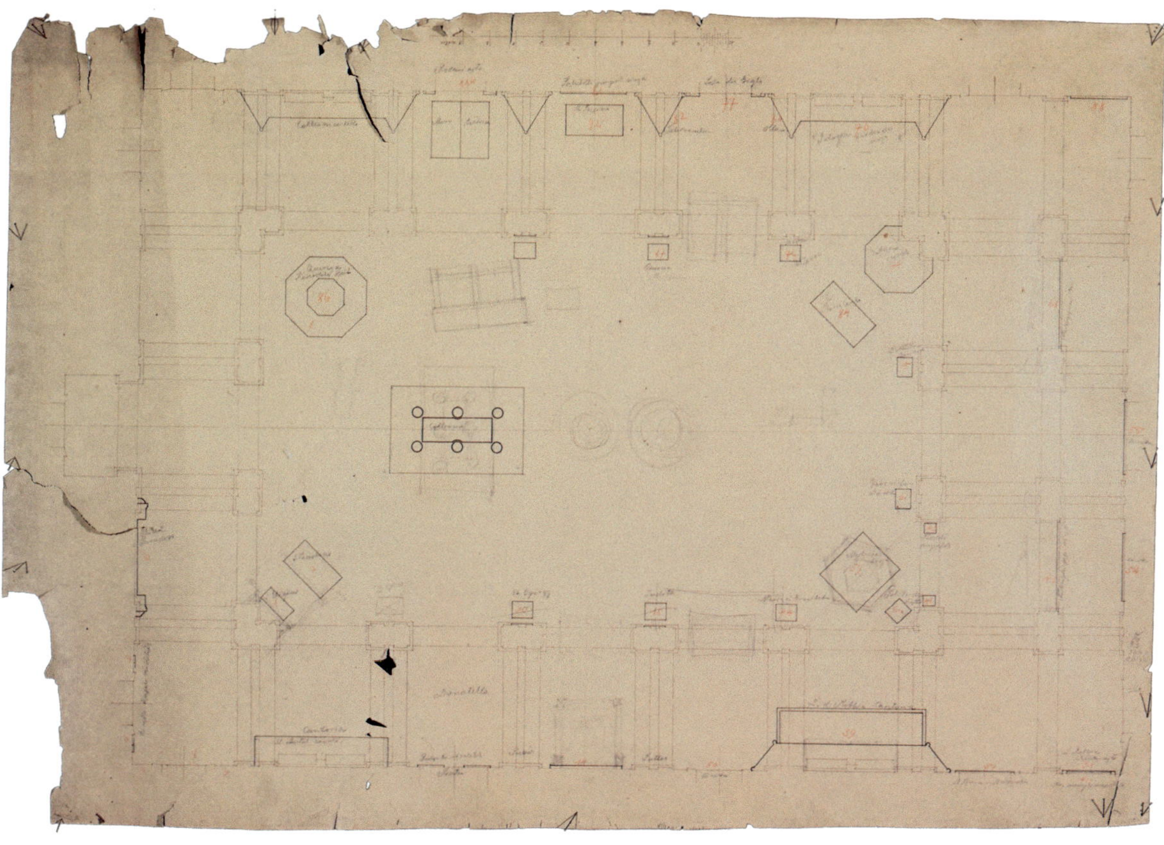

Fig. 6

Survey of the Colleoni pedestal
made by Kálmán Lux, Venice, 20 November 1907

Fig. 7

Layout of the Renaissance Hall
of the Museum of Fine Arts with the casts
arranged after the plans of Gábor Térey,
Budapest, ca. 1906

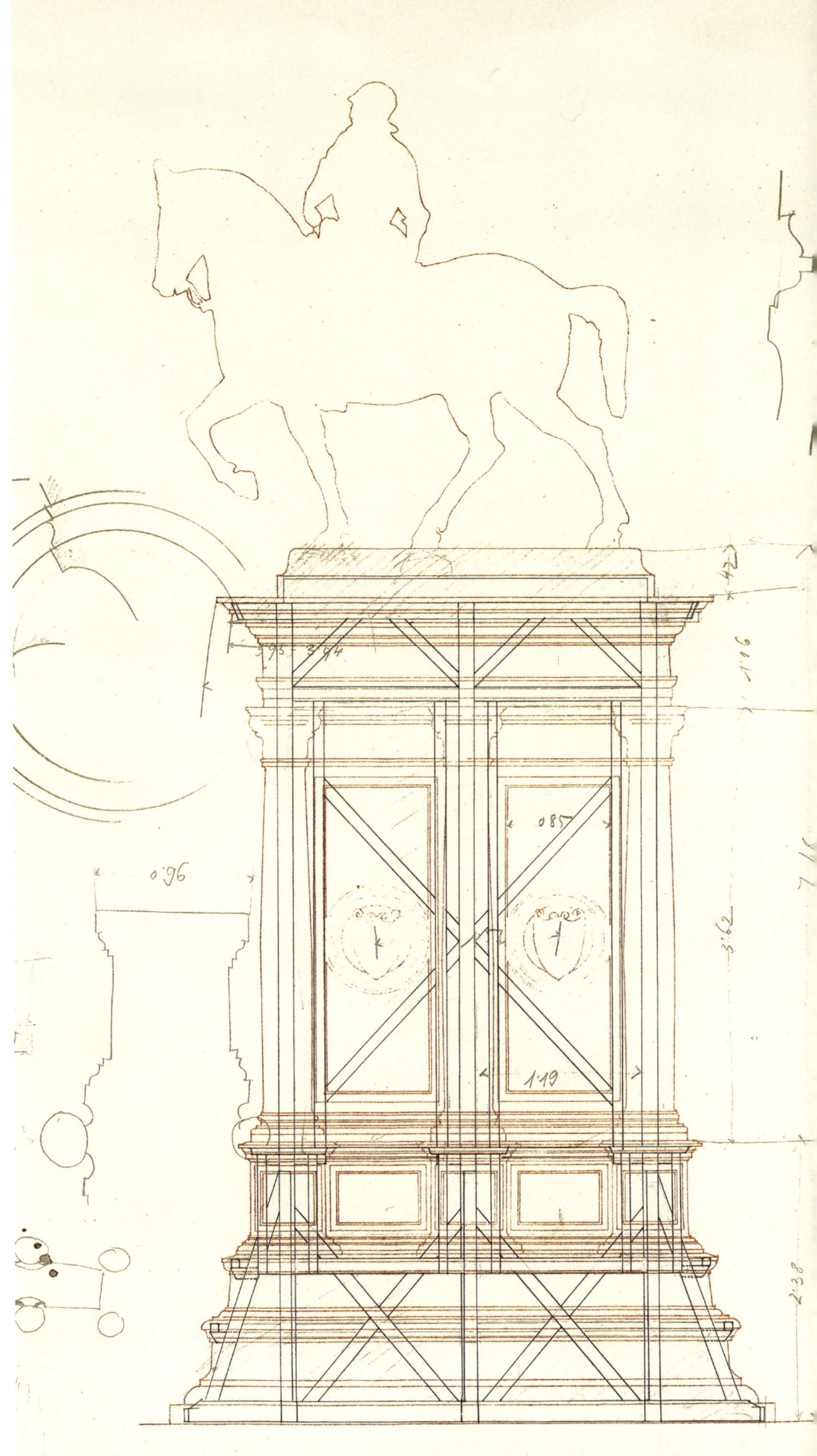

Fig. 8

Plans by Kálmán Lux of the wood armature
for the Colleoni pedestal, 1907–1908

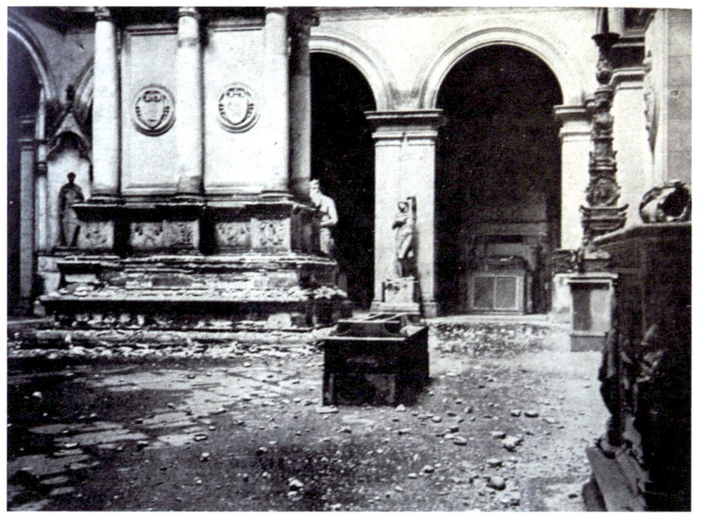

Like the *Medici Tombs,* the *Colleoni Equestrian Monument* was also ordered in 1905, in this instance from the casting workshop of the Kaiser-Friedrich-Museum, Berlin. The cast arrived in Budapest in April 1906.[23] While the initial idea was to purchase a copy of the equestrian statue's original pedestal, surviving documents reveal that other possibilities for a plinth were also taken into consideration. When the casting workshop in Berlin was asked about a suitable pedestal on which to exhibit the statue, they offered a plinth measuring a few centimetres in height, which they would produce and send with the cast.[24] Apparently, however, this solution did not comply with the original concept of the Budapest museum, nor with the architectural design of the Renaissance Hall. The precise evolution of the museum's decision ultimately to acquire a copy of the original pedestal cannot be traced, but more than half a year later, in January 1907, the Austro-Hungarian Embassy at the Palazzo Venezia in Rome was contacted for diplomatic help to obtain a cast of the original base of the *Colleoni Horseman*.[25] The museum's letter of gratitude from 6 July 1907 indicates that the ambassador of the Austro-Hungarian Monarchy, Heinrich Graf von Lützow (1852–1935), intervened personally with the Italian authorities to obtain permission for taking a mould of the pedestal in Venice. The notes in the documents also show that besides the official and diplomatic requests, the director of the museum, Ernő Kammerer, informally asked the help of the Hungarian politician and diplomat

József Somssich (1864–1941), then consul in Genoa.[26] The documents also provide insight into the process of installing the casts in the Renaissance Hall. The museum asked for permission to copy the Colleoni pedestal to be granted as urgently as possible, as the other casts planned for the hall could only be mounted after its monumental centrepiece, the equestrian statue, was in place. The first steps for obtaining the copy of the pedestal almost exactly coincided with the arrival in Budapest of the architectural parts of the *Medici Tombs*. This coincidence suggests that acquiring full copies of the *Medici Tombs* reinforced the museum's initial intention to obtain the pedestal of the Colleoni equestrian statue.

The museum also contacted the Venetian *Uffizio regionale per i monumenti del Veneto*, which commissioned the company of the stone carver Giuseppe Longo to make the copy of the pedestal.[27] As the permit was restricted to the reliefs on the pedestal, with thirty-six pieces being cast from the pedestal by Giuseppe Longo, the museum insisted on sending Hungarian specialists and architects to make precise measurements and layouts of the pedestal itself. In November, the architects Lajos Rauscher (1845–1914) and Kálmán Lux (1880–1961)

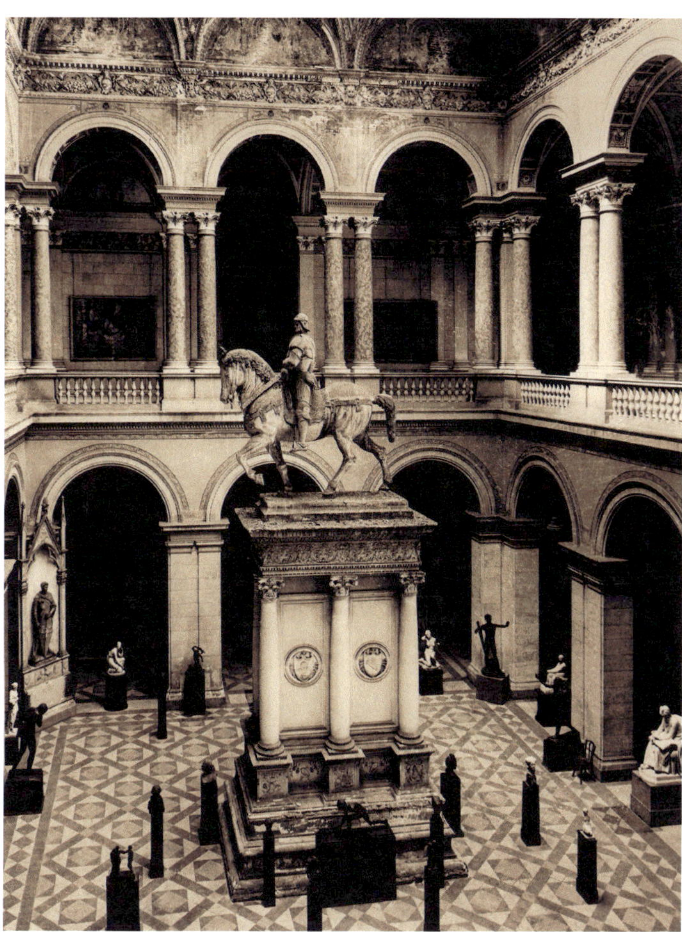

Fig. 9

The Renaissance Hall after World War II
with the pedestal of the Colleoni statue
and with the Michelangelo casts, 1945–1946

Fig. 10

The Renaissance Hall of the Museum of Fine Arts, Budapest, ca. 1951

travelled to Venice to conduct the architectural survey of the pedestal, and several drawings by the latter are now preserved in the archive of the museum (fig. 6).[28] After completing the survey, the architects submitted a request for further casts deemed necessary for recreating the base in Budapest. The casts arrived in Hungary at the end of 1907, and the whole *Colleoni Monument* was installed in the Renaissance Hall in 1908 (fig. 6 in the paper by Eckart Marchand).

Gábor Térey not only compiled the list of the casts but also drew plans for the arrangement of the works: layouts and wall view sketches for the Renaissance Hall have also survived from this period. Comparing these drawings with the final layout of the exhibition, it can be seen that certain interim modifications were made, and one sheet records how the positioning of the *Colleoni Monument* was altered during planning (fig. 7). In the early phase of planning, the *Colleoni Monument* was positioned with the head of the horse and the *condottiere* facing the main entrance, with the longer sides of the pedestal running parallel to the long sides of the hall. Given the proportions of the Renaissance Hall and the rectangular layout of the monument's pedestal, this seemed the ideal position. Ultimately, however, when the casts were installed, this monument and its pedestal were turned ninety degrees.

A full team of architects, cast makers, and decorative painters worked on installing the casts in the museum. Wooden armatures were generally constructed for the monumental casts, and the armature for the Colleoni pedestal was designed by Kálmán Lux (fig. 8), one of the architects who had visited Venice to survey the original plinth.[29]

The *Colleoni Monument* was installed in a remarkably short period of time, after which some of the other Renaissance casts were also put in place, enabling the hall to be opened to the public in 1908. Over the next few years, further Renaissance casts were added to the hall, and the exhibition of casts was only finalised in 1913.[30] Even when the hall was first opened in 1908, the contemporary press emphasised how significant it was that Budapest held the only copy of the Colleoni statue complete with its pedestal.[31]

As we have seen, all three monumental plaster casts – the replica of the *Colleoni Equestrian Monument* and the copies of *Lorenzo and Giuliano de' Medici tombs* – were delivered to the museum in their entirety: the first with its pedestal, and the second group with their architectural elements.

When the museum was established and in the first years of its existence, the museum strove to present the history of architecture alongside that of the fine arts. This concept is reflected in archive documents and early publications, and it can also be observed in the different architectural styles of the building's ground floor halls and in the museum's firm intention to have a separate department for architecture.[32] Ultimately, this separate department did not come to fruition, and the presentation of architecture received less attention in later periods of the museum's history. Nevertheless, in addition to the *Colleoni Monument* and the *Medici Tombs,* a few other casts purchased by the museum in its founding years bear witness to this initial desire to include architectural works among the exhibits, including complete copies of Ghiberti's *Gates of Paradise* and the *Golden Gate* of Freiberg Cathedral.[33] The *Colleoni Monument* is furthermore exceptional as the cast of its pedestal is the only known copy, while the architectural elements of the *Medici Tombs* are not (and never have been) present in any other cast collections.

After World War II, these three monumental Renaissance casts suffered a similar fate to that of the museum's other casts. The copies had remained in the exhibition halls during the siege of Budapest in late 1944 and early 1945. Although the museum was damaged during the war, the building remained structurally intact, but large parts of the skylights collapsed due to the air pressure caused by bombardments (fig. 9). In consequence, rain and snow penetrated the halls, especially where the casts were installed. Despite the fact that the casts were no longer regarded as valuable pieces for the museum, there was no suggestion of discarding them.[34] Over the following years, several plans were put forward for establishing a separate cast museum, but none was implemented at the time. In 1951 most of the casts, apart from the massive *Colleoni Monument,* were transferred from the Renaissance Hall to the Romanesque Hall. The equestrian statue remained in place, with an exhibition of nineteenth- and twentieth-century Hungarian sculpture installed around it (fig. 10). In 1953, the museum's collection of Venetian wellheads was arranged in the Renaissance Hall, and in preparation for this, around the end of 1952, the *Colleoni Monument* was dismantled and moved to the Romanesque Hall.[35] Unlike the *Colleoni Monument,* the *Medici Tombs* remained for a longer period in the Michelangelo Gallery, even after it was converted into a conservation workshop. While the other Michelangelo casts were removed to provide space for the conservators, the wall-mounted *Medici Tombs* could stay, as they did not obstruct the conservation work (figs. 4–5). Only in the late 1960s or early 1970s were the *Medici Tombs* finally removed from the conservation workshop, its components stored variously in the Romanesque Hall or in the basement of the building. In 1976, at the initiative of the Hungarian sculptor Miklós Melocco, the Michelangelo casts were restored and exhibited in the former synagogue in the regional city of Kecskemét, where they are still held today.[36] Due to a shortage of space, only the main figures of the *Medici Tombs* could be exhibited in their new home, while the architectural parts were left in storage in the Romanesque Hall. The pieces of the *Colleoni Monument* remained in the Romanesque Hall until 2015, when projects were launched to reconstruct the museum's Romanesque wing and to rehabilitate the museum's erstwhile plaster cast collection. As part of this process, a new exhibition of the plaster casts, including the *Colleoni Monument,* was envisaged in the renovated nineteenth-century Star Fortress in Komárom.[37]

According to the conservators who reassembled the copy of the equestrian statue in Komárom, some parts of its pedestal were lost, but the surviving pieces have been preserved in a way that will facilitate an eventual reconstruction of the whole cast. The *Colleoni Monument* was installed in Komárom in 2020, forming the centrepiece of the great hall, now named the Colleoni Hall. The same exhibition space also houses the *Gates of Paradise* (fig. 11). The new Colleoni Hall in Komárom, displaying the Colleoni statue with its pedestal and the *Gates of Paradise* complete with the work's frame, recalls the milieu of the former, hundred-year-old plaster cast exhibition in Budapest. As such, the new display also pays tribute to the original concept of the Museum of Fine Arts as an institution dedicated to presenting the history not only of the fine arts, but also that of architecture.

Fig. 11

The Colleoni Hall in Komárom, the casts of the equestrian statue of Colleoni and the *Gates of Paradise* among the installed artworks

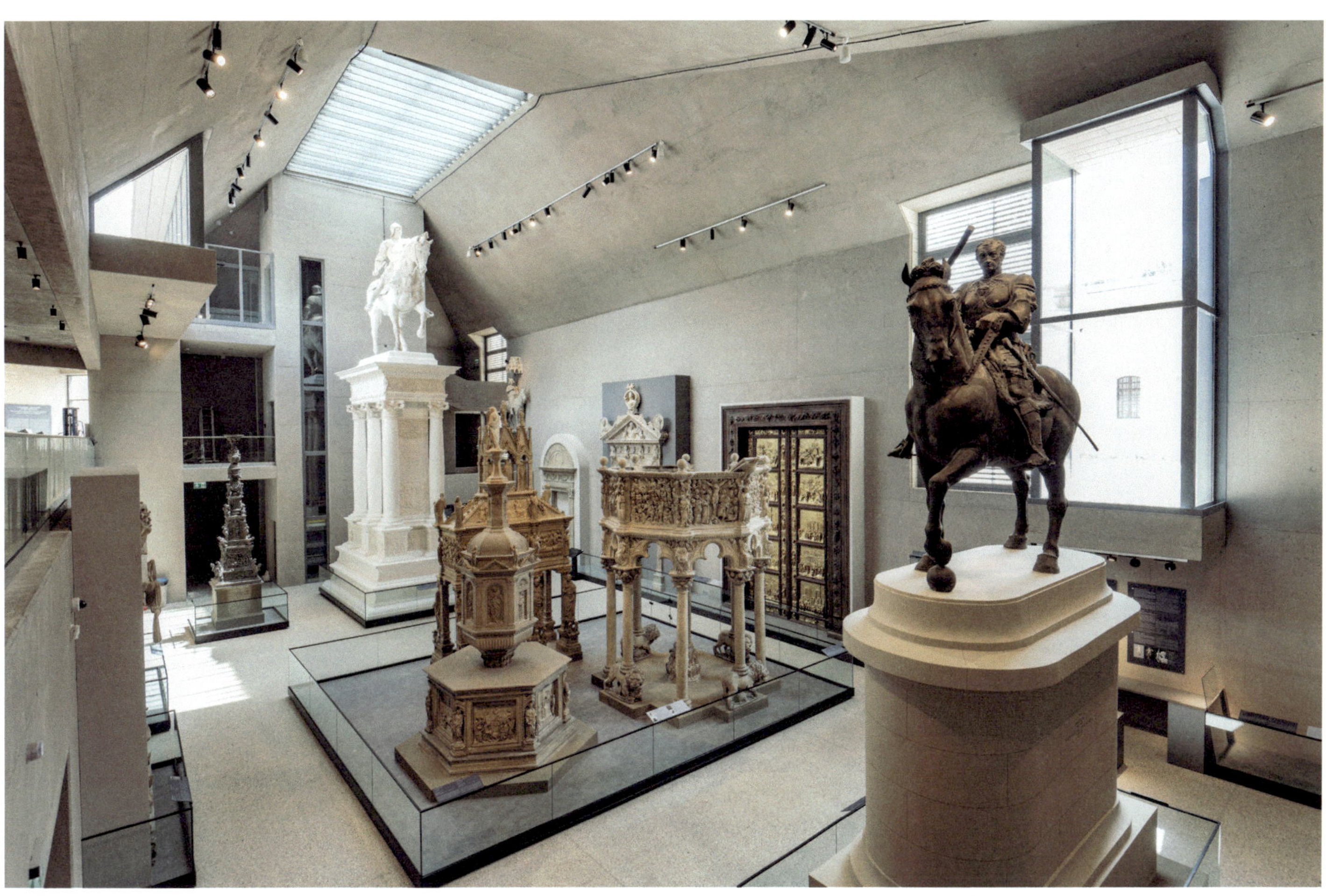

Notes

1   For the early history of the Museum of Fine Arts, Budapest see Bacher 1956; for the creation of the cast collection see Andó 2021 and Rózsavölgyi 2021, here esp.: 90–103 and respectively: 135–44.

2   For the original pedestal of the *Colleoni Monument* see Butterfield 1997, 183, 235–36.

3   One other whole copy of the Colleoni statue, made of stone and bronze, exists in Newark, New Jersey; the statue, placed in Lincoln Park, was ordered from the Scottish born sculptor John Massey Rhind by the local brewer Christian Feigenspan on the occasion of the 250th anniversary of the city in 1916. See http://www.newarkhistory.com/colleoni (accessed 25 August 2022).

4   The correspondence was discovered and published first by Edit Szentesi. See Szentesi 2006B, 36. Cited in English by Rózsavölgyi 2021, 136.

5   The Hungarian state at this time already owned the collection of the Esterházy family, the greatest noble family in Hungary; this collection was institutionally integrated into the Országos Képtár (National Picture Gallery), in addition to which the Hungarian National Museum also had significant fine art collections. These artworks later constituted the core of the Museum of Fine Arts, founded in 1896. Bacher 1956, 5–22.

6   See Wlassics 1900, 8 (for the *Medici Tombs*), 9 (for the Colleoni copy).

7   Radványi 2006, 12–14; in the English summary: 169–71.

8   Rózsavölgyi 2021, 143.

9   *Dr Térey Gábor jelentése a Szépművészeti Muzeum olasz renaissance plasztikai osztálya számára megszerendő gypsöntvények tárgyában, az öntvények jegyzékével* [Report of Dr Gábor Térey on the subject of the plaster casts to be acquired for the Italian Renaissance sculpture department of the Museum of Fine Arts, with a list of the casts], compiled 15/05/1901. Archives MFAB, 232/1901.

10   *Maiano, Gigli gipszöntvény felállítása* [The installation of the Maiano, Gigli plaster cast], Archives MFAB, Layouts, T-10. I would like to thank László Nagy for all his help in my researches in the Archives MFAB.

11   Térey listed 17 works by Michelangelo to be ordered in copies; except for 4 artworks from this list, the museum finally commissioned casts of all of them, as well as 3 other sculptures by Michelangelo not mentioned in Térey's list. See Térey 1901 (see note 9): IX, and Miriam Szőcs, Zsófia Vargyas and Márton Tóth, *Medieval and Renaissance Plaster Casts. Online Database of the Budapest Museum of Fine Arts' Cast Collection*, see: https://gipszek.szepmuveszeti.hu/en.

12   *Épitő Ipar* 1901, 6.

13   *Jegyzőkönyv a Szépművészeti Múzeum építőbizottságának üléseiről. II.* [Minutes of the Construction Committee of the Museum of Fine Arts, Part II], Archives MFAB, 766/902, 181.

14   *Jegyzőkönyv a Szépművészeti Múzeum építőbizottságának üléseiről. I. Hátsóépület.* [Minutes of the Construction Committee of the Museum of Fine Arts, Part I. Rear Section of the Building], Archives MFAB, 230/1899.

15   For the acquisition of the Renaissance and medieval casts see Szőcs 2016, here esp.: 139–40, in the English summary: 147 and Rózsavölgyi 2021, 142–44.

16   Archives MFAB, 56/1906. The untitled document contains the notes of August Gerber's previous letter and a draft of Ernő Kammerer's answer sent to Gerber dated 16 January 1906.

17   *August Gerber Köln a Medici-sírok építészeti részei mintázásáról jelent* [August Gerber from Cologne reports on the casting of the architectural elements of the *Medici Tombs*] Archives MFAB, 905/1906; the documents contain the letter of August Gerber dated 23 June 1906 and the draft of the reply from the museum director, Ernő Kammerer, dated 25 June 1906.

18   Szőcs 2018B, here esp. 143–45.

19   *August Gerber (Cöln a. Rhein Belfortstrasse 9.) 6527 Más cheque-nek átvételéről értesít az öntvényekre vonatkozó egyéb közlésében.* [August Gerber (Cöln a. Rhein Belfortstrasse 9.) acknowledges receipt of the cheque for 6527 marks as well as other information on the casts]. Archives MFAB, 1476/1906. Although the letter informs the museum that August Gerber died, in the museum's records they later refer to the workshop under the name of August Gerber.

20   *August Gerber közli, hogy a Medici-sírok architektúrájának öntvényeit legkésőbb f. é. april végéig szállíthatja* [August Gerber notifies that the architectural casts of the Medici tombs can be delivered at the latest by the end of April of the present year], Archives MFAB, 54/907.

21 *August Gerber (Cöln a. Rhein) közli hogy a Medici-sírok architektúrája egy részének egy waggonnyi öntvényét elküldötte; a felső és részek lehető gyorsan készülnek* [August Gerber (Cöln a. Rhein) sends notification that a railway wagon of casts constituting part of the architectural elements of the *Medici Tombs* has been despatched, and that the upper part elements will be cast as soon as possible] and *August Gerber (Cöln a. Rhein) 4220.- és 518.- Más számla beküldésével értesít, hogy a Michelangelo-féle Medici-sírok architecturájának és a Barberini-féle Faun és Tiberius mellszobránák öntvényeit elküldte* [August Gerber (Cöln a. Rhein), enclosing invoices for 4220 and 518 marks, sends notification that they have despatched the casts of the architectural elements of Michelangelo's *Medici Tombs* and those of the Barberini's Faun and Tiberius bust], Archives MFAB, 559/1907 and 1276/907.

22 We know from the records of the copies that the museum paid for wooden structure and assembly in 1907 and in 1908, although as most of the original documents are untraced, we are aware only of the registration numbers of the documents: 1915/1907, 1391/1908; 310/1908.

23 *A m.á.v. Budapest dunaparti teher pálya-udvarának értesítő és vétlevele egy Charlottenburgból érkezett gipszküldeményről.* [Notification from the Danube riverbank station of the Hungarian State Railways of the arrival of a consignment of plaster casts from Charlottenburg], Archives MFAB, 542/1906. For the history of the casting workshop of the Kaiser-Friedrich-Museum see Berlin 2019B.

24 *Generalverwaltung der koeniglichen Museen a Colleoni lovasszobor öntvényének méreteire vonatkozó adatokat közli, küldvén egyszersmind a rajzot is.* [The direction of the Königliche Museen sends measurements and drawings of the cast of the Colleoni horseman], Archives MFAB, 265/1906.

25 *Intézkedés a Colleoni-emlék felvétele tárgyában.* [Measures regarding the copy making of the Colleoni monument], Archives MFAB, 143/1907.

26 *K. u. k. össter.-ungar. Botschaft (am kgl. ital. Hofe) válasza a Colleoni-emlék talapzata ügyében írt megkeresésre.* [The answer of the Imperial and Royal Austro-Hungarian Embassy in regard to the (museum') request concerning the Colleoni pedestal], Archives MFAB, 591/1907.

27 *Ufficio regionale per la conservazione dei monumenti del Veneto (Venezia) válasza a Colleoni-emlék másolata ügyében 1068/907 sz. a. kelt itteni megkeresésre.*
[The answer of the Ufficio regionale per la conservazione dei monumenti del Veneto (Venezia) regarding our request no. 1068/907 concerning the copy of the Colleoni monument], Archives MFAB, 1101/1907.

28 Bacher 1956, 34. Among the layouts of the pedestal of the Colleoni horseman preserved from this period in the archives of the museum, several were made during, or soon after the survey was made in Venice, Archives MFAB, Layouts, T-24, T-36, T-43, T-98 (dated and signed by Kálmán Lux: *Venezia 1907 november 20. Felmérte: Lux Kálmán műépítész* [Venice 20 November 1907. Survey made by Kálmán Lux architect]).

29 In the archive of the museum, the plan for the wood armature was also preserved. Archives MFAB, Layouts, T-99.

30 The exhibition of casts in the Renaissance Hall was first opened in 1908, and further casts were installed in the hall in subsequent years, until the exhibition was completed in 1913. See Farkas 1913, 394 and Rózsavölgyi 2021, 144–49. A major rearrangement of all the cast exhibitions was carried out between 1923 and 1926. For this later refurbishment, see Hekler 1924, and Petrovics 1926.

31 Rózsavölgyi 2021, 143; Erdey 1908.

32 Wlassics 1900, 2–3; on the general interest in architectural casts see Lending 2017.

33 Rózsavölgyi 2021, 143; Szőcs 2016.

34 On the history of the cast collections in Budapest after World War II see Szőcs 2021B, esp. 161–67.

35 No documents have been preserved about the dismantling of the *Colleoni Horseman* and its pedestal; we are aware of this process only from documents and reports pertaining to the installation of the exhibition of Venetian wellheads. See Balogh 1954.

36 Szőcs 2021A, 166.

37 On the rehabilitation project of the plaster casts collection and on the exhibition in Komárom see Szőcs 2021A.

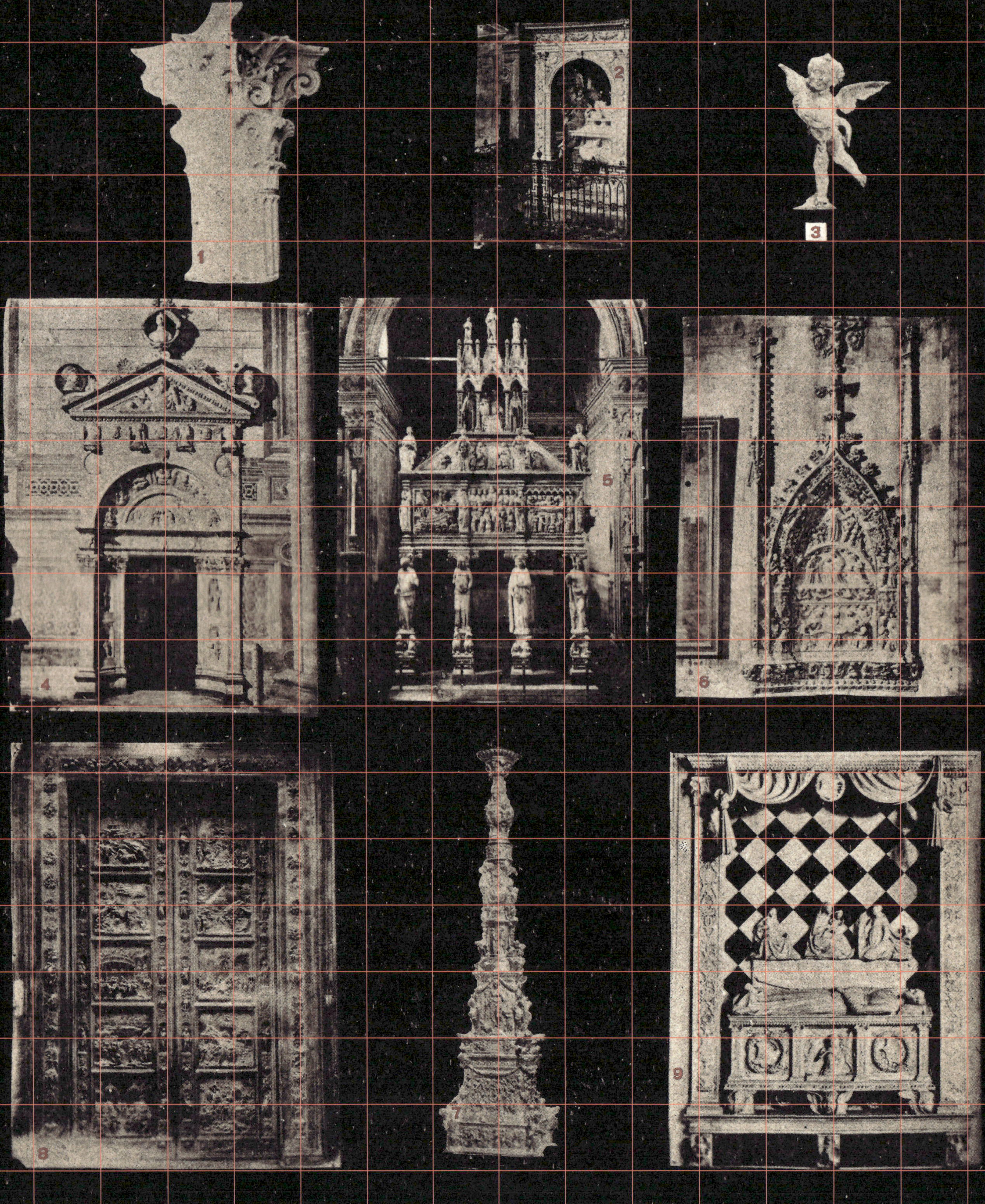

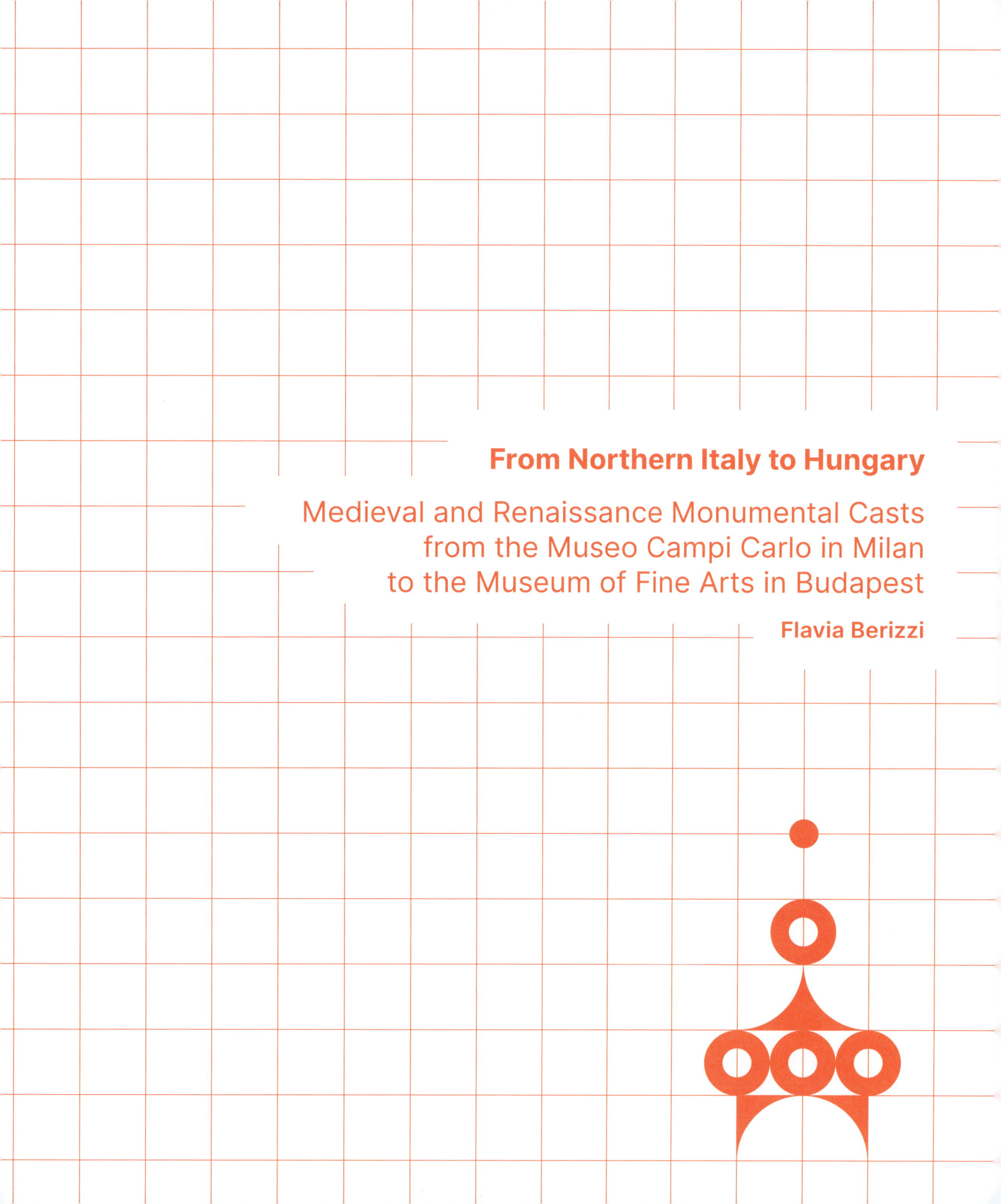

From Northern Italy to Hungary

Medieval and Renaissance Monumental Casts
from the Museo Campi Carlo in Milan
to the Museum of Fine Arts in Budapest

Flavia Berizzi

From Northern Italy to Hungary

Medieval and Renaissance Monumental Casts from the Museo Campi Carlo in Milan to the Museum of Fine Arts in Budapest

Flavia Berizzi

Among the *formatori*[1] who contributed to the improvement of the moulding technique in the second half of the nineteenth century, working in the most important surveys of sculptural and monumental works in Northern Italy, a leading role was assumed by the master Carlo Campi.[2] In the first decade of the twentieth century, his Milanese workshop was one of the main suppliers of the newly established Museum of Fine Arts in Budapest, collaborating in the extensive acquisition campaign of plaster casts reproducing masterpieces of Italian medieval and Renaissance art.

Born in Milan in mid-August 1841,[3] Campi was initiated into the profession of *formatore* under the aegis of the most successful sculptors on the Milanese scene of his time, including professors of the Brera Academy of Fine Arts. From the early 1870s, they introduced him to the operational dynamics of the School of Sculpture, where the young master was called upon to translate into plaster the didactic clay models of the most deserving students[4] and to immortalise anatomical details cast from live models.[5] In 1871 he opened his own workshop,[6] initially dedicating himself to the reproduction of plaster casts for educational purposes. This marked the founding of the first nucleus of the *gipsoteca* (fig. 1). Over time, he began working on the ancient models exhibited in the Gallery of Statues and those used in the Schools of Sculpture, Figure and Ornament, where maintenance interventions were required, or where there was a desire to obtain further copies.[7] From the 1880s, he became the privileged and almost exclusive *formatore* of the Academy. Campi's prestige grew hand in hand with the expansion of his manufactory's range, to which he progressively annexed the objects taken from the Brera Historical Collections.

Fig. 1

Anatomical models on display in the Carlo Campi workshop
at 37 via Moscova, Milan
In *Riproduzione d'oggetti d'arte Campi Carlo* (Milan, 1884–1887)

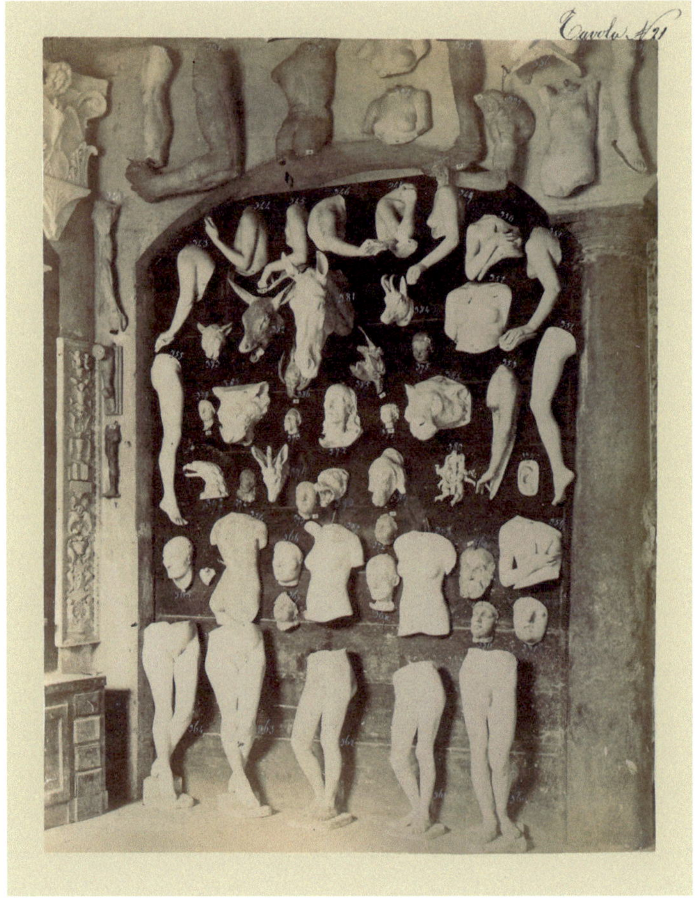

Fig. 2 | next page

The sequence known at present of the catalogues and illustrated albums of the Carlo Campi workshop dated to the end of the nineteenth century

Conservation locations:
Superintendence of Archeology, Fine Arts and Landscape
for the metropolitan city of Milan (1);
New Library, State Archive of Turin (2, 6);
Kunstbibliothek, Staatliche Museen, Berlin (3, 4);
Cantonal Library of Bellinzona (5);
Victoria and Albert Museum Archive, London (7);
State Archive of Canton Ticino, Bellinzona (8, 9)

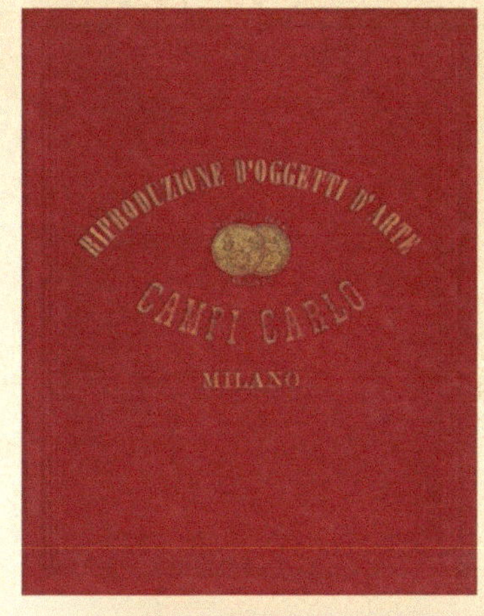

1   *Illustrated Album 1884–1887*

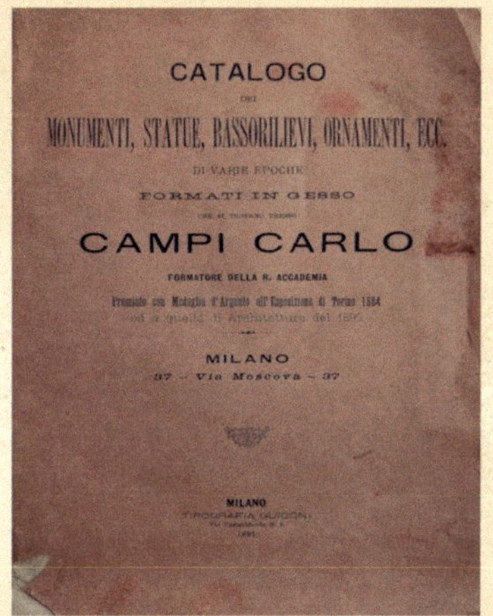

2   *Catalogue 1891*

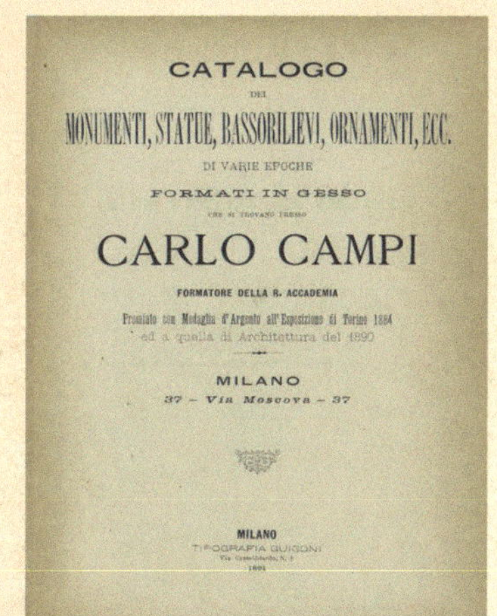

3   *Catalogue 1891–1892*

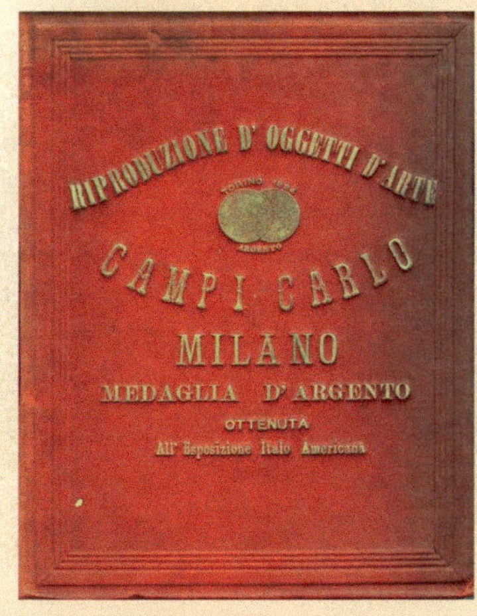

4   *Illustrated Album 1891–1892*

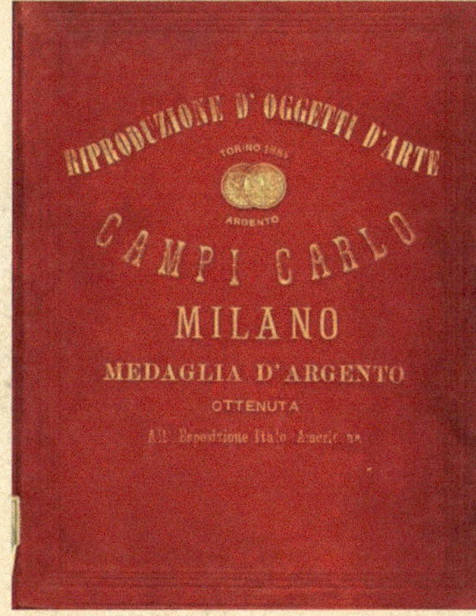

5   *Illustrated Album 1891–1893*

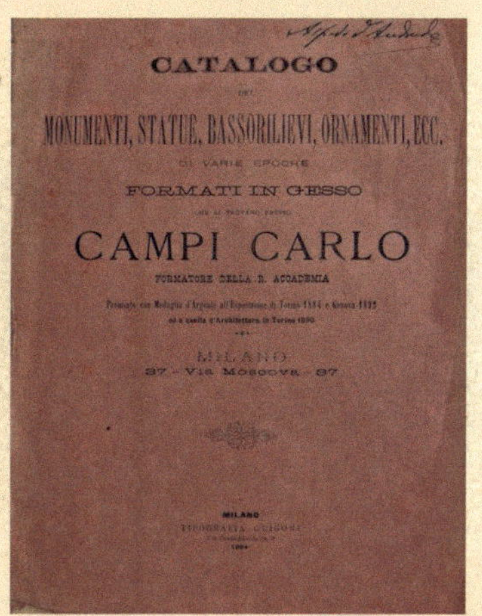

6   *Catalogue 1894*

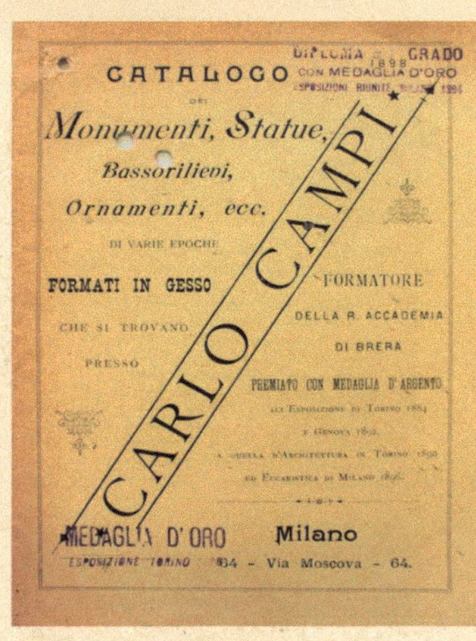

7   *Catalogue 1898*

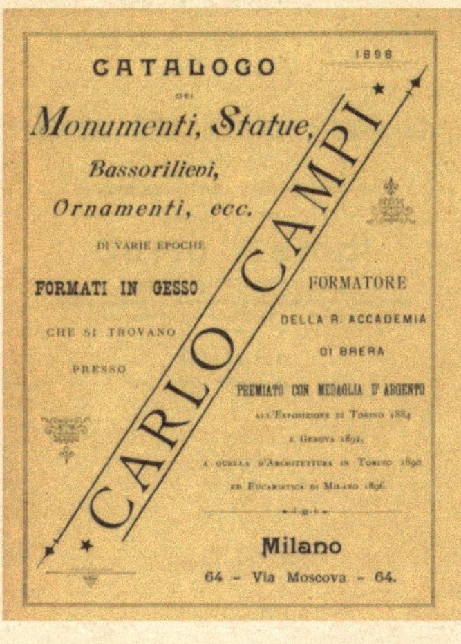

8   *Catalogue 1898–1900*

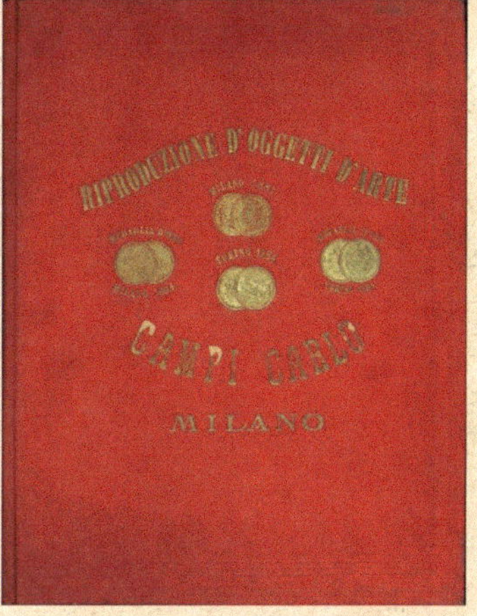

9   *Illustrated Album 1898–1900*

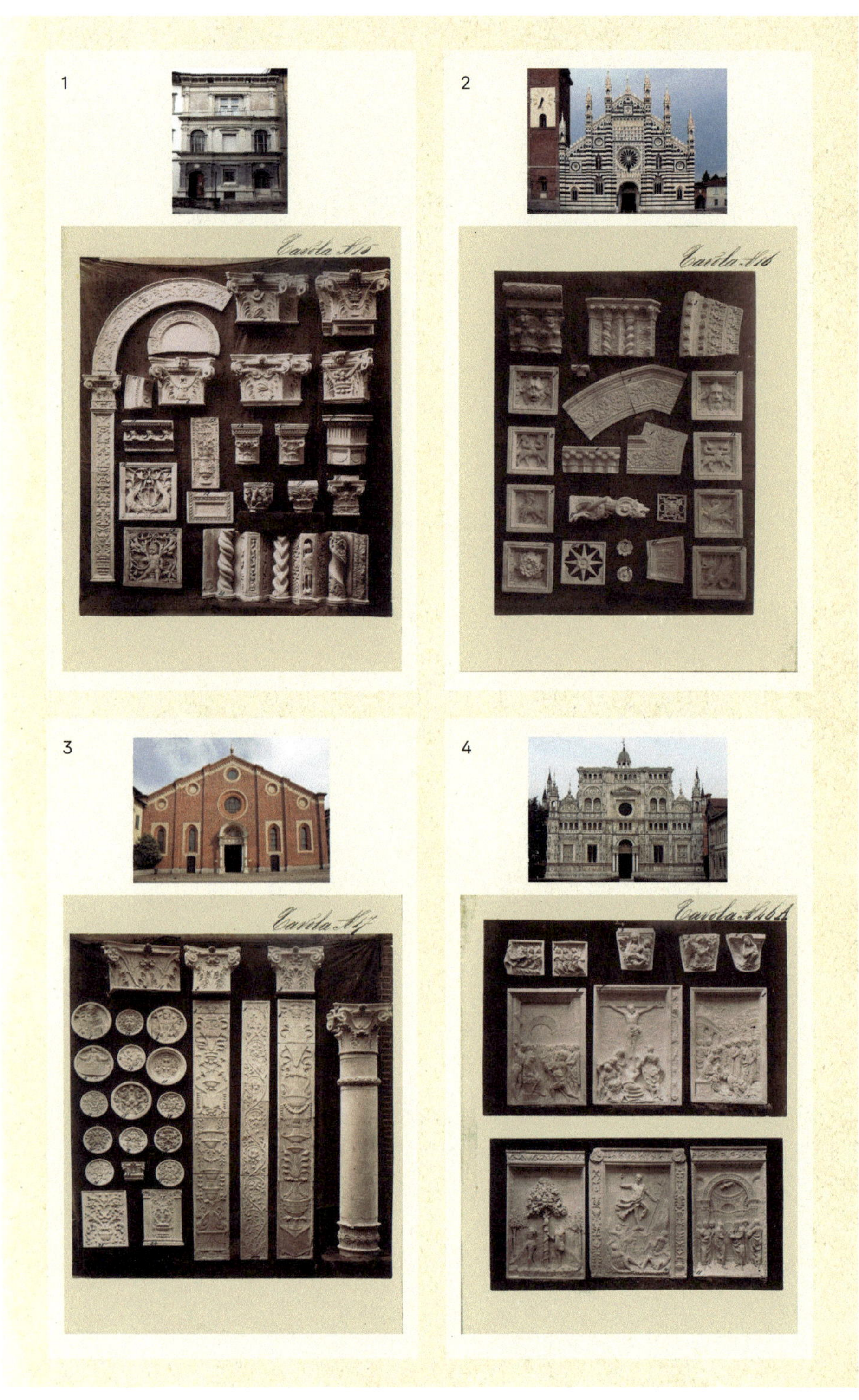

Fig. 3

Photographic plates showing casts after architectural details derived from the façades of buildings undergoing restoration in the last decade of the nineteenth century:

Casa Focaccia, Bergamo (plate no. 15 [1]);
Duomo di Monza (plate no. 16 [2]);
Santa Maria delle Grazie, Milan (plate no. 17 [3]);
Certosa di Pavia (plate no. 46A [4])
In *Riproduzione d'oggetti d'arte Campi Carlo* (Milan, 1898–1900)

With his proven reliability, in the last decade of the nineteenth century, Campi's services were sought after by local institutions responsible for the protection of monuments. The sequence of the precious catalogues and photographic albums[8] of the Campi workshop – only recently found in various Italian and European locations (fig. 2) – bears witness to the progressive acquisition of details taken from the most exemplary architectural complexes in the region between Milan, Monza, Bergamo and Pavia, fully corresponding chronologically with the restoration sites coordinated by the Ufficio Regionale per la Conservazione dei Monumenti in Lombardia (fig. 3). These study tools also provide evidence of the re-evaluation and critical success that surrounded the sculptural productions of the great Lombard masters of the past. Campi's perfect plaster casts, created in the era of the great Universal Exhibitions, played a crucial role in introducing these works to the general public. These events always earned the *formatore* recognition in the form of medals and acknowledgements, which were proudly emblazoned on the title page of the company's promotional material.

It was due mainly to the trust earned from the two authoritative institutions, as well as to the support received from the most influential personalities in Milan's cultural and artistic scene, that a rich collection of plaster casts was built up at Campi's workshop, located at 37 via Moscova. In this collection, effigies of classic masterpieces of Greco-Roman antiquity coexisted with replicas taken directly from the most excellent works of the Middle Ages and the Lombard Renaissance. The latter constituted the speciality of the Campi *gipsoteca*, attracting the interest of some major European museums, which, at the turn of the century, were building up their respective collections. These institutions, aspiring to a conception of universality, aimed to establish collections that incorporated both original artworks and spectacular plaster replicas. Among these, the Museum of Fine Arts in Budapest came late to the race. Upon its foundation in 1896, the experts commissioned by the Hungarian government to establish the collections had, on one hand, the opportunity to travel all over the continent, drawing on the experience of as many as 65 museums and exhibition venues.[9] On the other hand, they had access to a rich selection of reproductions already available in the moulding workshops, thanks to the huge surveys commissioned in the preceding decades. Although the Hungarian delegates did not include Italian destinations in their itinerary,[10]

they were able to witness the degree of technical excellence achieved by the Italian *formatori* through the monumental casts exhibited in London in the Architectural Courts of the South Kensington Museum. They then made their selection of objects through the catalogues of the various manufactories. Initially, the Campi workshop did not receive particular consideration: according to a report drawn up in 1901 by the art historian Gábor Térey, one of the museum's most authoritative professionals, the first programme for acquiring casts of Renaissance masterworks[11] envisaged commissioning from Campi a single work

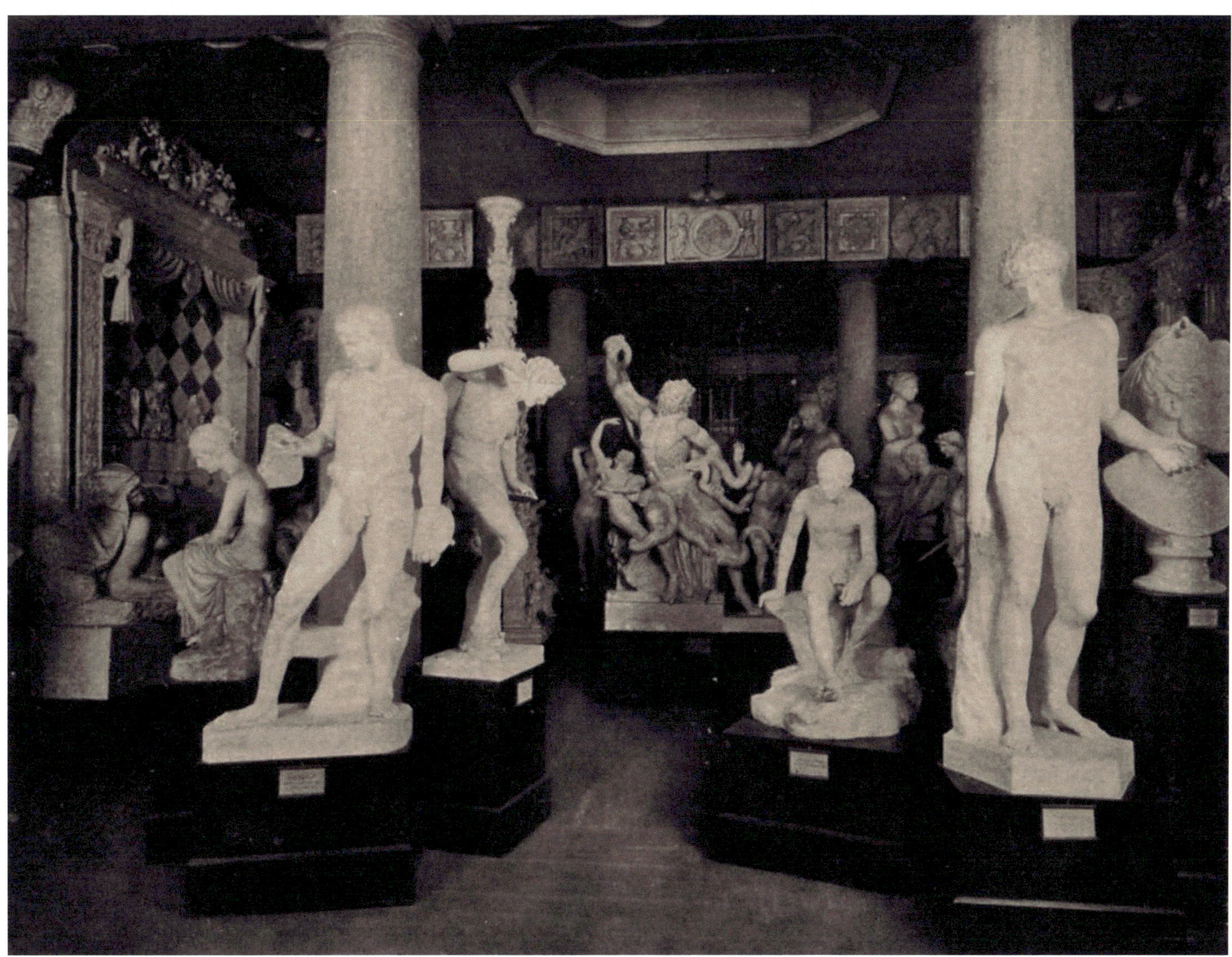

Fig. 4

The entrance hall of the Museo Campi Carlo at 17–19 via Brera, Milan

On the left, the plaster cast of the *Tomb of Medea Colleoni* and the *Paschal Candlestick* from the Basilica del Santo

of small dimensions, which was not even of Lombard but Tuscan origin. In this first phase, the offer of the Pierotti company was preferred among the Milanese, while in the Florentine region, substantial orders were placed with the Lelli atelier, where the founder Oronzio was succeeded by his son Giuseppe.[12]

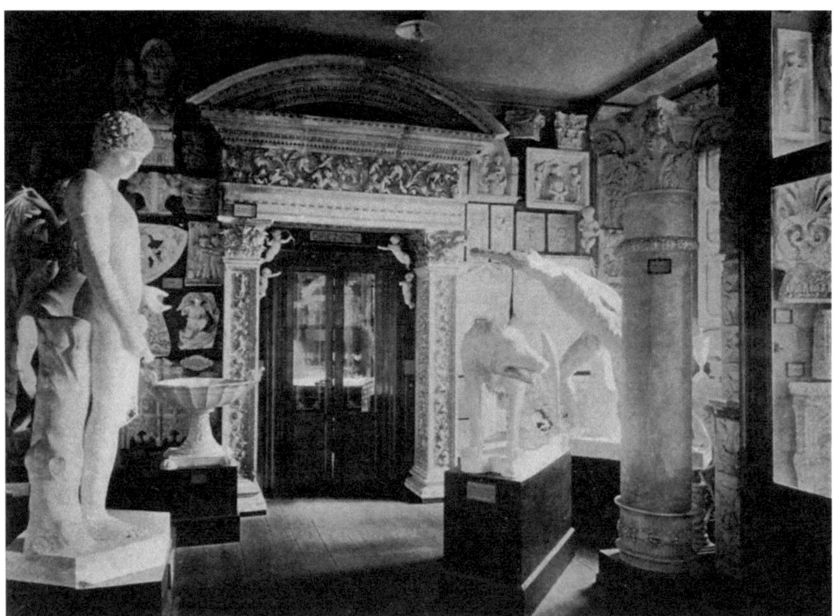

Six years later, when the time came to make specific purchases, the situation changed: in May 1907, Ernő Kammerer, a public official and lawyer with a special interest in history and art history, took over as director general of the museum and tried to establish relations with Pierotti, only to fail in his attempt.[13] This can only be explained by the rearrangements affecting the Milanese moulding workshops in the years around 1907: Edoardo Pierotti – son of Pietro, founder of the renowned company – was at the time involved in winding up the family business.[14] Similarly to what had been arranged with the Certosa di Pavia in 1891, when the manufactory gave 149 reproductions of the monastic complex free of charge,[15] at the beginning of 1907, the generous heir decided to offer as a gift to the Ministry of Education – and to the Brera Academy – the spectacular reproductions still in his possession, many of which would have aligned perfectly with the desires of Hungarian specialists. Moreover, the *formatore*, Edoardo Pierotti seemed to have done his best to make himself untraceable: in addition to having removed his own name

in favour of that of his more famous father, on the title page of the catalogue, updated in 1906, he also chose to omit the address.[16] The letter, not surprisingly, had a generic destination in "Milano", so that the envelope addressed to the deceased "Pietro Pierotti" was stamped as "Unknown by the postman" and returned to the sender. It was thus by mere twist of fate that mutual interests could not be met. Furthermore, due to lack of space in the Palazzo di Brera, Edoardo Pierotti's proposed donation failed to materialise; the beneficiary was the Campi workshop, which seized the opportunity to add the precious models to its already rich collection.[17] A written notice of the acquisition survives from the most authoritative supporter of the practice of plaster casting at the time: the illustrious architect and newly elected Senator Luca Beltrami. Beltrami was among the most eminent personalities of the Milanese and Italian artistic-cultural panorama. He supported the Campi company during a critical moment when, on 18 June 1905, the esteemed founder passed away following a long illness, leaving the business to his daughter in a will he had issued as early as 1903.[18] Emma Campi

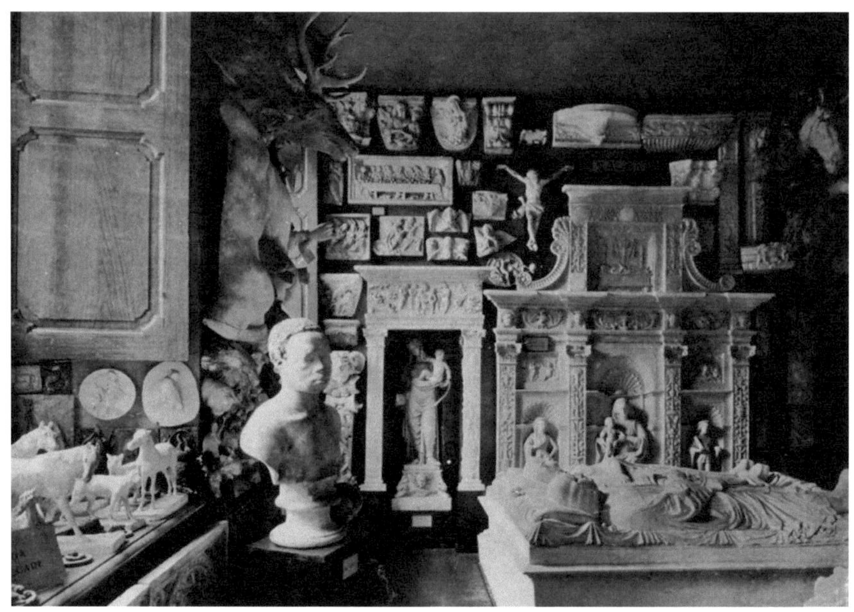

took over the management of the company, the Ditta Campi Carlo, choosing to continue operating under her father's name, supported by an accounting partner, Silvio Sironi. Both became authorised signatories; Sironi, in charge of administrative management, continued to sign correspondence in the name of the deceased master. During this transitional phase, Beltrami played a crucial role in ensuring the survival of the manufactory and the enhancement of the collection, supporting its transfer to 17 via Brera, right in front of the Academy. Thus, in October 1907, the Museo Campi Carlo was established as a city *gipsoteca*, perceived as a natural extension of the Braidense heritage. It was open to the public free of charge and eventually developed into the largest collection of plaster casts ever to exist in Italy,[19] finding a global counterpart – in numerical terms – only in Paris.[20] Some views of the museum's interior have come down to us thanks to a brochure that Beltrami dedicated towards the end of 1910 to the memory of his esteemed collaborator,[21] to whom the architect often resorted both in an institutional capacity, as first director of the Ufficio Regionale per la Conservazione dei Monumenti in Lombardia, and subsequently as a professional, as well as for private needs. In one of the photographs showing the entrance hall (fig. 4), juxtaposed with numerous casts of classical statuary in an eclectic ensemble, two very particular objects can be seen. These replicas of Renaissance masterpieces were acquired through a commission received from Budapest: unique reproductions in the panorama of the great European museums, they stand out from the more recurring models because they are owned only by the Museum of Fine Arts.

But how did this dynamic come about? If, as mentioned earlier, the Hungarian experts decided to limit their selection to models already available in the catalogues of moulding workshops, why did the Ditta Campi find itself making reproductions *ex novo*, deriving the moulds directly from the original monuments? Only an examination of the rich correspondence preserved in the Archives of the Museum of Fine Arts,[22] combined with information gleaned from documents held in the Lombardy region, has allowed us to fully understand the reasons and to reconstruct the negotiations that led to the sale of ten monumental replicas from Milan to Budapest.

The first documented contact dates back to April 1906, when Director Kammerer, engaged in finalising the acquisition programme, sent an initial message to the Campi administration on an exploratory basis. He informed them of the ambitious project and requested an updated catalogue with complete pricing information and estimates for packaging costs.[23] Sironi replied with the diligence that distinguished him and, after only four days, the illustrated album and its catalogue were already on their way to Budapest.[24] While the printed catalogue was considered cheap promotional material, the photographic albums were very expensive bound volumes produced in limited editions, loaned by the company for perusal by customers, whether in Italy or abroad, for a strictly limited time period necessary for making their choices. The albums were expected to be returned within a few days to be made available to other customers. However, the longer decision-making process of the museum professionals ended up clashing with the attitude of the accountant – on the one hand, obsequious and ceremonious, and on the other, impatient and insistent – who wrote several times in the following months soliciting orders and asking for the album back.[25] For their part, the Hungarian specialists intended to keep the photographs at their headquarters, not only to have effective visual support readily available, but also because they already envisaged using them as a tool for recording data, useful for taking measurements and identifying details of interest within complex monumental structures. This approach aimed to make communication more effective and to overcome the limits represented by geographical distance and language.[26] By mutual agreement, the solution was found to reprint and send the complete sequence of 66 loose photographic plates, which were specifically requested as unbound. This allowed a more functional mailing of only the images reproducing the selected objects. In return, the Campi administration promised that these would be provided free of charge in exchange for an important order, which, as it later transpired, would exceed 5,000 Italian lire (hereafter £5,000).[27] The sequence of numbered photographs was accompanied by the updated catalogue,[28] which, on the express recommendation of the director, was supposed to offer a rigorous numerical correspondence with the plates and, above all, to provide detailed dimensions, indispensable for setting up the exhibition project in advance.

It was not until September 1907, a few months after the aforementioned attempt to contact Pierotti, that the museum management was ready to define the details of the important commission, which was confirmed in November. The price specifications were requested for eight monumental reproductions, a part of which was chosen not from the Campi firm's proposals, but from the Pierotti catalogue: with explicit notification of the failed delivery of the correspondence to the competing manufactory. Kammerer asked the Campi administration if they could handle the entire mandate, trusting that they would be able to cover the duties of their now inactive colleague and envisaging further future orders.[29] Sironi promptly assumed the task, guaranteeing that he could also supply what had been offered by Pierotti. He submitted a detailed estimate, using the aforementioned method of recording dimensions on a photographic support.[30] He went out of his way in promising to supply no less than six of the eight monumental replicas within just six months of confirmation, having perfect models available in the workshop from which to derive the moulds. However, he immediately made it clear that for the remaining two objects, the process would have to be completely different: although the *Tomb of Medea Colleoni* from the eponymous chapel in Bergamo and the *Paschal Candlestick* from the Basilica of Sant'Antonio da Padova (fig. 4) were included in the Pierotti company's offer, the accountant explained that as the two Renaissance masterpieces had been replicated years ago in a single copy on the express order of the Italian government, they were not included in the offers of any *formatori*.[31] The issue likely arose because Pierotti had a tendency to include objects in his catalogue for which he did not have models. He did, however, take care to label them as "to be done".[32] These works must have been assumed to be potentially commissionable, and they were certainly worthy, since they had attracted the attention of art critics. It would have posed little effort for Pierotti to obtain authorisation to reproduce them before the strict monument conservation regulations issued in Italy in the first decade of the twentieth century.[33] However, the real meaning of the annotation must have escaped the notice of Kammerer and Térey: only in the light of this ambiguity is it possible to explain the source of the complications that arose from the commission of the two objects in question, regarding which Sironi initially maintained a cautious reserve, but eventually took a proactive attitude. Strengthened by the institutional support of Senator Beltrami and the Milanese Academy, he initiated the procedures for having the necessary authorisations issued by the competent authorities.[34]

While waiting for the permits, during the last two months of 1907, the workshop – at the time coordinated by the master Leonino Romani – operated at full capacity to complete the first six replicas. Among these, the *Door Frame* from San Lorenzo Cathedral in Lugano (fig. 5) had been included in the workshop's range for the longest time. The *Door Frame* had been part of the first important survey of medieval and Renaissance works carried out by Carlo Campi in the international arena, being selected among the most excellent Ticino sculptural works presented at the *Swiss National Exhibition* in Zürich in 1883, where it had been exhibited in perfect plaster reproduction. Another piece that Campi personally moulded directly from the original marble was the *Altar Table from Carpiano* (fig. 7)

The Romanesque Hall of the Museum of Fine Arts, Budapest in 1913

In the centre, the replica of the *Altar Table from Carpiano*

by Giovanni da Campione, whose replica, successfully shown at the *Sacred Art Exhibition* of Turin in 1898, was the recipient of prestigious awards. Pietro Pierotti, meanwhile, should be acknowledged for extracting the matrices from the *Tomb of Gaston de Foix*, a prodigious work by Agostino Busti, also known as Il Bambaia, on view at the *Exhibition of Ancient Art* held in Brera in 1872. In all probability, on this occasion, the Ditta Campi had to resort to the ancient plaster model still preserved today in the holdings of the Brera Academy. Twenty years later, in 1893, it was his son, Edoardo Pierotti, who carried out the reproduction of the *Sepulchre of Ludovico il Moro and Beatrice d'Este* after the marble original by Cristoforo Solari conserved in the Church of the Certosa di Pavia. The model available at the Museo Campi (fig. 6) must have been the result of this moulding undertaking, or alternatively a so-called second copy cast. Further research would be necessary to reconstruct the circumstances that led the company to replicate the *Sepulchre of Thomas II Count of Savoy* from Aosta Cathedral, of unknown dating. Last in the series, and certainly the most finely elaborated of all, is the cast of the base of the *Trivulzio Candelabrum* (fig. 8), after the bronze original in Milan Cathedral. It had been available for several years in the workshop and was likely reproduced by Carlo Campi deriving the moulds from the plaster model owned by the Brera Academy, which he had restored in 1894.[35] This object is fully documented in the earlier catalogues of the competing firm and would therefore be attributable to Pierotti senior.

On a practical level, the demanding commission was successfully completed due to the advanced moulding methods developed in the preceding decades, and in particular thanks to the technical perfection achieved through the gelatin moulding technique, skilfully mastered by Campi and his company. According to a practice shared with the Florentine workshop,[36] the *formatori* did not use piece moulds, but created, from time to time, flexible and perishable negatives composed mainly of animal gelatin, which could be exploited to obtain a very limited number of copies.[37] The museum's experts had little cause to worry, who, following repeated recommendations on the use of quality materials, with the express request for alabaster gypsum, were reassured by Sironi regarding the well-defined and precise rendering of the casts, obtained from very fine-grained raw material.[38] In compliance with the estimated times, by April 1908, the various components of the six reproductions were ready and awaiting complete drying.[39]

In the meantime, the company emerged victorious from the bureaucratic procedures and managed to obtain the necessary authorisations, which, however, had required significant diplomatic efforts. Thanks to the usual support

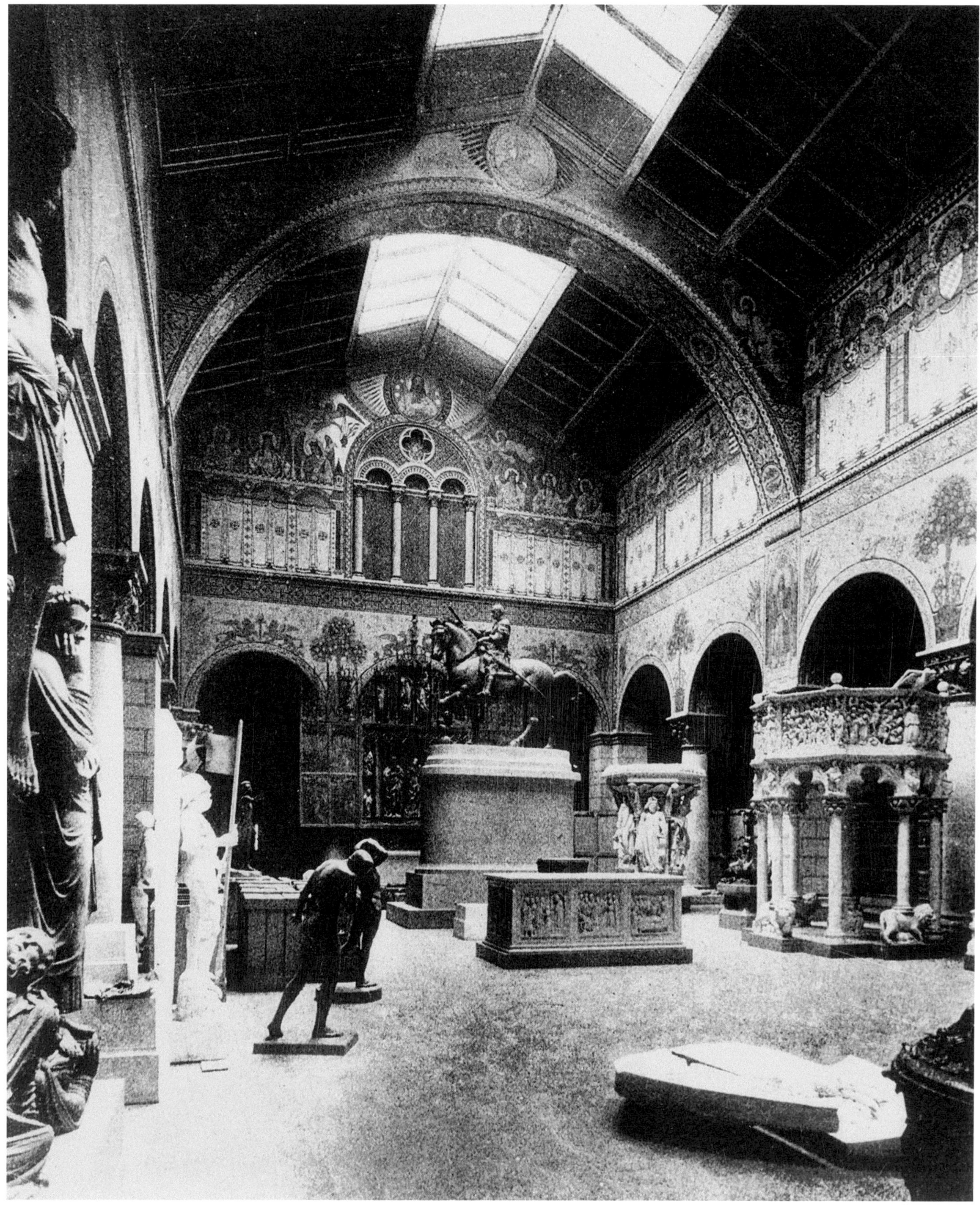

from the Lombardy Ufficio Regionale, whose leadership had in the meantime been taken over by the architect Gaetano Moretti, the local authorities of Padua and Bergamo had initially proven willing to consent to the reproductions.[40] So much so that Sironi, at the beginning of 1908, went too far in announcing the start of the works. In both cases, he proposed a processing time of eight months and set the beginning of the Paduan mission to April – just in time to complete the first six casts – and then the planning of the Bergamo enterprise to June. However, this optimistic forecast was followed by a sharp setback, which forced the Campi administration to escalate negotiations to ministerial level and follow the legal procedure which had been bypassed until the previous year.[41] At this juncture, the architect Massimiliano Ongaro, director of the Ufficio Regionale per la Conservazione dei Monumenti del Veneto, was also consulted. Ongaro had in recent times supervised the moulding of the Venetian *Equestrian Monument to Bartolomeo Colleoni* by Andrea del Verrocchio, and could have provided explanations on the practices and precautions outlined in the new regulations.[42] In addition to the obligation to deposit a large sum as a security – certified in the order of £2,000 – the Ditta Campi was required to deliver two copies free of charge for each replicated work, one for the Ministry and the other – as per long-established practice – for the institution responsible for the protection of the respective monuments, i.e., the Veneranda Arca del Santo di Padova and the Luogo Pio della Pietà Colleoni in Bergamo. Faced with fifty letters exchanged between Padua, Milan, Rome and Venice in order to be able to reproduce only Riccio's work, Kammerer had to give up the originally agreed 10% discount.[43] The effort paid off when, well ahead of the estimated schedule, in July 1908, the cast of the *Paschal Candlestick* was ready to join the first six replicas and leave for Budapest.[44] Following the example of the Gipsformerei in Berlin, an entire railway carriage was reserved for the purpose, but it was not sufficient to accommodate all the materials. Of the 21 crates prepared, 6 were retained, containing the casts of the Milanese candelabrum and the Aostan sarcophagus. Several months of negotiating and completing the laborious replica of the *Tomb of Medea Colleoni* passed before the casts were entrusted to the well-known Casa di spedizioni Innocente Mangili, which Carlo Campi himself had used for important international consignments.[45] In March 1909, the casts finally departed from Milan.[46] The methods and costs of the delivery had been the subject of protracted discussions in the preceding months,[47] since the museum management did not intend to assume the risks of any damage incurred during the journey. On the other hand, exemption from liability had been an explicit premise of both Milanese workshops in their respective catalogues for decades. Furthermore, the limited resources made available for the packaging, equal to 5% of the value of the casts – a much lower percentage than the usual 15% adopted by Campi (already considered modest when compared to Pierotti's standard of 20%)[48] – forced the *formatori* to create cost-effective protection systems. It was the two slenderest works, i.e., the two candlesticks, that paid the price due to fragile packaging. They reached

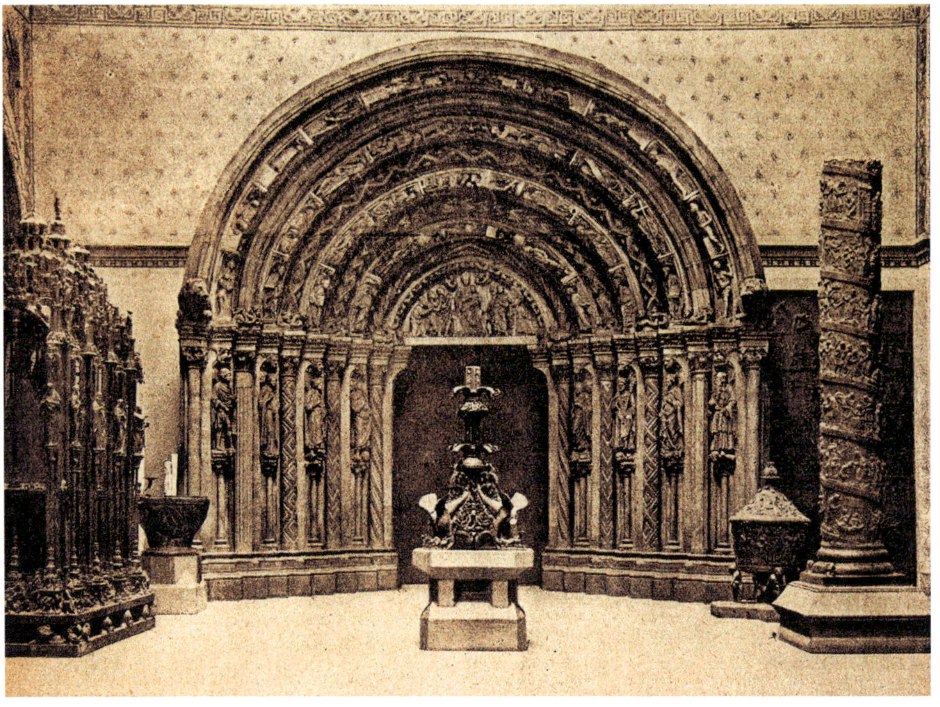

Fig. 8

The Romanesque Hall of the Museum of Fine Arts, Budapest in 1913

In the centre, the reproduction of the *Trivulzio Candelabrum*

Fig. 9 | next page

Printed plate showing the four "first copy" replicas, directly extracted from the original monuments:

The *Door Frame of the Sacrestia del Lavabo* (4); the *Tomb of Saint Peter Martyr* (5); the *Paschal Candlestick* from the Basilica del Santo (7); and the *Tomb of Medea Colleoni* (9)

Their target was the *Tomb of Saint Peter Martyr*, the fourteenth-century masterpiece by Giovanni di Balduccio, which had been included in the Pierotti catalogue for several decades. Despite one of the fundamental principles of conservation and protection laws, which prohibited working on originals where a plaster cast already existed and could be adopted as a model for moulding further copies, the Campi administration submitted a request to derive the matrices directly from the marble. Benefiting from the path already laid by the two completed operations and thanks to the intervention of an influential member of the clergy, the company was granted two months to work at the Basilica of Sant'Eustorgio. Given the enormous amount of work and the tight deadlines, between April and June 1909, the work team was supplemented by new forces, which resulted in the completion of all the components by July. They were packed in 23 crates and transported via railway. Due to the high number of elements, it was necessary to number them with reference to a construction scheme.[51]

Finally, it was thanks to a packet of photographs reproducing different sections of the Certosa di Pavia, delivered by Emma Campi's husband, Giovanni Mambretti, on a trip to Budapest,[52] that the Milanese workshop received the last commission from the Museum of Fine Arts. It involved replicating the marble *Door Frame* of the Sacrestia del Lavabo, from the circle of Giovanni Antonio Amadeo, today attributed to Tommaso Cazzaniga and Alberto Maffioli, which had never been moulded before. Encouraged by an initial verbal agreement from the local authorities, the Campi administration confidently made the deposit and arranged for the materials to be transported to the site. Once the suitability of the encumbrances had been ascertained through the usual system of notes on photography, the museum confirmed the commission in June 1909.[53] However, the optimistic plans were rejected and the procedure for issuing permits met with strong resistance from the Roman authorities. Following numerous updates on the unchanged situation, more than a year passed before the work team could undertake the operation, deriving the moulds on site

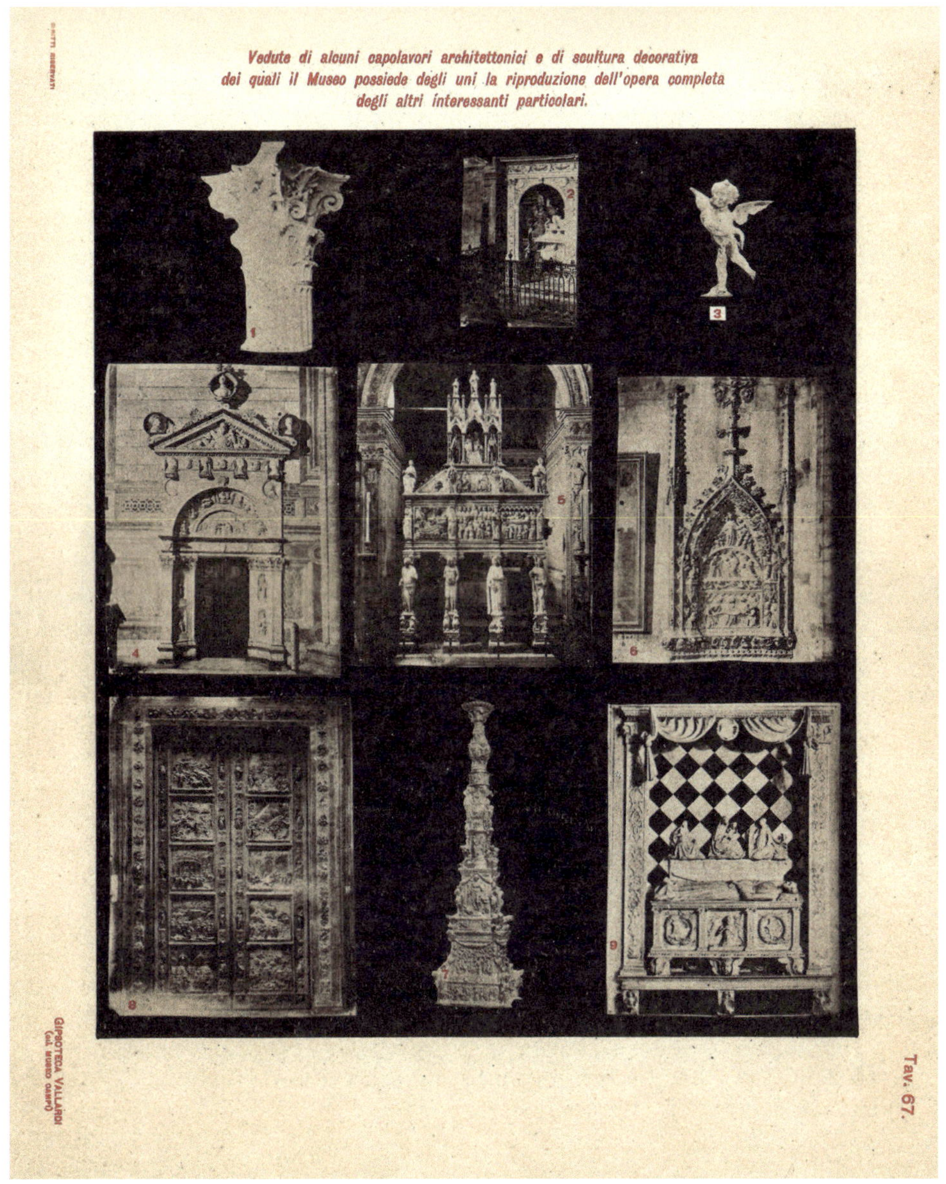

their destination with cracks and detachments due to the crates being too thin and flexible, so the wood shavings used as material cushioning were not sufficient to protect them.[49] Recognising the perfect rendering of the details, the museum professionals decided to proceed with the installation and subsequent bonding of the damaged parts, without requesting their replacement. The aesthetic choice of giving the two replicas a *patina* in imitation of bronze, carried out by local craftsmen, must have also served the purpose of masking the repairs.

Still, however, the acquisition campaign could not be considered concluded: the experts in fact aimed to enrich the collection with a further monumental masterpiece, grandiose enough to justify an investment comparable to that sustained up to now for the other eight replicas.[50]

between June and November 1910. The subsequent execution of the casts in the workshop must have been particularly laborious as it was only in July 1911 that the company was ready to entrust the last precious cargo, comprising 9 crates, to the forwarder Mangili.[54] Beltrami must have played a decisive role in breaking the stalemate. After more than two decades of commitment, in 1911, he finally managed to realise his dream of founding a museum at the Certosa destined to house the casts taken from the monastic complex. This museum offered a suitable exhibition space for the aforementioned group of Pierotti casts, donated since 1891 precisely on his encouragement, combined with the more recent reproductions deposited by Campi. About four years after the inauguration of the Museo Carlo Campi in Brera, he now succeeded in setting up a *gipsoteca* with the aim of effectively witnessing the conservation vicissitudes of the marbles displayed on the façade, which were at the time subject to rapid deterioration. The museum also facilitated a closer study of the details that would have escaped observation from a distance. This idea was part of Beltrami's peculiar sensitivity, refined in his youth during his time in Paris. Introduced by Charles Garnier at the École Nationale des Beaux-Arts, he received the position of assistant in the construction works of the Trocadéro building alongside Gabriel Davioud. He was strongly influenced by the layout of the Musée de Sculpture Comparée, designed by Viollet-le-Duc at the end of the Universal Exhibition of 1879. Returning to Italy, he waited a long time for the opportunity to create a Lombard equivalent, albeit to a much more modest extent, of the exhibition of the great *moulages* of French cathedrals, predecessor of today's Musée des Monuments Français.[55] Of the two replicas of the portal given by the Ditta Campi as a deposit, the one destined for the Certosa is still installed in its original form today, complete with internal wooden reinforcements, in the only room where the 1911 layout has been kept intact. The vicissitude described represents an important new element in revising the hypothesis of the current attribution of the Pavia replica, which cannot be ascribed to the Pierotti donation, but to the operation carried out by the Campi company on commission from the Museum of Fine Arts.

As for the conclusion of relations between Milan and Budapest, the months following the confirmation of the last order were marked by a series of letters in which Sironi continued to insistently update Kammerer on the company's new proposals. This communication included photographs and functional estimates for potential additional tasks.[56] No further orders came from the museum, which abruptly broke off contact. This prompted the accountant himself to undertake a desperate journey to re-establish relations.[57] Although this extreme attempt certainly did not produce the desired effect, it must have been an opportunity to admire the spectacular results of the great operational effort carried out by the Milanese *formatori* over almost four years, installed in the Romanesque and Renaissance Halls of the Museum of Fine Arts.

Among the replicas that survived the devastation of World War II, five casts from the Campi workshop were selected for the museum's new exhibition:[58] the four monumental reproductions made last (fig. 9). They derive directly from the marble and bronze originals, and for this reason they deserve recognition for their high value as so-called first copy casts. They are on display now in the large hall of the inner courtyard (fig. 10) of the Star Fortress in Komárom.

Fig. 10 | next page

The monumental replicas from the Campi workshop
on display in the Colleoni Hall, Star Fortress, Komárom

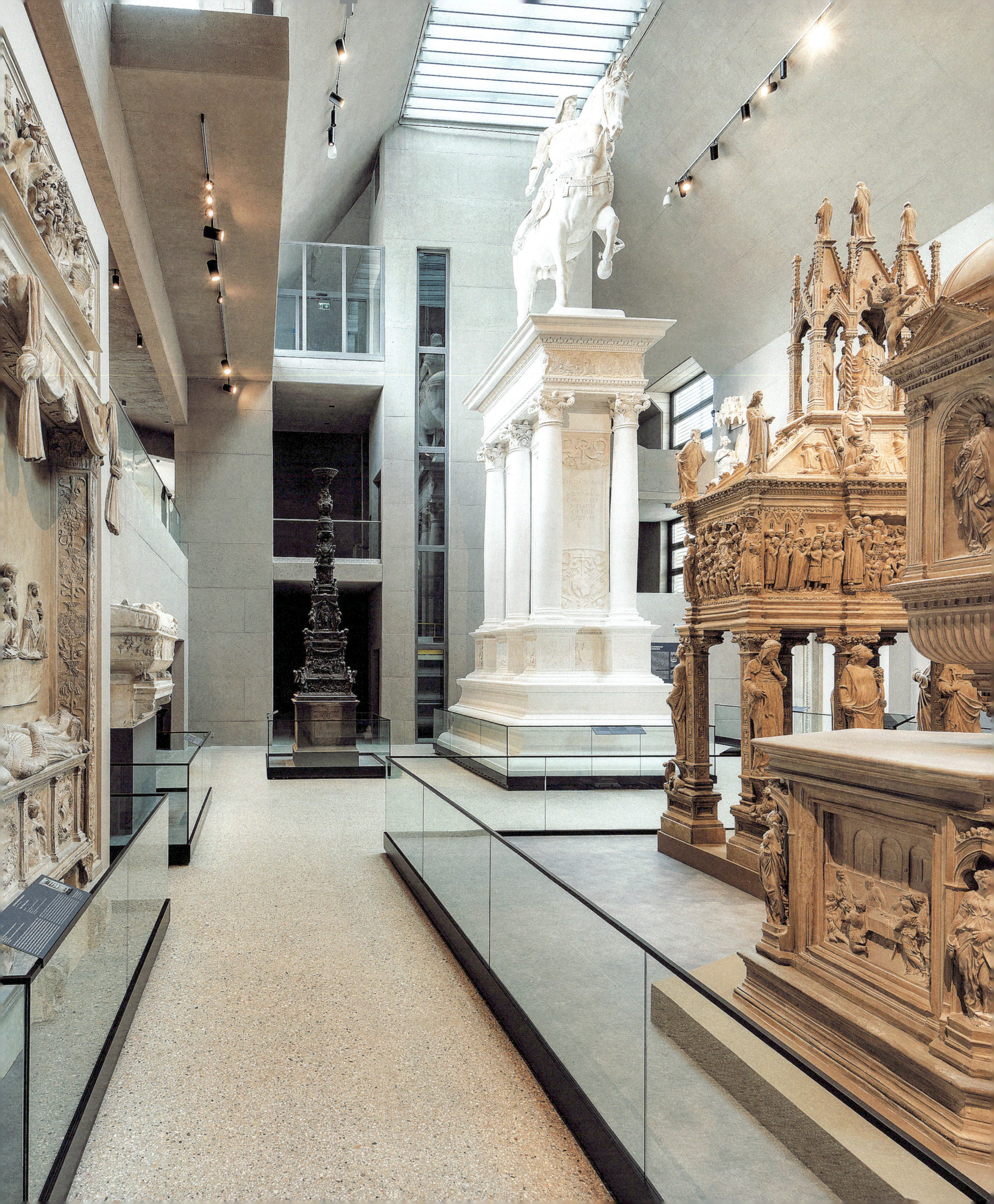

Notes

1 Cast makers.

2 The reconstruction of Carlo Campi's activity is extensively covered in: Berizzi 2020/2021A. This research, which contains specific bibliographic and archival references not mentioned here, represents the beginning of a systematic study that will be the subject of a future publication.

3 Monumental Cemetery of Milano, Archive, Rep. XX, Giard. 203, Campi Carlo. Municipality of Milan, Funeral and Cemetery Services, Archive, Family Tombs unit, via Larga – Monumental Cemetery, Rep. 20, Giard. 203, Carlo Campi.

4 Brera Academy of Fine Arts (Milano), Historical Archive, Tea, N.III.20, 15.08.1872; 29.08.1872; 16.09.1872.

5 Brera Academy of Fine Arts (Milano), Historical Archive, Tea, N.III.20, 2.07.1872; 9.07.1872.

6 Beltrami 1910, 15.

7 Brera Academy of Fine Arts (Milano), Historical Archive, Tea, N.I.24 - Formatore (1869–1923), 22.02.1882; Tea, N.IV.20, 17.05.1887; Tea, N.IV.23, 10.12.1888.

8 For complete references to the printed catalogues and illustrated albums identified to date, see: Berizzi 2020/2021A, Appendix II. The only previously known catalogue of the Campi manufactory documents the state of the collection up to 1906 and is kept in Florence at the Porta Romana Artistic High School Library, consignee of one of the most incredible plaster cast collections in Italy: *Catalogo riproduzioni in gesso*... 1906. To date, there is no album that can be associated with the catalogue in question; the only possibilities of visual confirmation are offered by the printed album of the Vallardi gallery of plaster casts, which at the beginning of the 1920s made use of the same photographic plates following the acquisition of the Campi Museum.

9 Bognár and Rózsavölgyi 2016.

10 Tóth F. 2012, 66–75.

11 In the detailed list of 180 works of the Tuscan and Lombard Renaissance, there is a single reference to the Campi catalogue (at no. 152), namely "Mezza colonna ornata esistente in un altare nella Chiesa di S. Trinità a Firenze, opera di Benedetto da Rovezzano. Altezza m. 1.70, larghezza m. 0.35, 25 £", estimated at the price of £30. Archives MFAB, 232/1901, 15.05.1901; cf. *Catalogo riproduzioni in gesso*... 1906, 5, Plate no. 56, 50. I would like to thank László Nagy in the Archives MFAB for all his help during my research.

12 Monumental reproductions supplied by the three Italian manufactories still dominate the Weston Cast Court of the Victoria & Albert Museum.

13 Archives MFAB, Budapest, 30.05.1907.

14 The workshop appears to have been based at 9 via Commenda in 1907. Brera Academy of Fine Arts (Milano), Historical Archive, Carpi, A.V.10.

15 Vedovello 1992, 128.

16 *Catalogo dei monumenti*... 1906.

17 Beltrami 1910.

18 Chamber of Commerce of Milano Monza-Brianza and Lodi, Historical Archive, Section "ditte" 1786–1920, File 02190, Campi Carlo.

19 *Gipsoteca Vallardi* n. d.; *Gipsoteca Vallardi* 1930.

20 Hofman 2010.

21 Beltrami 1910.

22 I would like to thank the curators, Miriam Szőcs and Márton Tóth, for their constant support and for sharing bibliographic and archival materials; special thanks to László Nagy in the museum's archive for providing the documents. Although the Museum offered to handle correspondence in Italian, the Campi administration continued to communicate in German. In this regard, I would like to thank Elisabetta Solca and Veronica Bonanno in the International Relations – Erasmus Office of the Brera Academy for their precious support in the translation. Concerning the Bergamo front, I would like to express my appreciation to Ing. Giuseppe Berizzi for having granted consultation of the correspondence related to the reproduction of the *Tomb of Medea Colleoni*. The documents, shared by Dr. Gabriele Medolago, were simultaneously included in the catalogue of the exhibition *I, Medea. The white legend of the Lombard Renaissance* (Bergamo, 16 March – 4 June 2023). This fortunate concurrence has made it possible to cross reference the news from both archives and to deal with them in the respective publications.

23 Archives MFAB, 02.04.1906. On the same date, the same request was also sent to the famous Malpieri workshop in Rome, where Leopoldo had been succeeded by his son Cesare (located at via del Corso 54). This contact, however, does not appear to have been followed up.

24 Archives MFAB, 512/1906, 06.04.1906.

25 Archives MFAB, 512/1906, 18.06.1906, 25.07.1906; 1512/1906, 20.10.1906; 1524/1906, 05.11.1906.

26 This method had to correspond
to a practice of the museum when
dealing with other suppliers,
as employed by the Campi
administration itself in its foreign
relations. Archives MFAB,
1088/1907, 30.09.1907, 4.11.1907.

27 Archives MFAB, 1524/1906,
08.11.1906; 1591/1906, 16.11.1906;
1809/1906, 27.12.1906; 254/1907,
15.02.1907, 22.02.1907;
335/1907, 01.03.1907.

28 Archives MFAB, 1591/1906,
16.11.1906; in all probability it was
precisely to favour the important
commission that the Ditta Campi
invested effort in producing
the updated version of its catalogue, printed in October 1906,
adding the "New reproductions"
section at the end. Cf. *Catalogo
riproduzioni in gesso…* 1906.

29 Archives MFAB, 1088/1907,
30.09.1907; 1701/1907, 15.11.1907.

30 Archives MFAB, 1088/1907,
30.10.1907, 4.11.1907; 1820/1907,
27.11.1907; 1827/1907, 29.11.07.

31 The content turns out to be
an interesting contribution to
our limited knowledge on the
campaigns for the acquisition
of plaster casts implemented
by the Italian Ministry of Public
Education in the second half of
the nineteenth century. Archives
MFAB, 1088/1907, 30.10.1907.

32 Cf. as an example: *Catalogo
dei monumenti…* 1883, 5–7.

33 Among the various provisions
adopted by the Italian Government,
the following is particularly
significant: Regio Decreto,
Regolamento per l'esecuzione
della Legge 12 Giugno 1902,
N. 185 sulla conservazione dei
monumenti e degli oggetti di
antichità ed arte e della Legge 27
Giugno 1903, n. 242 sull'esportazione degli oggetti di antichità
ed arte (Rome, 1904), 10, 96–99.

34 Archives MFAB, 1820/1907,
27.11.1907.

35 Brera Academy of Fine Arts
(Milano), Historical Archive,
Tea, N.I.24, 12.09.1894.

36 Bernardini and Mastrorocco
1985, XXXV.

37 An in-depth study of the Milanese
method was reported in: Berizzi
2020/2021B. Part of the content
was presented by the author
on the occasion of the international conference *Celebrating
Reproductions: Past, Present and
Future* (Victoria & Albert Museum,
London, 17–19 January 2019), with
a speech entitled "Gelatine Molds –
The Case-Study of the Restoration
of the Cast of the Brivio Monument
in Brera" and will be the subject of a
forthcoming and larger publication.
For more general references to
the gelatin mould technique,
see: Turco 1961; Millar 1897.

38 Archives MFAB, 1701/1907,
15.11.1907; 752/1908, 01.05.1908;
1820/1907, 27.11.1907;
826/1908, 11.05.1908.

39 Archives MFAB, 752/1908,
22.04.1908; 826/1908, 11.05.1908.

40 Archives MFAB, 296/1908,
19.02.08; 752/1908 22.04.08.
Luogo Pio Colleoni (Bergamo),
Archive, serie Cappella Colleoni,
fald. 10, fasc. 33, 19.03.1908;
20.03.1908; 21.03.1908;
23.03.1908; 07.04.1908; 14.04.1908.

41 Archives MFAB, 1820/1907,
27.11.1907; 882/1908, 23.05.1908,
30.05.1908; 1118/1908, 06.07.1908;
1907/1908, 27.11.1908. Luogo Pio
Colleoni (Bergamo), Archive, serie
Cappella Colleoni, fald. 10, fasc. 33,
11.11.1908; 19.11.1908; 20.11.1908.

42 Archives MFAB, 1260/1908.
Luogo Pio Colleoni (Bergamo),
Archive, serie Cappella Colleoni,
fald. 10, fasc. 33, 17.05.1908.

43 Archives MFAB, 882/1908, 2.06.08;
1118/1908, 06.07.1908; 1260/1908.

44 Archives MFAB, 1118/1908,
06.07.1908; 1168/1908, 13.07.1908.

45 Victoria & Albert Museum
Archive, ref. MA/1/C280, Campi
Carlo (1891–1907) 19.10.1894;
01.06.1895. Archives MFAB,
826/1908, 11.05.1908.

46 Luogo Pio Colleoni (Bergamo),
Archive, serie Cappella Colleoni,
fald. 10, fasc. 33, 25.11.1908.
Archives MFAB, 199/1909,
28.01.1909; 514/1909, 20.03.1909.

47 Archives MFAB, 1088/1907,
30.09.1907; 1701/1907, 15.11.1907;
1820/1907, 27.11.1907; 1827/1907,
29.11.07, 29.12.07; 71/1908,
14.01.08; 752/1908, 01.05.1908;
826/1908, 11.05.1908.

48 Cf. *Catalogo riproduzioni in gesso…* 1906, 4; Catalogo dei monumenti… 1906, 15. The Lelli firm in Florence, according to Director Kammerer, offered a packing service equal to only 3.5% of the cost of the casts. Archives MFAB, 1827/1907, 29.12.07.

49 Archives MFAB, 1260/1908, 15.08.1908; 689/1909; 697/1909, 27.04.1909; 768/1909, 30.04.1909; 1200/1909, 26.08.1909.

50 The cast of the *Tomb of Saint Peter Martyr* (1909) was acquired at a cost of £8,250 (plus £412 for shipping), today equivalent to about €35,000; Archives MFAB, 233/1908, 02.07.08; 752/1908, 05.01.1908. The total cost of the first eight reproductions amounted to £9,350 (plus £420 for shipping), which is approximately €40,000 today. The breakdown of the costs is as follows: *Door Frame* from the San Lorenzo Cathedral in Lugano (1908): £475; *Altar Table from Carpiano* (1908): £400; *Tomb of Gaston de Foix* (1908): £1,000; *Sepulchre of Ludovico il Moro and Beatrice d'Este* (1908): £800; *Sepulchre of Thomas II Count of Savoy* (1908): £675; *Trivulzio Candelabrum* (1908): £1,000; *Tomb of Medea Colleoni* (1909): £3,000; *Paschal Candlestick* from the Basilica del Santo (1908): £2,000; Archives MFAB, 1820/1907, 11.27.1907. The replica of the *Door Frame* of the Sacrestia del Lavabo (1911) cost £4,800 (shipping costs included), today equivalent to almost €20,000; Archives MFAB, 840/1909, 06.22.1909.

51 Archives MFAB, 737/1909, 25.04.09; 1199/1909, 12.07.1909; 1200/1909, 19.07.1909, 18.08.1909.

52 Archives MFAB, 514/1909, 20.03.1909.

53 Archives MFAB, 768/1909, 30.04.1909; 840/1909, 11.05.1909, 22.06.1909.

54 Archives MFAB, 1199/1909, 12.07.1909; 1200/1909, 26.08.1909; 1726/1909, 19.10.1909; 905/1910, 17.05.1910; 1542/1910, 26.09.1910; 1834/1910, 10.11.1910; 384/1911, 28.02.1911; 1249/1911, 07.07.1911.

55 Lodi 2008.

56 Archives MFAB, 1726/1909, 19.10.1909; 2120/1909, 17.12.1909; 1542/1910, 26.09.1910; 1249/1911, 07.07.1911; 1675/1911, 04.10.1911; 540/1912, 05.04.1912; 1069/1912, 13.05.12; 1204/1912, 29.05.1912; 2146/1912, 09.11.1912.

57 Archives MFAB, 2146/1912, 16.11.1912.

58 Szőcs 2021A. Unfortunately, it seems that three reproductions (the *Altar Table from Carpiano*, the *Tomb of Gaston de Foix,* and the *Sepulchre of Thomas II Count of Savoy*) have been destroyed or dispersed; the reidentification of the fragments of the replica of the *Door Frame* from San Lorenzo Cathedral in Lugano is recent news; the cast of the base of the *Trivulzio Candelabrum* is highly valued in the recently inaugurated visible storage at the National Museum Conservation and Storage Centre in Budapest.

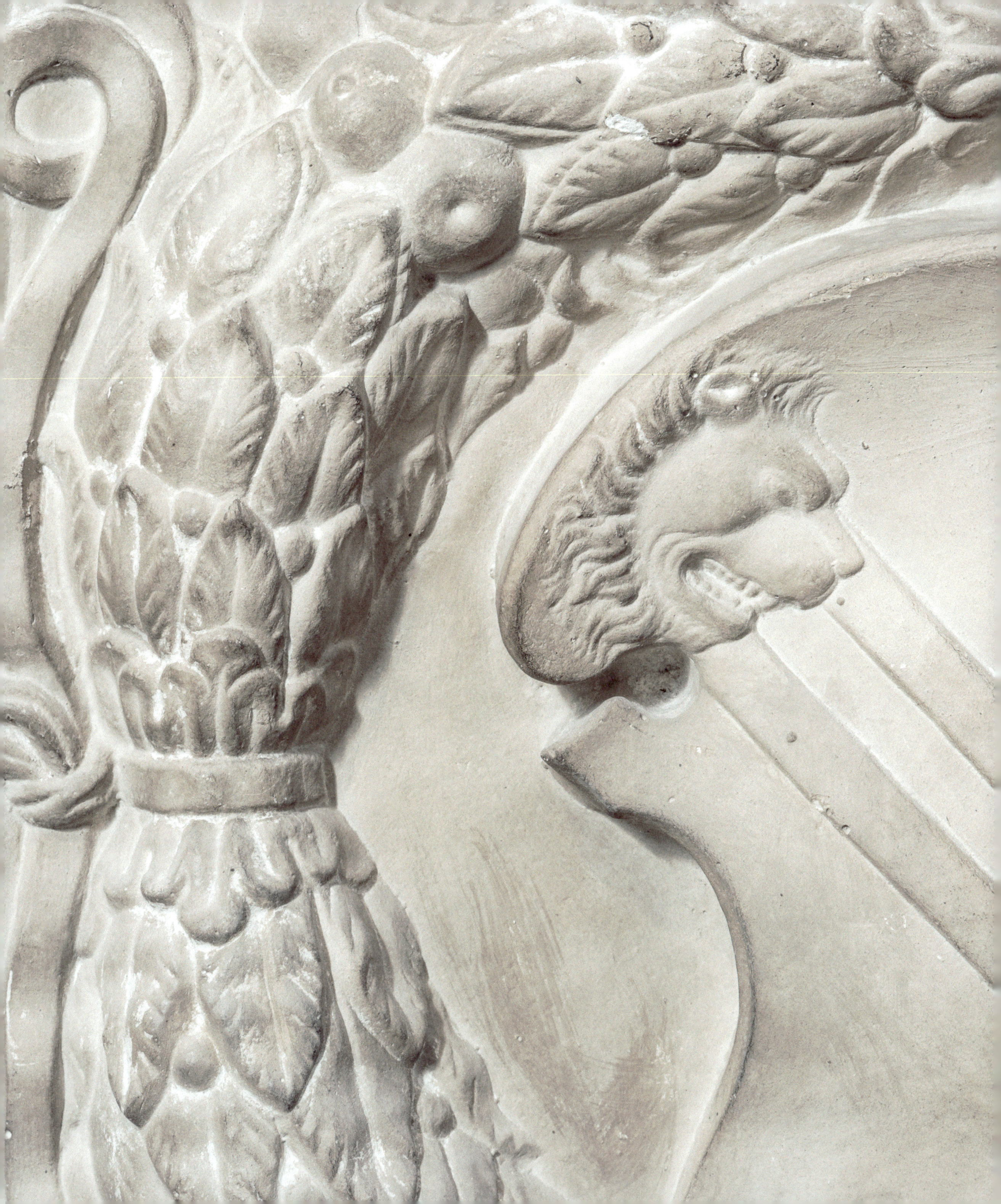

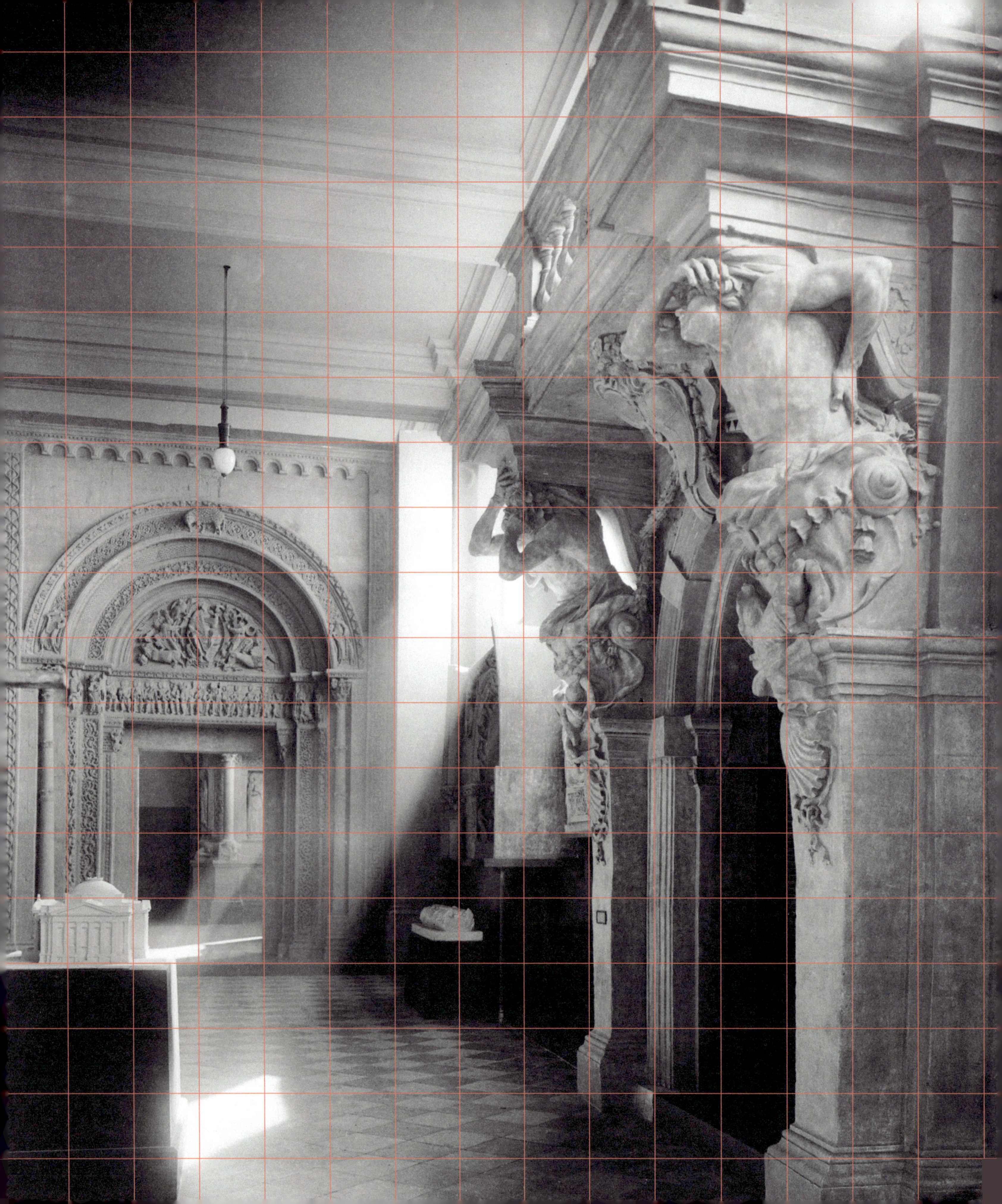

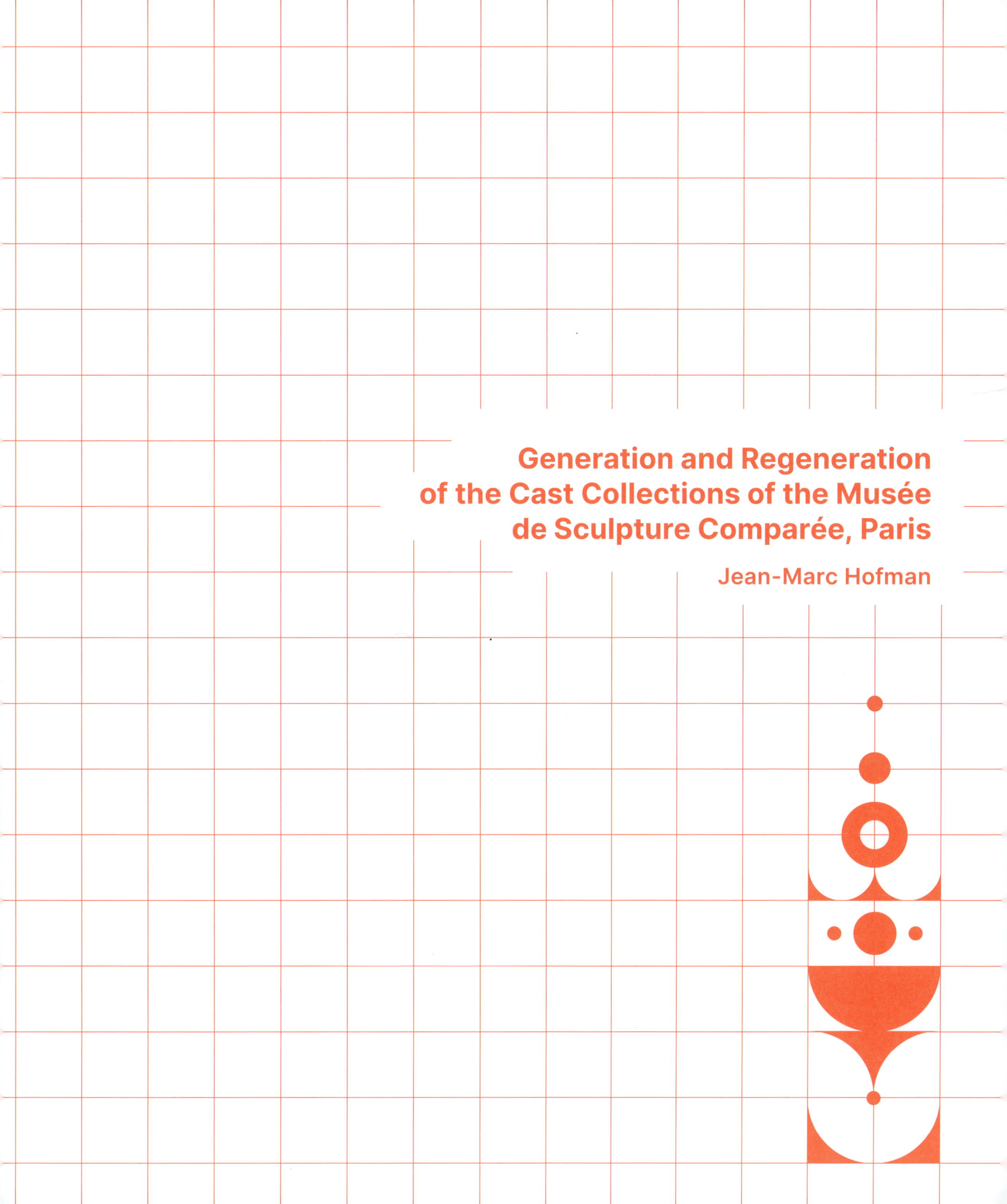

Generation and Regeneration of the Cast Collections of the Musée de Sculpture Comparée, Paris

Jean-Marc Hofman

Generation and Regeneration of the Cast Collections of the Musée de Sculpture Comparée, Paris

Jean-Marc Hofman

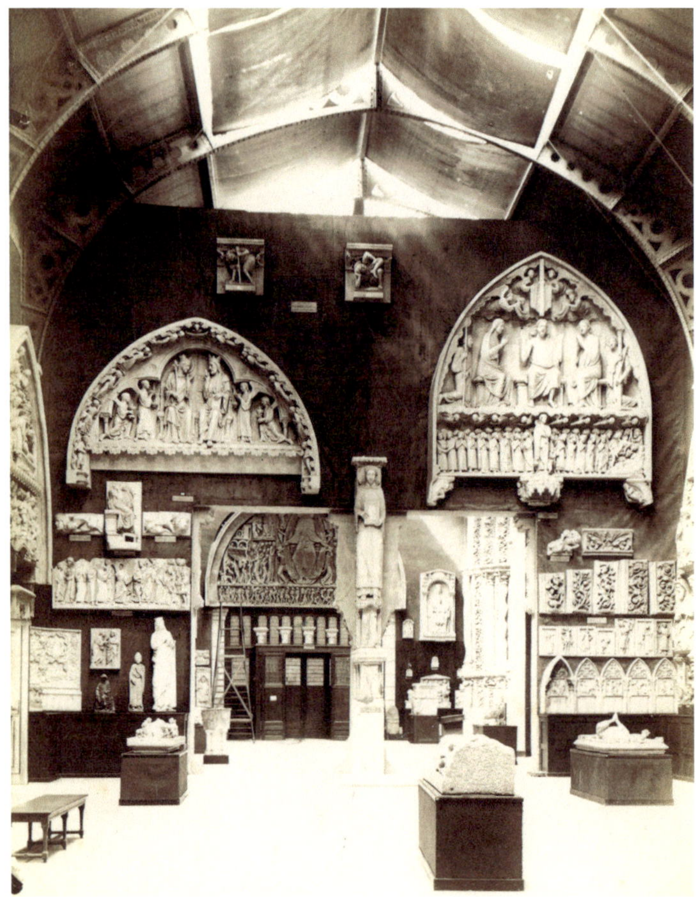

Fig. 1

The Musée de Sculpture Comparée, Paris

Room of early Gothic monumental sculpture, ca. 1900

On 19 September 2007, the Cité de l'architecture et du patrimoine (City of Architecture and Heritage) opened its doors in the western wing of the Palais de Chaillot in Paris, an institution created to promote the beauty of French heritage, as well as contemporary French architecture and its actors. While the Cité is a recent foundation, its collections of plaster casts are much older, preceding it by more than a hundred and thirty years. They found their origin in two successive museums on the same site: the Musée de Sculpture Comparée (Museum of Comparative Sculpture), opened 28 May 1882, was renamed the Musée des Monuments français (Museum of French Monuments) in the 1930s, after a thorough reorganisation. This collection of casts is exceptional for its chronological coherence and its size. It is a collection of architectural casts, sometimes of colossal dimensions, made after French heritage monuments from the Middle Ages to modern times, with a strong predominance of the Gothic period (fig. 1). Since its creation, and in its various forms, it has been one of the best means of exhibiting and popularising French architecture through the presentation of its most famous monuments.[1]

This paper intends to examine the formative period of creation of the collections of casts, within the context of the foundation of the Musée de Sculpture Comparée (1879–1935), including certain aspects of its philosophy as well as its material history. It also explores the paths by which the collections were diffused within France and abroad, with the main thread focusing on casts of monumental size.

The history of the museum and its collection of casts are inseparable from that of the Committee on Historical Monuments, a state department founded in 1837 to examine the restoration works to be carried out on monuments after decades of neglect. The members of the Committee – archaeologists, historians, architects – were the founders of the museum's collection of casts; the very same people, through their writings and their dedication, also contributed to forging medieval archaeology as a scientific discipline. The first of them was the architect and theorist on historical monuments Eugène Viollet-le-Duc

(1814–1879), the founding father of the Musée de Sculpture Comparée in 1879. Viollet-le-Duc championed the creation of a museum of plaster casts of French monumental sculpture for more than three decades. The earliest evidence of his commitment to such an institution dates back to 1848. His name appears in a petition from cast makers calling for the formation of a national casting workshop, with the aim of creating a collection of national sculptures for study and research.

Another testimony of his commitment took place in 1855, when the architect, speaking on behalf of a humble cast maker, Auguste Malzieux (1820–1873), appealed to the political authorities to have his extraordinary collection of casts installed in the Musée du Louvre.[2]

Malzieux was undoubtedly one of the very first cast makers to produce plaster copies of French monuments on a very large scale, a practice regulated in France by a circular dated 16 December 1842, five years after the creation of the Committee on Historical Monuments and two years after the publication of the first list designating French historical monuments. In response to the destruction caused by artists unable to cast without damaging the sculptures they wanted to reproduce, it was deemed necessary to impose controls on the practice. Any casting operation was therefore subject to authorisation, which was systematically rejected for commercial reasons.[3] Permits were only granted to experienced cast makers who were mainly active in the official sphere of historical monuments. On this subject, two months before the promulgation of these rules, a columnist in *Le Journal du Cher*, reporting on highly official casting works in the Cathedral of Saint Stephen in Bourges (Centre-Val de Loire), praised the extreme skill and ability of the Parisian cast maker Giuseppe Barsugli (1804–1860) to preserve "de toute mutilation les objets qui sont confiés à sa dextérité".[4] Barsugli was to show no less dexterity over the years, but in the practice of artistic counterfeiting, in which he distinguished himself on many occasions.

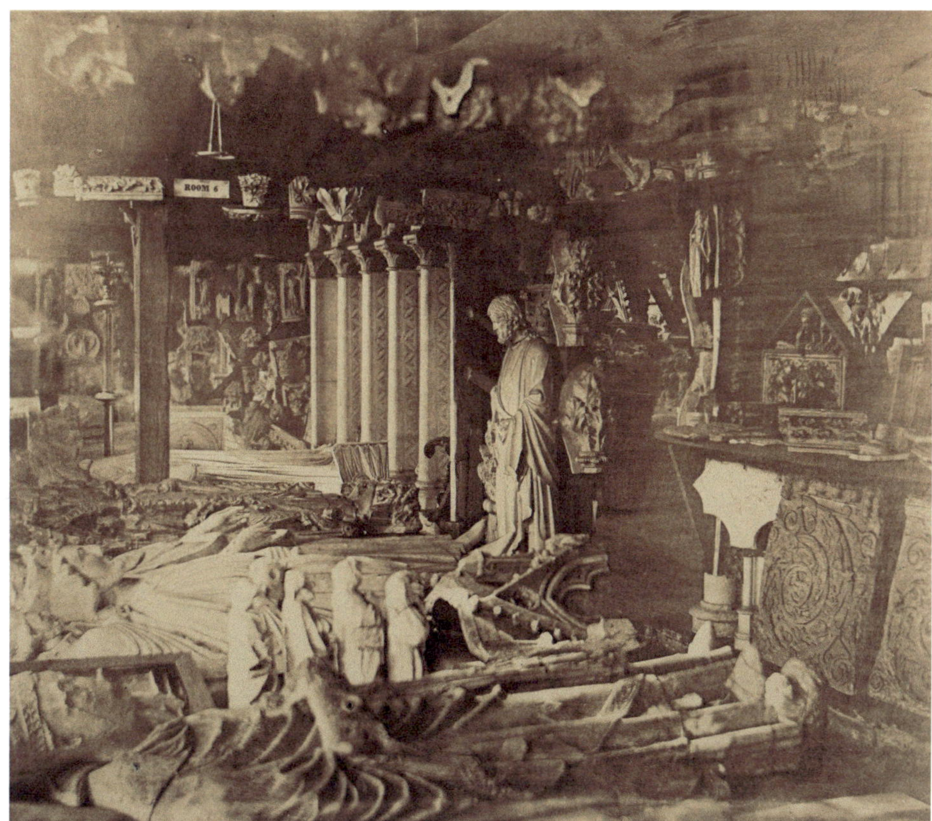

Fig. 2

The Architectural Museum,
Cannon Row, Westminster, London
Room 6: casts of French and German
sculpture, 1851–1857

On the right are the casts of an apostle
of the Holy Chapel and of door hinges
of the Cathedral of Notre-Dame in Paris
executed by Auguste Malzieux

Auguste Malzieux's collection contained several thousand casts made on the restoration sites of historical monuments. It also included the replication of the casts he had made of French monuments at the request of the Architectural Museum in London, an institution founded in 1851 by a group of architects led by George Gilbert Scott (1811–1878) in the context of a deep reflection on architectural education in England, unfolding against the backdrop of the Gothic Revival movement (fig. 2).[5] The name of Malzieux is also associated with the Medieval Court in the Crystal Palace in Sydenham, where plasters of a selection of six arcades from the choir of the Cathedral of Notre-Dame in Paris were exhibited. In the French literature of the second part of the nineteenth century, Malzieux's casting of the choir was regarded as a significant achievement: it was probably one of the first French monumental architectural ensembles to be moulded in its entirety. Although Malzieux's collection was never installed in the Musée du Louvre, he arranged them in his own temporary Musée d'Archéologie du Moyen Âge on the Île Saint-Louis between 1856–1857/1858, one of Viollet-le-Duc's major attempts to create a museum of French monumental sculpture.

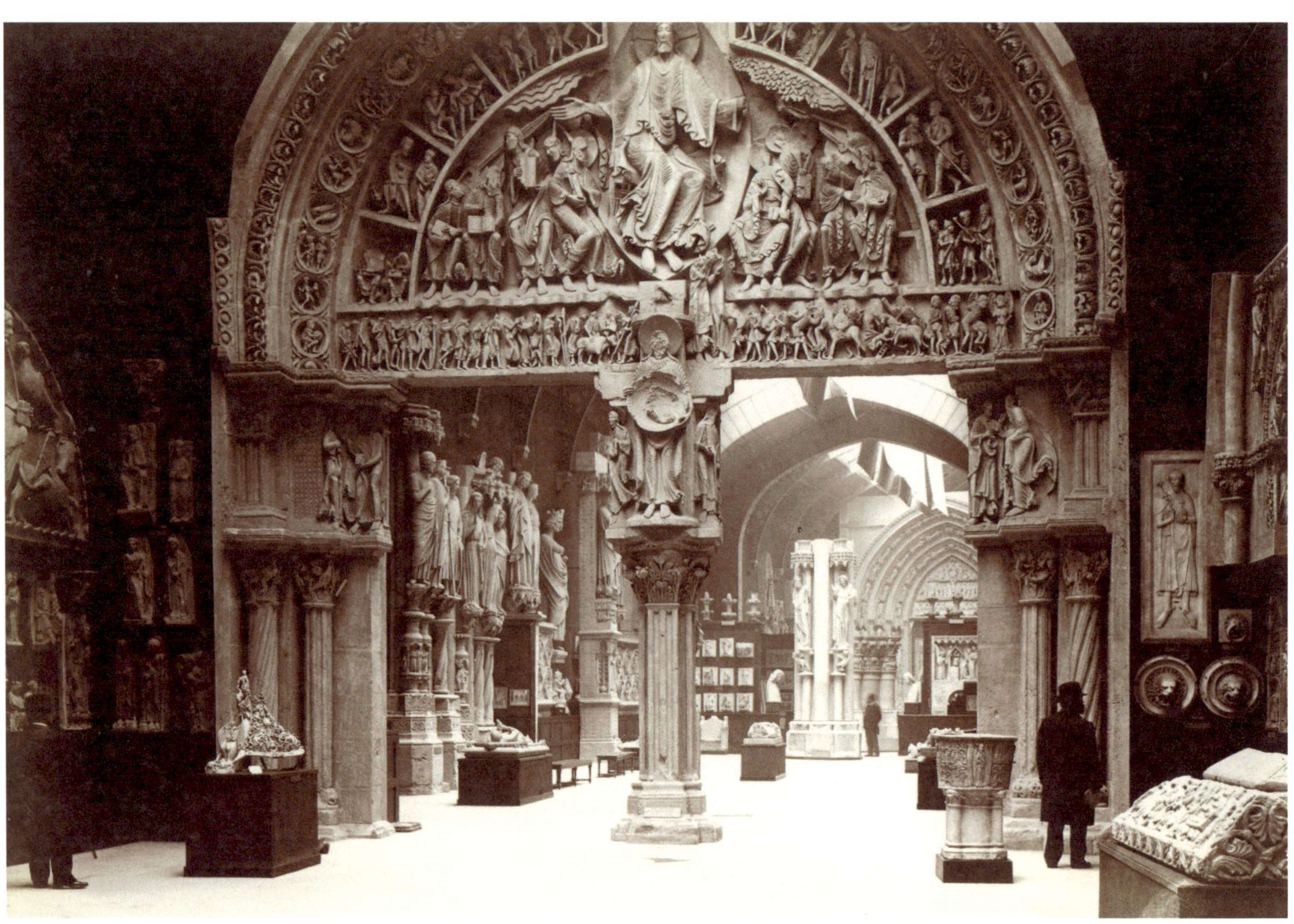

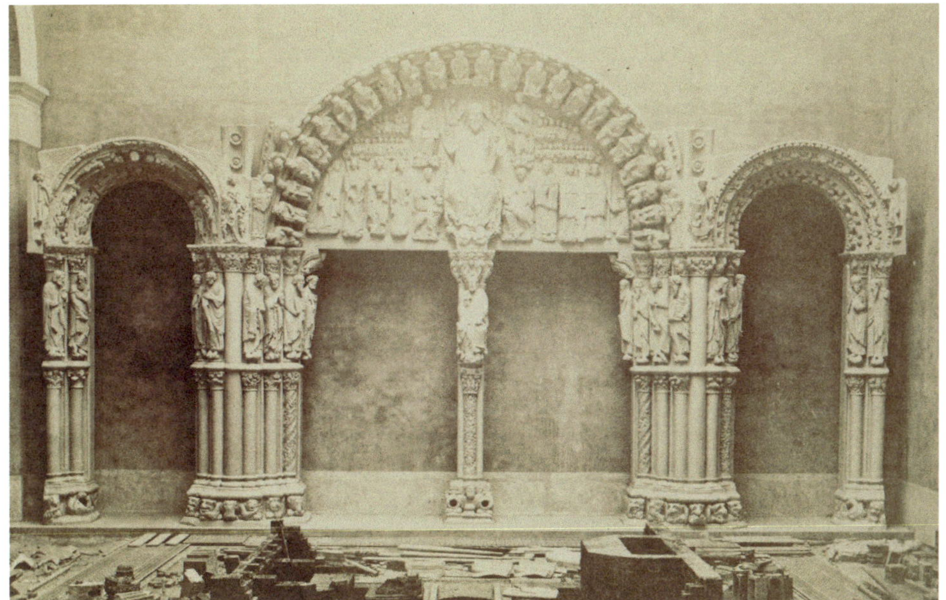

Generation

The project of a Musée de Sculpture Comparée was finally approved in 1879, a year that also saw the death of Viollet-le-Duc, who was therefore never able to witness the implementation of the museum that he had advocated for thirty years. Nevertheless, he did have the time to set out the main guidelines in two reports. Viollet-le-Duc planned to gather in the Palais du Trocadéro, predecessor of the Palais de Chaillot, the life-size casts of the main types of French sculpture, from the Romanesque period to modern times. His intention was to gain recognition for the artistic value of this heritage, in particular that of Gothic sculpture, disdained by the teachings of the Académie des Beaux-Arts (Academy of Fine Arts). For Viollet-le-Duc, the art of different civilisations had evolved following similar phases of development that could be unveiled by comparing them. He thus proposed establishing parallel series of casts of ancient and medieval sculpture from France and abroad, to dispel any idea of alleged inferiority in the art of the Middle Ages.

Monumental casts, such as the central portal of the narthex of the Basilica of Sainte-Marie-Madeleine in Vézelay (Yonne) – 10 metres high, 9.6 metres long – were already on display when the museum opened its doors in 1882 (fig. 3). Most of these "outsize casts" of the collections were made before the end of the century, some of them

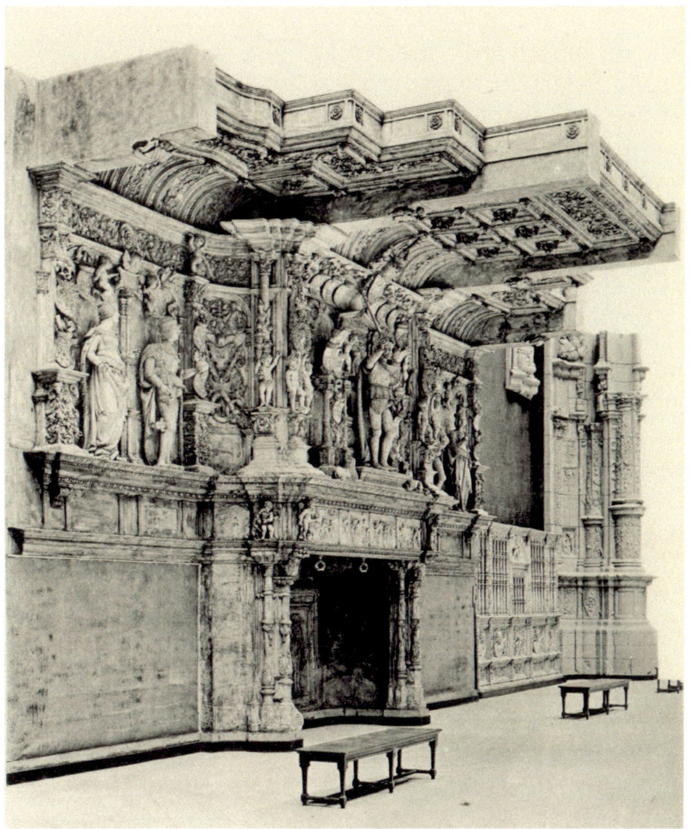

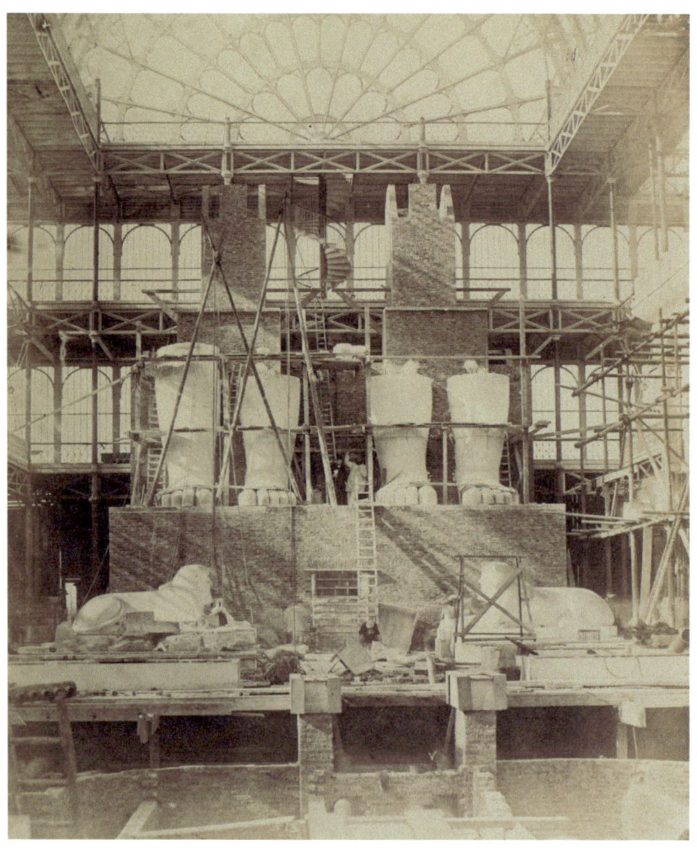

des épreuves de moulage, the name of the British architect Owen Jones (1809–1874) was included with that of Desachy as inventor. On 17–18 April 1857, a patent practically similar was registered in Belgium and France under the title *Mousselino-plastie ou léger plastique,* widely known by the name "staff", by Desachy's brother-in-law, Eugène Denis Arrondelle (1824–1907), head of the casting workshop of the Louvre.[7] This took place a few days before the publication of Desachy's patent specification, on 23 April 1857.

In both cases, the principle consists of combining plaster (or any plastic material) with fabric to obtain extremely durable yet lightweight proofs. In their patent, Desachy and Jones specify that the casts obtained from their invention are a twentieth of the weight of ordinary proof; in Arrondelle's, he promises the creation of casts "d'une légèreté extraordinaire".[8] Before the second half of the nineteenth century, plaster casts were indeed usually thick or even plain, sometimes fitted with metal to make them more solid, and therefore much heavier. Nonetheless, according to Ernest Albert Velten (1871–1949), head of the casting workshop of the Musées nationaux from 1927 until his death, this type of manufacturing still persisted in the first third of the twentieth century in German, Spanish, and even Italian casting workshops.[9]

in connection with the World Fairs of 1889 and 1900, as the Palais du Trocadéro was located within their area. These remarkable casts constituted an attraction in their own right: they invited nineteenth-century visitors on a wonderful tour through monumental France, in a unique, immersive experimental journey.

The type of casts of colossal size is in line with those executed by the South Kensington Museum (now Victoria and Albert Museum) in London from the 1860s onwards. The portal of the Glory of Santiago de Compostela, moulded in its entirety in 1866 by Domenico Brucciani (1815–1880) for the South Kensington Museum, is the prototype of the monumental plaster architectures of the Musée de Sculpture Comparée (fig. 4).

Their execution certainly relied upon the use of the fibrous plaster, first patented in England on 23 April 1856 by Alexandre Desachy (1817–1886), head of the casting workshop of the Academy of Fine Arts in Paris, under the title *Improvements in Producing Architectural Mouldings, Ornaments and Other Works of Art Formed with Surface of Plaster or Cement.*[6] When the invention was patented in France a few months later, on 22 November 1856, under the sober title *Perfectionnements apportés au tirage*

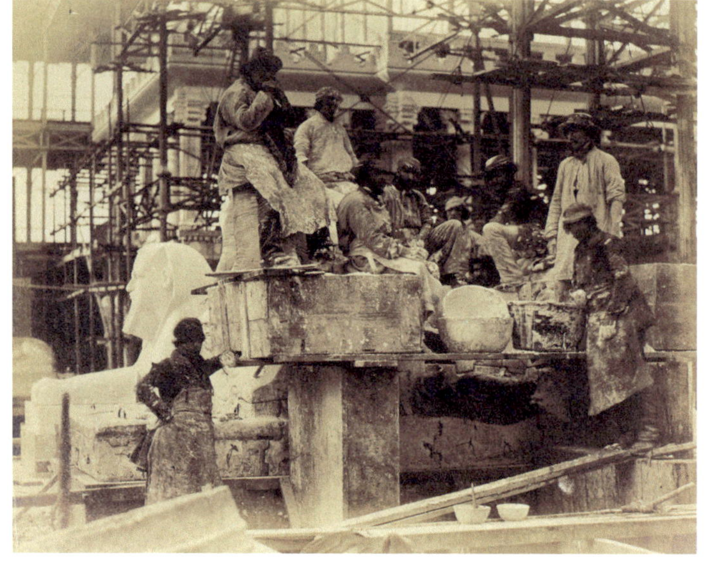

These technological innovations certainly opened up new horizons in the field of large and monumental casts. Casts of this type were nonetheless already known in the first part of the nineteenth century, such as the one of the Renaissance fireplace and ceiling of Brugse Vrije (Liberty of Bruges, fig.5). The latter was commissioned by King Louis-Philippe in 1838 for exhibition in the Musée du Louvre, and was moulded by François Henri Jacquet (1778–1857), head of the casting workshops of the Academy of Fine Arts in Paris and the Louvre. According to an essay on the monument by Jacques Olivier Marie de Mersseman (1805–1853), a Bruges practitioner fond of historical studies, the fireplace was completely dismantled to carry out the casting. The operation seems to have caused significant damage: loss of the original colours, whitish colouring suggesting the presence of mould on some parts of the sculpture, blackish on others, anarchical reassembly...[10] Of the cast, which was exceptional in its dimensions – 5.76 metres high, 10.44 metres long –, not a single fragment remains. In August 1891, the Musée du Louvre donated the fireplace to the Musée de Sculpture Comparée, where it was reassembled, before being dismantled and destroyed around 1935, when the Palais du Trocadéro was transformed into the Palais de Chaillot for the Exposition Internationale des Arts et Techniques dans la Vie Moderne in 1937.[11]

While Arrondelle and Desachy both claimed to have invented fibrous plaster, it should be noted that both were trained by Jacquet, who, as head of two state casting workshops, was renowned in his own times for the excellence of his technical skills and ingenuity.[12] Considering the chronology, one might wonder if was not in fact Jacquet who fathered the process, which was subsequently perfected and patented by Desachy and then by Arrondelle.

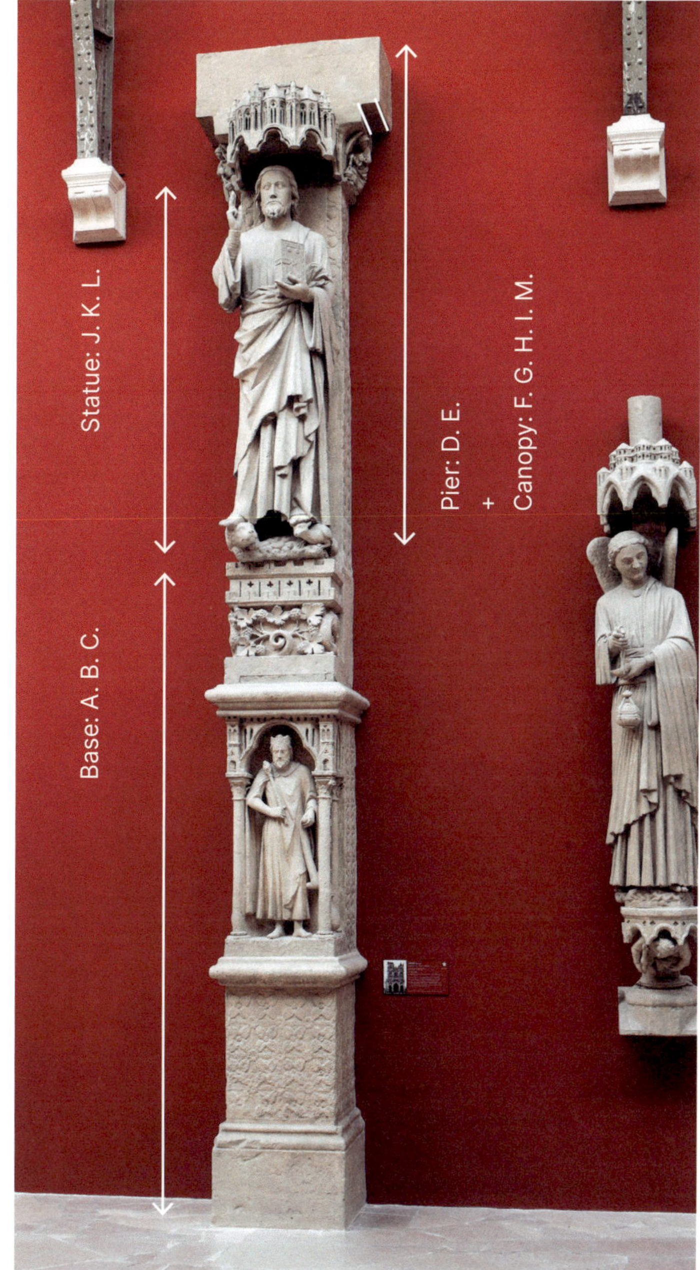

Whatever the truth of this, one thing held in common by Alexandre Desachy, Owen Jones, and Eugène-Denis Arrondelle was their work in the Crystal Palace, in its second life in Sydenham (1854–1936), where they experimented with the use of fibrous plaster. It was under the direction of Jones, joint director of decoration of the Crystal Palace, that Desachy, as general superintendent, laid out the spectacular Egyptian, Greek, Roman, and Alhambra Courts. Eugène-Denis Arrondelle was at his side as foreman; Auguste Alexandre Arrondelle (1835–1866), the latter's brother, also worked as cast maker on the site.

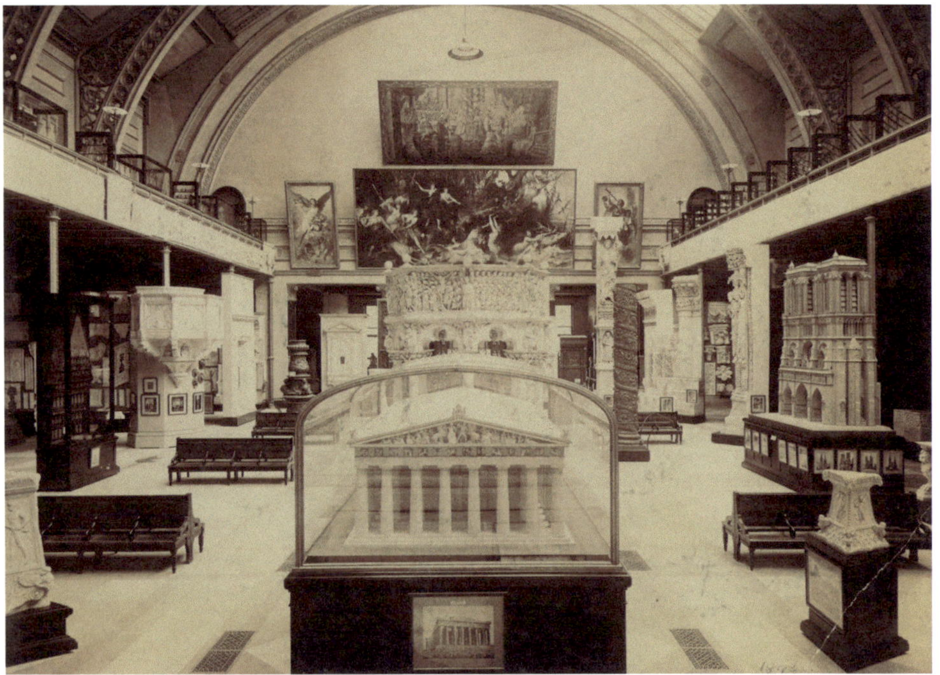

Fig. 9

The Metropolitan Museum of Art, New York
The Hall of Architectural Casts, 1895

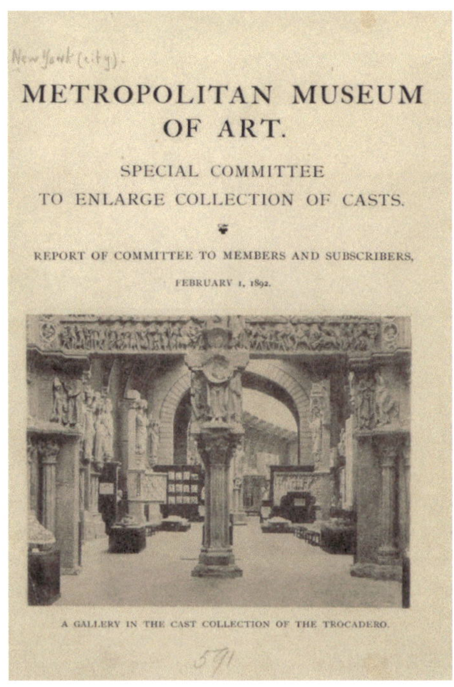

Fig. 10

Cover of *Special Committee to Enlarge Collection of Casts: Report of the committee to Members and Subscribers,* (New York, The Metropolitan Museum of Art, 1892)

Philip Henry Delamotte (1821–1889) may have immortalised them in photography, in particular during the setting up of the Egyptian Court. Owen Jones, with his top hat, appears in several *clichés,* alongside members of the workshop in charge of installing these incredible courts (figs. 6–7).[13] The figure beside Jones between the monumental *Colossi of Abu Simbel* could perhaps be Desachy or Arrondelle.

The casts commissioned by the Musée de Sculpture Comparée were all the outcomes of these technological innovations.

After Viollet-le-Duc's death, a Subcommittee of the Musée de Sculpture Comparée was created within the Committee on Historical Monuments, to give substance to the museum. Their members initially had mouldings made of the French artworks mentioned in Eugène Viollet-le-Duc's reports. They also relied on the illustrations in the *Dictionnaire raisonné de l'architecture française du XIe au XVIe siècle*, Viollet-le-Duc's renowned encyclopaedia published between 1857 and 1868. The works chosen by the architect to illustrate his dictionary were almost in-

evitably destined to be replicated in three dimensions for the collections. The reference to Viollet-le-Duc's dictionary is obvious when comparing its engravings of certain architectural fragments with the casts in the collections. The Subcommittee was very attentive to the question of which framing to adopt. Casts had to promote the architectural value of the element they reproduced. In the case of column capitals, cast makers were instructed to mould the start of the vaults on one side and part of the column on the other.

The casts exhibited in the museum were not treated as substitutes of the original works: they had to appear as such and not be mistaken as the originals. It was therefore expressly requested by the members of the Subcommittee that the seams on the casts should be left visible, "comme témoins irrécusables de l'exactitude du travail".[14] This philosophy differed from that of other institutions, which often specified a casting technique that avoided seams in order to reinforce the illusion of the original. In winter 1869–1870, when Henry Hardy Cole, Superintendent of the Archaeological Survey in India, moulded the Eastern Torana of the Great Stupa of

Sanchi (Raisen District, Madhya Pradesh) for the South Kensington Museum, he opted for the gelatine technique, which not only reduced the time required, but also avoided the pattern of seams generated by other processes.[15]

The rejection of illusionism is also manifest in the reluctance to reproduce the tones of the original materials on the casts, based on the argument that it would take away much of their finesse and delicacy.[16] The philosophy of the Musée de Sculpture Comparée differed from the practice in other European institutions (London, Berlin), where some of the casts on display recreated the shade and colour of the originals. When the Parisian museum opened its doors, the casts were left raw, slightly tinted by the colour of the clay used to make the mould. The clay from the region of Laon (Aisne) was particularly appreciated by the members of the casting workshop because it gave the casts a beautiful greenish tinge.

The members of the museum's committee expected the casts to fully reproduce the volumes of the original sculptures, down to their most minute details, and to testify to the high degree of technical skill with which they were created, as well as to the ability of the cast makers, first and foremost those of the casting workshop of the Musée de Sculpture Comparée.

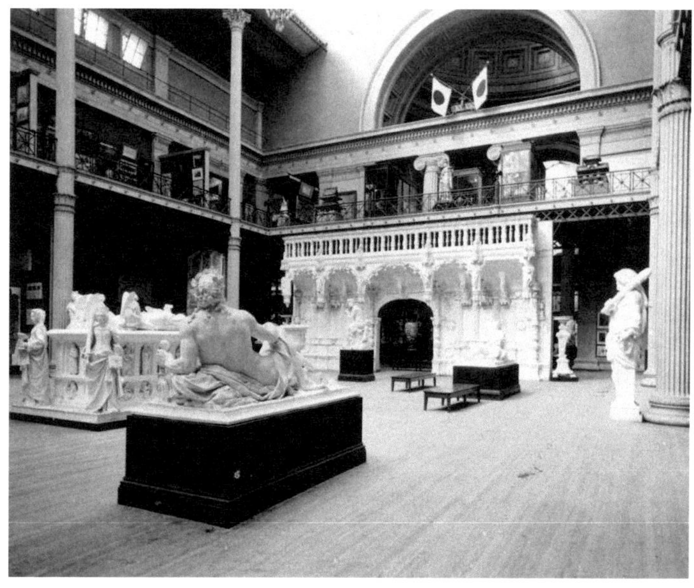

Fig. 11

World's Columbian Exposition
of Chicago, 1893
The East Court of the Palace of Fine Arts

In the foreground are casts of sculptures
of the park of the Palace of Versailles;
in the background is the cast of the rood
screen of Saint Stephen Cathedral,
in Limoges (6.30 metres high;
11.4 metres long)

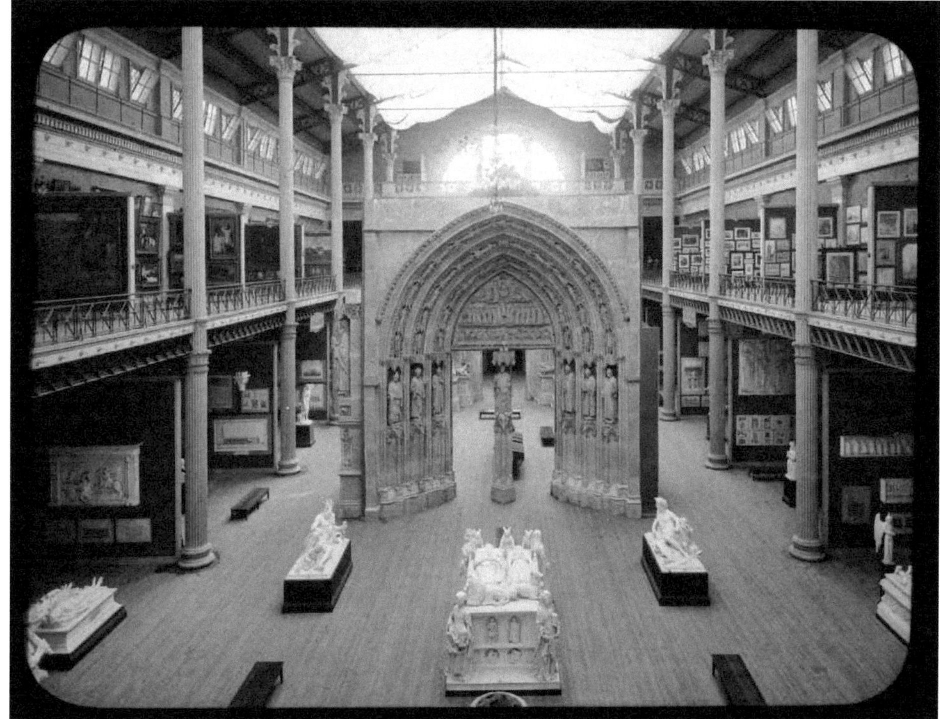

Fig. 12

World's Columbian Exposition
of Chicago, 1893
The East Court of the Palace of Fine Arts

In front of the cast of the north transept
portal of the Saint Andrew Cathedral,
Bordeaux (11 metres high; 10.68 metres long),
are the casts of sculptures of the park
of the Palace of Versailles, and that of the
Tomb of Francis II, Duke of Brittany
from Nantes Cathedral

Regeneration

A part of the cast collections of the Musée de Sculpture Comparée, which reached 1,259 casts in 1890 and 6,945 in 1937, was widely distributed in France and abroad thanks to its casting workshop, founded and directed by Jean Pouzadoux (1829–1893), and later led by his son Edouard Charles (1860–1940).

The diffusion of cast collections was officially encouraged from 1867 onwards with the *Convention for Promoting Universal Reproductions of Works of Art for the Benefits of Museums of All Countries*, initiated by Henry Cole, director of the South Kensington Museum. This convention is one of the first international treaties to promote the mutual benefits of sharing reproductions of works of art relating to historical monuments for educational purposes. This intention was reiterated on several occasions during the century and afterwards, such as in 1885, at a conference for the international exchange of reproductions of works of art, organised in Brussels. The implementation of the exchanges planned eighteen years earlier had encountered certain difficulties, including serious doubts about the harmlessness of certain casting methods.[17]

In France, the Ministry of Public Education and Fine Arts also encouraged the distribution of the casts of the Musée de Sculpture Comparée to high schools, universities and departmental museums. In the 1900s, it offered to the latter a list of casts, covering the twelfth, thirteenth, and fourteenth centuries, to fill the gaps in their collections of French monumental sculpture. This list is a kind of "digest" of French medieval monumental sculpture, reflecting the recognition accorded to certain sculptures by proponents of medieval archaeology at the turn of the century.

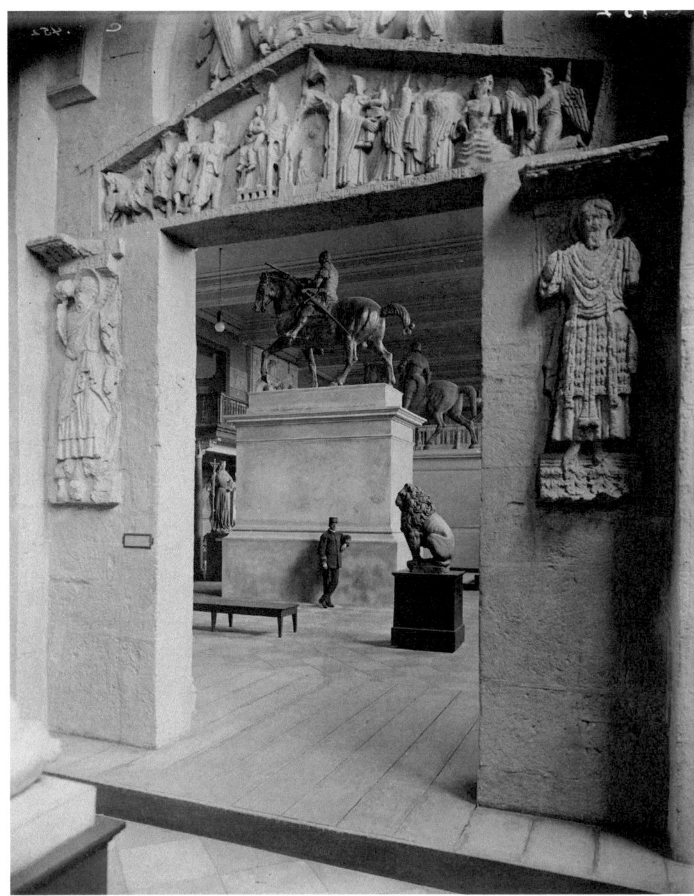

Fig. 13

The Art Institute of Chicago
Interior of the Blackstone Hall, ca. 1905

In the foreground is the cast of the portal
of the south front of the Church of Notre-Dame-du-Port,
in Clermont-Ferrand, in the background, are casts
of equestrian sculptures by Donatello and Verrocchio

Fig. 14 | next page

The Art Institute of Chicago
Interior of the Blackstone Hall, ca. 1905

In the foreground is the cast of the portal
of the City Hall of Toulon, by Pierre Puget;
in the background is a cast of a part
of the west front of the Abbey of Charlieu
(11 metres high; 11.50 metres long)

These international treaties and initiatives contributed to the diffusion and popularisation of the most famous monuments of French art, and thus served the purpose for which the Musée de Sculpture Comparée had been conceived by Eugène Viollet-le-Duc and realised by his followers.

The dissemination of the casts in the collections was also the result of specific orders executed with the aim of creating large collections of architectural casts or enriching existing collections. These also led to the making of moulds from the most renowned and impressive casts exhibited in the museum. With the clay squeezing technique used by cast makers to replicate monumental sculptures and architectural elements, the clay piece moulds are not reusable, so they only allow for the creation of a unique cast. Over the years, some of these casts were moulded by the casting workshop for commercial purposes using techniques that facilitated the preservation of the moulds – plaster piece moulding or gelatine moulding. For the period of activity between 1880 and 1902, the inventory book of the casting workshop of the Musée de Sculpture Comparée numbered 501 moulds. This "treasure of matrix" probably represented more than a third of the collections on display in the museum at the beginning of the twentieth century. The museum was nonetheless resistant to the practice of *surmoulage* due to the risk of deterioration of its collection, even by the means of clay squeezing, as it was also reluctant to mould on monuments that it considered too fragile to withstand the operation.

In Europe, the South Kensington Museum was the first institution to request this type of special order, outside the workshop's sales catalogue, making use of this opportunity sixteen times between 1889 and 1892. For instance, in 1889–1890, the South Kensington Museum financed for its collections the making of a mould of the pier of the central portal of the western front of the Cathedral of Notre-Dame in Amiens, widely known as *Le Beau Dieu d'Amiens*, taken from the museum's unique cast made in 1880. The moulds, which in this case were composed of thirteen pieces, each marked with a letter from A to M, remained the exclusive property of the casting workshop of the Musée de Sculpture Comparée, which thus, by this means, enriched its sales catalogue with a new "must-have" of French monumental sculpture. The lettering, which is sometimes visible on the surface of the casts, matched the minimalist description in the assembly instructions given to purchasers. In the case of the *Beau Dieu,* these were the following: "Superposer A. B. C. D. E. F. M.; Adjoindre G. H. I. à F. Placer la base de la statue J. sur C. et monter ensuite sur J. les K. et L."

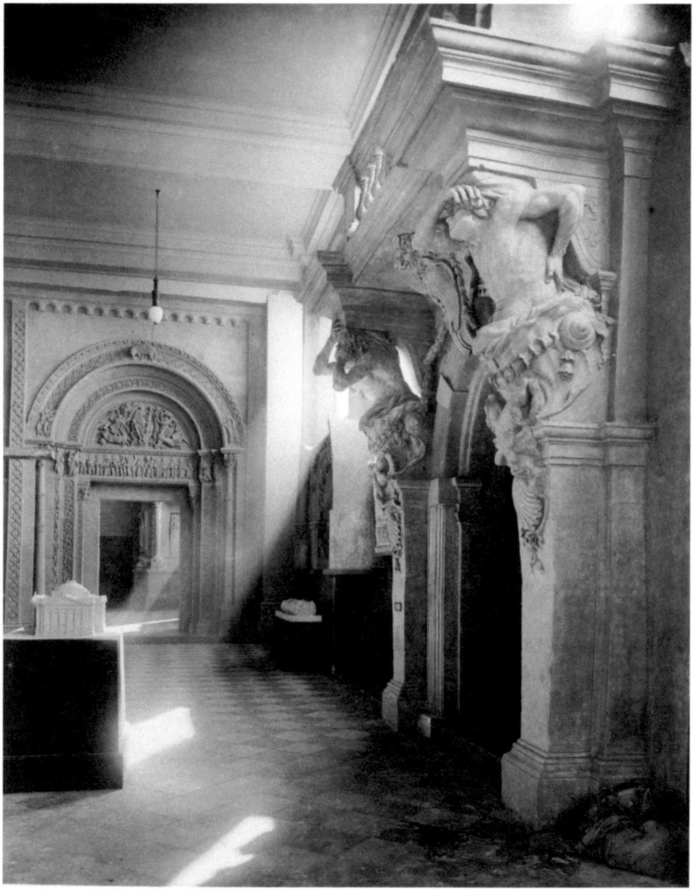

(fig. 8).[18] The assembly of colossal casts was obviously much more complex due to the higher number of pieces. The cast of the rood screen of the Cathedral of Saint Stephen in Limoges (Nouvelle-Aquitaine), for example, was delivered in more than a hundred pieces.[19]

The diffusion of the collection of the Musée de Sculpture Comparée and the making of moulds on some of its casts of monumental sculpture mainly resulted from specific requests by American museums and for the Chicago World's Fair of 1893. Of the 501 moulds, 36 were specifically created and financed by the latter. Opened in 1872, The Metropolitan Museum of Art in New York was, together with the Boston Museum, one of the very first North American institutions to acquire casts of French monumental sculpture. Of the 300 casts of the Willard Architectural Collection owned by The Metropolitan Museum of Art, 76 came from the casting workshop of the Musée de Sculpture Comparée.[20] These were capitals, door hammers, statues, or keystones taken from the most outstanding French monuments. The moulds of 6 of these casts were specifically created in connection with the opening of The Metropolitan Museum's Hall of Casts (Architecture Hall) in 1889 (fig. 9). For the Metropolitan Museum, which aspired to create the most important collection of casts in the world, the Parisian museum represented the model to follow and imitate, as the photography chosen for the cover of the *Report of the Special Committee to Enlarge Collection of Casts*, dated February 1892, explicitly shows (fig. 10). Until 1895, 11 other moulds were created at the New York museum's request, among them, in 1889–1890, that of the wooden doors of the portal of the western front of the Cathedral of Saint Savior in Aix-en-Provence (Bouches-du-Rhône). The creation of a new entry in the sales catalogue led immediately to high demand from other institutions. Ordered in 1892, the cast of this portal kept in the collection of the Victoria and Albert Museum also came from this mould. A third exemplar of this cast was on display one year later in the World's Columbian Exposition in Chicago, among dozens of masterpieces from the Musée de Sculpture Comparée.

Some moulds financed by the South Kensington Museum and The Metropolitan Museum of Art between 1889 and 1893 found new fortune in the context of the World's Columbian Exposition (1 May 1893 – 3 October 1893), a world fair devoted to the 400th anniversary of the discovery of America (figs. 11–12). In 1891, Halsey Cooley Ives (1847–1911), founding director in 1879 of the Saint-Louis School and Museum of Fine Arts, was commissioned to organise the fine arts section of the exposition. In the same year, he met Antonin Proust (1832–1905), meteoric Minister of the Fine Arts (1881–1882) and chairman of the Subcommittee of the Musée de Sculpture Comparée. With Roger Ballu (1852–1908), French principal commissioner for Fine Arts in the Chicago World's Fair, they selected a large number of casts in the collections of the museum that could be replicated for the event. The section of the catalogue dedicated to French historic sculpture on display in the East Court of the Palace of Fine Arts lists 116 entries representing even more casts of sculpture, mostly as applied to architecture from the eleventh to the nineteenth century. Of these, 72 entries concern casts that came from the casting workshop of the Musée de Sculpture Comparée, 23 from the casting workshop of the Musée du Louvre, and the rest from that of the Union centrale des Arts décoratifs. Representing 82 entries, the Renaissance and modern periods were particularly well illustrated, predominantly with sculptures from the Palace of Versailles and from the Louvre.[21]

A comparison with archival sources reveals that this list falls short of the number of casts made by the casting workshop of the Musée de Sculpture Comparée.[22] This order, amounting to a total value of 115,000 francs, 50,000 francs of which was financed by France, was the most important ever placed with the workshop. It was executed in record time, between June and December 1892, largely from the collection of moulds housed in the casting workshop. It also led to the creation of 19 new moulds of monumental casts, such as that of the famous rood screen in Limoges Cathedral. *Surmoulages* were also made with the clay squeezing technique for at least three casts: the central portal and part of the west front of the Abbey Church of Saint-Gilles (Gard), the portal of the north transept of the Cathedral of Saint Andrew in Bordeaux, and part of the west front of the Abbey Church of Charlieu (Loire). These casts were therefore unique doubles.[23] The importance of the cast numbers and the complexity of the assembly required the presence in Chicago of Jules Fontaine, a member of the casting workshop with thirty-five years of experience. Accompanying the 225 cases of casts, he embarked on the USS Constellation for an eleven-day voyage.[24] With all these casts, the East Court was a kind of avatar of the Musée de Sculpture Comparée – a "museum in mirror". As initially stated, at the end of the event, the collections were transferred to the Art Institute of Chicago, where they were reinstalled in the Blackstone Hall, inaugurated on 20 October 1903 (figs. 13–14). For this new layout, Edward J. Finley Timmons (1882–1960), who was then student there, stained the casts of the carved wooden doors of the cathedrals of Aix, Beauvais, and Rouen in imitation of oak.[25] This illusionist approach prefigures what was carried out on a much larger scale when the Musée des Monuments français was founded in the 1930s from the existing collections of the Musée de Sculpture Comparée.

The exhibition of casts of the masterpieces of French heritage in the World's Columbian Exposition certainly inspired the industrialist and philanthropist Andrew Carnegie (1835–1919) to fund a collection of architectural casts in the museum that bears his name, in Pittsburgh (Pennsylvania). As for the Casts Courts in the South Kensington Museum, an extension of the Carnegie Museum was custom-built to house, amongst other things, the Hall of Architecture, opened in 1907 (fig. 15). Between 1905 and 1907, 14 casts were delivered to the Pittsburgh Museum, commissioned by John W. Beatty (1851–1924), director of Fine Arts, with the art dealer Roland F. Knoedler (1856–1932) as intermediary. Despite the reluctance of the members of the Musée de Sculpture Comparée, a mould of the Well of Moses in the Chartreuse of Champol (Côte-d'Or) was specially made from the museum's unique cast executed in 1881.[26] The latter may have suffered during the procedure, as the first cast taken from the mould replaced it. The exemplar in the Carnegie Museum is the second produced. The cast of the Well of Moses kept in the collection of the Museum of Fine Arts, Budapest, ordered in 1908, also comes from this mould.

The Carnegie Museum also aspired to obtain monumental casts: the portal of the north transept of the Cathedral of Saint Andrew in Bordeaux and the portal of the west front of the Church of Saint-Gilles, two of the most impressive casts, which were on display at the Chicago World's Fair. Regarding the former, in 1906 a *surmoulage* was made on the cast at the Art Institute of Chicago, following the rejection in 1905 of a project for a second casting campaign on the original, due to the fragility of the stone.[27] For the front of the Church of Saint-Gilles, a new campaign of casting was specifically performed on the original, which was moulded by Edouard Charles Pouzadoux in its entirety. In 1908, a *surmoulage* was made on the wooden doors of the central portal of the latter to complete the cast on display in the Art Institute of Chicago.[28]

Through its partial replication, the mother collection of the Musée de Sculpture Comparée has continuously regenerated itself, fulfilling the mission that Viollet-le-Duc and the pioneers of the protection of French historical monuments had sworn to accomplish. The task of enumerating its surviving children in North American museums still remains. The architectural casts of the Art Institute of Chicago were packed away in the 1950s; those that were deemed "deteriorated beyond repair" were destroyed.[29] In the early 1930s, The Metropolitan Museum of Art's Hall of Casts suffered a similar destiny. Over the years, its casts collections were gifted to other American institutions or sold; the last auction took place in 2006.[30]

Nowadays, the cast collections of the Carnegie Museum are the most important in quantity and value in America. The cast of the front of the Church of Saint-Gilles, with its three porches, is unique, as is the cast of the portal of the north transept of Bordeaux Cathedral, since the one in the Musée de Sculpture Comparée was dismantled in the 1930s. All that remains of the latter – the tympanum with its voussoirs and only three statues – is held by the Musée des Monuments français in the Cité de l'architecture et du patrimoine. The number of surviving moulds from the casting workshop of the Musée de Sculpture Comparée within the invaluable collections of the casting workshop of the Réunion des musées nationaux – Grand-Palais likewise remains to be assessed.

Fig. 15

Carnegie Institute, Pittsburgh. The Hall of Architecture, ca. 1908

On the left, the cast of the portal of the north transept of the Saint Andrew Cathedral in Bordeaux;
on the right, the cast of the portal of the west front of the Church of Saint-Gilles

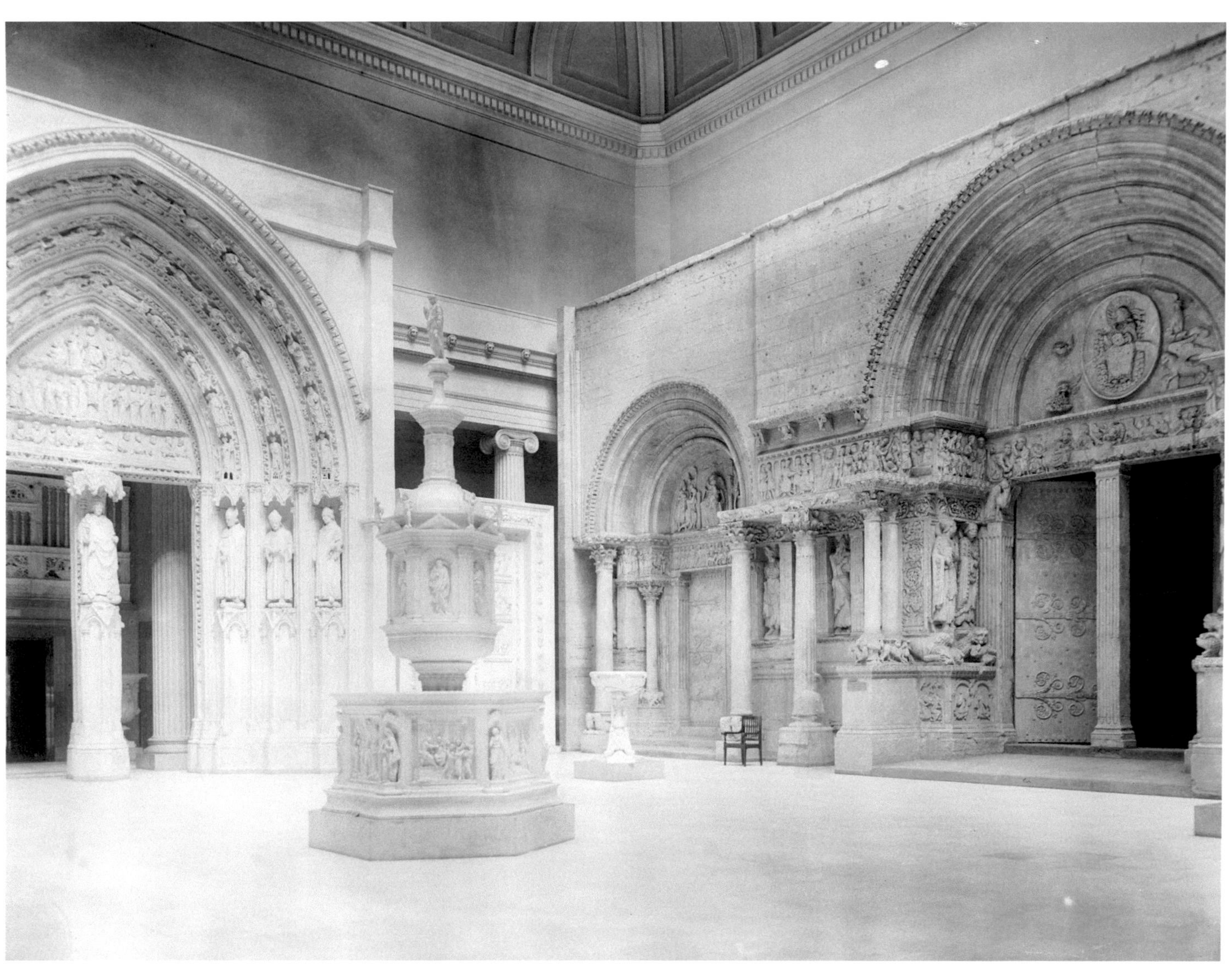

Notes

1 See Lending 2017.

2 Hofman 2016.

3 *Note, circulaires et rapports…* 1862, 23.

4 "… from any mutilation the objects entrusted to his dexterity." *Le Journal du Cher* 1842, n. p. These works were carried out in the context of a project for a museum of French monuments in Paris, which dates back to 1848. Viollet-le-Duc was strongly involved in this project, led by the Committee on Historical Monuments. On this subject, see Hofman and Lancestremère 2013, 207–13.

5 Wagstaffe Yapp 1853, 51–52.

6 *English patents…* 1856.

7 The French patents are respectively registered by the Institut national de la propriété industrielle under the ratings 1BB29873 and 1BB31773. Desachy's name is misspelled Desachi. On their family ties, in 1851, Eugène Denis Arrondelle married one of the sisters of Alexandre Desachy, Joséphine Théodorine (1830–1870).

8 "… of an extraordinary lightness." See *English patents…* 1856.

9 Archives du Musée des Monuments français, Paris, CAPA/MSC 6.

10 Messermann 1845, 22–25.

11 Archives du Musée des Monuments français, Paris, *Carnets de Paul Deschamps* 1934–1940.

12 *Nécrologie* [Alexandre Desachy] 1886, 293; Pontarmé 1901, 1–2. They both were aged about thirteen when they entered Jacquet's workshop. Regarding Jacquet's ingenuity, see Lebrun 1838, 61.

13 Delamotte 1855. Construction, displays, and the opening ceremony are documented by 160 mounted salted paper prints.

14 "… as irrefutable witnesses to the accuracy of the work." Musée des Monuments français, Paris, Collection A. V. Geoffroy-Dechaume, box 14: *Instruction concernant les travaux de moulages à exécuter pour le Musée de Sculpture Comparée*, 1881.

15 *First Report…* 1882, VIII: "What can be done with gelatine in one day takes 14 days to accomplish by Piece Moulds; The object, will moreover, be covered with seams or divisions, whilst with an elastic mould the object is cast solid in one piece."

16 Archives du Musée des Monuments français, Paris, Records of the Subcommittee of the Musée de Sculpture Comparée, session of 27 November 1880.

17 *Échanges internationaux…* 1885.

18 "Superpose A. B. C. D. E. F. M.; Add G. H. I. to F. Place the base of the statue J. on C. and then assemble K. and L. on J. "; Archives du Musée des Monuments français, Paris, inventory book of the Casting workshop, mould n°234.

19 Archives du Musée des Monuments français, Paris, inventory book of the Casting workshop, mould n°98.

20 *Tentative List of Objects…* 1891, 96–121.

21 *World's Columbian Exposition…* 1893, 261–76. In this publication the casts are listed between the numbers 1196 and 1311; one number may include several casts.

22 Médiathèque de la photographie et du patrimoine, Charenton-le-Pont, 80/8/6.

23 In 1892, a mould of the left part of the portal of the north transept of Bordeaux's Cathedral was financed by the South Kensington Museum. Archives du Musée des Monuments français, Paris, inventory book of the casting workshop, mould n°318.

24 McKee 1964, 18. Crates in the East court of the Palace of Fine Arts during the installation or deinstallation are visible on a photograph that was published in *The American Architects and Building News* dated 24 March 1894.

25 *The Art Institute of Chicago…* 1904, 27, 58. The name Blackstone Hall was given after a gift of 75,000 dollars by Mr and Mrs T.B. Blackstone devoted to the acquisition of architectural casts.

26 Archives du Musée des Monuments français, Paris, inventory book of the casting workshop, mould n°518.

27 Archives du Musée des Monuments français, Paris, CAPA/MSC 8. *Avis du Comité des Inspecteurs généraux des édifices diocésains et paroissiaux*, dated 6 June 1905. The recommendation was signed by the architects on historical monuments, Louis Sauvageot (1842–1908) as rapporteur and Anatole de Baudot (1834–1915), with the head of the casting workshop of the Musée de Sculpture Comparée, Edouard Charles Pouzadoux.

28 *Bulletin of the Art institute of Chicago* 1908, 9.

29 *The Art Institute of Chicago…* 1954–1955, 6.

30 *Historic Plaster Casts from the Metropolitan Museum of Art*, Sotheby's, New York, 26 February 2006.

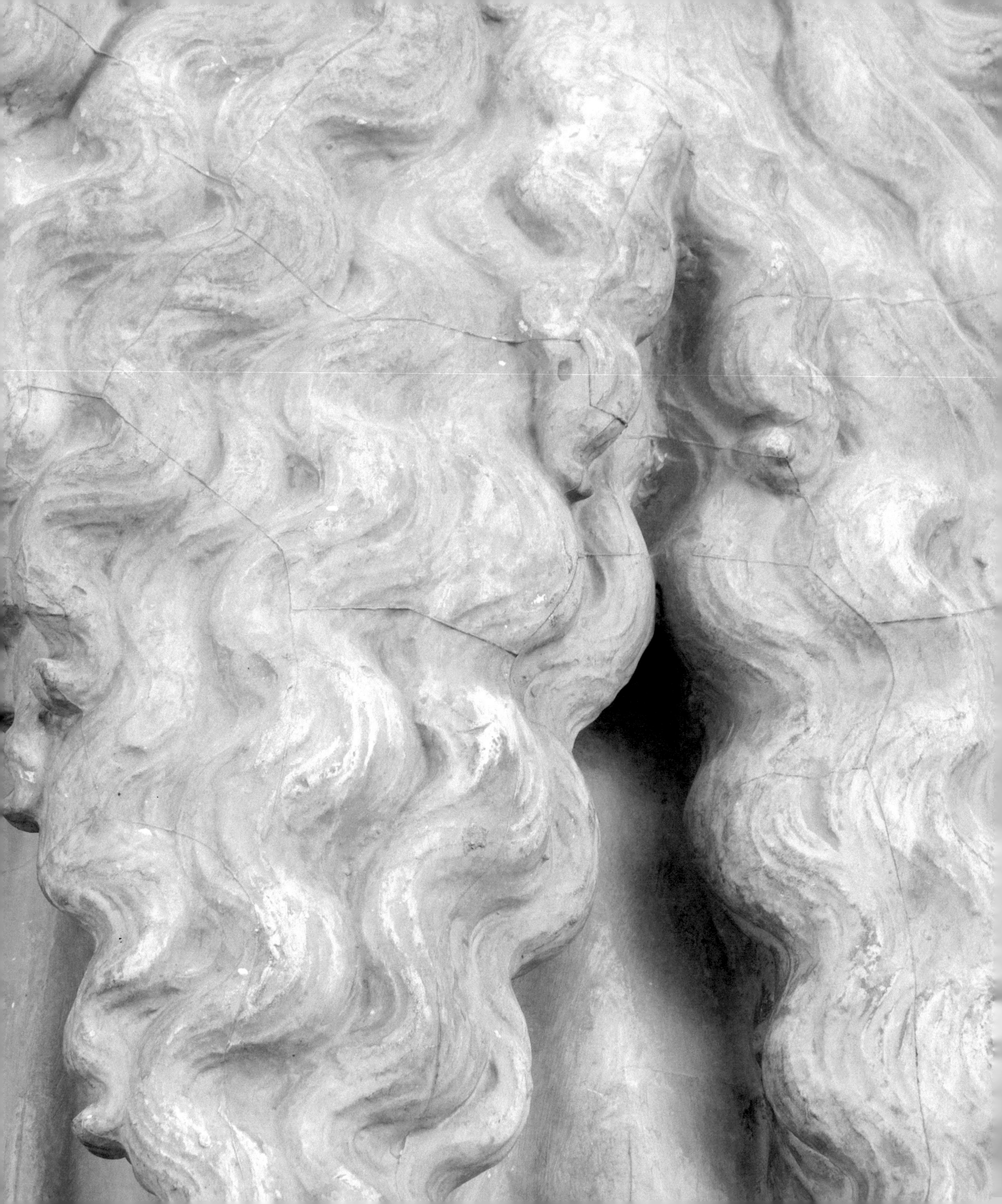

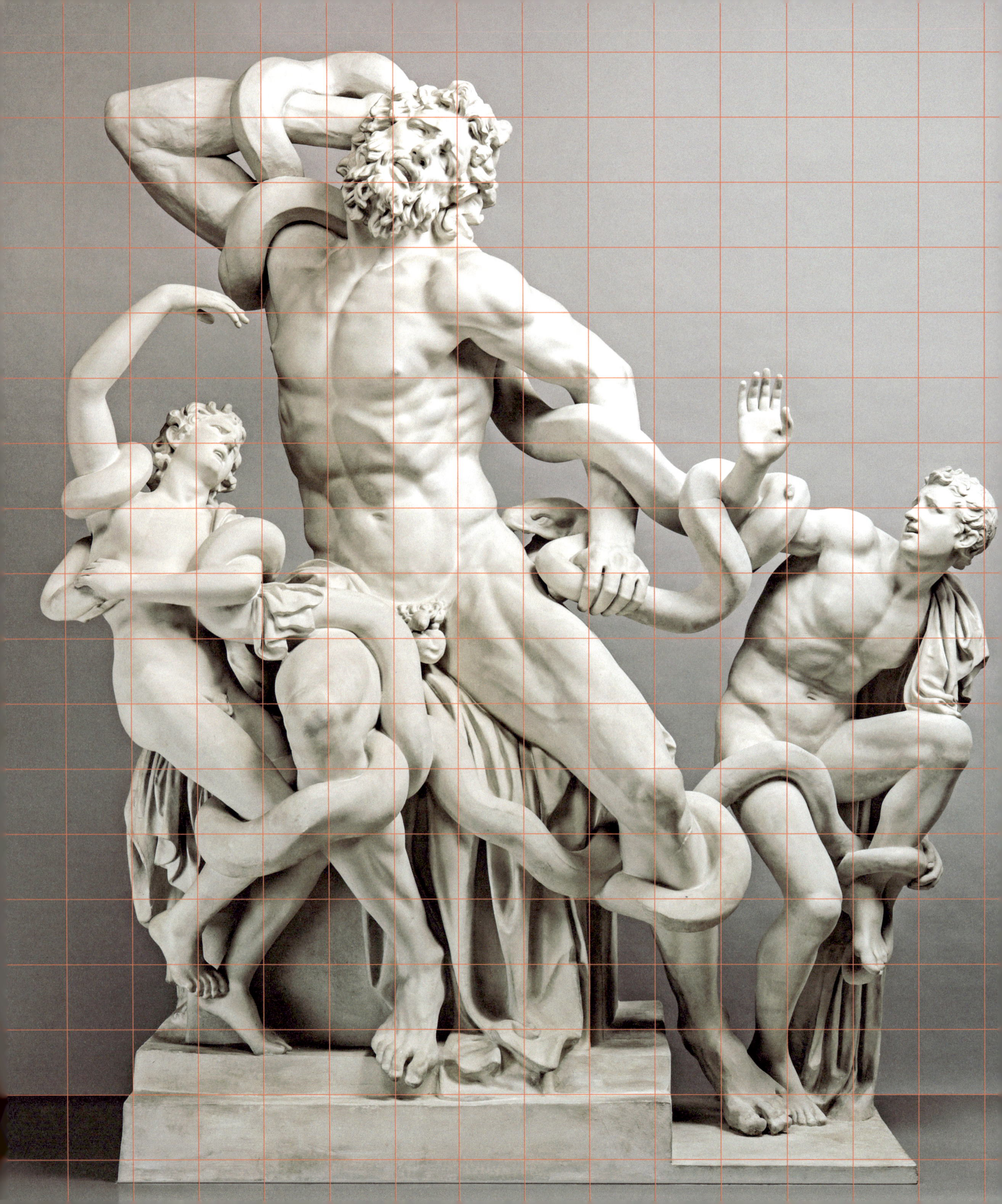

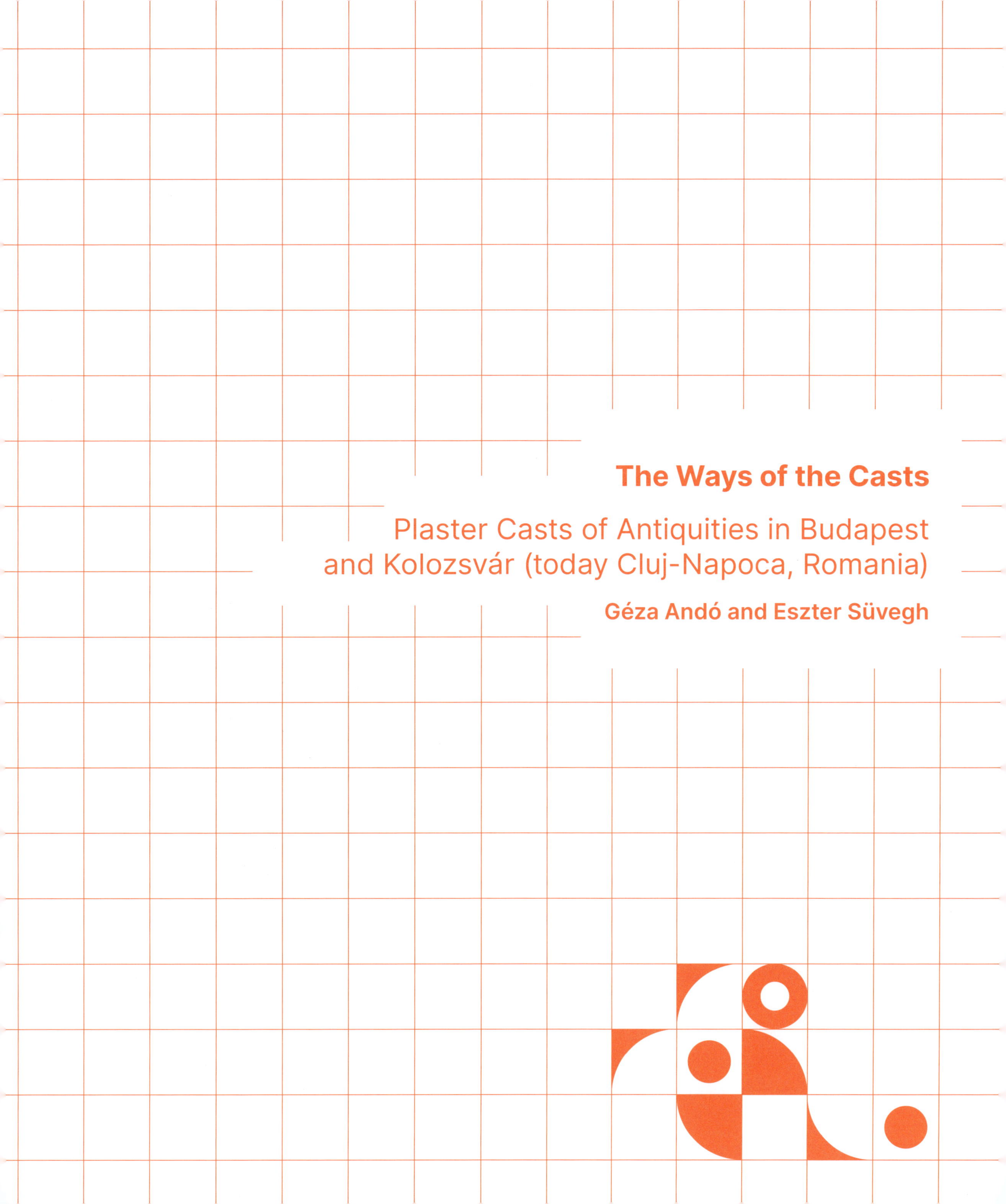

The Ways of the Casts

Plaster Casts of Antiquities in Budapest
and Kolozsvár (today Cluj-Napoca, Romania)

Géza Andó and Eszter Süvegh

The Ways of the Casts

Plaster Casts of Antiquities in Budapest and Kolozsvár (today Cluj-Napoca, Romania)

Géza Andó and Eszter Süvegh

Through a forgotten episode in the past of the historical plaster cast collection in Budapest, in this paper, the reader will be given a glimpse into its particular history and its curious circumstances. Furthermore, through an example, we will also explore the important role played by such a collection in scholarship and education.

Unlike the major museums of Europe, large public collections in Hungary did not grow out of royal collections but were established by aristocrats' contributions, private donations, and with budgetary resources voted for by the Hungarian Parliament.

Even around the time when the Museum of Fine Arts in Budapest was established, in the late nineteenth and early twentieth century, Hungary did not have a substantial collection either of original ancient sculpture or of European medieval and Renaissance sculpture. The lack of these collections in museums or universities teaching fine arts or classical archaeology prompted the establishment of a cast collection.

It is thanks to Ferenc Pulszky[1] (fig. 1) that a plaster cast collection of classical sculptures was formed in Hungary. Ferenc Pulszky was a politician, classical archaeologist, writer, art collector, and director of the Hungarian National Museum.[2] While forced into exile in London,[3] he expounded in a reading, held in the British Museum in 1851,[4] that an "ideal" museum should give a picture of the completeness of the art of mankind. He stood by the view of expanding the traditional approach of presenting the ancient world exclusively through works of Greek and Roman art and argued that collecting and exhibiting should extend to objects from the great empires of the Near East and cultures of the Far East, among others. He proposed that in order for an exhibition to be comprehensive, it was essential to display originals alongside plaster casts.

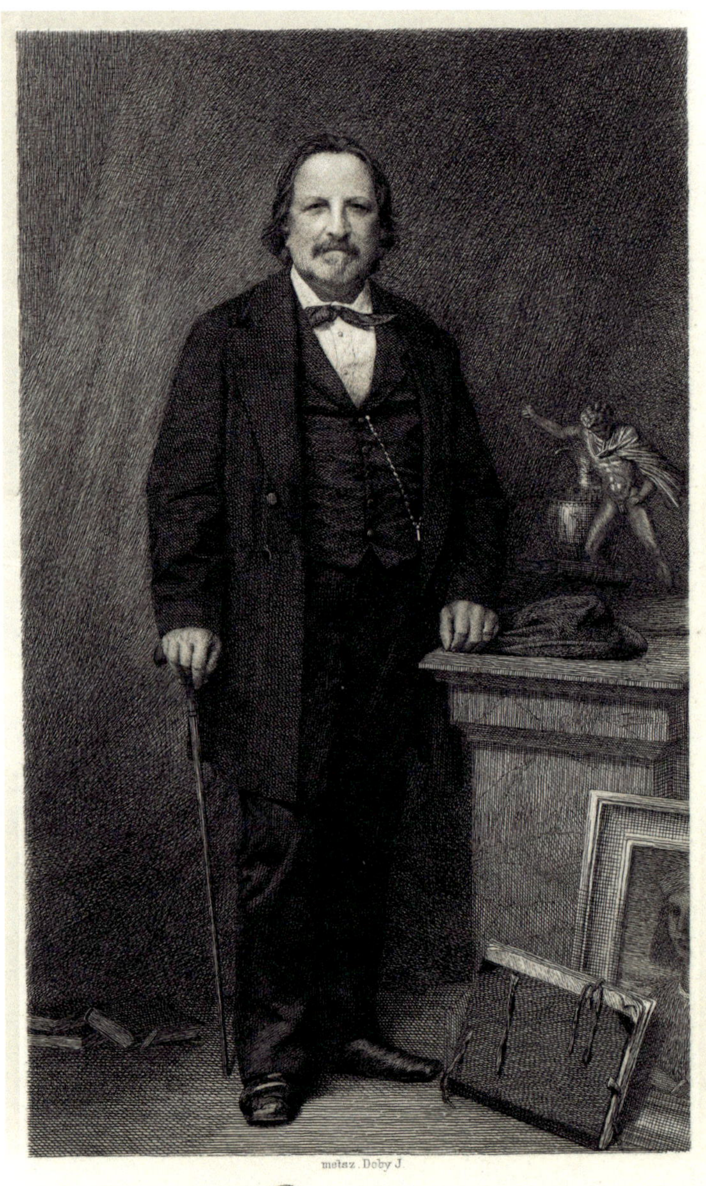

Fig. 1

Jenő Doby, Ferenc Pulszky, 1884

The Plaster Cast Collection
of the Hungarian National Museum

Ferenc Pulszky became director of the Hungarian National Museum in 1869 and immediately started compiling a plaster cast collection (fig. 2). A series of casts, made of sculptures unearthed in excavations at the time in Greece, which he purchased at the 1873 Vienna World's Fair,[5] lent uniqueness to the collection: this ensemble of casts, made by Felice Napoleone Martinelli of Rome working in Athens, fundamentally defined its character.[6] Pulszky formed and expanded the collection methodically, on the one hand with copies of famous and well-known sculptures, such as the *Laocoön* (fig. 3), that were obligatory from a didactic point of view, and on the other, with pieces that served the study of the works of art and their comparison.

The Hungarian public could also learn about Pulszky's progressive ideas about museums, as he published them several times in various journals in the 1870s.[7] The concept was in line with what had already been formulated in London, and we see this spirit reflected in the early versions of the designs of the Museum of Fine Arts.

By the 1880s, the much-welcomed growth in the number of its original works of art brought the National Museum face to face with the ever graver problem of a lack of space. However, by this time the plan was already progressing towards the foundation of a new museum of fine arts, which would not only display paintings but would also present the history of sculpture from antiquity to the eighteenth century, featuring original works and plaster casts as well. This institution would later become the Museum of Fine Arts, Budapest.[8]

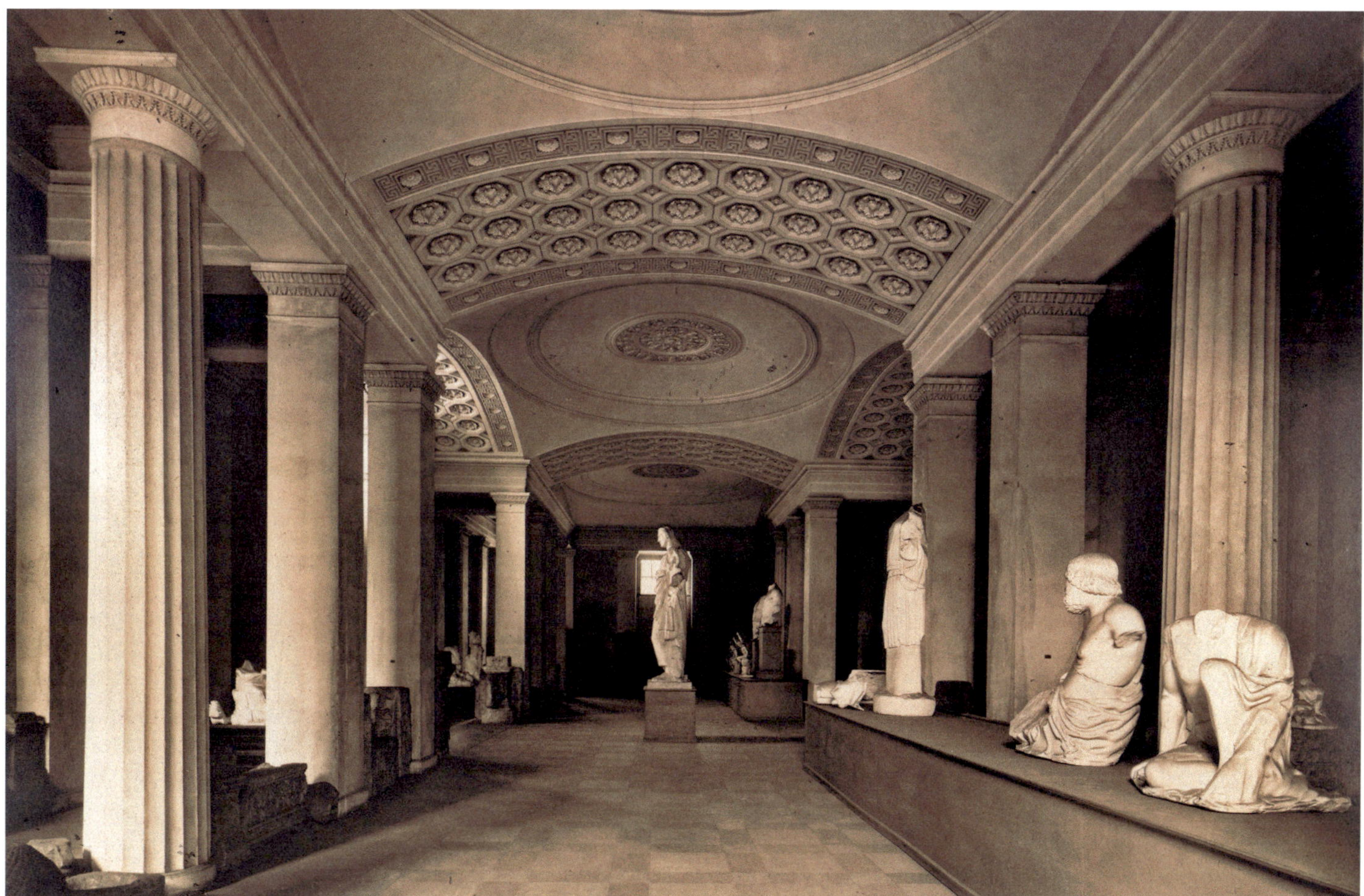

Fig. 2

The lobby of the Hungarian National Museum

In the centre is the cast of Mausolus, in the foreground and background are casts of the sculptures of the east pediment of the Temple of Zeus in Olympia. The casts shown in the photograph are currently in the National Museum of Transylvanian History in Cluj-Napoca

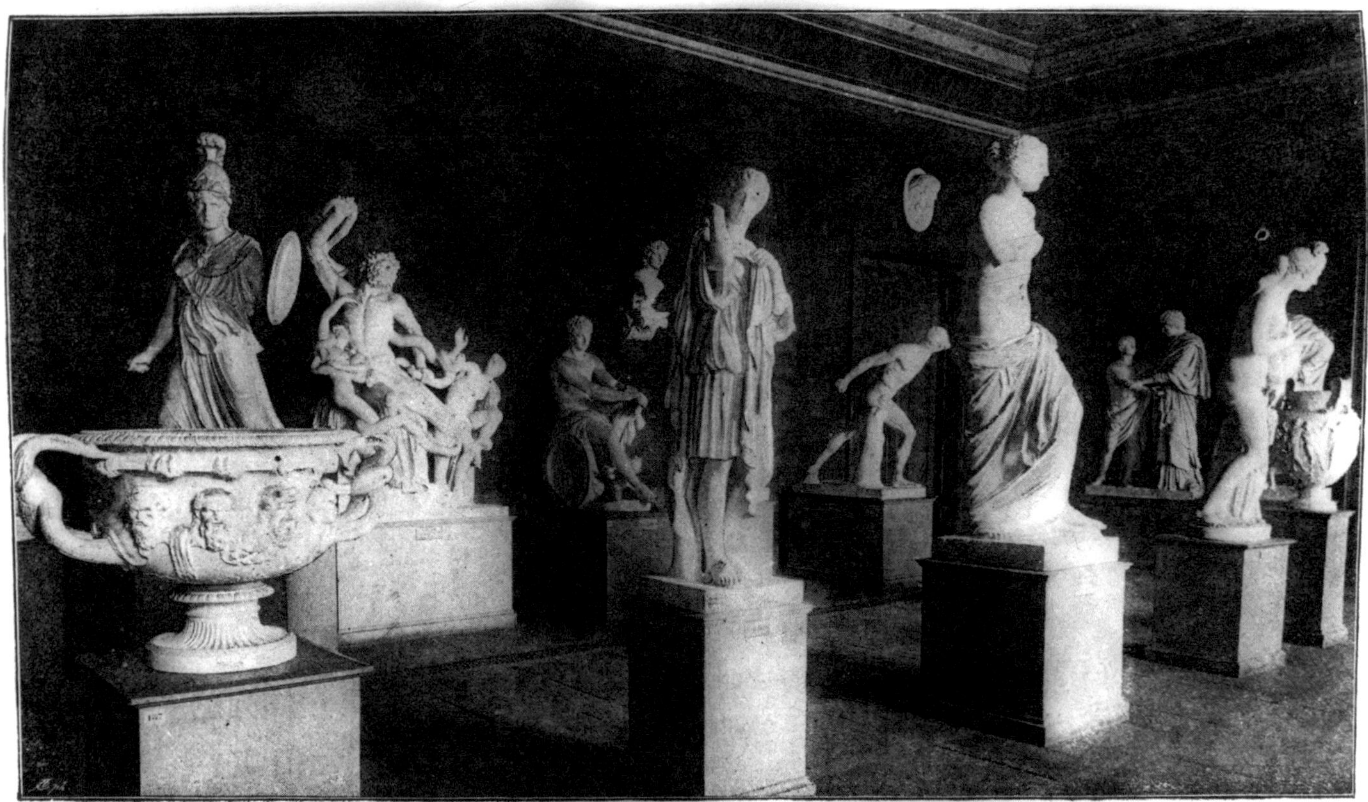

The Plaster Cast Collection of the Museum of Fine Arts, Budapest

The enormous ground floor halls of the Museum of Fine Arts were constructed to house the plaster casts (fig. 4). The museum opened in 1906 and the first plaster cast exhibitions were in 1913.[9] Why so late? A museum's worth of copies had already existed for eight years at that point, the museum itself had been opened for six years, and the well-informed press seemed to know as early as 1908 that the exhibitions were almost finished.[10]

And this is where a remarkable plot twist took place. A forgotten episode of the plaster casts, left out of the historiography of the museum, will be recounted now.

Fig. 3

Exhibition of casts in the Hungarian National Museum

Room of Hellenistic sculpture (Room VIII). In the background is the *Laocoön Group*. This plaster cast is currently on display in Matthias Corvinus House (birthplace of Hungarian King Matthias Corvinus), which since 1950 has served as the headquarters of the University of Art and Design in Cluj-Napoca

Plaster Casts in Kolozsvár (today Cluj-Napoca, Romania)[11]

Although the basis of the collection consisted of casts from the Hungarian National Museum, only some of these pieces were included in the exhibitions opened at the Museum of Fine Arts.

No sooner had the exhibition of casts of ancient art opened than the museum handed over 106 plaster casts[12] to the Royal Hungarian Franz Joseph University in Kolozsvár.[13] It was common practice to enrich the Transylvanian collections, as well as the collections of other parts of the country, with deposits from large public collections in Budapest. The dean of the University of Kolozsvár, János Csengeri, wrote a letter in November 1909 to Ernő Kammerer, director of the Museum of Fine Arts, Budapest, saying that he knew that the museum "might be willing" to hand over its precious plaster casts, "no longer indispensable for the Museum", to the University of Kolozsvár, to help facilitate education in aesthetics and art history. This request was fulfilled with surprising rapidity.[14] Both parties emphasised the cultural

Fig. 4 | next page

Exhibition of casts in the Museum of Fine Arts, Budapest, organised by Antal Hekler and Zoltán Oroszlán in 1923

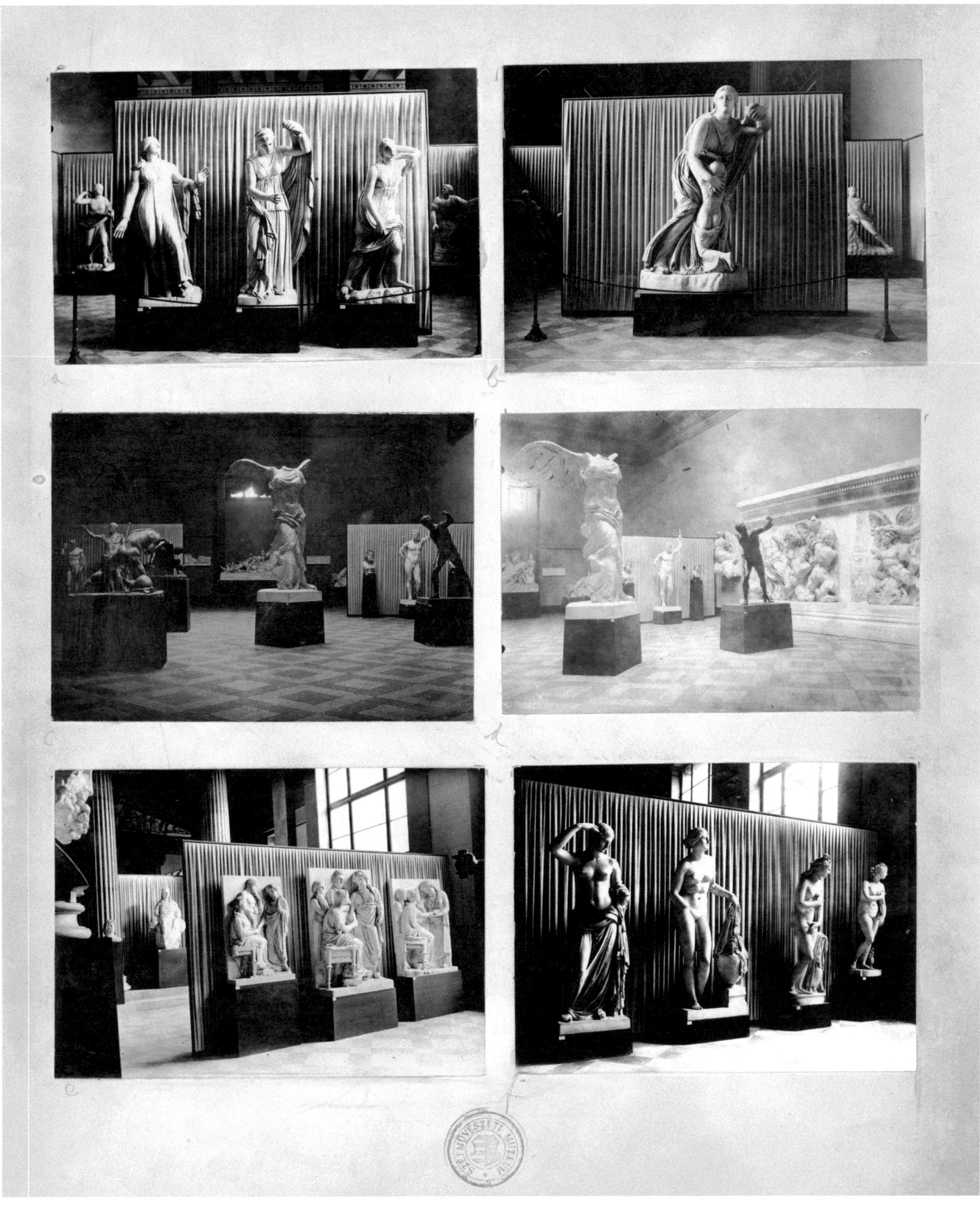

importance of this transfer. Based on the documentation, the Museum of Fine Arts wanted to keep only the part of the collection that was purchased by Ferenc Pulszky at the 1873 Vienna World's Fair, saying, "no reproduction is available since then" of these casts.[15] The articulated reason stated in the documents for handing over the other casts, that is, most of the collection, was the poor and damaged condition of the "much hauled" sculptures which, even after conservation, would have been rather conspicuous next to the new plaster casts ordered at the time.

Among the documents of the handover, there is an additional noteworthy clause: the collection to be transferred must be housed in the new building of the Transylvanian Museum Association.[16] However, both the University of Kolozsvár and the Transylvanian Museum Association were struggling with a lack of space at this time, and the placement of the large number of artefacts that arrived in 1910 posed considerable difficulties. In a telegram, Dean Csengeri requested a temporary cessation of further deliveries,[17] but the reply from the Museum of Fine Arts explained that they could not store the plaster casts and chests in Budapest any longer, so their dispatch had already taken place.[18] New casts of almost all the sculpture reproductions given to Kolozsvár were commissioned by the Museum of Fine Arts between 1905 and 1912, in a process that started even before the handover.

Another story also seems to be taking shape behind this transaction. In order to understand this, we need to take a look at the historical, social, and cultural situation of Hungary and Transylvania at the time.[19]

During the era of reform, the awakening and strengthening of national consciousness was a Europe-wide trend, which also involved the establishment of independent national institutions. The idea of creating an independent Transylvanian-Hungarian scientific collection was born as early as the second half of the eighteenth century.[20] Forming a museum collection symbolising the national sovereignty of Hungarians in multi-ethnic Transylvania was not only a cultural issue, but also a political one. This effort, however, was not successful until the mid-nineteenth century. The ambitions of the Transylvanian Hungarians and Székelys (a Hungarian subgroup in Transylvania) were inspired, among other things, by the founding of the Brukenthal Museum in Nagyszeben (today Sibiu, Romania), which was the first museum, and also the oldest institution of its kind in Transylvania, and was the institutional basis for significant cultural and scientific activity.[21]

In 1859 the Transylvanian Museum Association was established,[22] whose goal was to centrally house, professionally preserve, and scientifically process the important private

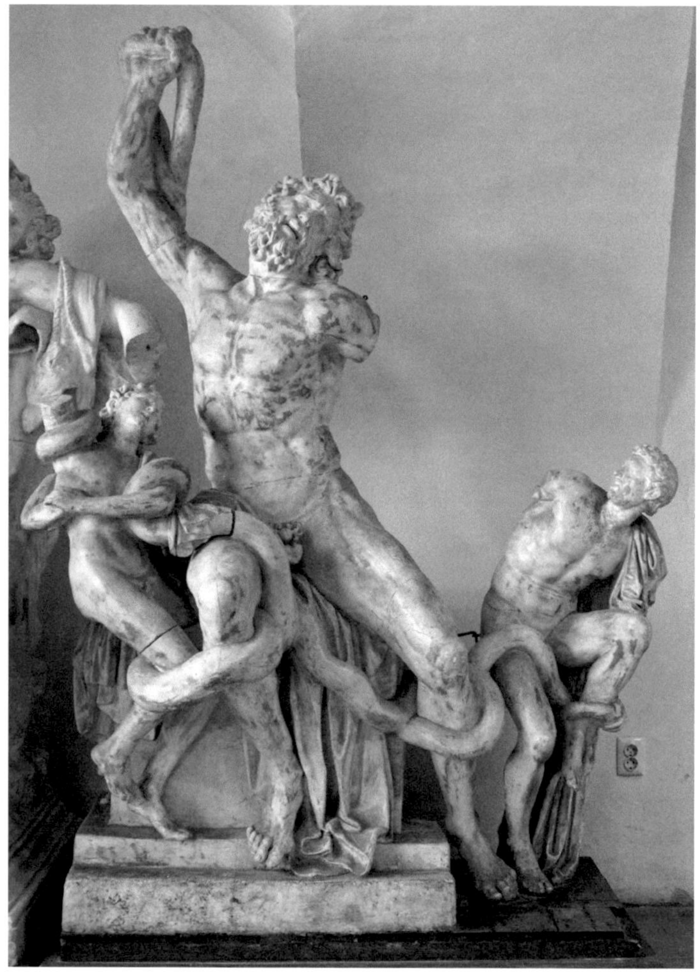

collections of Transylvanian-Hungarian aristocrats and people belonging to other layers of society. The archaeological holdings of the museum, organised according to type of find, comprised more than 10,000 objects. As the organisation of the collections started, so did the research management work of the association. By 1906 the final structure, constructed according to discipline, was born.

Kolozsvár gained high significance due to the continuously growing collection and the vibrant scholarly activity. When the Hungarian government planned to establish a regional university, Kolozsvár won the contest over Pozsony (today: Bratislava, Slovakia). The decision was based on the fact that a significant public collection already existed there at that time which could provide a background for scientific activity. The Royal Hungarian Franz Joseph University of Kolozsvár was established in 1872. In that same year, the association signed an agreement with the Hungarian government to hand over its right of handling its collections to the University of Kolozsvár. This gave the Hungarian state access to the scientific material essential for the establishment and functioning of the university. Then followed

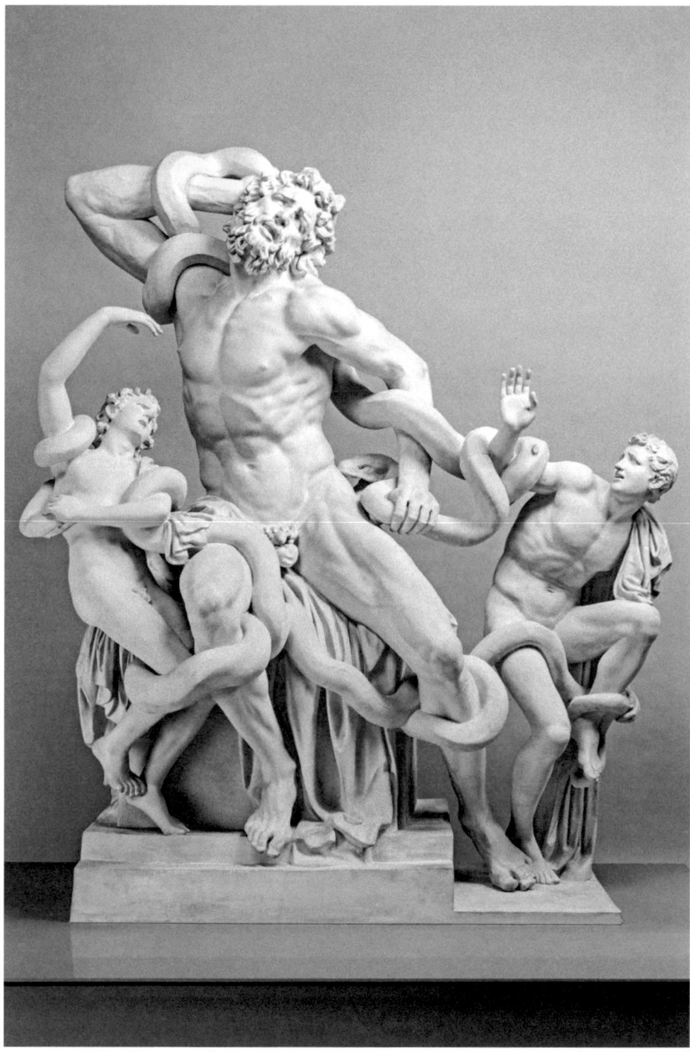

modelled after the Musée de Sculpture Comparée in Paris, where, in addition to plaster copies of outstanding sculptural works from the Transylvanian region, plaster casts of masterpieces of universal art were also to be included.[25] In addition to copying Transylvanian monuments, in 1905 Pósta ordered fifteen casts of Egyptian statues from Brucciani in London. He knew and understood exactly the scientific, educational and museological importance of the National Museum's former collection of plaster casts, and he advocated the acquisition of this material for Kolozsvár. Zoltán Vincze gives a brief account of the further fate of the plaster casts that went to Kolozsvár: "Another list (2 May) refers to 106 pieces of 'wrapped plaster casts from the National Museum'. The copies were packed in 101 crates. Recalling the minister's instruction, Kammerer emphasised: 'this plaster collection is to be placed in the new building of the Transylvanian Museum'. He strictly instructed that it can only be unpacked and assembled after the final equipment has been completed, until then it must be stored in a dry, fire-proof place. From April to autumn 1910, Pósta placed it in the warehouse of the Takarékpénztár és Hitelbank [Savings Bank and Credit Bank], and in October it was moved to the old theatre building. In accordance with the instructions he received, he did not open the chests, did not see their contents, and since the museum building was not built, they were not exhibited. In 1925, the management of the Romanian university transferred them to a site in the yard, and when it was repaired in 1929, the three wagonfuls of crates were finally transferred to the museum. The report on the transfer only mentions 98 crates. The list of plaster casts released from their box prison and finally visible includes copies of classical Greek works …"[26]

The circumstances of the origin of these plaster casts have hitherto been largely overlooked. They are referred to only once in the publications of the Museum of Fine Arts.[27] Before Vincze, the volume dealing with the history of the University of Kolozsvár mentions the collection of plaster replicas in one sentence: "The government laid the foundation for the university's fine arts museum on 23 January 1910, with a collection selected from the art historical gypsum objects of the Museum of Fine Arts, and sent the statues down in April."[28]

the golden age of the association and the university, up until World War I, as the university became an important institution in Hungarian scientific life.

János Csengeri, the organiser of the transaction, was himself a classical philologist university professor and translator of classical authors.[23] Béla Pósta[24] must also be mentioned here for a complete picture of the story. He started his career at the Hungarian National Museum in Budapest. Ferenc Pulszky and József Hampel also helped him – among other things, by supporting him to travel to Hungary and Europe – to gain as much knowledge as possible of the museum conditions of the time. He was appointed university professor of archaeology at the University of Kolozsvár in 1899. This meant that he was also director of the collection of the Transylvanian Museum Association, handled by the university. Among his plans was to create the "Musée de Trocadéro of Transylvania" in the soon-to-be-opened Department of Coins and Antiquities,

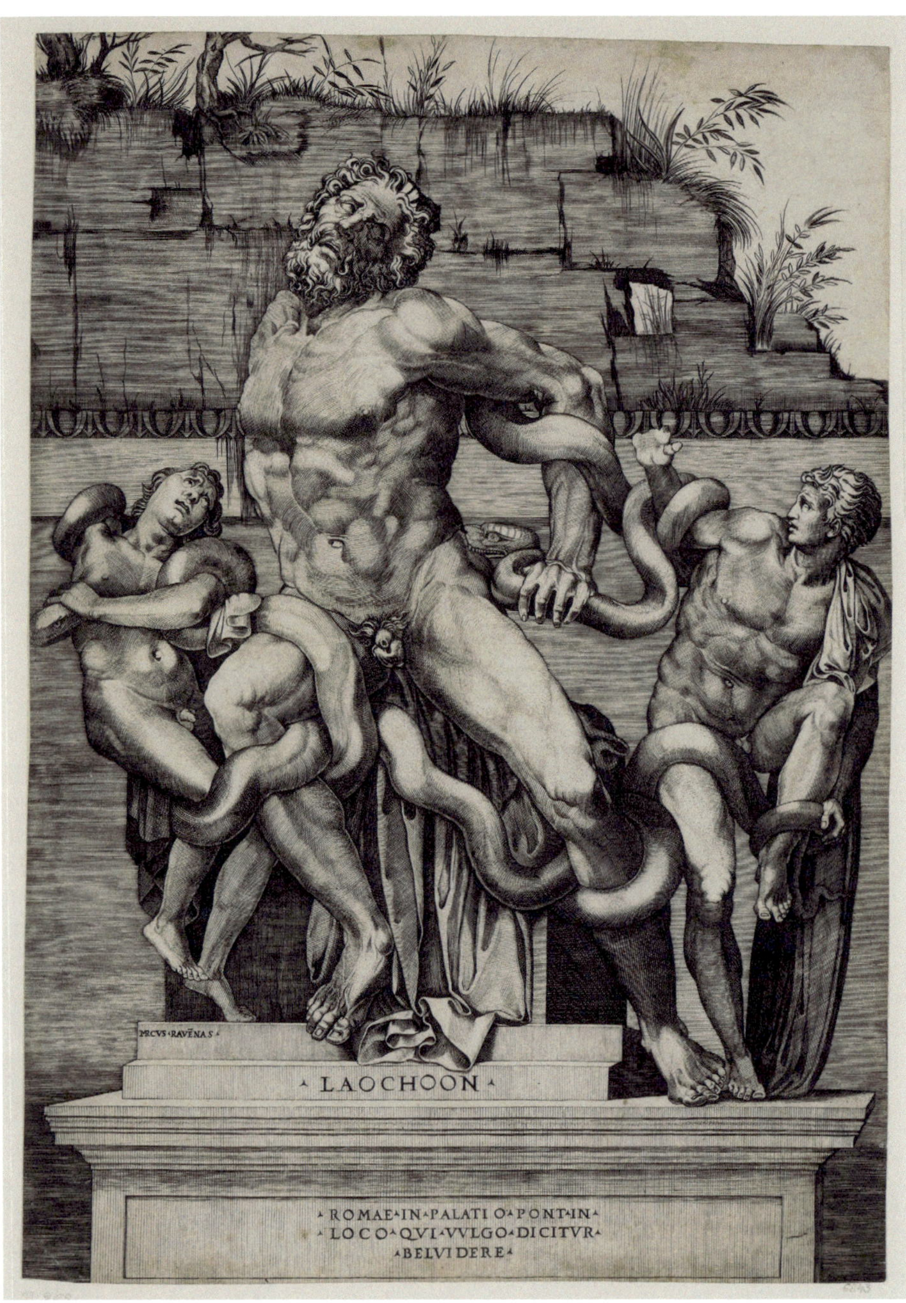

Fig. 7

The *Laocoön Group*
before Montorsoli's restoration,
engraving by Marco Dente, ca. 1515–1523

Throughout its history, the question of where the plaster cast collection should be housed instead of the Museum of Fine Arts, Budapest has arisen several times. Antal Hekler wrote about the fleeting idea of relocating the plaster cast collection to a suitable place: "In 1914 … we were still justified in entertaining the idea of reserving the ground-floor halls of the museum for the dynamically growing collection of original sculptures, while relocating the plaster museum and ascribing it a scholarly function under the auspices of the university. In 1918, we had to discard this plan as well."[29] The collection that stayed in the Museum of Fine Arts never made its way to the environs of a university, to a place where it could have served its true purpose. The collection handed over to the University of Kolozsvár eventually became part of a university, but it seems that it could not fulfil the hoped-for educational or scientific role that a consciously compiled and conceptually presented collection can provide.

Thanks to a comprehensive restoration program, the collection of plaster casts of the Museum of Fine Arts, Budapest, which has survived many vicissitudes, can be seen again

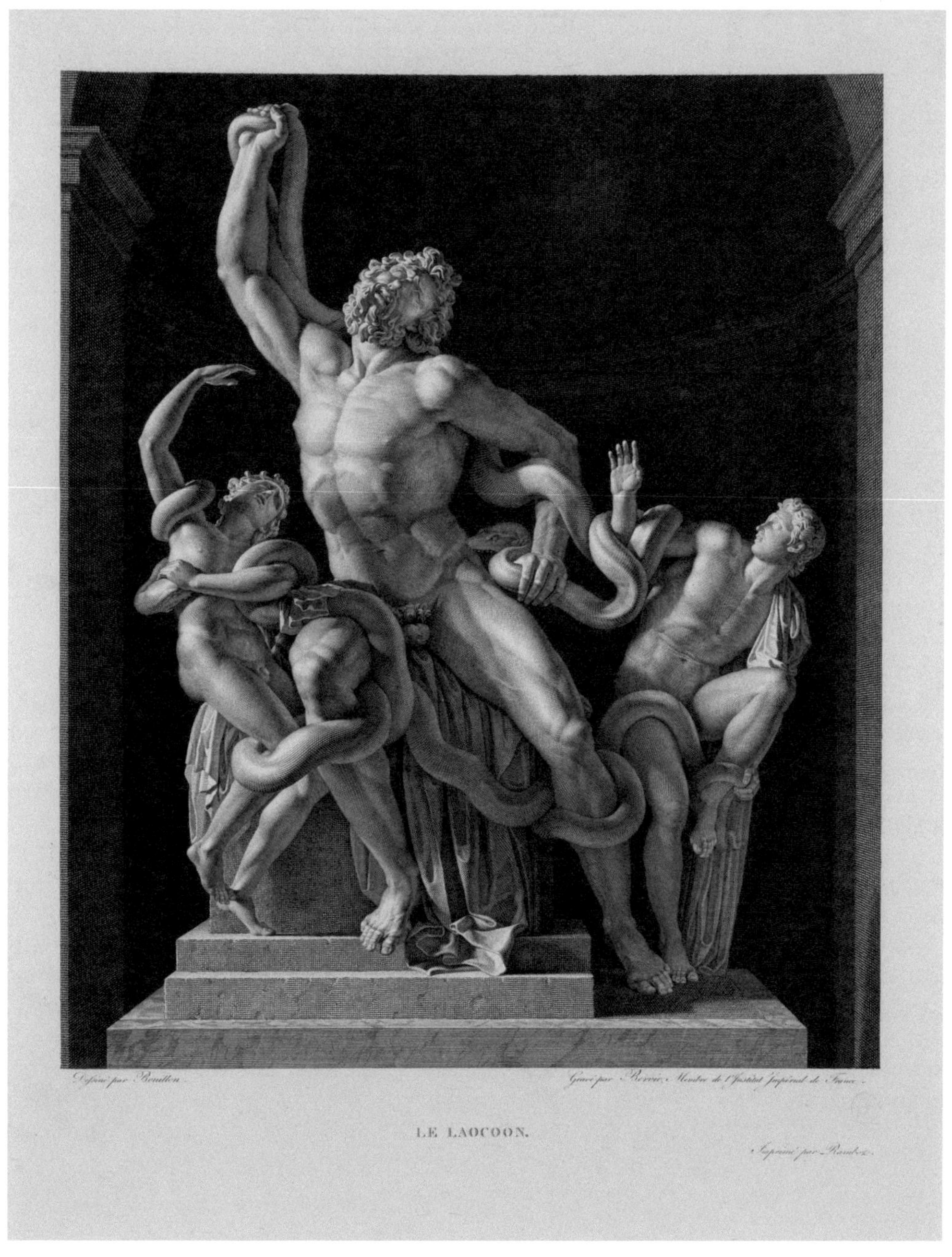

Fig. 8

The *Laocoön Group* in Paris with additions modelled after François Girardon's version, designed by Pierre Bouillon, engraving by Charles Clément Bervic, 1807

after many decades in two locations: in Komárom in the Star Fortress and in Budapest in the ground floor exhibition space of the NMCSC.[30] Among the pieces transferred to Kolozsvár that have thus far been recovered, one group can today be found in the National Museum of Transylvanian History, with additional casts in the Art and Design University, both in Cluj-Napoca.[31]

Antal Hekler's definition of the role of these and other similar plaster cast collections is also valid for the curators of the collections today: "A museum of plaster casts that does not have its own field of concern, that does not serve research work with its material collection and objectives, does not fulfil its true vocation. Our museum of casts also offers an invaluable benefit from the point of view of university teaching. By supporting the needs of research work in university seminars with its scope of collecting, our cast collection must also become a venue of autonomous significance generating added value for art historical research, following the example of related institutions abroad. Even in today's difficult conditions, we are not willing to forfeit this primary vocation of the plaster cast museum."[32]

Laocoön in Budapest

In this last section, let us take a closer look at two pieces from the Budapest plaster cast collection; today, one of them is on display in Cluj-Napoca, Romania the other in Komárom, Hungary.[33] They are two different versions, reconstructions of the same well-known work of art, and illustrate the role of plaster casts in scientific research.

Being one of the most important works of antiquity, acquiring a cast of the *Laocoön Group* was indispensable for the Budapest collection.[34] Two quite different copies were exhibited in Budapest: one by the Hungarian National Museum in the last third of the nineteenth century (fig. 5),[35] and the other by the Museum of Fine Arts in the early twentieth century (fig. 6).[36] Each of them represents a different stage in the sculpture's post-antique history.[37]

According to contemporary accounts, when the *Laocoön Group* was unearthed in 1506 in Rome, the right arms of the father and the smaller boy were missing (fig. 7).[38] In the centuries that followed, the lost parts were completed with additions.[39] Laocoön's figure was first restored in the 1530s by Giovanni Angelo Montorsoli, a pupil of Michelangelo, with his arm stretched upwards as he tries to wrest himself free of the sea serpents. It was supplemented in this form over several centuries: in the early eighteenth century, Agostino Cornacchini remade the additions with only minor modifications. Later, in the 1780s, the younger son received a new, more rigid, almost straight right arm. For a short episode, between 1800 and 1815, during the *Laocoön*'s stay in Paris, the earlier additions were replaced again with plaster pieces modelled after the seventeenth-century *Laocoön* adaptation by François Girardon (fig. 8). In this reconstruction, the right arm of the Trojan priest was slightly bent, with the forearm almost vertical and the right arm

of the younger son was bent again, like before the 1780s. However, from 1816 until the middle of the twentieth century, the statue was once again displayed with the Cornacchini arm of Laocoön and the straight arm of the younger son.[40]

Based on a contemporary photograph (fig. 3), the version presented to the public at the Hungarian National Museum's plaster cast exhibition seems to be that of Girardon: note the shape of the right arms of the father and son. The short-lived Paris reconstruction of the group was moulded between 1800–1815; our cast might derive from this mould and might have been purchased from Paris,[41] but for the moment we do not have concrete evidence to prove this. It was handed over to the Museum of Fine Arts with the material of the Hungarian National Museum, but later was taken to Kolozsvár in 1910,[42] as the Museum of Fine Arts had ordered a new plaster cast from the workshop of August Gerber in Cologne in 1907 (fig. 6).[43] In the latter cast, the figure of the father is depicted in accordance with new findings: with his arm bent back completely as it is bound by the sea serpents. It follows the composition of the sculpture in the Vatican as we know it today. In 1903, Ludwig Pollak, an archaeologist, art collector and art dealer, found the original ancient fragment of Laocoön's arm in a stone-cutter's workshop in Rome.[44] The arm was joined to the marble sculpture as late as 1957,[45] but Pollak had published a drawn reconstruction in 1905,[46] and the director of the Dresden Albertinum, Georg Treu, had already created the new reconstruction in 1906 using plaster replicas (fig. 9).[47] This may have been the model of the second plaster cast that came to Budapest. Interestingly, even though August Gerber was the maker of our second cast, a few years after it arrived in Budapest, in 1910, the Laocoön in his catalogue was still illustrated with the previous version:[48] in the picture, Laocoön has the right arm attributed to Cornacchini and his son is stretching his hand to the sky in desperation.

Fig. 9 │ next page

Laocoön Group

Plaster cast reconstruction with the "Pollak arm"
by Georg Treu, 1906, Albertinum, Dresden

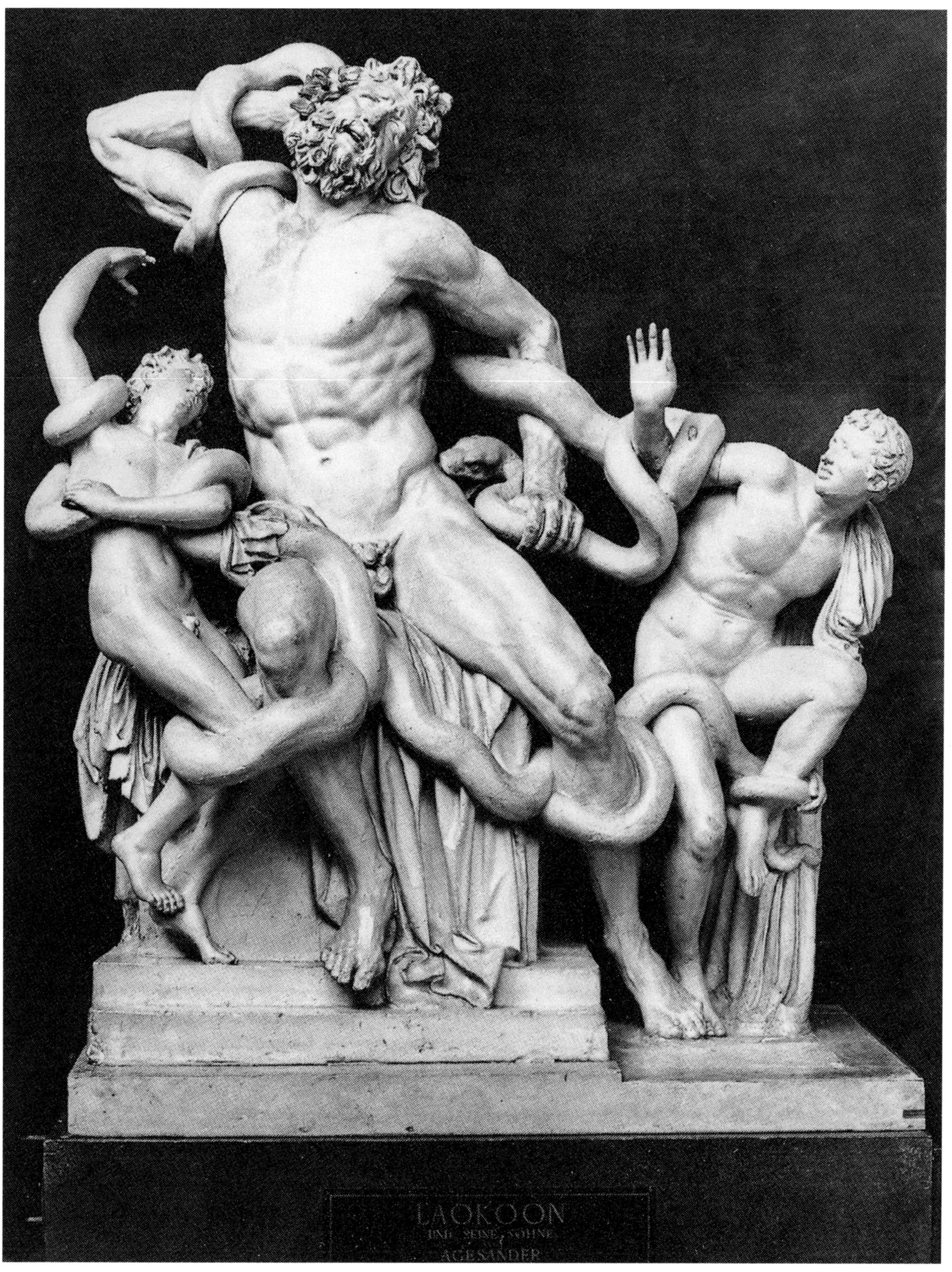
LAOKOON
UND SEINE SÖHNE
AGESANDER

Notes

1 On Ferenc Pulszky, see
Szilágyi 1997; Szilágyi 2007,
I, 91–110; Wilson 2010.

2 On the plaster cast collection of the
Hungarian National Museum, see
Szentesi 2006A, Szentesi 2006B,
Szentesi 2006C and also Andó 2021.

3 Newmann 1888; Kabdebo 1979.

4 Pulszky 1852. Speech quoted
in Wilson 2010.

5 Edit Szentesi found the handwritten
list of Martinelli's material presented
at the world's fair and purchased by
Pulszky: *Catalogo dei getti in gesso
di diversi oggetti di scultura greca
antica esposti da Felice Napoleone
Martinelli nella sezione greca al
Espozione (sic!) Universale di Vienna
1873* entitled handwritten list (MNM
ÉRT, without date, signature or reference number, a file cover or any other
documentation, on top of the box
containing the documents of 1873)."
Cf. Szentesi 2005, 402, note 12.

6 Szentesi 2006B, 11–14,
and notes 118–149.

7 Pulszky 1875.

8 Andó 2021, 99–101,
and notes 24–34.

9 The exhibition of antique sculpture
copies was opened in the Doric Hall
and the Doric connecting corridor,
while that of medieval and Renaissance copies was opened in the
Romanesque and Renaissance
Halls, and the Michelangelo Room.

10 Nagy 2013, 74, note 197.

11 As before 1918 the city was part of
Hungary when we talk about the
period before the end of World War I,
we refer to the city as Kolozsvár
(Hungary), when referring to the
period after 1918, we use its current
name, Cluj-Napoca (Romania).

12 Andó 2021, 106–7; the documents
report that the objects were then
packed in crates, but it is suspected
that at least a large proportion of
the sculptures from the Hungarian
National Museum had not been
unpacked since the transfer in 1904.

13 For the history of the university,
see Gaal 2001.

14 János Csengeri's letter requesting
the transfer of casts is dated 8
November 1909. Archives MFAB,
1828/1909, the document number
in Kolozsvár: 103-1909/10. The
letter written to the minister supporting the request of the University of Kolozsvár (Archives MFAB,
1828/1909, 13 November 1909)
reads as follows: "Only a small part
of the plaster collection taken over
from the National Museum can be
included in the antique sculpture
department of the Museum of Fine
Arts. It is appropriate to know the
pieces that were cast by the Greek
government for the 1873 exhibition
in Vienna, but of which a different
reproduction has not been available
since then. However, the overwhelming majority cannot be used,
because it would disturb the unified
effect of the collection here to a
great extent. When assembled and
put together, it forms an instructive
and valuable series, but among
casts of a different type, moulded
from newer plaster, the nearly forty-
year-old, often hauled, mutilated
and damaged pieces cannot be
placed without their condition being
disturbingly conspicuous. Likewise,
I am very happy to accept the attached request from the University of Kolozsvár, in which it requests
the future transfer of the collection
to the University of Kolozsvár, because such a treasure, lying here
in the wasteland and irretrievable
from ruin, can be beneficially put to
the service of culture." (Translated
from Hungarian by the authors.)

The ministerial authorisation is
dated 23 January (Archives MFAB,
232/1909). József Reichenberger's
invoice issued about the packaging
was approved by Kálmán Lux on 30
April (Archives MFAB, 745/1910).
Notification of the delivery of the
entire material was written on 2 May
1910 (Archives MFAB, 715/1910).

15 Archives MFAB, 232/1910.

16 For the request for placement,
see Archives MFAB 232/1910.
This clause is also included in the
ministerial approval letter (135784-
1909). On the Transylvanian Museum
Association, see Szabó 1942;
on the collections: Sipos 2009.

17 Archives MFAB, 715/1910
(16 April 1910).

18 Archives MFAB, 715/1910
(2 May 1910).

19 For the events preceding the
establishment of the Transylvanian
Museum Association and the details
of its establishment, see the six volumes of *Az Erdélyi Múzeum-Egylet
Évkönyvei* 1860–1873.

20 From the beginnings to the
establishment, cf. Szabó 1942, 3–26;
Egyed 2006, esp. 233–34;
Egyed and Kovács 2009.

21 Today Brukenthal National Museum /
Muzeul Național Brukenthal. The collection of the Brukenthal Museum
preserves the private collection
of Baron Samuel Brukenthal (also
Bruckenthal, 1721–1803, Habsburg
governor of Transylvania from 1774
to 1787). He died in 1803, and according to his will, his art collection
– as a family fee tail – was to be kept
together and made accessible to the
public; in the event of the family's
death, he bequeathed it to the
Lutheran parish in Nagyszeben.
The collection was open to the
public from 1817. In the 1850s,
the Lutheran Church became the
owner of the collection until World
War II, when it was nationalised by
the Romanian state. See Paris 2009.

22 It was established thanks to the efforts of Count Imre Mikó, who said at the inaugural session on 23 November 1859, "Our goal is to create as an association a new temple for scientific work." *Az Erdélyi Múzeum-Egylet Szabályai* 1859.

23 Tar 2007.

24 Banner 1963; Csorba 1971.

25 Vincze 2014, 282–84, and notes 1263–1269. Vincze does not accurately describe the origin of the significant part of the National Museum's plaster casts, acquired at the Vienna World's Fair in 1873. The plaster replicas handed over to Kolozsvár are not from the 1873 Vienna World's Fair, which were cast by Felice Napoleone Martinelli, but pieces commissioned by Ferenc Pulszky for the National Museum. The Martinelli casts were kept by the Museum of Fine Arts. (See also notes 14 and 28 in this paper). The details of the story are known thanks to Edit Szentesi's research, see: Szentesi 2006B, 11-14 and notes 118-149; Szentesi 2006C, 22; Szentesi 2006A. Here we would like to thank Edit Szentesi – with whom we started working on plaster casts together at the time – for drawing our attention to the volume.

26 Vincze 2014, 283–84, and notes 1268–9.

27 "In this final brochure of volume III of the 'Collections of the Museum of Fine Arts' primarily the sculptural works processed since the establishment of the Museum of Fine Arts are listed, and secondly the paintings belonging to the increase in 1913.

They are therefore not included in this:

...

II. from the gypsum copies, the casts that are: a) obtained as copies of sculptural masterpieces according to Sándor Wekerle's October 1894 directive and are partially not yet assembled and b) those from the National Museum's collection of antiquities, some of which, with the exception of those commissioned by the Greek government for the purposes of the 1873 Vienna World Exhibition, were transferred on permanent deposit to the Faculty of Humanities of the Royal Hungarian Franz Joseph University of Kolozsvár by the Minister of Religion and Education, in accordance with decree no. 135784-909 and dated 23 January 1910." (Translated from Hungarian by the authors.) See Peregriny 1915.

28 Márki 1922, 89.

29 Hekler 1924, 102. (Translated from Hungarian by the authors.)

30 For the entire collection see Szőcs 2021A; for the antique collection: Andó 2021.

31 In searching for the material transported to Kolozsvár, we received a lot of help from Melinda Mihály, who found many sculptures based on the available documents. We are grateful for her useful contribution. We would also like to thank the management of the National Museum of Transylvanian History (Erdélyi Nemzeti Történeti Múzeum / Muzeul Național de Istorie a Transilvaniei) and The Art and Design University (Universitatea de Artă și Design, UAD) in Cluj-Napoca for making it possible to study the casts.

32 Hekler 1924, 107. (Translated from Hungarian by the authors.)

33 For the *Laocoön* cast in Komárom, see Süvegh 2021.

34 Szentesi 2006B, 16.

35 Formerly: Hungarian National Museum, inv. no. 164. Now displayed at the Ion Andreescu University of Art and Design, Cluj-Napoca, Romania.

36 Museum of Fine Arts, Budapest, inv. no. Ag.283. Now exhibited in the Star Fortress, Komárom, Hungary. Cf. note 33.

37 For an analysis of the correlations between the successive stages of restoration of the *Laocoön* and the different types of its casts, see Zahle 2010.

38 Buranelli 2006, 49; Rebaudo 2007, 7.

39 For a detailed history of the restorations of the *Laocoön,* see Rebaudo 2007 and Frischer 2009. Jan Zahle gives a short synopsis in Zahle 2010, 144, table 7.1.

40 Rebaudo 2007, 42–55, 65–75; Frischer 2009; Zahle 2010, 151–52.

41 Zahle 2010, 150–52.

42 Andó 2021, 108–9, fig. 11.

43 Süvegh 2021.

44 Pollak 1905; Liverani 2006.

45 Magi 1960.

46 Pollak 1905, figs. 1–2.

47 Raumschüssel 1994, fig. 2.

48 Gerber 1910, nos. 31–33.

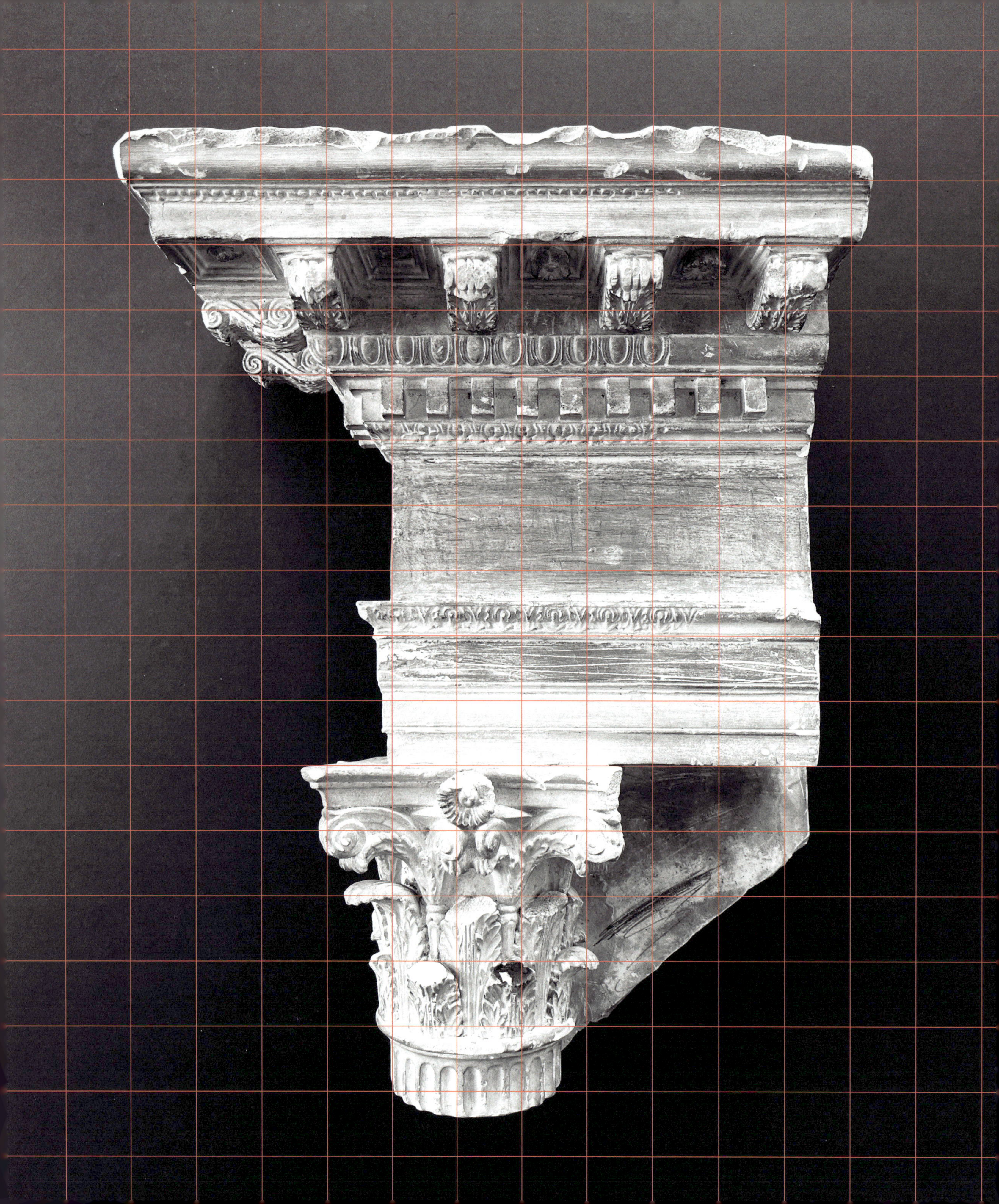

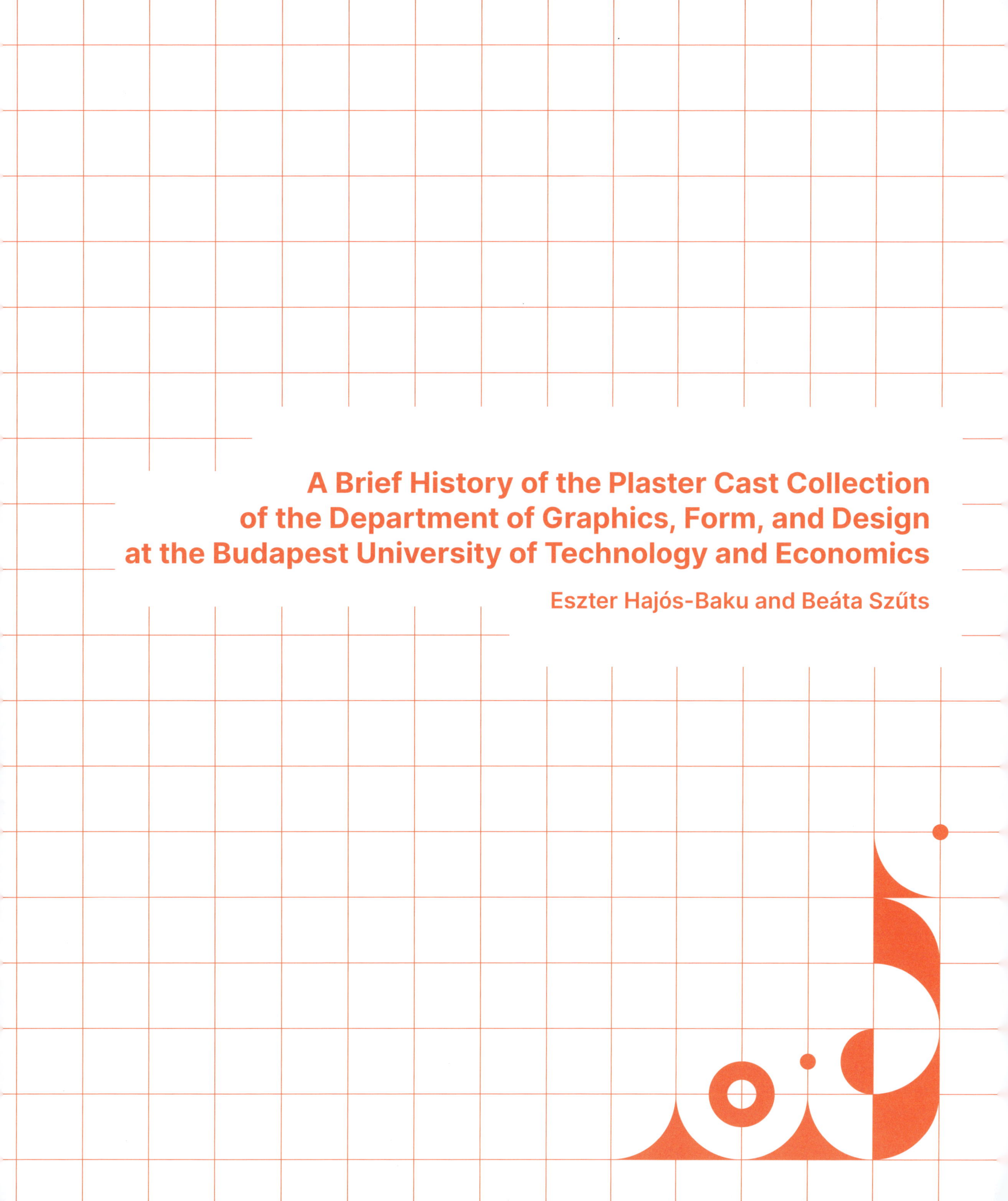

A Brief History of the Plaster Cast Collection of the Department of Graphics, Form, and Design at the Budapest University of Technology and Economics

Eszter Hajós-Baku and Beáta Szűts

A Brief History of the Plaster Cast Collection
of the Department of Graphics, Form, and Design
at the Budapest University of Technology and Economics

Eszter Hajós-Baku and Beáta Szűts

The creation of modern plaster cast collections dates back to the eighteenth and nineteenth centuries. Their history in Hungary coincided with that of the larger international collections, the only difference being that while representative exhibitions in London or Berlin had started by the second third of the nineteenth century, no significant plaster cast collection in Hungary was put on display until the beginning of the twentieth century, when the Budapest Museum of Fine Arts (hereinafter referred to as MFAB) unveiled its plaster cast exhibition in its specially designed premises.[1] At first, plaster copies of classical antiquities were used primarily in education, and later, during the great museum building boom of the nineteenth century, the predominant historicist tendencies extended the scope beyond antiquity to include replicas of medieval and Renaissance artworks, bringing plaster casts into the service of understanding the history of art to its fullest extent.[2]

The historical plaster cast collection of the Faculty of Architecture at the Budapest University of Technology and Economics (Budapesti Műszaki és Gazdaságtudományi Egyetem, hereinafter primarily referred to as BME) is one of the largest, if not the most extensive educational plaster cast collection in Hungary.[3] It lists hundreds of casts, the majority belonging to the archive of the BME Department of Graphics, Form, and Design (hereinafter referred to as Dept. of Graphics). Most items are located on site (fig. 1), while a group of 62 plaster casts, mostly copies of Renaissance sculptures, is on long-term loan at the Castle Museum of Ozora, Hungary.

The collection grew to its current dimensions in the course of decades-long development, primarily in parallel with reforms of the teaching of drawing at the university. In addition to items cast in the university's own workshop, a significant part of the collection was acquired from plaster casting workshops both in Hungary and abroad, or as donations. Regarded as essential tools in art and architecture education, the collection includes copies of important artworks from ancient Greece and Rome, Italian Renaissance and baroque art, as well as outstanding examples of Romanesque and Gothic pieces.

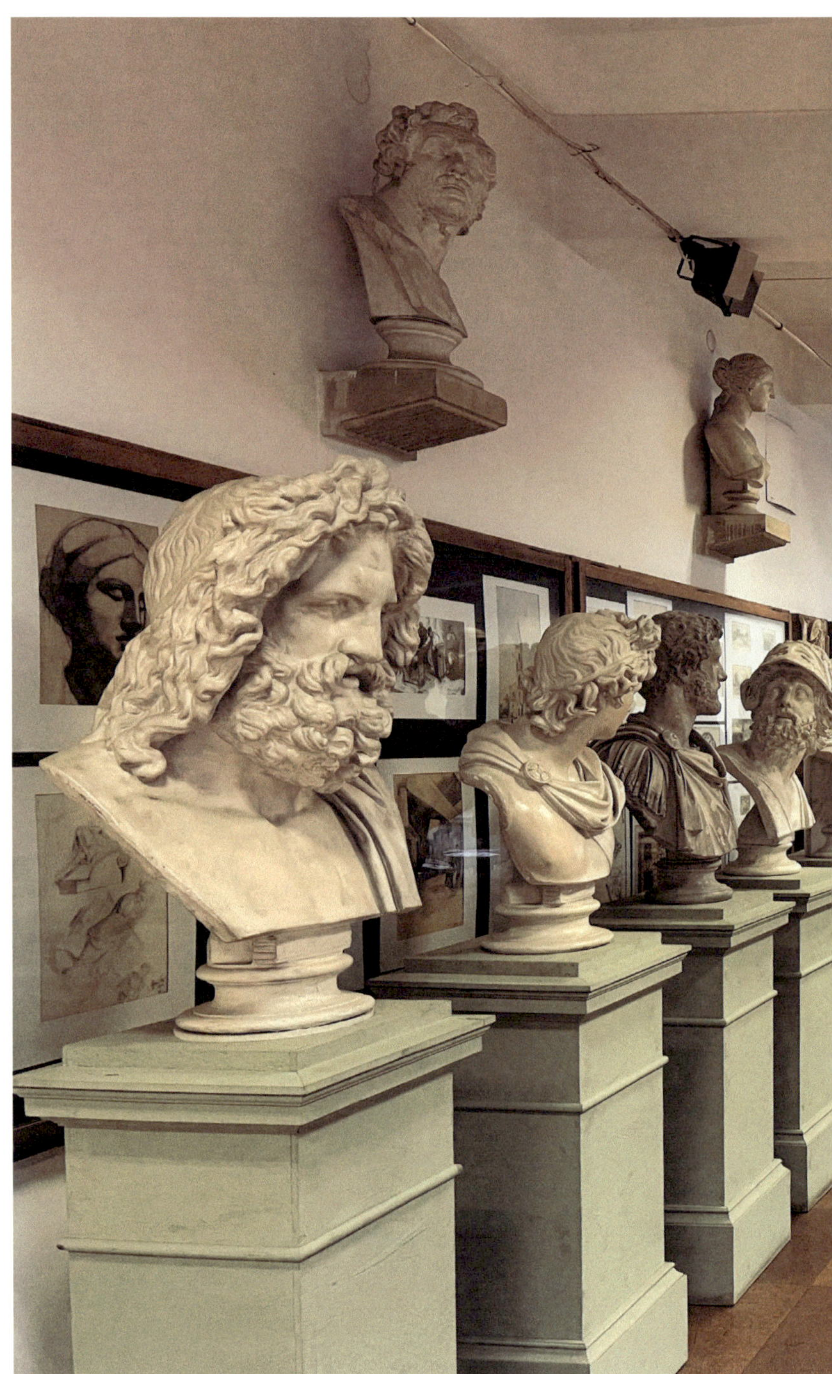

The adverse fate of the collection was no different from that suffered by similar collections. Plaster casts, once indispensable accessories of educational reforms, eventually became oversized disposable objects, relegated to remote storage rooms, and replaced by more up-to-date demonstration tools and techniques. The revived research interest in plaster casts, however, has brought the BME collection into the limelight as well, this time from an entirely novel perspective. Commenced in 2016, the underlying research of this paper approached the items in this unique collection of impressive richness and quality both as historical documents of education and as objects of heritage value. The scientific survey and cataloguing were followed by a series of studies into the provenance of the casts. Building from fragments, this paper seeks to unfold the brief history of the formation of a once significant collection, the plaster cast museum and moulding studios, and by doing so, to enrich the history of architecture education and – even more directly relevant to the casts – the history and methodology of drawing education.

I History of the Collection from the Beginnings

Worn and weathered by the storms of history, like the casts themselves, the archival records have yielded scarce, yet extremely useful information about the collection. The continuous restructuring of the institution and its faculties and departments throughout the past have made it practically impossible to uncover comprehensive, department-specific lists of purchases and inventories. From the very early period, inherently lacking in sources, two documents stand out, which through careful research have provided adequate answers to a number of questions. One of the documents is entitled *Pénztári könyv* (Cash Book), the other *Inventárium* (Inventory Book), and they contain a complete list of assets of the Freehand Drawing Storeroom of the Császári és Királyi József Műegyetem (Imperial and Royal Joseph Technical University) – the predecessor of today's BME Dept. of Graphics. Relying on these documents, it is safe to assume that the extant collection, extensive as it is, may only constitute half of the originally purchased quantity. Present research has resulted in a comprehensive catalogue of the current collection, continuously updated with new data. This paper focuses on the brief history of the reconstruction of the collection, the plaster cast museum at the university and the moulding studios, while subsequent research aims at investigating their role in teaching, as part of an analysis of historical teaching methodologies in architecture education.[4]

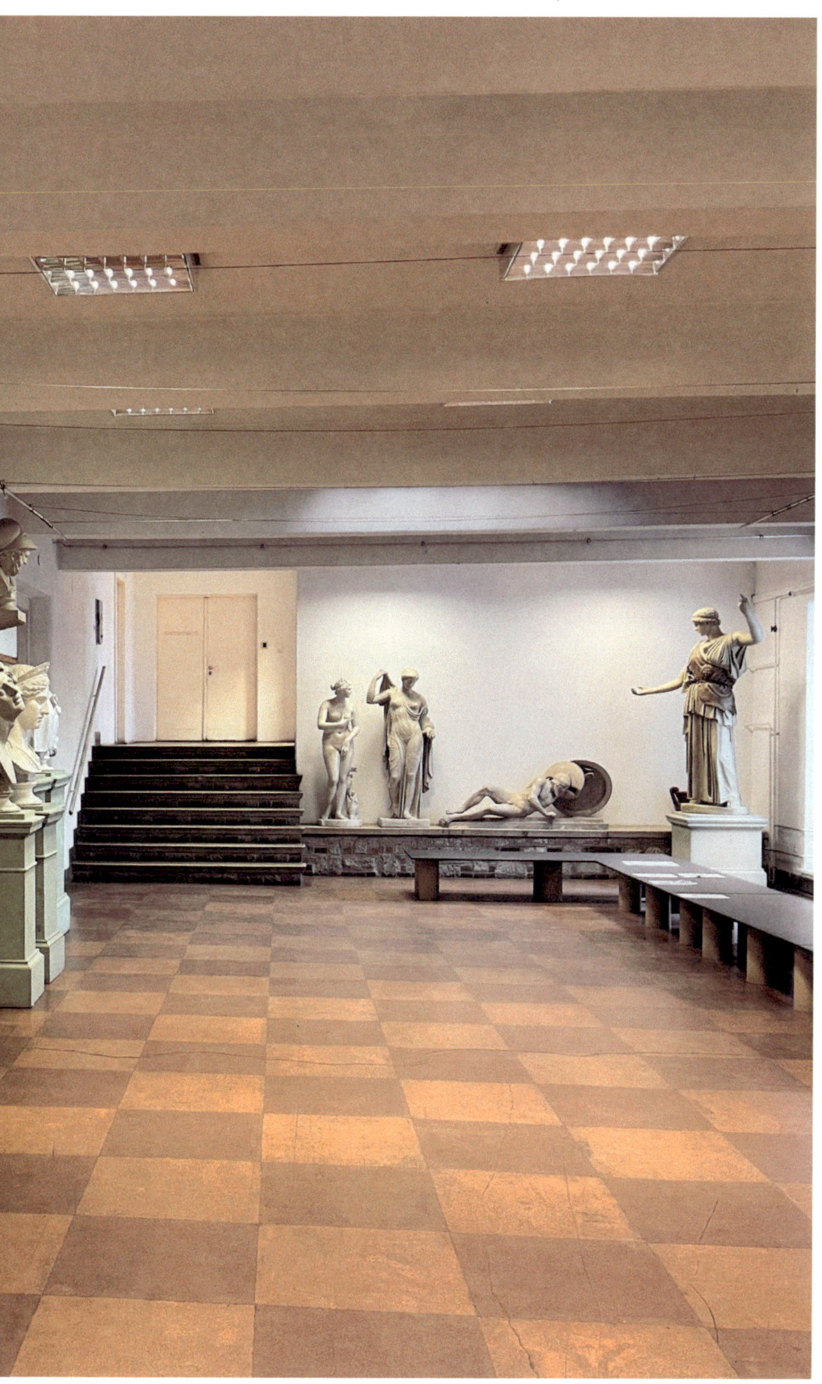

Fig. 1

The Department of Graphics, Form, and Design, Budapest University of Technology and Economics

I.1 First Casts of the Collection, Inventory "E" (1853–1861)

The earliest data to indicate the acquisition of plaster casts was found among the inventories of the József Ipartanoda (Joseph Industrial School),[5] which recorded in one of its entries the purchase of the first plaster casts, during the academic year 1852–1853.[6] The document, along with five additional inventories, was unearthed in the library of the Dept. of Graphics. From these inventories one can follow the changes in the stock of teaching aids and accessories of the Joseph Industrial School and its successor institutions, the Joseph Polytechnicum, and subsequently the Imperial and Royal Joseph Technical University, during a period between 1847 and 1875. The inventories provide a summary of drawing templates and model collections acquired for the "General Drawing Storeroom" of the Industrial School, recorded in both Hungarian and German. Prior to being entered in the inventory and admitted to the storeroom, teaching aids and accessories were sorted into groups and marked accordingly with different letters. Groups "A" to "D" contained template drawings: ornamental patterns used for ornamentation studies were in group "A";[7] templates for architectural typology and descriptive geometry, as well as architectural sample books, were compiled in group "B";[8] group "C"[9] contained landscaping plans and site plans;

and mechanical drawings were assigned to group "D"[10]. Their descriptions also reveal that during the initial period of education, significant emphasis was placed on expanding the collection of template drawings and sample books, i.e., group "B". In terms of quantity, this was the group that expanded most intensively over the years. By the 1870s, the number of items in the collection already exceeded four hundred. Closely connected to this part of the collection is a group marked in the inventories with the letter "F",[11] which lists a mixed assortment of additional drawing templates and sample books. These items entered the collection in the years 1853–1854, most likely by donation, since the items are registered in groups along with the name of the donor or donating institution. Forming another extensive group in the collection, geometric model bodies and plaster casts are registered in the inventories under the letter "E".[12] Two surviving sheets in the inventory dated between 1851 and 1861 sum up in serial numbered order the various geometric bodies used for freehand drawing. From the academic year 1852–1853 onwards, plaster cast items were also added to the register. The 1853 inventory sheet describes three plaster cast items. Their number gradually increased with time, and by 1861 there were 17 pieces in the possession of the General Drawing Storeroom.[13] These were, in general, smaller samples of building decoration (e.g., ornaments, rosettes, acanthus leaves) and architectonic details (e.g., consoles).

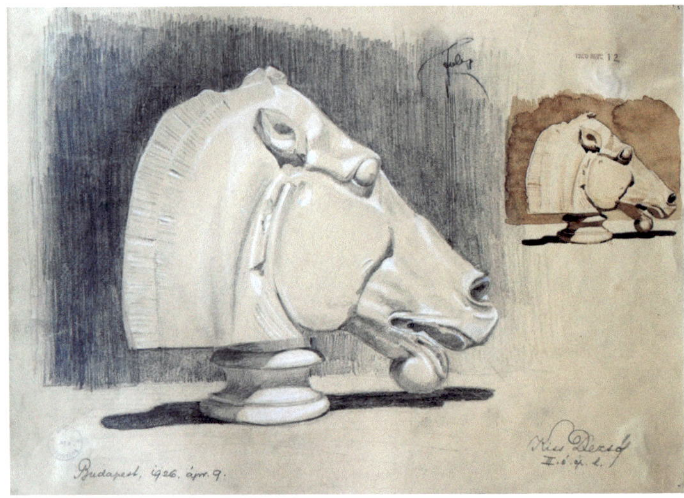

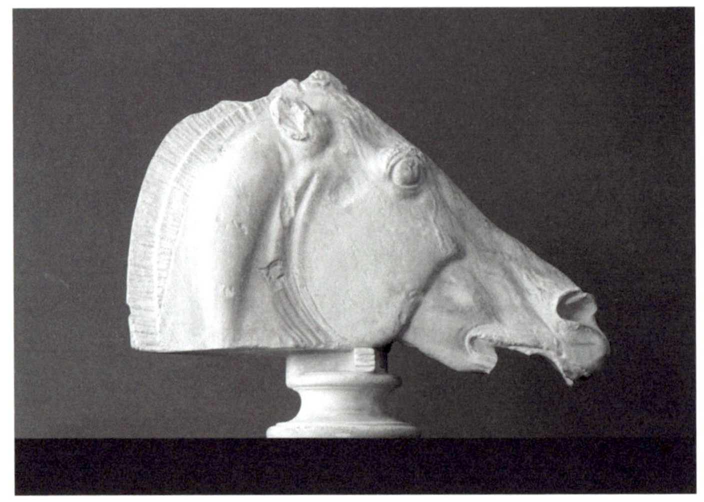

I.2 Acquisitions of the Moulding and Architectural Storerooms between 1864 and 1870

Despite the absence of inventory books between 1859 and 1871, the growth of the cast model stock can still be followed from the annual statistical reports made by the university. These have played a vital role in the provenance research of the plaster casts, since analysis of these reports provides precise information on changes in the number of drawings and plaster casts stored in the various storerooms and departments throughout the university. The reports encompass the contents of the library and a total of 12 storerooms.[14] Among them, statistical data refer to plaster cast models stored in the General Drawing Storeroom and the Moulding Storeroom from the academic year 1859–1860,[15] as well as in the Architectural Storeroom from the academic year 1869–1870.[16]

Analysis of the database has revealed a significant expansion in the stock of the Moulding Storeroom during the academic year 1863–1864. The number of plaster cast items that year alone increased from 25 to 34.[17] The following years brought no significant increase in the number of plaster casts in the Moulding Storeroom, although the Architectural Storeroom, which began to show up in the reports from the academic year 1865–1866 onwards, is first mentioned as containing plaster casts in the academic year 1869–1870, then totalling 70 items.[18] The same records show a growth in the number of plaster casts in the Moulding Storeroom, an increase by 10 items compared to the previous year.[19] The growth could be related to an 1869 acquisition from the Imperial and Royal Museum of Art and Industry (k. k. Museum für Kunst und Industrie) in Vienna.[20] The surviving invoice evidences a 96-item order. Two additional documents associated with this invoice reveal that 14 out of the 96 items were intended to be ordered for the Moulding Storeroom ("Modolier Kabinet [*sic*]") and 81 items for the Architectural Storeroom ("Architektonisches Kabinet [*sic*]") of the Polytechnicum.[21]

Fig. 2 | previous page at left

Student drawing of *Selene's Horse* from the east pediment of the Parthenon, 1926
Archive of the Department of Graphics, Form, and Design

Fig. 3 | previous page at right

Plaster cast of *Selene's Horse* from the east pediment of the Parthenon, early 20th century
Unknown cast maker. Department of Graphics, Form, and Design

I.3 The Cast Collection of the Freehand Drawing Storeroom, Acquisitions between 1884 and 1902

The so-called *Inventory "E"*, along with five additional inventories introduced in the first chapter, followed the cataloguing system established in the 1850s. Presumably, however, the growing number of items and the transitions in the education system also affected the administration, necessitating the simplification of the inventory system. From 1883, a new classification was developed for the items and the former "A" to "E" cataloguing system was replaced with inventory groups "A", "B" and "C". The Inventory Book and Supplementary Inventory of Freehand Drawing Storeroom (hereinafter primarily referred to as *Inventárium*) recorded the assets of the Freehand Drawing Department's storeroom according to this newly introduced cataloguing system.[22] Most relevant to the present research, group "B" contained the plaster casts, initially under inventory numbers B181 to B192, totalling 61 items, described as "ornaments".[23] In the 1890 inventory their number had increased to 345.[24] Added in 1896, a segment of the Parthenon frieze was inventoried under number B193, and a replica of the temple frieze from Phigalia under number B194.[25] With these additions the number of catalogued items reached 347, and together with the items financed from the supplementary inventory lump sum of 1897, the 1898 inventory listed a total of 383 plaster casts.[26]

While the *Inventárium* recorded the assets of the Freehand Drawing Storeroom (previously the Storeroom of the General Drawing Studios), i.e., the assets affiliated with today's Dept. of Graphics, until 1903, another unique document details acquisitions made between 1883 and 1902: the *Pénztári könyv*[27] (Cash Book) is probably the most exciting source discovered within the context of the research of plaster casts at BME. The document records acquisitions of teaching aids, supplies, accessories and equipment for the Freehand Drawing Storeroom, as well as for the staff and teaching premises of the Dept. of Graphics.

For almost every year during the period from 1884 to 1901, there are records of acquisitions of plaster casts. Most of the items came either from Hungarian or international plaster casting workshops or from other workshops affiliated to educational institutions.

The first entry in the Cash Book to register an actual acquisition of plaster casts is a March 1884 invoice connected to Gusztáv Kelety, the "founder" of the Országos Magyar Királyi Mintarajztanoda, later Mintarajziskola (Hungarian Royal Drawing School, hereinafter referred to as Drawing School) – the predecessor of today's Hungarian University of Fine Arts. The 1884 acquisition can presumably be linked to the school's workshop. Two further purchases were made for the Dept. of Graphics from the Drawing School: one for 42 plaster cast items (marked as ornaments) in 1886, and another for 61 items in 1891. In addition to the Drawing School, the workshop of the Állami Paedagogium (Teacher Training School of Buda) provided schools around the country with the necessary teaching supplies, including plaster casts. A single purchase was made from the Paedagogium in September 1887. This entry records the acquisition of more than 80 items for a remarkably high amount. In addition, the Cash Book mentions acquisitions of plaster casts from the Museum für Kunst und Industrie (today Museum für angewandte Kunst) in Vienna: 33 plaster casts in 1886, 40 items in 1897 and 48 pieces in 1899 were added to the collection. In 1901, another plaster cast-related invoice was paid, although further details on this purchase are unfortunately not disclosed.

Besides institutions and their affiliated plaster casting workshops, orders were placed to private individuals as well, although to a significantly lesser extent.

Based on the summarised invoice details, the general impression is that the period between 1884 to 1901 witnessed a large-scale wave of acquisitions, which expanded the collection of the Freehand Drawing Storeroom with a total of 674 plaster casts. The significant increase in the collection is due to the 1884 reform in drawing education initiated by Lajos Rauscher, head of the Drawing Department.[28]

Fig. 4 | next page at upper left

Plaster cast of a segment of the Corinthian order
(column capital and entablature)
Renaissance variation, early 20th century
Made by the plaster casting workshop of the
Budapest National Higher School of Industry, Budapest
Department of Graphics, Form, and Design

Fig. 5 | next page at upper right

Plaster cast of an acanthus leaf, early 20th century
Unknown cast maker. Department of Graphics, Form, and Design

II The Current Collection

II.1 Provenance of the Collection

As outlined above, we can track the growth of the university's plaster cast collection from archival records between 1850 and 1900. Unfortunately, none of the listed objects from this period have survived to the present day.

The vast majority of the extant casts came into the university's possession between 1900 and 1930; however, relatively few written sources survive from this period. In the absence of invoices and inventory books, any estimation of the acquisition dates of the plaster casts has, in general, relied on the illustrated appendices of contemporaneous catalogues issued by plaster casting workshops and on student drawings held in the archives of the Dept. of Graphics. The surviving historical sales catalogues and price lists have greatly aided the identification of the plaster casts, but it should be noted that the ranges of items presented in both Hungarian and foreign catalogues often overlap. The majority of the plaster casts in the department's collection are not imprinted with any seals or stamps, making it impossible to determine their exact provenance or date of acquisition. Nevertheless, certain unmarked items have been approximately dated with the help of old student drawings. For example, the dates written on respective student drawings (fig. 2) confirm that the plaster cast of the *Discobolus* and that of *Selene's Horse* from the eastern pediment of the Parthenon (fig. 3) were undoubtably in the collection before the 1920s.

In the case of the plaster casts bearing seals or stamps, meanwhile, the provenance of most of these has been clarified with relative certainty by comparing the imprints with the available catalogues. Research has revealed that a number of plaster casts were acquired from international suppliers, primarily from German and Italian casting workshops, while Hungarian workshops also made a considerable contribution.

Most plaster casts in the latter category are assumed to have been crafted in the early 1900s by the casting workshop of the Állami Felső Ipariskola (Budapest National Higher School of Industry) in Budapest.[29] Established by the Royal Hungarian Ministry of Commerce through a merger with the former workshop of the Paedagogium, the casting workshop mostly produced architectural elements for educational purposes.[30] Located at the school's building in Budapest (8 Népszínház Street), the casting workshop published a catalogue in 1904, illustrated with black-and-white photos, catering for the needs of various levels of educational institutions with a wide selection of plaster casts.

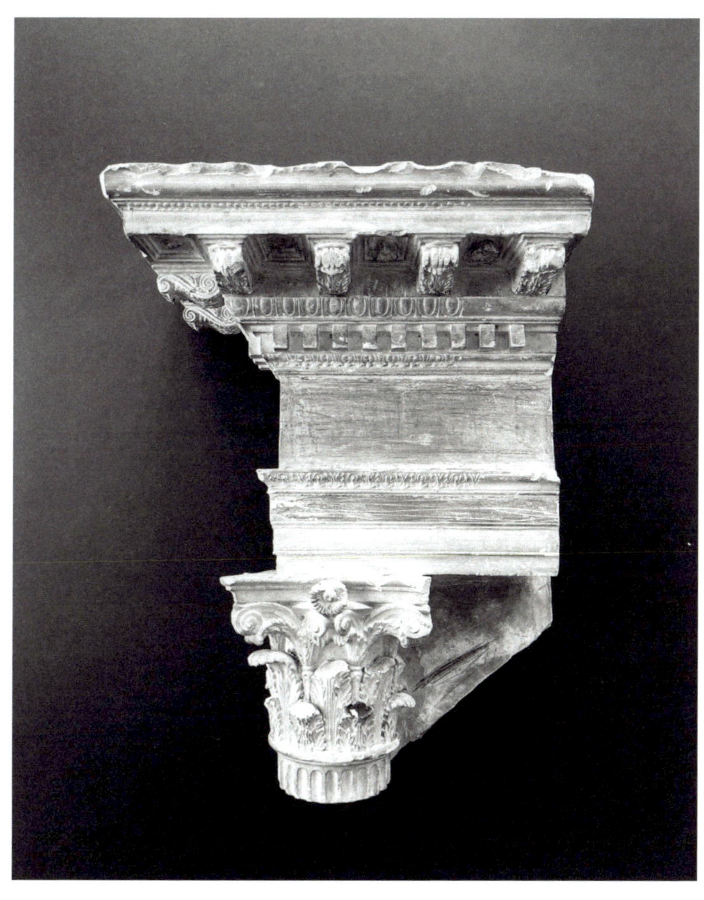

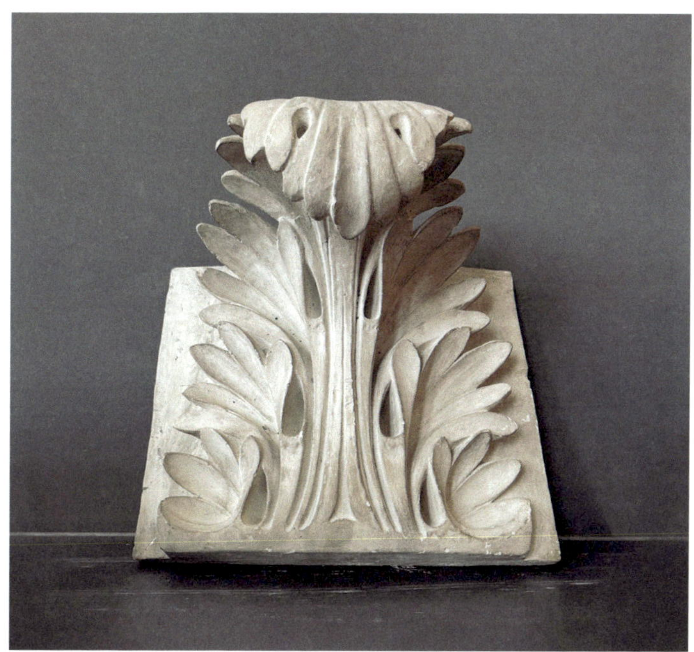

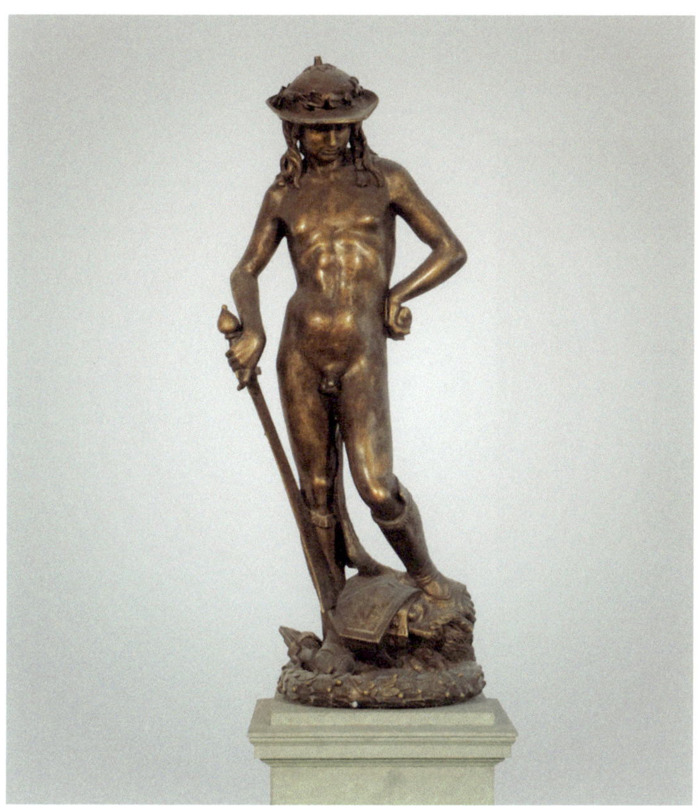

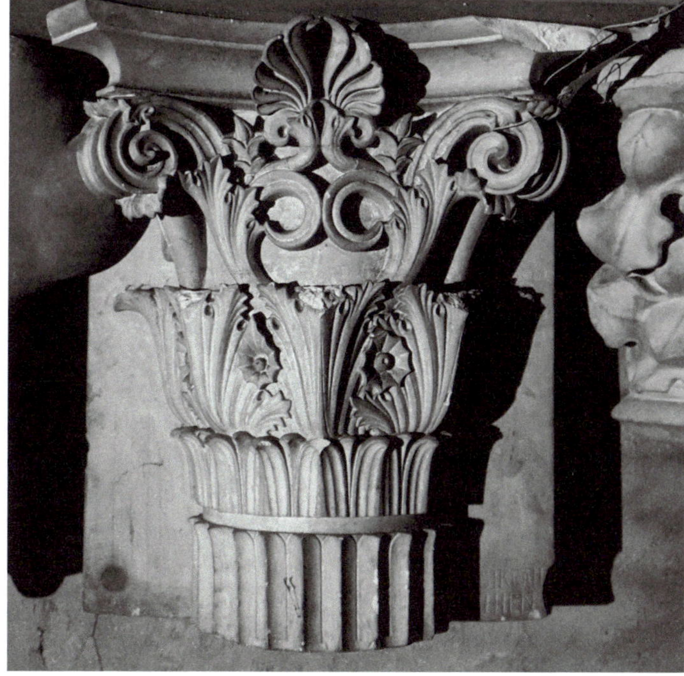

Fig. 6 | lower left

Plaster cast with bronze-imitation painting of Donatello's *David*
Early 20th-century, made by August Gerber, Cologne
Department of Graphics, Form, and Design

Fig. 7 | lower right

Plaster cast of a pilaster capital (with acanthi and volute)
from the Choragic Monument of Lysicrates in Athens, end of 19th century
Made by the casting workshop of Kaiser-Friedrich-Museum, Berlin
Department of Graphics, Form, and Design

Two copies of their sales catalogues survive in the library archives of the department. Both copies contain several handwritten marks and marginal notes in pencil next to photos of the casts. The surviving plaster casts and the catalogues together confirm that a large number of items were ordered from this particular casting workshop. The bulk of the ordered samples are architectonic plaster casts, consisting of, among others: demonstrative segments of classical column orders (bases/shafts, capitals/entablatures, fig. 4); Romanesque, Gothic, and Renaissance column and pilaster capitals; antique, archaic, and Renaissance entablature details; and various decorative elements, including antique acroteria, Gothic finials, keystones, ornate consoles, and gables with vine motifs.

In addition to the architectonic details, a great number of illustrative plaster casts of Renaissance, baroque, and rococo ornamentation have also survived. A distinct group among the plaster casts from this supplier contains naturalistic or stylised illustrations of organic forms, mostly plant ornamentations, floral motifs, fruits and leaves, with a particularly large number of stylised foliage motifs from different eras, and variations of palmettos and acanthi (fig. 5). Among the remaining Hungarian-made plaster casts, busts and full-length figures are the most significant in quantity.

A number of items were acquired from German plaster casting workshops, including that of sculptor August Gerber in Cologne, the Munich-based cast maker Rappa & Co., and the workshop of the Kaiser-Friedrich-Museum (today Bode Museum) in Berlin.

Twelve of the highest-quality pieces in the current collection can be attributed to August Gerber's workshop. All but two of these are copies of the most exquisite sculptures from Greek antiquity and the Italian Renaissance, and they constitute the most valuable objects in the BME collection. There are also painted and patinated sculptures among the Gerber plaster casts, such as the copies of Donatello's *David* (fig. 6) and the *Candle-bearing Angel* by Veit Stoß.

Three items are associated with the plaster casting workshop of the former Kaiser-Friedrich-Museum in Berlin: an antique Corinthian capital copied from a column of the Tower of the Winds in Athens, a composite pilaster capital from the Monument of Lysicrates in Athens (fig. 7), and a late Gothic canopy of a statue's niche from Strasbourg Cathedral. The latter was added to the collection in 1923, placed on deposit by MFAB.

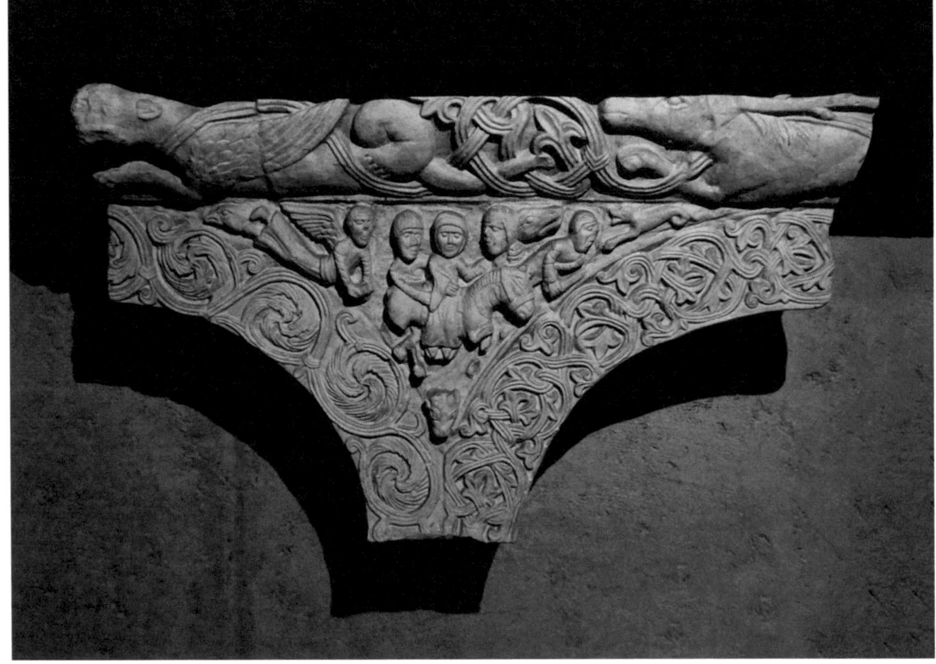

Fig. 8

Plaster cast of an early medieval relief segment
Detail from the pulpit substructure
of Sant' Ambrogio church in Milan, ca. 1910
Made by Carlo Campi, Milan
Department of Graphics, Form, and Design

Fig. 9 | next page

Plaster cast of a detail from the Parthenon frieze
Early 20th century, made by August Gerber, Cologne
Department of Graphics, Form, and Design

Among the German casts, a unique and rather diverse ensemble, in both genre and style, is made up of items produced by the Munich-based casting workshop Rappa & Co. A total of five plaster casts in the current collection came from this atelier: a large-scale archaic krater depicting female dancing figures, a tondo of the Madonna by Andrea della Robbia, a Renaissance pilaster capital, a lion's head mask, and a Gothic column capital. The quality and diversity of these items suggest that the Munich atelier must have had an extensive assortment of plaster casts on offer.

Besides the plaster casts of German origin, there are also pieces in the collection produced by Italian casting ateliers. The workshop of the Milanese Carlo Campi is credited with the crafting of three Romanesque relief segments with animal and vine scroll motifs, as well as a Byzantine capital fragment, which, according to their labels, are copies of details from Cremona Cathedral. Two remarkably high quality early medieval relief segments, replicas of the respective details on the pulpit substructure of Sant'Ambrogio church in Milan (fig. 8), are also works by the cast maker Carlo Campi.

On two occasions, in 1923[31] and in 1938,[32] the BME plaster cast collection was augmented with items transferred from the MFAB. Identification of the pieces concerned is extremely difficult, as the escrow agreement does not provide detailed specifications of the listed works. Their descriptions are limited to names and dimensions. In 2013, during the survey of the historical plaster cast collection of the museum, only seven items from this group could be identified with certainty.[33]

The collection expanded through private donations as well. Archive research has so far revealed information on one such group of objects from this period. Plaster casts of reliefs from Pécs Cathedral were donated to the Department of Medieval Architecture during the academic year 1938–1939 by the sculptor Géza Maróti,[34] instructor of moulding at BME.[35] The plaster casts are redesigned and modified versions of the reliefs made by the sculptor György Zala in 1887, during reconstruction of the cathedral, after the Romanesque originals lining the entrance stairs of the crypt.[36]

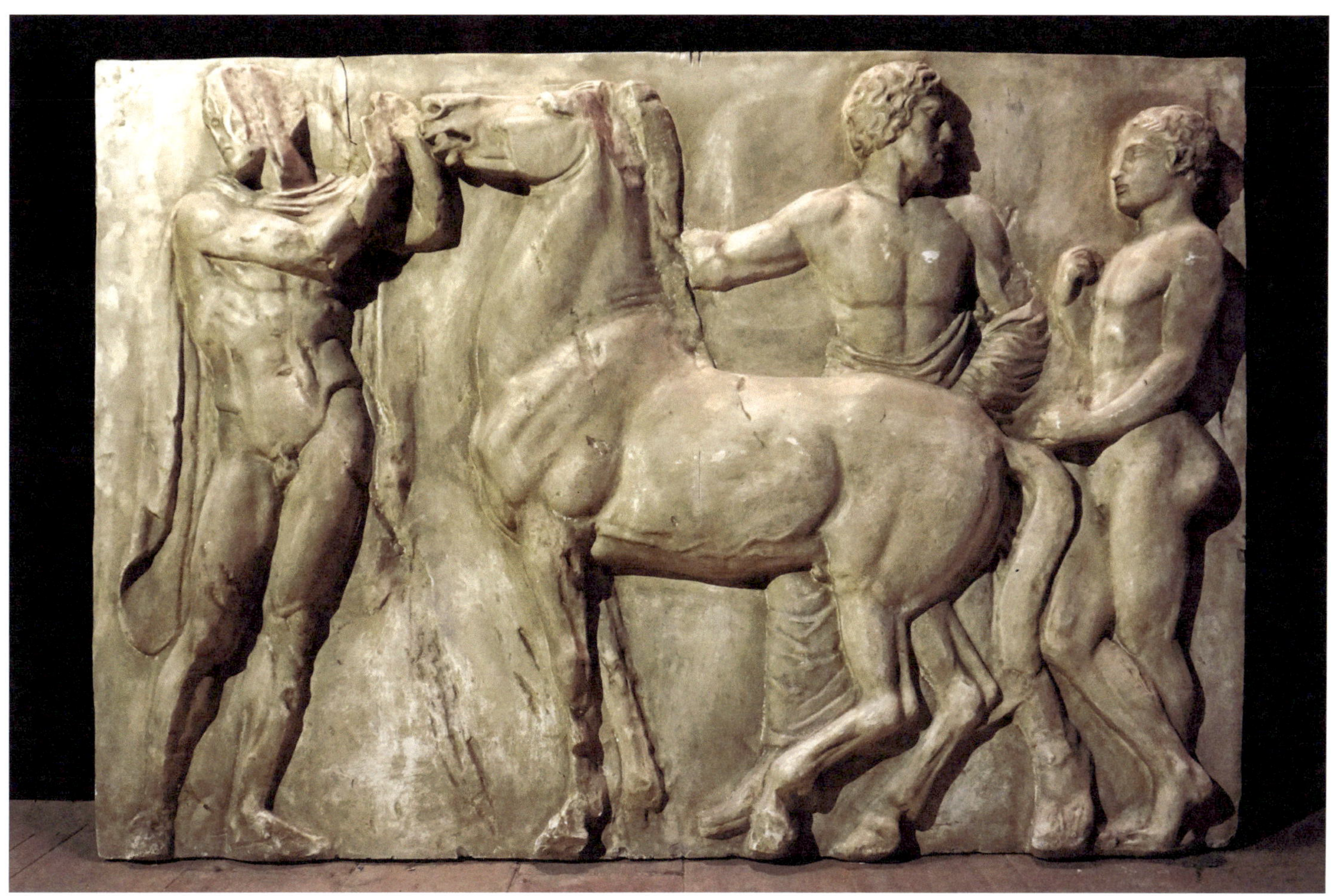

II.2 Typology

During the 2016 survey of the collection, the casts were classified into six distinct groups. One of the most spectacular groups – which is also the largest in quantity – contains the architectural casts: replicas of ancient Greek and Roman orders; details of bases, pedestals, capitals and cornices; capitals of Romanesque, Gothic, and Renaissance columns and pilasters; details of classical and Renaissance cornices; and various samples of embellishments, such as Gothic cross finials, keystones, ornamental canti-levers, wimpergs etc. Beside the architectural casts, another group comprises ornamental features of different architectural styles. Easily distinguishable from the various ornamental details of the Romanesque, Renaissance, and baroque periods is the group of floral and foliage patterns. The figural casts form a distinct category, subdivided into two groups: one includes the full-length figures (both reduced and full-size copies)

and busts, while the other contains replicas of narrative and figural reliefs. The majority of the latter are replicas of outstanding Renaissance artworks, primarily from the Italian quattrocento and cinquecento: pieces by Donatello, Verrocchio, Desiderio da Settignano and Michelangelo. Among the true gems is the cast of a section of the Parthenon friezes (fig. 9), as well as the copy of one of the relief panels of Luca della Robbia's *Cantoria,* made for Santa Maria del Fiore in Florence and preserved today in the Museo dell'Opera del Duomo.

The life-size, full-length figures and busts in the collection are mostly replicas of ancient Greek and Roman sculptures (fig. 10), but there are also a few copies of Renaissance artworks. A unique group in the collection encompasses the anatomical and descriptive geometry models. Besides the full-length figures, the few remaining anatomical models include different parts of the body, such as hands, arms, feet, facial features, and details of the human muscle system.

Fig. 10

Plaster cast of a fallen warrior figure from the east pediment
of the Temple of Aphaia II in Aigina, early 20th century
Unknown cast maker. Department of Graphics, Form, and Design

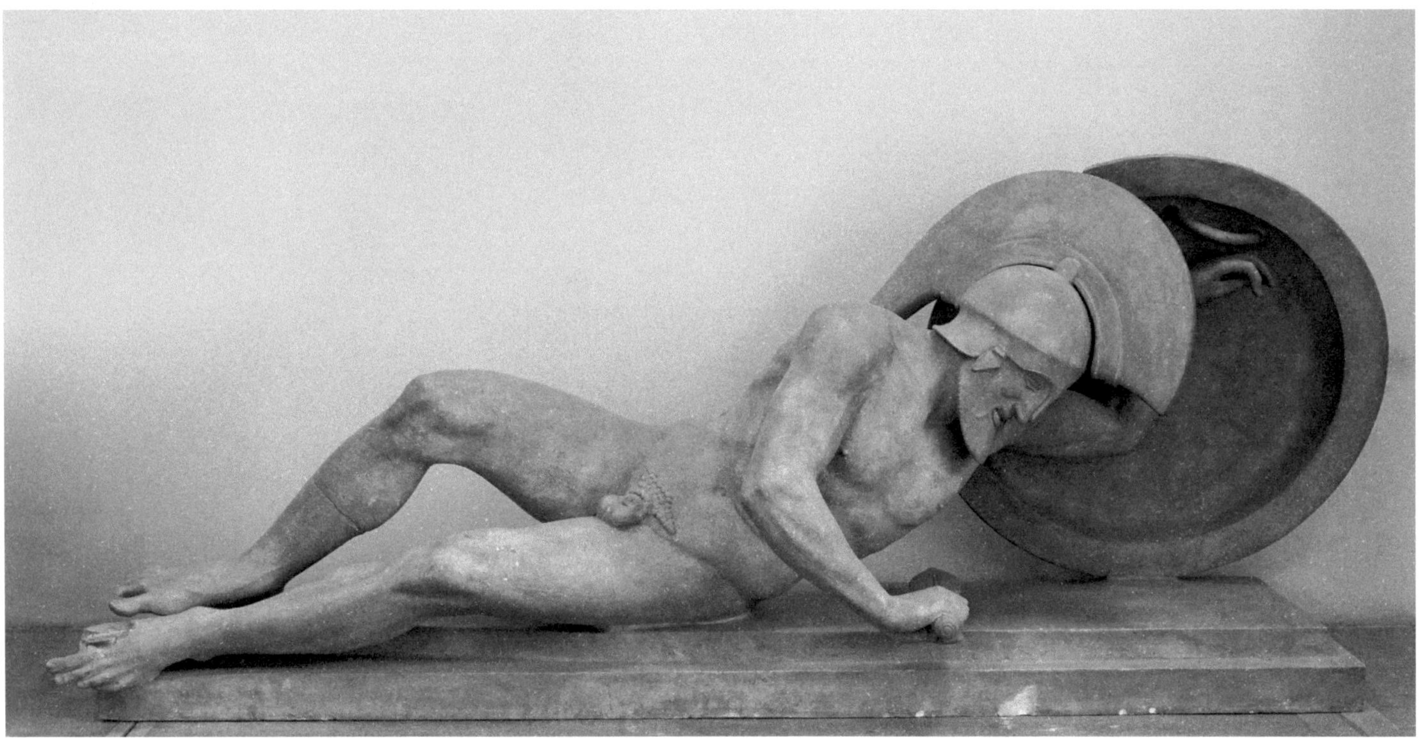

III The Plaster Cast Museum of BME

One of the most exciting yet most enigmatic chapters in the history of the collection is the creation of the Technical University's Plaster Cast Museum. The expansion of the collection is believed to have been prompted partly in response to the proposal to set up such a museum. In the absence of relevant sources, however, all we can do with regard to the founding of the museum and the evolution and make-up of its collection is to make assumptions. The initial calls for the establishment of a permanent, comprehensive collection covering all historical periods emerged relatively early. In 1884, a proposal by Lajos Rauscher, head of what was then the Department of Freehand Drawing, put forward in connection with the reform of teaching drawing at the university, was the first to posit the creation of an educational collection, comprising items encompassing all periods and styles of art.[37] The letter also makes mention of a dedicated room – adjacent to the drawing studios – where plaster casts would be on permanent display. This could be interpreted as a kind of visual repository attached to the storeroom, rather than a proper museum, as Rauscher's proposal itself focused on the reform of freehand drawing education, specifically the teaching of the newly introduced *Ékítményes alaktan* (an old-fashioned term for "ornamentation course"). Extant sources imply that the museum was intended to present characteristic pieces of universal art: ancient Greek, Roman, and Renaissance sculpture, including works by Donatello, Verrocchio, and Michelangelo, as well as architectural monuments from these eras, supplemented possibly with relics of Hungarian art. Beyond the overall concept, the actual pieces to be exhibited are unknown, as are the composition and number of items in the museum's collection. It is safe to assume (and confirmed by the organisational structure of the university) that the museum exhibited its own collection of plaster casts, and not those used in education. While certain plaster casts belonging to the different departments may occasionally have featured among the exhibits, as well as works by instructors or students, sources from later times rule out the possibility that the individual collections of the departments were merged into a single, university-level museum collection. It is nonetheless peculiar that there is no trace of any acquisition of plaster casts for the museum in the university's financial archives, and no records have yet been found substantiating the existence of a plaster cast museum in the university's organisational structure. For a while, Rauscher's proposal was the only document to corroborate at least the desire to establish a museum of such scope at BME.

The first tangible source to refer to the university's Plaster Cast Museum is the set of architectural plans for the new central building of the Imperial and Royal Joseph Technical University, designed by Alajos Hauszmann.[38] Based on the surviving blueprints, the plaster cast museum was located in a colonnade hall on the lower ground floor (today's ground floor), wedged between the two inner courtyards of the north wing.[39] Opposite the museum, the western side of the wing housed the Moulding Studio and the university's own Plaster Casting Workshop.

Unfortunately, the lack of any further written sources or photographs means that neither the configuration of the interior nor the layout of the museum premises are currently known. It is certain, however, that the Museum, together with the Moulding Studio and the Plaster Casting Workshop, remained at this location for almost thirty years, until after World War II, when they were relocated to another part of the building. Among the extremely fragmentary documents that have survived, the Hauszmann plans are essentially the only piece of information to suggest the actual existence of the museum. The decision to relocate the museum was taken at a meeting of the University Economics Committee on 13 February 1947.[40] According to the minutes of the meeting, the Plaster Cast Museum and the Moulding Studio were moved to rooms 14–16 on the second floor of the same wing. Further decisions were taken at the same meeting to create an exhibition hall for the Faculty of Architecture in the former premises of the Moulding Studio and to relocate the Department of Drawing to the third floor of the building.[41] To date, there is no reliable information about the later life of the museum – it was most likely closed down in the 1950s, and the exhibited casts were subsequently transferred to storage.

IV The Moulding Studio and the Plaster Casting Workshop of BME

There are no available data concerning when exactly the university's Moulding Studio and Plaster Casting Workshop were established. What is certain is that the idea of teaching moulding as a subject and of setting up a Moulding Studio for this purpose arose relatively early on. A letter survives written by Károly Juhbál, professor of drawing at the Joseph Industrial School, to the then-director of the institution, Mihály Karácson, giving a detailed account of his trip to Vienna and Munich.[42] The main objective of Juhbál's journey was to purchase template drawings for the Industrial School from the Imperial and Royal Museum of Art and Industry in Vienna.[43] From Austria he proceeded to Munich, where he studied the teaching methods at the local industrial schools. He observed relatively few practices that could be applied at home, as these institutions concentrated rather on artistic training and therefore bore little resemblance to the Hungarian Industrial School, whose profile was somewhat different. Nevertheless, he pointed out that the practical use of the moulding studio he had seen there could be beneficially followed by industrial schools in Hungary. With this in mind, he asked the director to request permission from the Hungarian Royal Governor's Council for Károly Juhbál to travel again to Munich in autumn that year in order to "study moulding to its full extent."[44] We can be sure that in the years when the Joseph Industrial School still existed, there was still no separate Moulding Studio or Plaster Casting Workshop. It can also be assumed that moulding was only incorporated into the curriculum for the teaching of drawing at a much later date.

The first reference to the subject of moulding can be found in the aforementioned annual statistical reports for the academic year 1859–1860.[45] The report reveals that moulding had by then been added to the timetable alongside the compulsory drawing subjects, and that the subject had its own dedicated teacher, and even its own collection of related equipment and stock of casts.

Information on the Moulding Studio and the Plaster Casting Workshop can be obtained from a letter of 1862 and its attachment, a handover report.[46] The letter, signed by József Stoczek, then-director of the Technical University, is addressed to the Hungarian Royal Governor's Council. It states that, following the death of the previous teacher of moulding, the Moulding Workshop, with its inventories and accessories, had been handed over to the interim teacher, Károly Szandház, as of 14 April 1862. The handover report attached to the letter contains four sections detailing the inventories of the hand tools in the Moulding Studio, its template drawings and its plaster casts. The plaster casts numbered 1–59 in the inventory were the works of the late moulding teacher, Ferenc Uhrl, or other masters, as well as pieces purchased by the university for use as "copy templates" during the lessons. The group of items numbered 60–95 contained student-made copies. Some of these were in a fragmentary or incomplete condition or copies of such poor execution that there was no longer any wish to use them for the purpose of instruction, so a request was made to remove them from the collection. A separate inventory would be compiled of the more successful student-made copies, as these could still be utilised by novice students when practising making plaster casts. This document is interesting to researchers for two reasons. Firstly, it mentions the origin and quality of the plaster casts that entered the collection, and secondly it offers insight into the role of plaster casts in education and into the teaching methods and processes in use at the institution.

Our earliest concrete "visual document" of the existence and arrangement of the Moulding Studio and the Plaster Casting Workshop is Alajos Hauszmann's design for the Central Building of the Lágymányos Campus, already mentioned in connection with the Plaster Cast Museum.[47] According to the floorplan, the Moulding Studio and Plaster Casting Workshop were located on the lower ground floor (today's ground floor) of the building, in the north wing, opposite the museum. Based on the available sources, the studio and workshop operated here for almost forty years; later, after several moves, they were transferred at some point in the mid-1950s to room IX of today's Dept. of Graphics.[48] Surviving timetables reveal that Moulding remained among the compulsory subjects for architecture students for many decades, until it was abolished sometime in the 1970s.

Drawing after plaster casts, as a method of improving students' comprehension of the different stylistic eras and architectural forms, was introduced relatively early at the Technical University. The methodology had found legitimacy in practice and in its successful application over decades, and it prevailed until education reforms were finally passed, leading to the adoption of new techniques. The practice of drawing after plaster casts was revived in the 1950s, in the educational methodology of socialist-realist architecture.[49]

Based on the sources uncovered to date, it has unfortunately not been possible to reconstruct with any accuracy the chronological evolution of how many items were held in the collection over its almost century-long history, or to keep track of how the stock was distributed among the various storerooms of the university. Surviving acquisition documents seldom disclose exactly which storeroom of the Faculty of Architecture each specific purchased or donated plaster cast enriched. From the 1850s until the turn of the century, a large number of plaster casts were acquired for the Moulding Storeroom, the storeroom of the General Drawing Studios, and the Architectural Storeroom. Among these, the most significant increase took place in the storeroom of the General Drawing Studios, which later became the storeroom of the Dept. of Graphics. Based on cash book and inventory records, the number of plaster casts held by the department by the early 1900s was close to 700. By estimation, the plaster cast collection of the Moulding Storeroom must have been similar in size. Most other departments of the faculty had their own storeroom collections, which may have contained plaster casts as well. Unfortunately, in the absence of relevant sources, any assumptions about additional plaster casts are merely hypothetical.

The original location of the items raises multiple questions. Judging from the available sources, the educational collections belonging to the different departments were redistributed from time to time. This is exemplified by a dean's proposal made at the Rector's Council on 11 July 1945, which suggested the reorganisation and reallocation of the architecture history and design departments within the Faculty of Architecture.[50] The proposal also addressed the redistribution of the different collections and teaching equipment among the departments. When institutional reorganisations were enacted, items from discontinued collections were often transferred to other departments. One thing is certain: the vast majority of the items in the collection today, which contains almost 400 pieces, were always owned by the Dept. of Graphics and its institutional predecessors (General Drawing Storeroom of the Industrial School and Freehand Drawing Storeroom of the Imperial and Royal Joseph Technical University). After World War II, this collection was united with the plaster cast collections of the other departments of the Faculty of Architecture, and the items were transferred to storage. The exact date of the merger is unclear at present, but it is assumed to have occurred at the time of educational reforms, which gave a continuously diminishing role to plaster casts. The resolution of these questions requires further research. As the main focus of the present paper is the early history of the BME's plaster cast collection, specifically the acquisitions of casts and the ateliers that produced them, and due to limitations in scope, the role of plaster casts in the teaching of architecture must be discussed in a separate article. The ongoing research has left no doubt that, beyond its historical value, the current collection once played an essential role in education, and plaster casts were once assets of fundamental importance in the teaching of drawing, moulding, and architectural typology.

Notes

1 For more information on the history of the plaster cast collection of MFAB, see Szőcs 2021A.

2 In the case of the most representative collections around the world, the thorough survey of plaster casts coincided with revived scientific interest. In addition to the cited comprehensive studies and handbooks, which give detailed descriptions of several collections, there are also individual publications dedicated to the survey of specific collections. For these reasons, the present paper does not intend to analyse exhaustively the history of plaster cast collecting or the scope of collections in general, confining itself instead to mentioning a few selected notable examples. See Frederiksen and Marchand 2010; Schröder and Winkler-Horaček 2012; Meyer and Savoy 2014; Nichols 2015; Lending 2017.

3 For the history of the university, see note 5.

4 Hajós-Baku and Szűts 2021; Hajós-Baku and Szűts 2022.

5 The history of the plaster cast collection is nearly as old as the history of the university itself. The royal decree to officially establish József Ipartanoda (Joseph Industrial School, named after Archduke Joseph of Austria, Palatine of Hungary), the earliest direct legal predecessor of BME, was issued on 12 June 1844, and the institute opened its doors to its first cohort of students on 1 November 1846. After a preliminary year, students could proceed with their studies in one of three fields (technology, commerce or economics). At the same time, growing interest arose in the creation of an independent Hungarian technical university. For a brief period from 1850, the class of technology was merged with the Institutum Geometricum, creating the Joseph Industrieschule.

In 1856 the school was elevated to university rank and was subsequently renamed Joseph Polytechnicum. In addition to the preliminary course, the university offered programmes in technology and in economics, and students could select the technical and economics courses that best suited their interests. It was also around this time that the programmes began to differentiate: the education of mechanical engineers, general engineers, and chemical engineers became practically separated into their own departments. In 1860, Hungarian was reinstated as the language of education and the name Polytechnicum was replaced with Császári és Királyi József Műegyetem (Imperial and Royal Joseph Technical University). Architecture as an independent discipline (and faculty) did not exist before the academic year 1873–1874, up until which time the education of architecture students was assigned to the Department of General Engineering. The first three faculties established in 1871 were "Universal Studies" (until 1882), "General Engineering" and "Mechanical Engineering", followed by "Architecture" and "Chemical Engineering" in 1873–1874. Frequent transitions in the institutional structure, which characterised the early history of BME, often concurred with campus relocations, until 1909–1910, when teaching finally began on its current grounds in the Lágymányos neighbourhood of Buda.

For more information on the BME Campus and its buildings, see Armuth and Lőrinczi 2013.

6 Inventory "E" 1851–1861, BME Dept. of Graphics.

7 Inventory "A" 1849–1875, BME Dept. of Graphics.

8 Inventory "B" 1847–1875, BME Dept. of Graphics.

9 Inventory "C" 1847–1860, BME Dept. of Graphics.

10 Inventory "D" 1847–1868, BME Dept. of Graphics.

11 Inventory "F" 1853, BME Dept. of Graphics.

12 Inventory "E" 1851–1861, BME Dept. of Graphics.

13 Inventory "E" 1851–1861, BME Dept. of Graphics, records between 2 November 1858 and 15 November 1861.

14 BME-OMIKK, fond 2/b, container 11, 14/1860/61.

15 BME-OMIKK, fond 2/b, container 11, 14/1860/61.

16 The earliest mention of the Architectural Storeroom as an individual unit has been found among the statistical data of 1865/66. BME-OMIKK, fond 2/b, container 16, 22/1865/66.

17 BME-OMIKK, fond 2/b, container 14, 79/1863/64.

18 BME-OMIKK, fond 2/b, container 20, 31/1869/70.

19 BME-OMIKK, fond 2/b, container 20, 31/1869/70.

20 Museum für angewandte Kunst (hereinafter referred to as MAK), Vienna, 85–1869.

21 Of particular interest are the discrepancies between the summary invoice and the split invoices of the two storerooms. For example, while there are altogether 96 items on the (pro forma) summary invoice, the total number of plaster cast items on the two split invoices is only 95. This change suggests that further negotiations must have taken place between the two institutions before the orders were finalised. MAK Vienna, 85–1869.

22 *A m. kir. József-műegyetem Szabadkézi rajz szertárának leltára és pótleltára* [Inventory Book and Supplementary Inventory of the Freehand Drawing Storeroom of the Royal Hungarian Joseph Technical University], 1883–1903, BME Dept. of Graphics.

23 *Pótleltár az 1889 évben a pótberu-házási alapból a „Szabadkézi rajz" czímén kezelt szertár részére enge-délyezett 300. forinton beszerzett taneszközökről* [Supplementary inventory of teaching aids acquired from the 1889 additional fund allocated to the Freehand Drawing Storeroom, in the amount of 300 Forints], BME Dept. of Graphics.

24 *Pótleltár a m. kir. József-műegyetem „szabadkézi rajz" czímén kezelt szer-tára részére a pótberuházási alapból az 1890. évben engedélyezett 300 forinton beszerzett taneszközök és berendezési tárgyakról* [Supplemen-tary inventory of teaching aids and equipment acquired from the 1890 additional fund allocated to the Free-hand Drawing Storeroom of the Royal Hungarian Joseph Tech-nical University, in the amount of 300 Forints], BME Dept. of Graphics.

25 *Pótleltár a m. kir. József-műegyetem Szabadkézi rajz szertárának 1897. évi átalányából beszerzett taneszközök és berendezési tárgyakról* [Supple-mentary inventory of teaching aids and equipment acquired from the 1897 lump sum for the Freehand Drawing Storeroom of the Royal Hungarian Joseph Technical Uni-versity], BME Dept. of Graphics.

26 *Pótleltár a m. kir. József-műegyetem Szabadkézi rajzi szertárának azon taneszközeiről és berendezési tárgya-iról, melyek a részére az 1898. évben az évi átalányból (=1140 frt.) beszerez-tettek* [Supplementary inventory of teaching aids and equipment acquired from the 1898 lump sum (of 1140 Forints) for the Freehand Drawing Storeroom of the Royal Hungarian Joseph Technical University], BME Dept. of Graphics.

27 *Pénztári könyv 1883–1902* (Cash Book 1883–1902), BME Dept. of Graphics.

28 BME-OMIKK Repository, fond 3/c, container 10, 577/1884/85.

29 *A Budapesti Áll. Felső Ipariskolával…* 1904.

30 Ibid.

31 *Letéti szerződés* [Escrow agreement], 1923, Archives MFAB, 349/1923.

32 *Átvételi elismervény* [Acknowledg-ment of receipt)], 11 November 1939, Archives MFAB, 36/1939; and the *Magyar királyi József nádor Műszaki és Gazdaságtudományi Egyetem jegyzőkönyvei* [Proceedings of the Royal Hungarian Joseph University of Technology and Economics], 1934–1949, BME-OMIKK 4/a., 4/b. *M. kir. József Nádor Műszaki és Gazdaságtudományi egyetem – rektori tanácsülések, 1938–1939* [Rector's Council meetings 1938–1939 – Royal Hungarian Joseph University of Technology and Economics], 2 March 1939 (115–124), point 19 (140–1939), 6–7 (120–121). Source: https://library.hungaricana.hu/hu/view/BME_RT_1938-39/?query=-gipsz&pg=121&layout=s (last accessed: 20 November 2022).

33 The survey in 2013 was initiated and coordinated by the Narmer Architec-ture Studio in collaboration with MFAB; the survey was conducted and the report on the evaluation of the plaster cast collection of MFAB was co-authored by museologist Géza Andó, art historian Eszter Baku and conservator-restorer Péter Módy. For the results of the survey, see Andó and Baku 2016.

34 For more on the education career of Géza Maróti, see Salamon 2016.

35 *A Budapesti M. Kir. József Nádor Műszaki és Gazdaságtudományi Egyetem 1939/40. tanévének megnyitásakor, valamint az 1938/39. tanév ünnepélyein tartott beszédek és az 1938/39. tanévi évkönyv* [Open-ing speeches in the academic year 1938–1939 and at the opening cer-emonies of 1939–1940, Almanac 1938–1939 – Royal Hungarian Joseph University of Technology and Economics], table 184/VII. Source: http://public.omikk.bme.hu/bme_evkonyv/weblap.php?step=2&-cat=beszedek&konyvtar=./besze-dek/1938_39/&alcim_id=261 (last accessed: 20 November 2022).

36 Szakács 2005.

37 BME-OMIKK Repository, fond 3/c, container 10, 577/1884/85, 5–6.

38 *Hauszmann Alajos, a Műszaki Egyetem Központi épületének terve, 1906-09* [Architectural plans of the Central Building of BME by Alajos Hauszmann, 1906–1909], The Muni-cipality of Budapest Repository, XV_17_f_401_a_119_6. Source: https://maps.hungaricana.hu/hu/BFLTervtar/27725/view/?pg=3&bbox=12494%2C-12729%2C23319%2C-7231 (last accessed: 20 November 2022).

39 These rooms are currently used by laboratories belonging to BME Faculty of Civil Engineering.

40 *Magyar királyi József nádor Műszaki és Gazdaságtudományi Egyetem jegyzőkönyvei* [Minutes of the Royal Hungarian Joseph University of Technology and Economics] (1934–1949), BME-OMIKK 4/a., 4/b. *Gazdasági Bizottság jegyzőkönyvei, 1945–1949* [Minutes of the Econom-ics Committee, 1945–1949], 13 February 1947, 165–82. Source: https://library.hungaricana.hu/hu/view/BMEjkv_GazdBiz_1945-1949/?pg=0&layout=s (last accessed: 20 November 2022).

41 Ibid.

42 BME-OMIKK, fond 1/a, container 1, 106/1846/47.

43 Today's Museum für angewandte Kunst in Vienna (MAK Wien).

44 BME-OMIKK, fond 1/a, container 1, 106/1846/47.

45 BME-OMIKK, fond 2/b, container 11, 14/1860/61.

46 BME-OMIKK, fond 2/b, container 12, 145/1861/62.

47 *Hauszmann Alajos, a Műszaki Egyetem Központi épületének terve, 1906–09* [Architectural plans of the Central Building of BME by Alajos Hauszmann, 1906–1909], The Municipality of Budapest Repository, XV_17_f_401_a_119_6. Source: https://maps.hungaricana.hu/hu/BFLTervtar/27725/view/?pg=3&bbox=2494%2C-12729%2C23319%2C-7231 (last accessed: 20 November 2022).

48 *Magyar királyi József nádor Műszaki és Gazdaságtudományi Egyetem jegyzőkönyvei* [Minutes of the Royal Hungarian Joseph University of Technology and Economics] (1934–1949), BME-OMIKK 4/a., 4/b. *Gazdasági Bizottság jegyzőkönyvei, 1945–1949* [Minutes of the Economic Committee, 1945–1949], 13 February 1947, 165–82. Source: https://library.hungaricana.hu/hu/view/BME-jkv_GazdBiz_1945-1949/?query=gipsz&pg=177&layout= (last accessed: 20 November 2022).

49 Bardon 1952.

50 *Magyar királyi József nádor Műszaki és Gazdaságtudományi Egyetem jegyzőkönyvei* [Minutes of the Royal Hungarian Joseph University of Technology and Economics] (1934–1949), BME-OMIKK 4/a., 4/b. *M. kir. József Nádor Műszaki és Gazdaságtudományi egyetem - rektori tanácsülések* [Rector's Council meetings 1938–1939 – Royal Hungarian Joseph University of Technology and Economics], 11 July 1945 (35–52). Source: https://library.hungaricana.hu/hu/view/ BME_RT_1945/ ?query=SZO%3D(%C3%BAjkori%20%C3%A9p%C3%ADt%C3%A9stani%20tansz%C3%A9k)&pg=47&layout=s (last accessed: 20 November 2022).

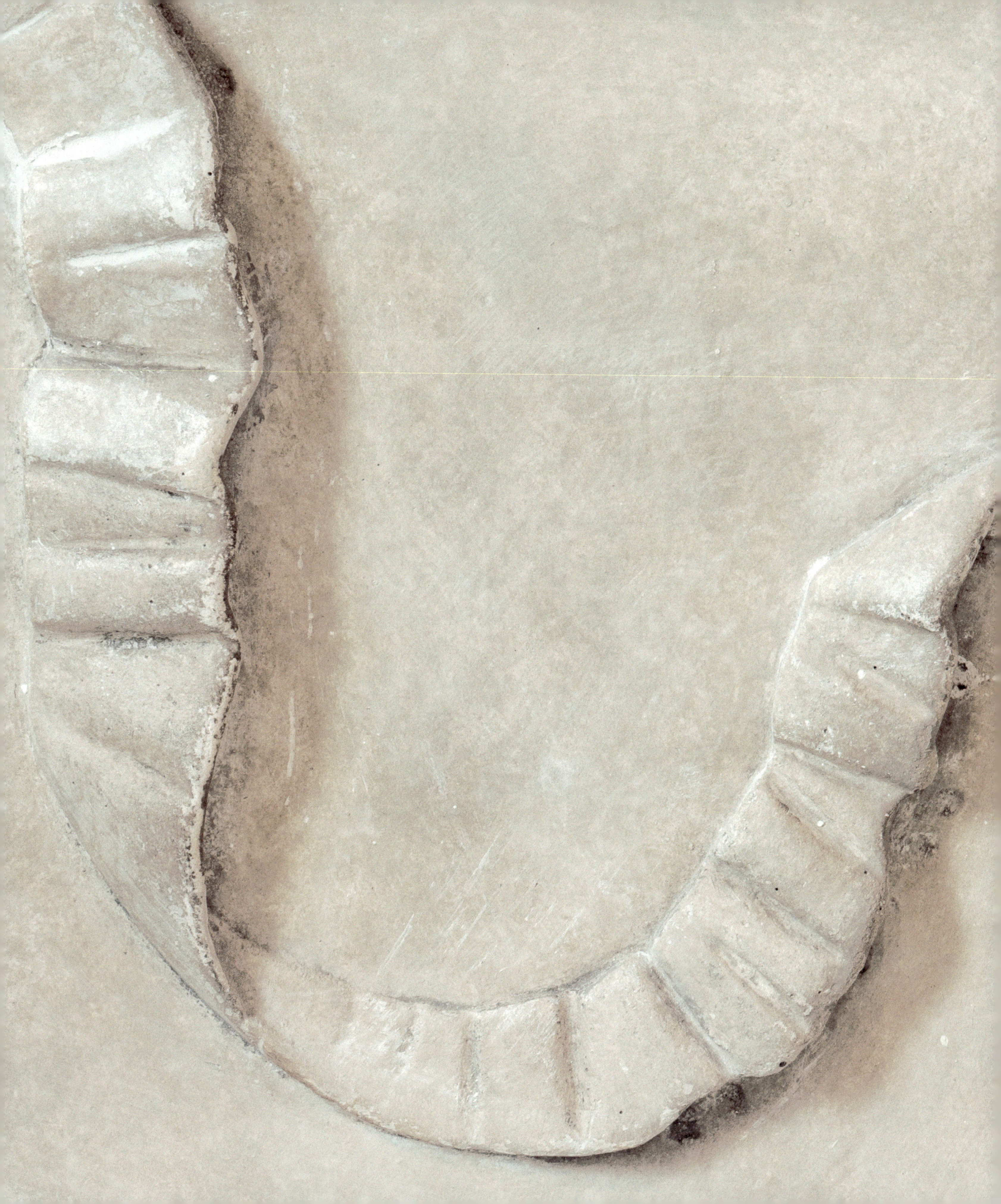

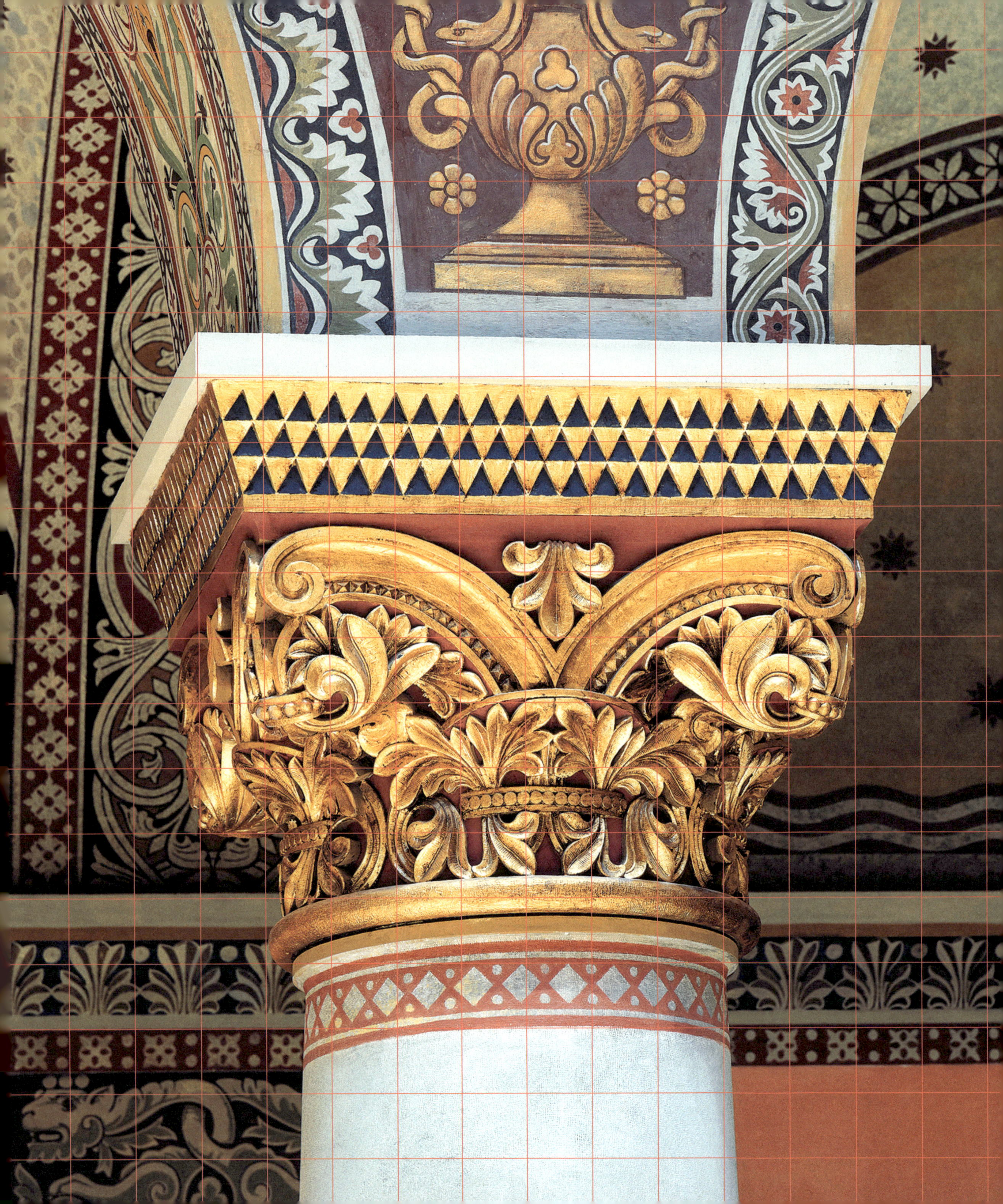

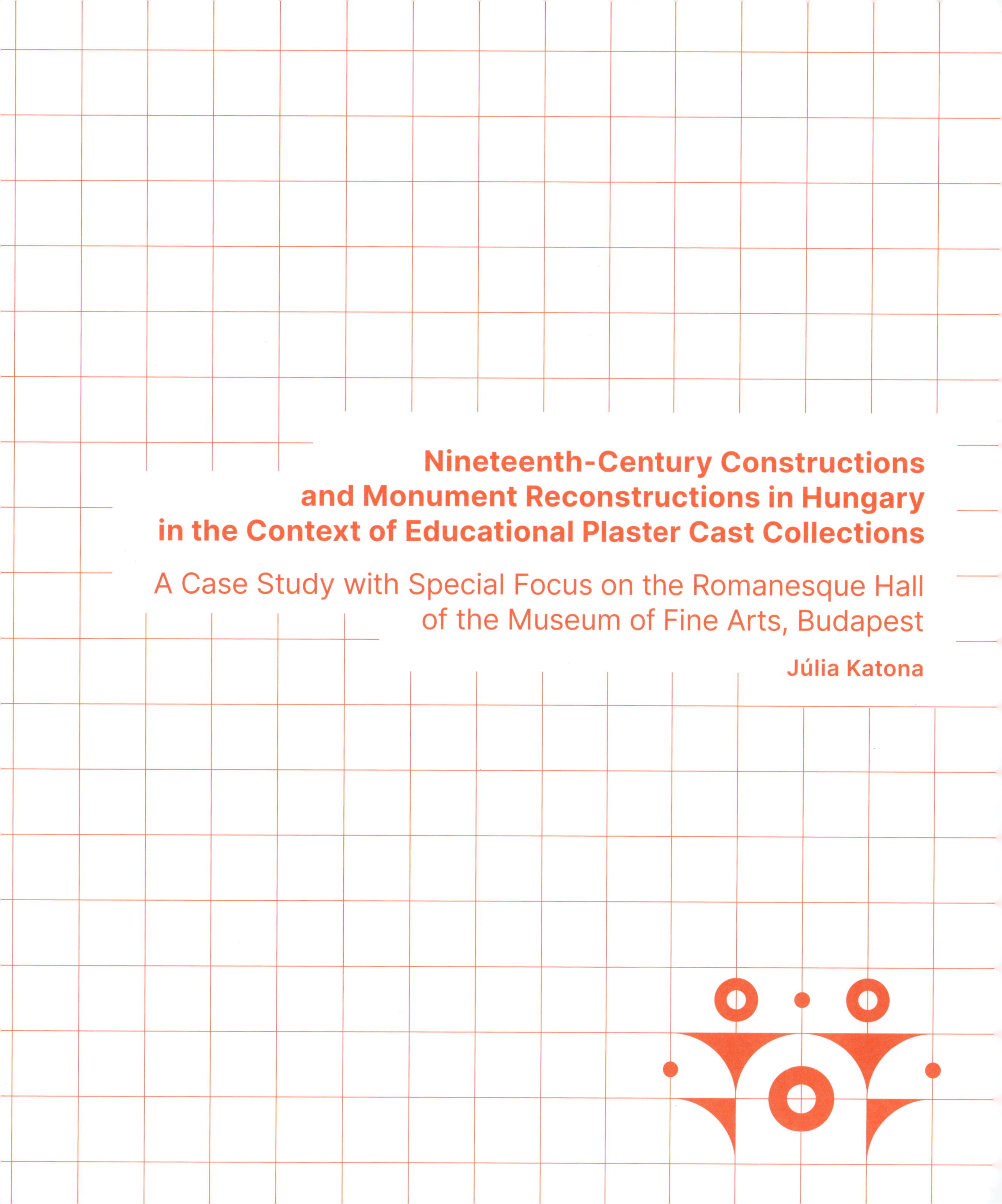

Nineteenth-Century Constructions and Monument Reconstructions in Hungary in the Context of Educational Plaster Cast Collections

A Case Study with Special Focus on the Romanesque Hall of the Museum of Fine Arts, Budapest

Júlia Katona

Nineteenth-Century Constructions and Monument Reconstructions in Hungary in the Context of Educational Plaster Cast Collections

A Case Study with Special Focus on the Romanesque Hall of the Museum of Fine Arts, Budapest

Júlia Katona

Architects, sculptors, and craftsmen working in the field of architectural ornamentation during the era of historicism used the formal elements of historical styles in very different ways compared with today, utilising them and "reapplying" them with diversity and creativity. This study examines one of the most remarkable Hungarian examples of historicism as the "reapplication" of historical elements in the context of educational plaster cast collections. How did such a significant turn-of-the-century construction relate to a unique plaster cast collection used for educational purposes? How was it connected to Hungarian monument protection in the period? In general, how did artists and craftsmen use plaster casts in the constructions and reconstructions of the era?

In connection with the venue for the conference entitled *Plaster Casts and Cast Collections Across Europe. History and Future*, the paper focuses on the design process of the architectural sculptures of the Romanesque Hall (fig. 1) of the Museum of Fine Arts, Budapest.[1]

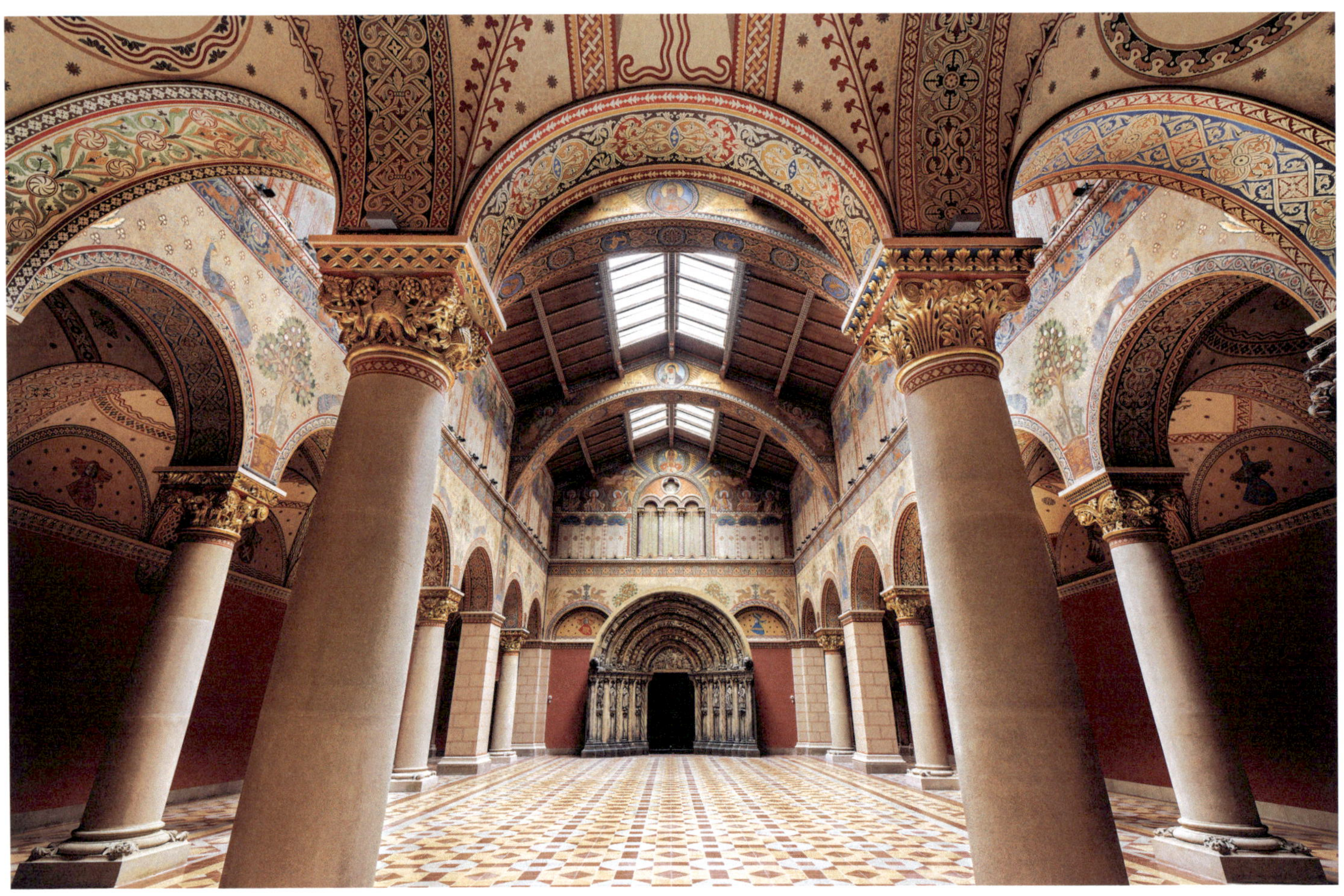

The Romanesque Hall is unique in that it remained intact after the damage of World War II. For the next seventy years, no further restoration or completion work was carried out either on the walls or in the sculptural decoration. Apart from severe water damage, the painted wall decorations and architectural sculptures were preserved almost in their original forms (fig. 2).

Construction of the museum building started on 1 August 1900, in line with the designs of two prominent architects, Albert Schickedanz (1846–1915) and Fülöp Herzog (1860–1925). Initially there was no mention of a courtyard named or designed in the "Romanesque" style. The appellation of the space as the Romanesque Hall or courtyard first appears in documents generated after the beginning of construction work. According to the minutes of the building committee, the architects originally intended to design the glass-roofed courtyard in the Renaissance style. It was considered far more expensive to build the space in the Romanesque rather than the Renaissance style, but as a result of savings in the budget, it was ultimately decided to construct the hall in the spirit of the Romanesque.[2] The medieval-like design extended not only to the arrangement of space, but also to the type and material of the supports, the shaping of the sculptural decoration, and the figural and ornamental elements of the wall painting. The release of additional financial resources meant that the masonry pillars originally planned for the axes of the triumphal arches could be substituted with columns made of granular sandstone, quarried from Besztercebánya (today Banská Bystrica, Slovakia), which was much more in keeping with the Romanesque style.[3]

According to archive documents, construction of the Romanesque Hall, including its architectural and painted design, began at the end of October 1900 and lasted until May 1904, with only minor additions and repairs made subsequently. The construction of the masonry and the supports took place between October 1900 and autumn 1901 (contractor: Ede Ney et al.), the stylistic design of the capitals of the supports was completed in 1902 (contractor: Ignácz Langer), and the wall painting works took place from the summer or October of 1903 until the end of May 1904 (contractors: architects Albert Schickedanz and Fülöp Herzog).[4]

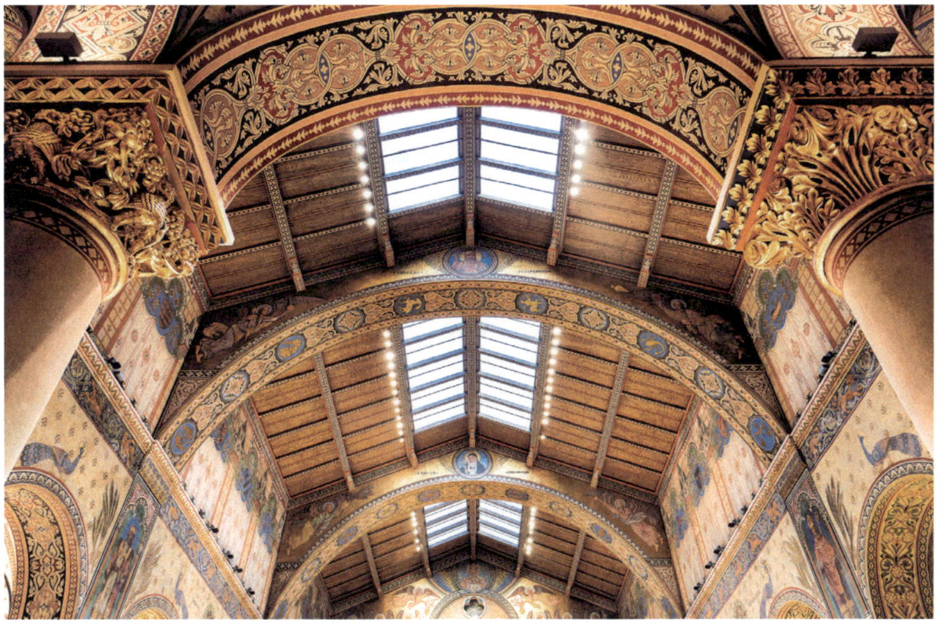

In the context of educational plaster cast collections, the programme and the models of the decorative sculptures were highly relevant. Both the design and execution processes were very well documented and can be followed in the extant archival sources. The tender for the sculptural works of the Romanesque Hall was announced in 1902 as part of the works to be carried out in the rear section of the building. The budget estimate for the sculptural plaster works for the Museum of Fine Arts can be read in the attachment to the tender announcement of 4 March 1902. Furthermore, the design process is described precisely in a separate document entitled "Sculptural works for the Romanesque Hall, required for the construction of the Museum of Fine Arts".[5]

Fig. 1 | previous page

The Romanesque Hall of the Museum of Fine Arts, Budapest after its restoration in 2015–2018

Fig. 2

Triumphal arches in the Romanesque Hall of the Museum of Fine Arts, Budapest, viewed from Dózsa György Street (formerly Aréna Street)

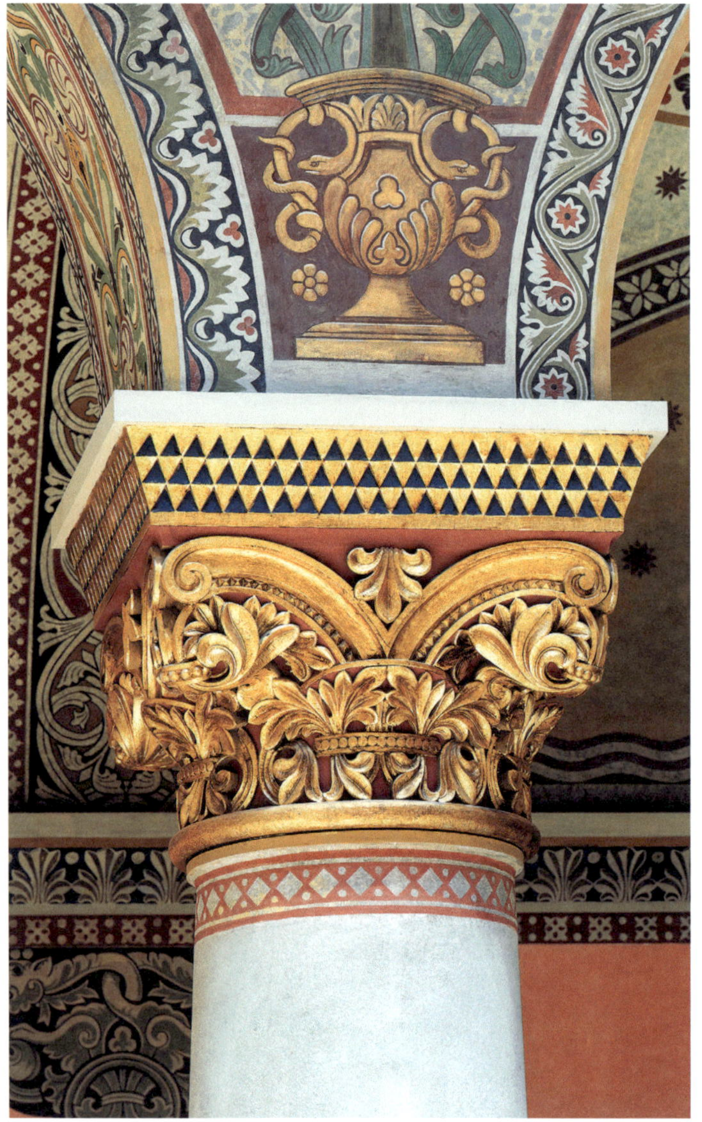

In the tender announcement for the sculptural works of the Romanesque Hall,[6] the building committee ordered, respectively, six and two "models of Romanesque column capitals" (the different numbers referred to the planned positioning of the capitals), and eight "models of Romanesque column bases", all made of plaster. The models had to follow "the character of various capitals in Pécs Cathedral" and be executed after drawings and photographs provided by the construction management. The tender announcement also called for the same number of "sculptural works in roughly carved Beszterce-bánya stone", which were to be "produced in accordance with" the plaster models.[7] As a result of the tender, on 4 May 1902, a contract was signed with Ignácz Langer (1857–1927) for the stone carving works of the Romanesque Hall.[8] This project, according to Langer's fourth income statement, lasted until September 1902.[9]

Six of the eight capitals had to be made in a "simple design" and two in a "more ornate design". This was justified by the originally planned spatial distribution of the hall's system of supports: the middle nave from Aréna Street (today: Dózsa György Street) and the cross-vaulted, U-shaped surrounding area were considered to be more "decorative". The 2 × 3 capitals between the pillars in the axis of the triumphal arches were ordered in a "simpler" design.

The description of the hall's sculptural works suggests that the decorative sculptural pieces were intended to be placed in the space, in the manner of Romanesque-style works. The document is an exceptional written source of the working method of "historicising" architecture that used and transformed specific samples, so it is worth citing here in full the part of the announcement that precisely prescribes the use of historical models:

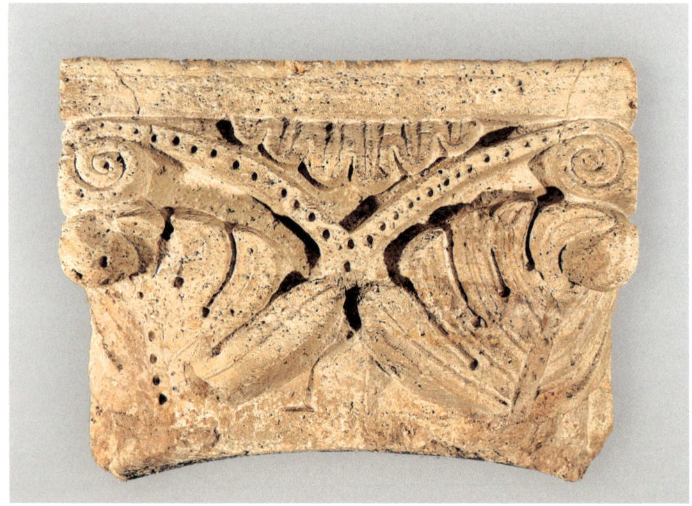

Fig. 3 | above

Tendril-leaf capital from the Romanesque Hall of the Museum of Fine Arts, Budapest, designed and carved by Ignácz Langer in 1902

Fig. 4

Southern capital from Pécs Cathedral

"Sculptural works for the Romanesque Hall, required for the construction of the Museum of Fine Arts

A) Models made of plaster. The models to be produced will be presented to the construction management and, if desired, will be amended according to their instructions.

1. 6 models of Romanesque column capitals to be produced with different motifs in the character of various capitals in Pécs Cathedral, based on drawings and photographs provided by the construction management, in a simple design. The models should be made in half size. The actual size of the capitals is 1.31 – 1.31 – 0.95 m.

2. 2 different models of capitals in the Romanesque style, described as in item 1, but in a more ornate design. Size as before.

3. 8 models of Romanesque column bases, described otherwise as in item 1, also in half size. The actual size is 1.24 – 1.24 – 0.56 m.

B) Sculptural works in roughly carved Besztercebánya stone, already delivered to the construction site, produced in accordance with the models detailed above under items 1, 2, and 3 and the instructions of the construction management.

4. 6 Romanesque column capitals, made after the models stated in item 1, in size 1.31 – 1.31 – 0.95 m, with the necessary scaffolding.

5. 2 Romanesque column capitals, made after the models stated in item 2, in size 1.31 – 1.31 – 0.95 m, with the necessary scaffolding.

6. 8 Romanesque column bases, made after the models stated in item 3, in size 1.24 – 1.24 – 0.56 m."[10]

The eight capitals in the hall all differ in decoration and are unique pieces of design "in style". Their ornamentation is limited to tendril-leaf and tendril-animal motifs typical of the Romanesque style. As specified in the tender announcement, the styling of the capitals in the central nave was carried out following specific examples, in the "character" of the capitals of Pécs Cathedral. Among the "drawings and photographs provided by the construction management", which were included in the tender, the latter are presumably those taken in the early 1890s by the art historian Péter Gerecze. Gerecze's photo documentation, held by the Collection of Photographs of the former Gyula Forster National Centre for Cultural Heritage and Asset Management,[11] captured numerous stone carvings, which could have served as examples for the design of the capitals. The stone carvings in Pécs are echoed in several versions in the capitals produced for the Romanesque Hall.

The capital on the south side of the hall's southeastern wall is a direct copy of the western capital of the southern triumphal arch pillar of Pécs Cathedral. The original leaf-shaped "Y shape with a pair of volutes"[12] was only slightly modified in the early twentieth-century version (figs. 3–4). The decorative friezes of birds pecking grapes in Pécs Cathedral, meanwhile, may have been the prototypes for the bird figures on the tendril-animal-shaped capital on the eastern side of the northeastern wall. In this case, Langer transformed the animal-shaped motifs from a flat representation into a spatial composition. Gerecze took photographs of both of the mentioned stone carvings in the 1890s, which may have served as starting points for the stylistic design (fig. 5).

There is also secondary photographic documentation of the plaster models made by Ignácz Langer, who carried out the work, in the 1904 catalogue of the Plaster Casting Workshop of the Budapest National Higher School of (Building) Industry, which supplied plaster casts to educational institutions of various levels and functions at the turn of the century.[13] Plate IX, with the title "Architectural and decorative elements in the Romanesque style",[14] presents mixed architectural details from the church in Bény (today Bíňa, Slovakia) and from Matthias Church (Buda Castle), mainly capitals, and copies of capitals designed by Ignácz Langer for the Museum of Fine Arts (fig. 6). The focus of the photomontage, which ignores scale, was a total of eight plaster models of the capitals made for the Romanesque Hall of the Museum of Fine Arts.[15] These are also numerically identical to the 6 + 2 plaster models listed in the tender announcement (cited above), but only two of them can be considered identical in every detail to those installed in the hall, and one can be identified as a design variant.[16] The rest may have been master specimens rejected by the construction committee and ultimately not implemented.[17]

The appearance of architectural and decorative plaster models used in constructions and re-constructions in nineteenth-century Hungary was much more general than it might seem at first sight. The above-mentioned plaster cast catalogue from 1904, illustrated with photographs, is a unique and rare visual and textual resource both for constructions and re-constructions and for the composition of educational plaster cast collections of the period. In this price list of plaster models, the plates compiling and mixing the "original" architectural and

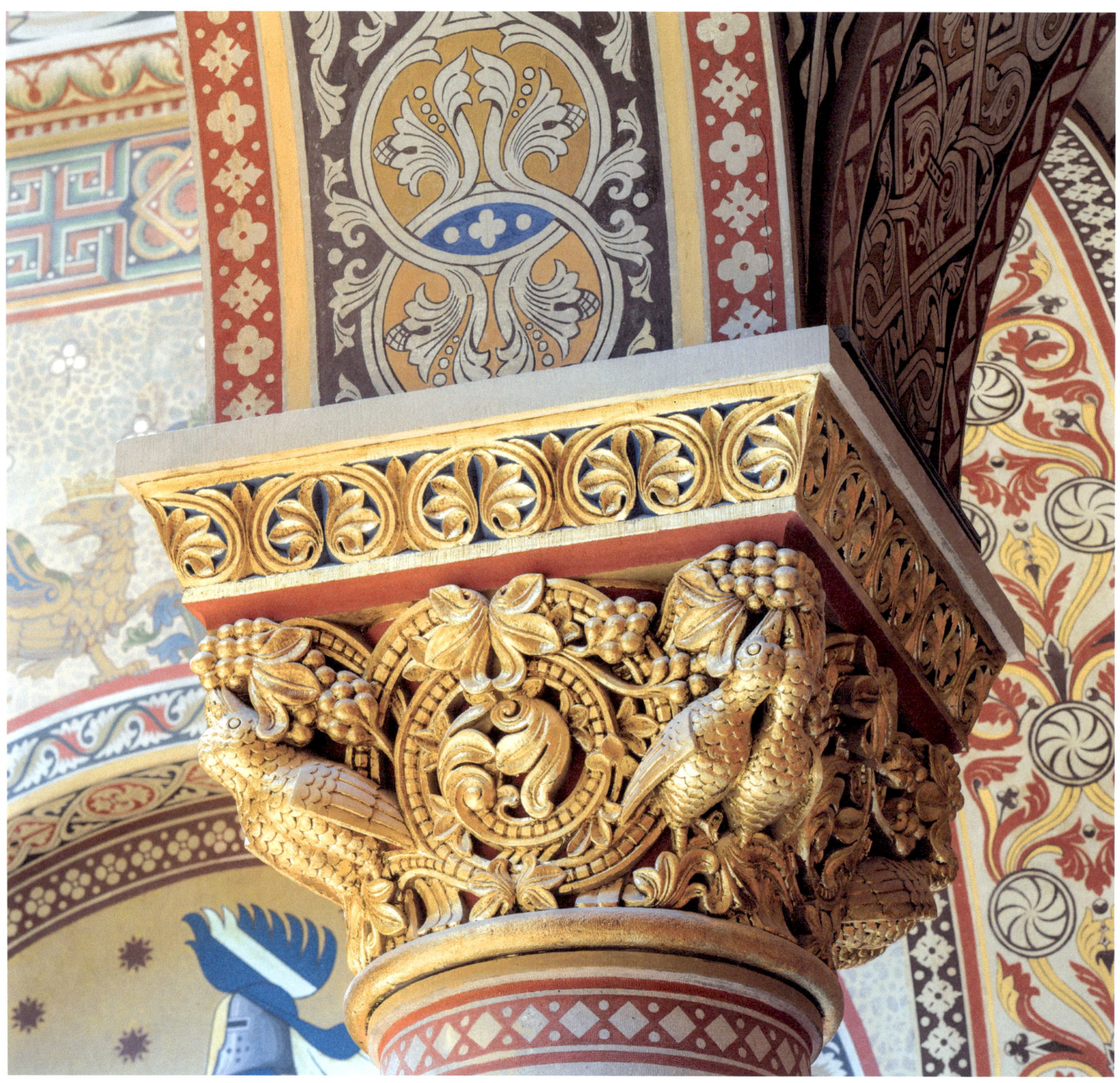

Fig. 5

Tendril-leaf capital from the Romanesque Hall of the Museum of Fine
Arts, Budapest, designed and carved by Ignácz Langer in 1902

Fig. 6 │ next page

Architectural and decorative elements in the Romanesque style
Price List of the Copies of Sculptures and Models
Made in the Plaster Casting Workshop
of the Budapest National Higher School of Industry, 1904, plate IX

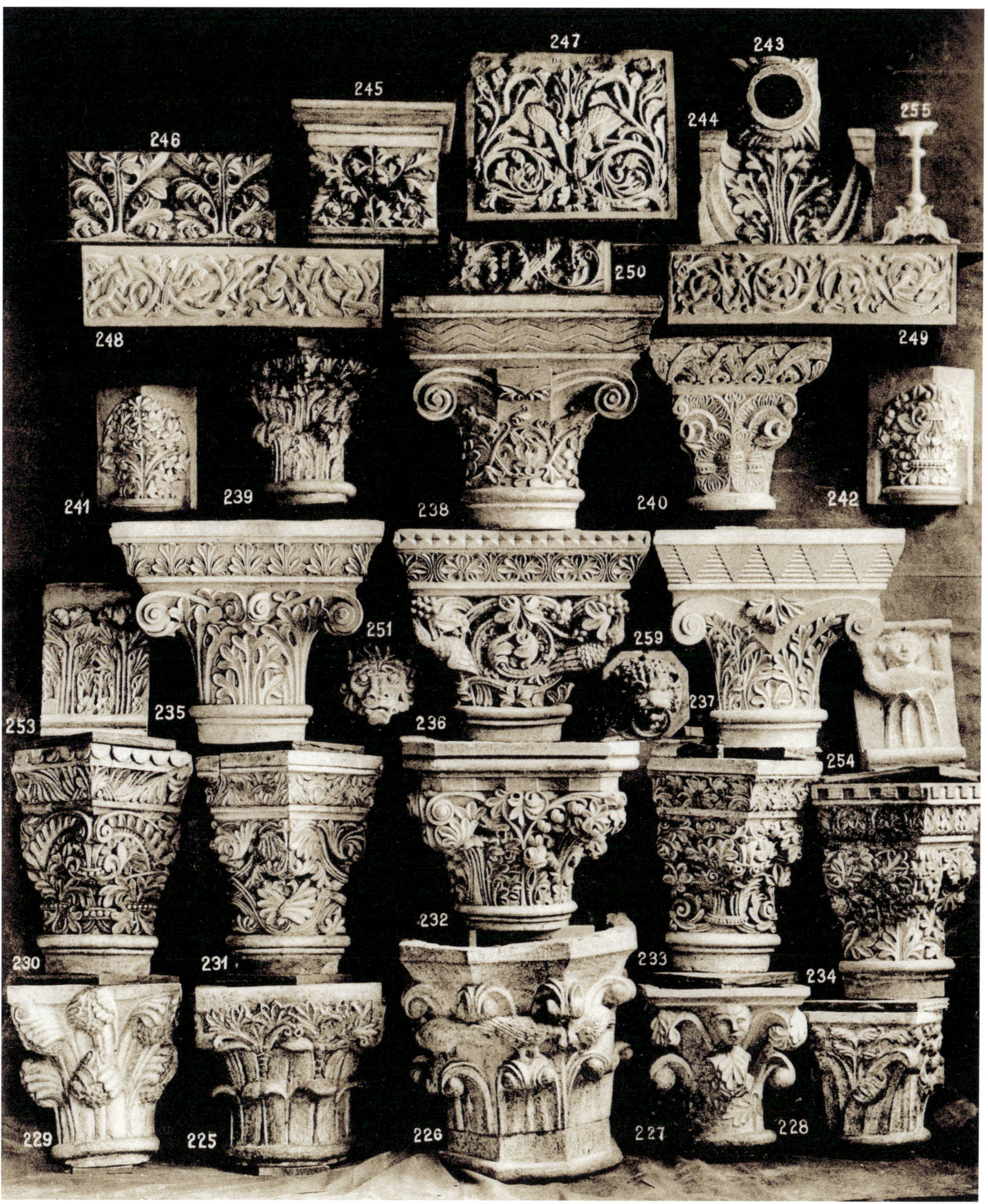

ornamental elements of the Middles Ages with the models executed in the Romanesque and Gothic styles are the most relevant to the topic of this study. On the plates representing examples from the Middle Ages, besides the plaster models made by Ignácz Langer for the Romanesque Hall, other medieval examples also appear, such as copies of two early Romanesque capitals and a unique relief with a human figure from the church in Bény (early thirteenth century), a base and a Gothic filial from the Church of Our Lady of Buda (Matthias Church, reconstructed by Frigyes Schulek, 1874–1896). A Gothic rosette "in late manners", from the neo-Gothic building of the Ministry of Finance designed by Sándor Fellner (1901–1904), also figures as a precedent for designing "in style" – in line with the typical design process of historicism. The text of the catalogue clearly distinguishes between casts copied after original medieval architectural parts and models designed "in style" and used in constructions and re-constructions of the nineteenth century. In its terminology, "early" indicates original elements from the Middle Ages, while "newer age" represents casts from the period of historicism (figs. 8–9).

Only a few specimens from abroad can be found among the plaster models representing the formal decorative sets of the Middle Ages. One of the rare examples is the cast named by the catalogue as "Romanesque Frieze. Old" (fig. 7), which is a copy of a detail from the Cathedral of Saint-Denis near Paris (twelfth century). Its modification over time is very instructive, showing how the process of copying resulted in significant changes to the original version. Provenance research has revealed that the original architectural element went through three known phases of copying and passed through three countries before it ended up in the Plaster Cast Collection of the Budapest Metropolitan Industrial Drawing School (1886–1945) at the very beginning of the twentieth century. It is worth tracing its journey from Paris to Budapest. Surprisingly, the original piece is a colonette from the Western portal of the Cathedral of Saint-Denis, a three-dimensional carving which is currently conserved in the collection of Musée de Cluny.[18] The first copy of the original colonette appears in the collection of musée de Sculpture comparée, displayed in la Salle d'ornementation. This unique museum, initiated by Eugène Emmanuel Viollet-le-Duc (1814–1879), opened in 1882 and focused on the architectural and sculptural monuments of the Middle Ages in France through a special collection of life-size copies made of plaster.

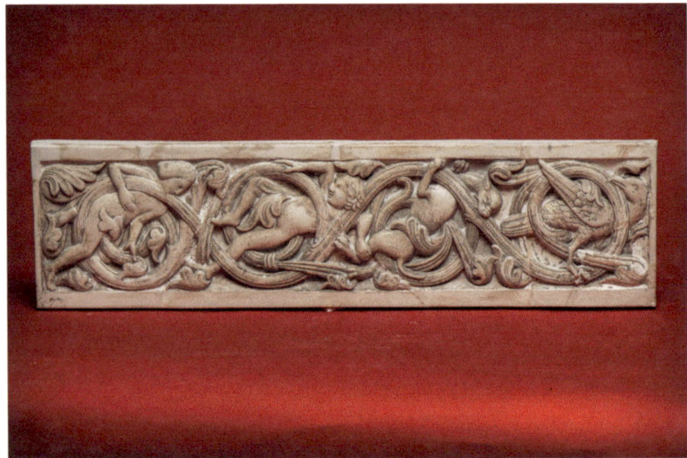

Fig. 7

Romanesque Frieze, early 20th century,
Plaster Casting Workshop of the Budapest
National Higher School of Industry.
Schola Graphidis Art Collection, Budapest

Fig. 8 | next page at upper left

Architectural and decorative elements
in the Romanesque and Gothic styles
*Price List of the Copies of Sculptures and Models
Made in the Plaster Casting Workshop of the Budapest
National Higher School of Industry*, 1904, plate X

Fig. 9 | next page at upper right

Architectural and decorative elements in the Gothic style
*Price List of the Copies of Sculptures and Models
Made in the Plaster Casting Workshop of the Budapest
National Higher School of Industry*, 1904, plate XI

Fig. 10 | next page at lower left

Architectural and decorative elements in the Renaissance style
*Price List of the Copies of Sculptures and Models
Made in the Plaster Casting Workshop of the Budapest
National Higher School of Industry*, 1904, plate XIV

Fig. 11 | next page at lower right

Decorative elements in the baroque and rococo styles
(Louis XIV and Louis XV)
*Price List of the Copies of Sculptures and Models
Made in the Plaster Casting Workshop of the Budapest
National Higher School of Industry*, 1904, plate XXIII

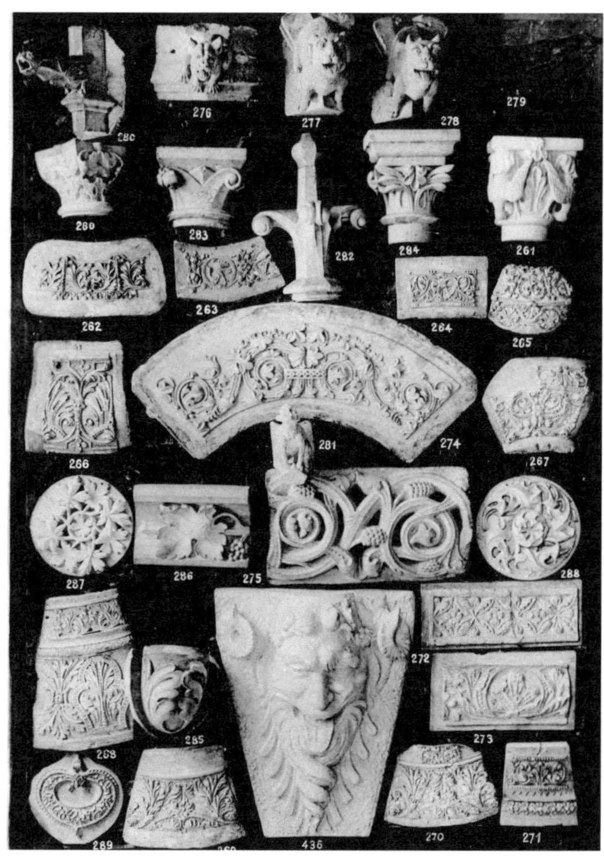

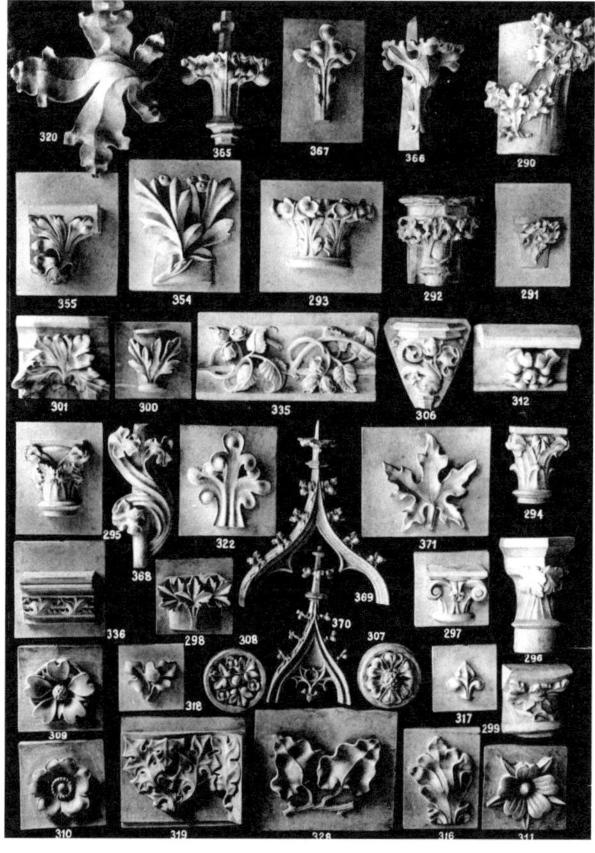

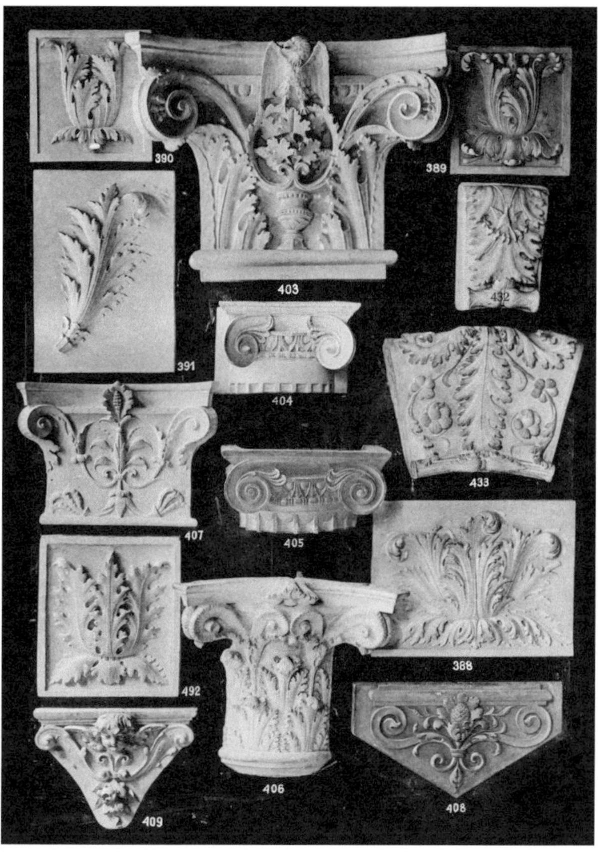

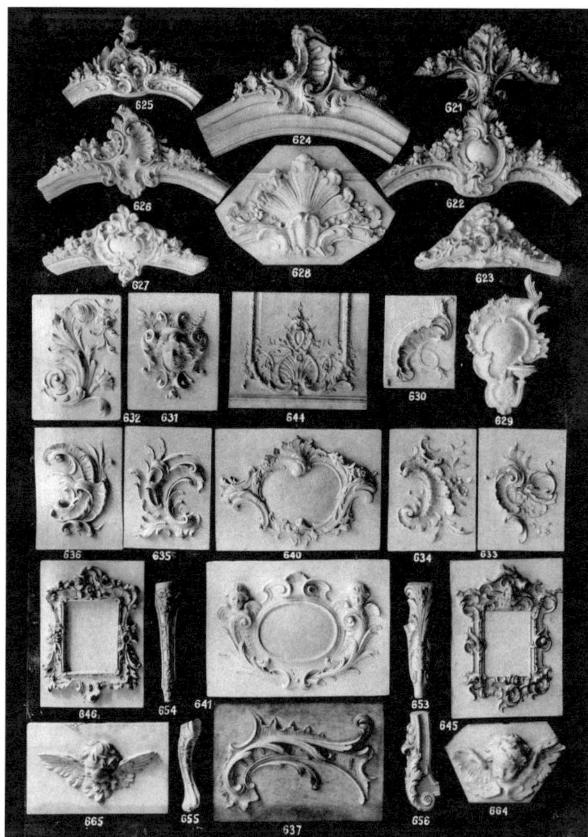

The model conserved in the Schola Graphidis Art Collection[19] may have come to Budapest from Vienna, from the plaster casting workshop run by Alexander Schroth and, after his death (1899), by his son Moriz Schroth. The workshop made plaster casts for the Museum für Kunst und Industrie in Vienna. Schroth's catalogue contains a two-dimensional copy of the twelfth-century carving of a tendril-animal-human figure from the Cathedral of Saint-Denis. It seems that a dimensional modification took place that spread across borders. This modification, which must have taken place somewhere between Paris and Vienna, changed the function, size (reduction) and "spatiality" of the original object. Thanks to the loss of spatiality and the additional flattening, the column decoration became suitable as an educational aid and was enriched with another feature: it could be viewed as a picture.

The Hungarian and foreign examples cited above, which derive from the Plaster Casting Workshop of the Budapest National Higher School of (Building) Industry, are currently part of the Plaster Cast and Sculpture Collection of the Schola Graphidis Art Collection. This special educational collection belongs to the Hungarian University of Fine Arts – High School of Visual Arts and contains objects from the end of the eighteenth century to the second half of the twentieth century. The set of plaster casts once belonged to the Budapest Metropolitan Industrial Drawing School (1886–1945). By 1896–1897, the number of plaster models used for educational purposes in this central Industrial Drawing School exceeded 1,800.[20] After World War II, many of these casts were destroyed or stolen, and now only approximately 100 objects from the late nineteenth and early twentieth centuries survive. The surviving casts exemplify the composition of the educational plaster cast collections that were once used all over Europe. During the art historical research and reconstruction of the once complete plaster cast collection of the Industrial Drawing School, the price list of plaster casts published in 1904 provided an important resource for identifying the models one by one.

At the same time, a new context has also emerged, in that this illustrated catalogue represents the encyclopaedic knowledge of the period. As the photographic illustrations of the 1904 catalogue show, the plaster cast collections used in various art or other educational institutions in the late nineteenth and early twentieth centuries were visual encyclopaedias of diverse knowledge reflecting the educational and cultural ideals of the era. The themes of the copies and sculptures conveyed the periods of art, applied arts, and architecture history spanning from antiquity to the modern era: mythological knowledge, familiarity with the history of culture through prominent figures of literature and history, as well as wide-ranging knowledge of botany, anatomy and geometry. The compilation of the plaster cast collections required a deep knowledge of history and cultural history, and the plaster casting workshops and their price lists/catalogues were the mediators of this common knowledge.

Studying this catalogue, it can be determined that the European plaster cast collections of the nineteenth century consisted of two distinct parts, one larger and one smaller. The larger set included elements of ancient Greco-Roman, Renaissance, baroque and rococo architectural and ornamental forms, representing a common cross-section of plaster collections across Europe, as well as full-figured representations, anatomical plaster models and busts (figs. 10–11). The smaller group consisted of plaster models representing the national art. These included representative pieces that made up a large part of the medieval set of forms.

The plaster casts representing the ornamental forms of each artistic style were mainly copies of European examples. Besides certain constant elements in the cast collections, however, the lists of architectural and ornamental plaster casts exemplifying medieval decorative motifs varied from country to country. In the 1904 catalogue, for example, almost half of the Romanesque and Gothic plaster casts were made up of pieces made after architectural elements of buildings located in Hungary. This points to the relationship between monument protection and education, since plaster casts created during the restorations and constructions of historical monuments in Hungary, which then became redundant, entered the bloodstream of the educational system through the Plaster Casting Workshop of the Budapest National Higher School of (Building) Industry at the turn of the century.

Regarding the function of plaster cast collections in the transfer of knowledge, replicas of architectural and decorative details originating from the Middle Ages played a very important role in this system. Casts of original medieval carvings – such as those from the church in Bény and from Matthias Church, the plaster capitals made by Ignácz Langer for the Romanesque Hall of the Museum of Fine Arts, and the Gothic-style rosette designed for the neo-Gothic building of the Ministry of Finance – all disseminated the most up-to-date nineteenth-century information about the art and architecture of the Middle Ages, and strengthened the idea of nationalism of the period.

This study has highlighted the close connection between nineteenth-century monument protection and the art and industry education of the era, and has revealed the special design process applied in the constructions and re-constructions of the period of historicism.

Notes

1 Katona 2018.

2 Archives MFAB, 515/1900 and *Jegyzőkönyv a Szépművészeti Múzeum építőbizottságának üléseiről. I. Hátsóépület* [Minutes of the Construction Committee of the Museum of Fine Arts, Part I. Rear Section of the Building], Archives MFAB, 636/1900, 7 December 1900. Throughout this text, the English translations of quotations from the original construction documents, tender announcements and contracts found in the Archives MFAB were made by the author.

3 *Jegyzőkönyv a Szépművészeti Múzeum építőbizottságának üléseiről. I. Hátsóépület.* [Minutes of the Construction Committee of the Museum of Fine Arts, Part I. Rear Section of the Building], Archives MFAB, 496/1900, 10 October 1900.

4 *A Szépművészeti Muzeum decorativ festése ügyében 157253.25 K. erejéig Schickedanz és Herzoggal kötött szerződés jóváhagyás alá terjesztetik. Ministernek* [Regarding the decorative painting of the Museum of Fine Arts, the contract entered into with Schickedanz and Herzog up to an amount of 157253.25 crowns is submitted to the Minister for approval], Archives MFAB, 475/1903, 18 July 1903.

5 The document *A szépművészeti muzeum építkezéséhez szükséges szobrászmunka a román teremben* [The sculptural works of the Romanesque Hall for the construction of the Museum of Fine Arts] is part of the main archival material on the design of the Romanesque Hall in the tender announcement; see *Árlejtési hirdetmény. Költségvetés. A Szépművészeti Muzeum építkezéséhez szükséges Fősz (Gyps) szobrász munkáról.* [Tender announcement. Budget. On the plaster (gypsum) sculptural work required for the construction of the Museum of Fine Arts], Archives MFAB, 143/1902, 4 March 1902.

6 *Tender announcement. Budget. On the sculptural work required for the construction of the Romanesque Hall of the Museum of Fine Arts.* See note 5.

7 Ibid.

8 Contract for stone carving works of the Romanesque Hall. Archives MFAB, 470/1902.

9 Ignácz Langer's fourth income statement about the sculptural works for the Romanesque Hall. Archives MFAB, 656/19.

10 See note 5.

11 Bakó 1993.

12 Tóth S. 2010, 47.

13 *A Budapesti Áll. Felső Ipariskolával...* 1904.

14 "Román stilü épitészeti és diszitő elemek" [Architectural and decorative elements in the Romanesque style], in Ibid., plate IX.

15 Ibid., cat. nos. 230, 231, 234, 235, 236, 237, 238.

16 Ibid., cat. nos. 235, 236, 238.

17 Ibid., cat. nos. 230, 231, 233, 234, 237.

18 Colonnette from the Cathedral of Saint-Denis, third quarter of the twelfth century, height: 149 cm. Musée de Cluny, Paris, inv. no. RF 1249 / Cl.19576.

19 The Schola Graphidis Art Collection is the collection of the Hungarian University of Fine Arts – High School of Visual Arts. On the history of the collection, see Katona 2016.

20 Vidéky 1897, 53.

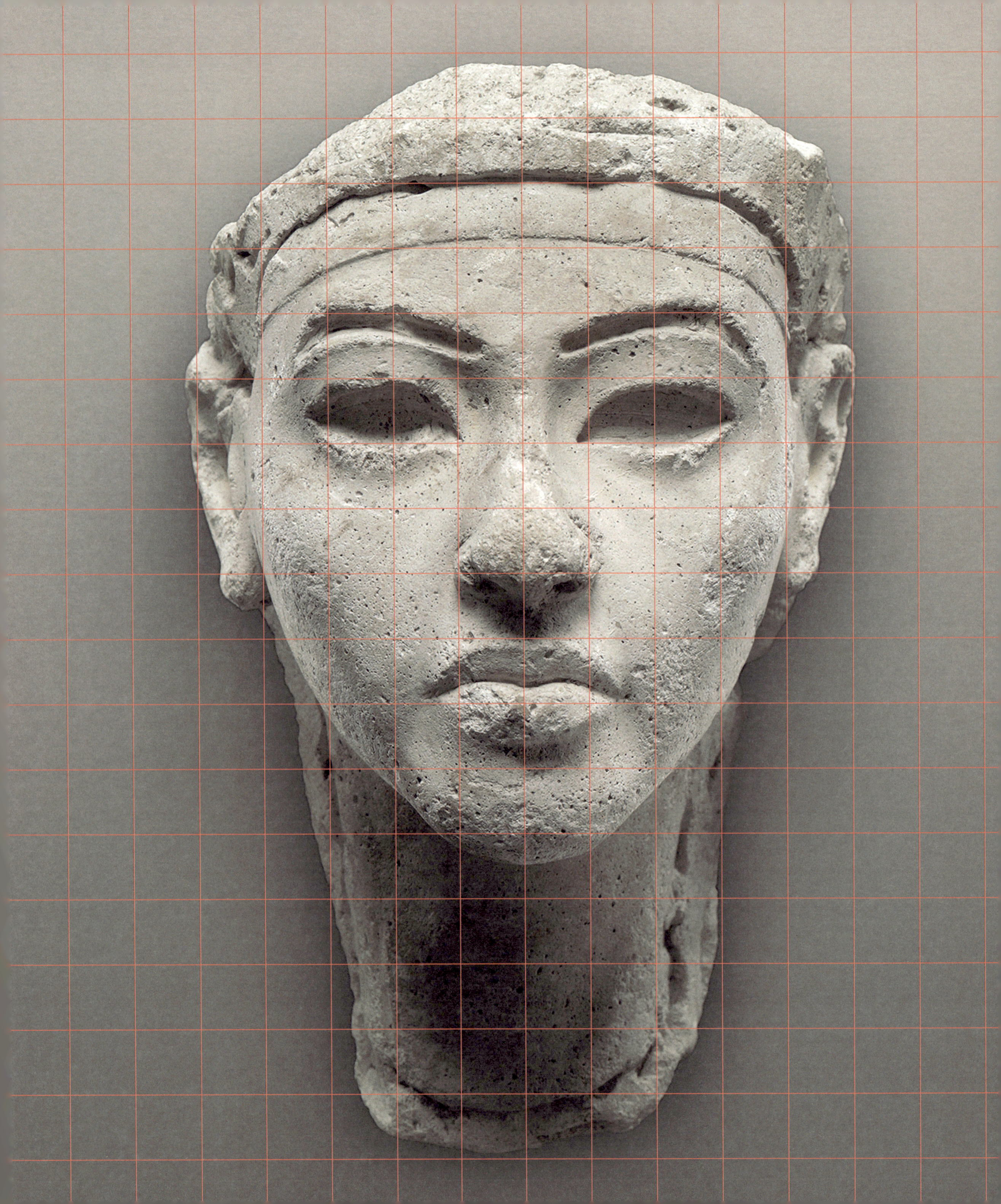

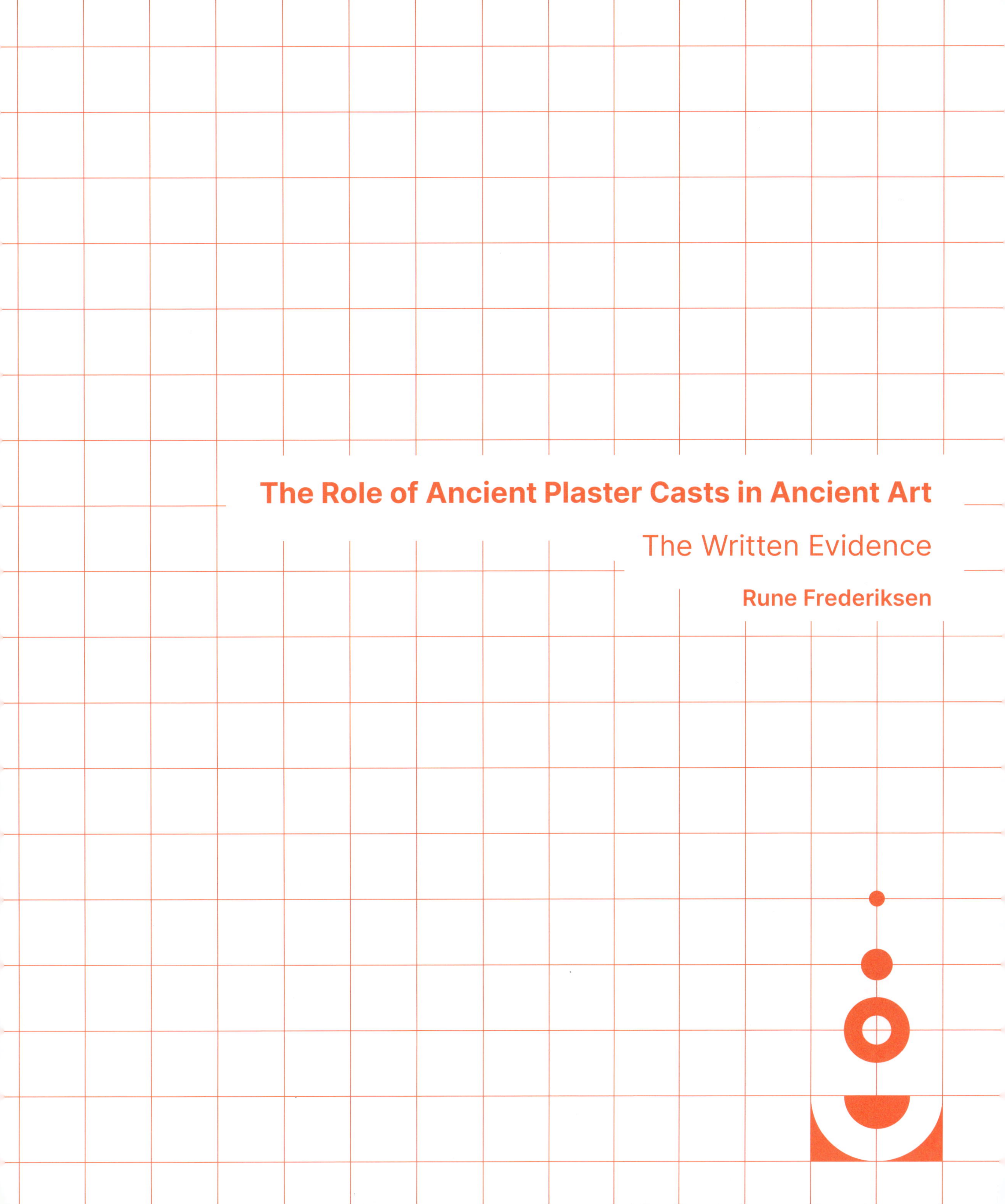

The Role of Ancient Plaster Casts in Ancient Art

The Written Evidence

Rune Frederiksen

The Role of Ancient Plaster Casts in Ancient Art

The Written Evidence

Rune Frederiksen

I would like to begin this article by congratulating the Museum of Fine Arts in Budapest on the great task of having re-installed and re-opened the old cast collection to the public in the two very different locations.[1] It is a reassuring experience to be able to witness an important European art institution taking all its collections seriously and it is a great honour to have been invited to speak at the seminar to mark this opening and likewise to publish in the present book.

Denmark has a collection comparable in nature to the one we are celebrating today, but much larger. The collection is stored in a warehouse built in 1784 (fig. 1), at a very prominent address in the harbour of Copenhagen and comprises some 2,000 casts (figs. 2–3).

The collection in Copenhagen was saved from destruction in the mid-1980s and the museum opened to the public in 1995, only to be shut down again and the staff to be dismissed in 2002. Since then, for the past twenty years, the collection has had to fight for its survival. This is despite the fact that Denmark is a very wealthy nation, and the collection, building, and location together offer such a potential that one wonders if there have been any greater missed opportunities in the whole of Europe in recent years.[2] Now to the topic of this article.

Studies on the technique of sculpture not only consider the role of plaster in the sculptural process as soon as the discussion moves beyond that of direct carving,[3] but also usually provide ample space to acknowledge the role of the ancient world in the developments of sculptural techniques.

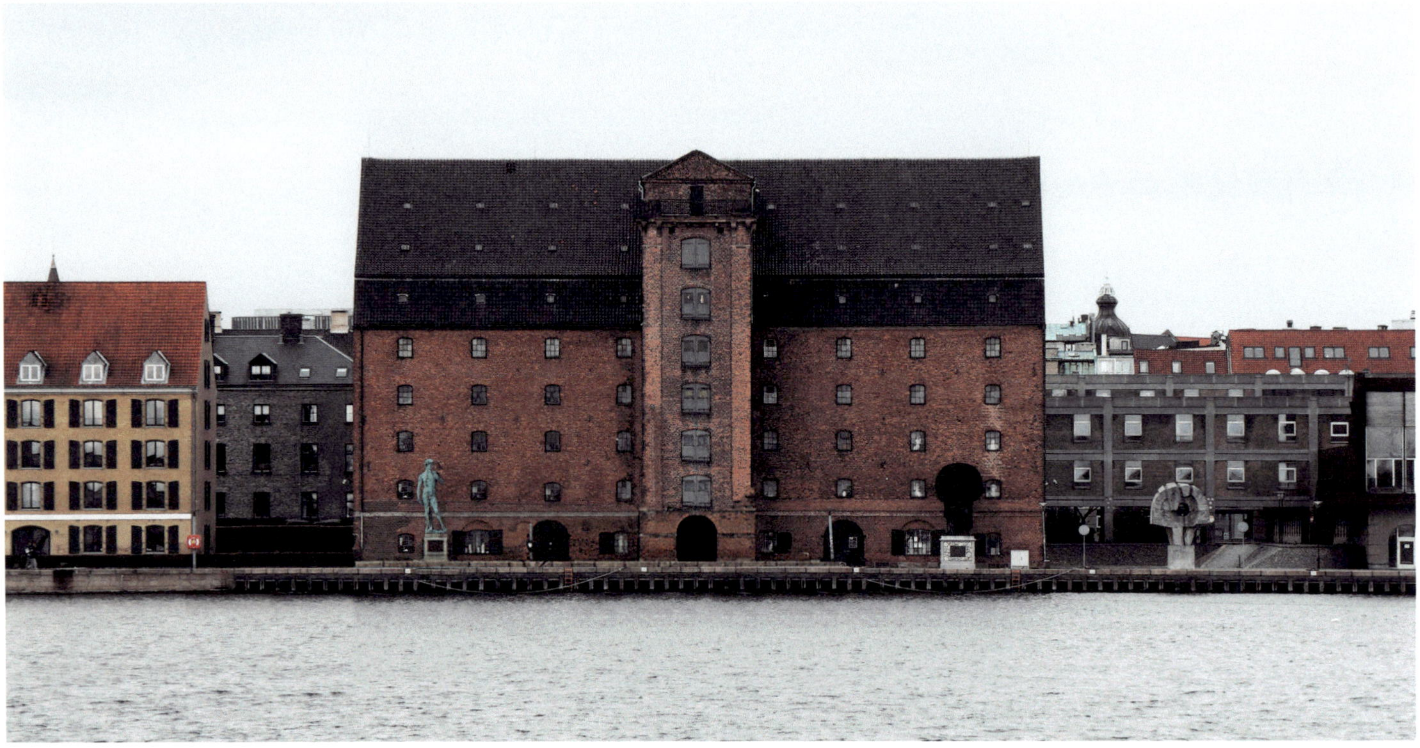

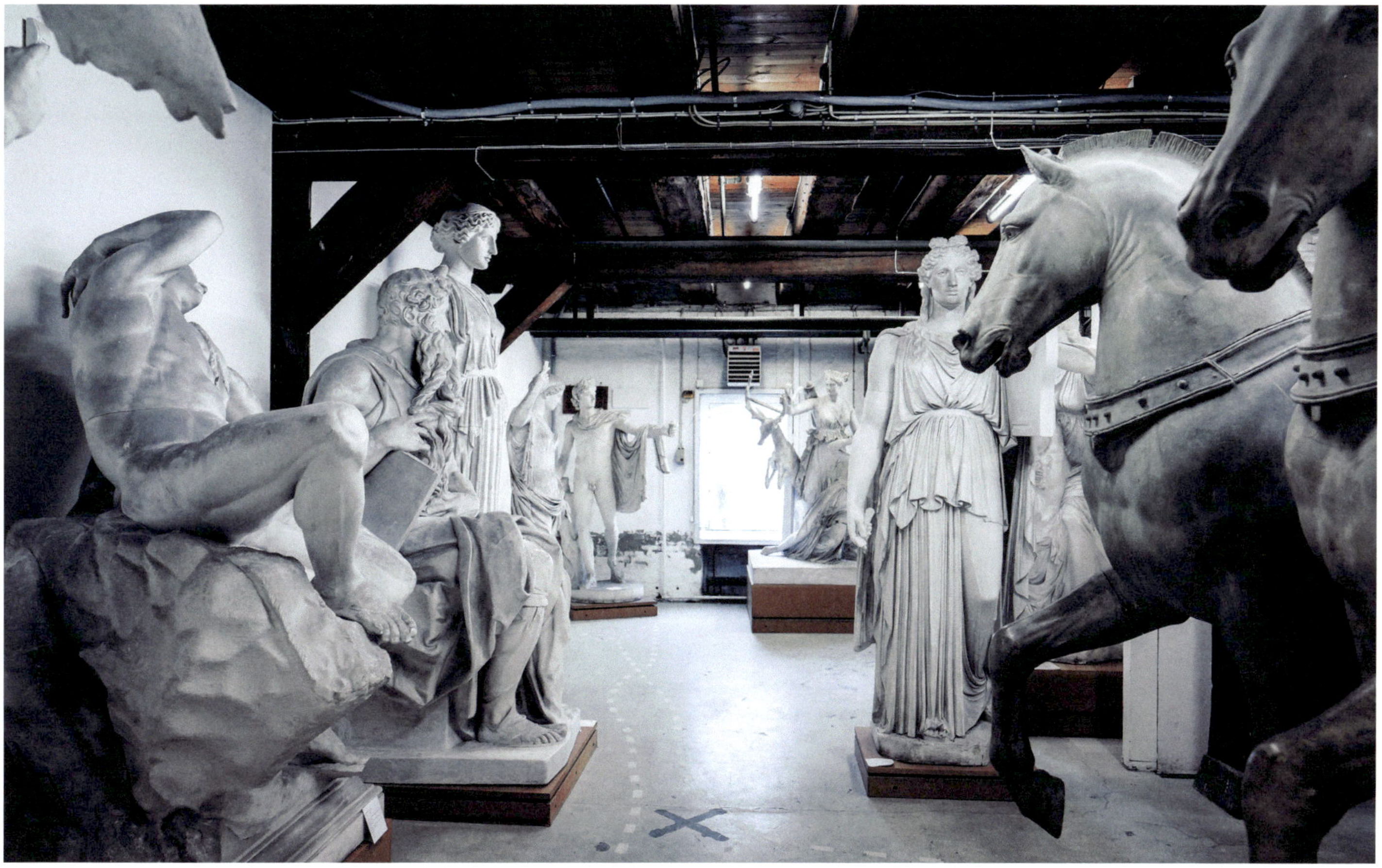

By contrast, discussions on the establishment of collections of plaster casts of sculpture, for good reasons, tend to only cover the centuries from the Renaissance up to modern times.[4]

Plaster casts were used extensively by artists and artisans in antiquity. This we know because of finds consisting of fragments of ancient casts, such as the famous Egyptian examples from the workshop of the sculptor Thutmose in Amarna in the Egyptian desert (fig. 4).[5]

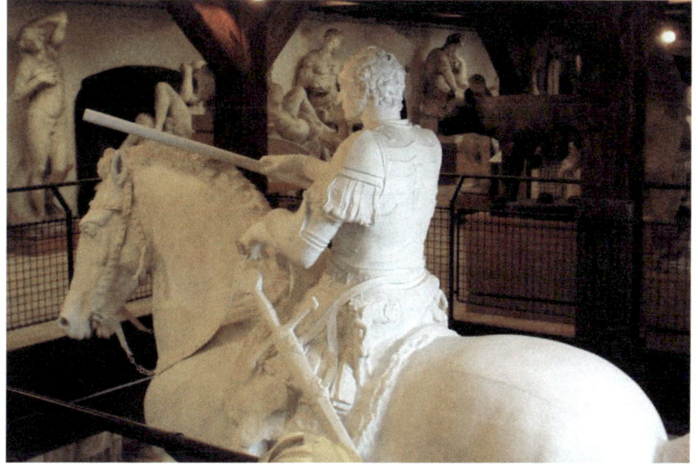

Fig. 1 | previous page

West Indian Warehouse in Copenhagen
(designed by C. F. Harsdorph, 1784)
housing the Royal Cast Collection since 1985

Fig. 2

View of the ground floor of the Cast Gallery, Copenhagen

Fig. 3

View of the second floor of the Cast Gallery, Copenhagen

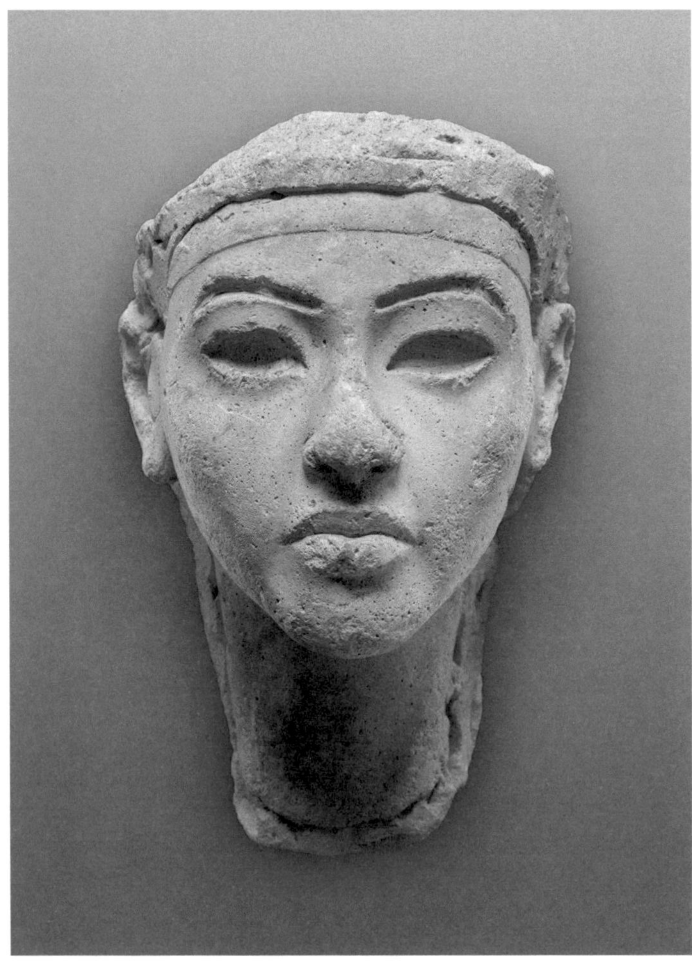

observation of preserved ancient sculpture in stone and metal. Before we take a closer look at these other sources, let us first consider what purposes casts served in ancient art. Plaster casts were used in all sorts of ways then, as they were later and still are today, primarily to transfer form from one material to another and from one place to another.

The transfer of form is an aspect of ancient art which cannot be underestimated. In the Egyptian and ancient Greek worlds, such transfers were constantly required when artists and craftsmen created sculpture,[6] both large-scale monumental sculpture as well as smaller-scale crafts such as toreutics.[7] Ornamental decorations on buildings were also produced in accordance with exacting standards, and we have every reason to believe that patterns used in architecture, which had to be precise in detail and proportion, must have been carried out with the aid of detailed templates, for example, in plaster.[8]

However, even though the ancient Greek world, encompassing at least one thousand city states,[9] generated more sculpture in pure numerical terms than any other culture in the entirety of world history, the vast majority of it comprised original works which were produced as grave markers, honorific monuments for victorious athletes and so forth; that is, monuments that were produced only once for a very specific purpose, never intended to be recreated in multiple versions or copies.

When the power of the Roman world started to gain momentum in the late Republic of the second and first centuries BC, the need for monuments increased, as did interest in the monumental art of the Greeks,[10] and this launched the most significant epoch for copying and reproducing sculptural art, at least until modern times. This was the period covering the later Republican era and the entire imperial period, until the third century AD, when the practice slowly waned. In those centuries, the Romans transferred an enormous number of Greek statues, reproductions as well as prototypes, from sanctuaries and public urban spaces in the Greek world to the main centres of Roman power, primarily in the Italian peninsula, especially Rome itself.[11]

Not until the late nineteenth century in Europe did the world see a similar rise in the numbers of replicas made of sculpture.[12] This was when all the major cast collections were established, including the one whose reinstallation we are celebrating in Budapest.

From the classical world, the most important find is the one made at Baia in the bay of Naples. Among the Baia fragments are a number of moulds directly cast from ancient Greek masterpieces, such as the bronze original to the *Apollo Belvedere* in the Vatican and the famous group the *Tyrant Slayers* (fig. 5).

One of the fragments from this group was the left half of the face of *Aristogeiton*, here inserted in a cast from another ancient Roman marble copy of the group (fig. 6).

A modern cast of the ancient face fragment of Aristogeiton from the cast of the group of the *Tyrant Slayers* fitted into a modern cast of a Roman marble copy of the original group. We are also informed about the use of plaster casts by written ancient Greek and Roman sources as well as from indirect

Fig. 4

Plaster cast of the portrait of Akhenaten
from the workshop of Tutmosis in Amarna, now in Berlin

Plaster casts played a key role in the workshops of Roman sculptors,[13] and we have already seen the remains of ancient plaster casts which provide hands-on proof of this phenomenon. If plaster casts played as significant a role in the ancient world as we have just determined, then we would expect to find plenty of sources describing such casts from various points of view, and indeed we do.

First of all, there was an awareness of plaster as a *material*. The famous pupil of Aristotle, Theophrastus, writing around 300 BC, relates in his book *On Stones* how plaster, called *gypsos*, exists in many places around the Mediterranean as a natural mineral. He also tells us how it behaves when pulverised and mixed with water.[14] There is no doubt that what he describes is what we know as *plaster of Paris* produced from burning certain stones, as he says the ancients did in Phoenicia and Syria, for example, marble. Etymologically, of course, the ancient Greek *gypsos* is what lives on in Latin as *gypsum*, in German as *Gips,* and in Italian as *gesso*, to mention just a few examples.

Almost contemporaneous with Theophrastus's text is this handsome little piece (figs. 7a-b), believed to be a third- or second-century BC cast of a nose piece from a harness (it would have rested on the muzzle of a horse). It is of plaster and depicts a seated warrior in front of a trophy. This is another example of ancient plaster casts, similar to the ones we saw earlier. What is interesting here is that it bears an inscription, incised while the plaster was still wet (fig. 7b).

The Greek text reads "Ἰσιδώρου τὸ γύψινον", which translates as 'the [work] of plaster [is] of Isidoros'.

The purpose of the inscription may have been to inform anyone intending to produce a new nose piece based on this plaster image of a warrior that the great artist who invented the design was named Isidoros. Another possibility is that the plaster was used for advertisement, perhaps one of a number of examples of works that could be ordered at the workshop of Isidoros. The text uses *gypsos* in its adjectival form, 'of plaster', rather than the noun *gypsos*, so from this inscription alone it is not clear whether the Greeks around 300 BC referred to a plaster cast as a noun, deriving from the name of the material *gypsos*. Luckily, other extant texts verify that indeed they did, but more on this later.

Texts from the Greek period that refer directly to plaster casts and the process of copying are few and far between – we have to search among the Greek and Latin texts of Roman times to learn more. The most likely reason for this is the fact that, as mentioned earlier, the art of copying practically exploded in the Roman world. The Greeks did produce copies, but this seems to have been mostly for precious metalware and toreutics, and for other intermediate processes of sculpture between the original modelling in clay or wax and the finished work in stone or metal.

This is also the impression we derive from the words of one of the greatest Roman connoisseurs of Greek art, namely Pliny the Elder. Pliny was the author of *Naturalis Historia* (NH), finished in the Flavian period, probably in the year 79 AD, and it contains long passages on Greek art, including sculpture.

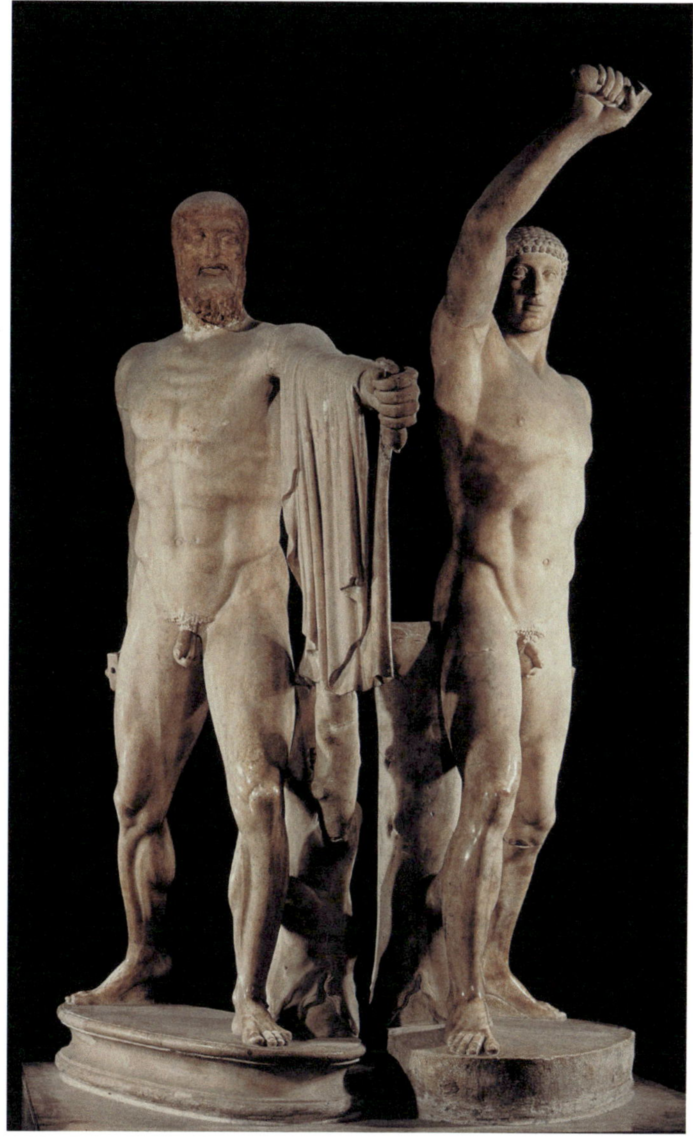

Fig. 5

Tyrant Slayers of Kritios and Nesiotes (Roman copy in marble)
Museo Archeologico Nazionale, Naples

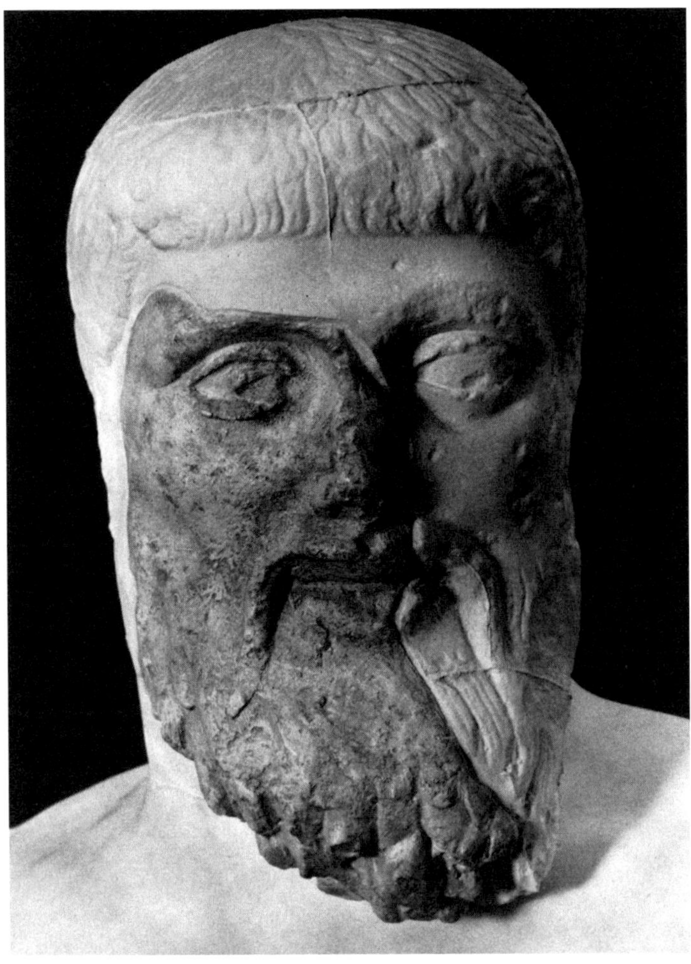

Pliny *NH* 35.153:[15] "The first person who modelled a likeness in plaster of a human being from the living face itself and established the method of pouring wax into the plaster mould and then making final corrections on the wax cast, was Lysistratus of Sicyon, the brother of Lysippus of whom we have spoken."

Here, in book 35, Pliny says that a certain Lysistratus of Sicyon, brother of the famous sculptor Lysippus, invented the practice of casting the face of a person, which we know as a life mask. Pliny also says that Lysistratus invented the very method to take a cast of a statue, and that this invention revolutionised the technique of sculpture completely.

Also in book 35, Pliny writes:[16] "The same artist also invented taking casts from statues [... *idem et de signis effigies exprimere invenit* ...], and this method advanced to such an extent that no figures or statues were made without a clay model. This shows that the knowledge of modelling in clay was older than that of casting bronze."

The important phrases are ... *gypso e facie ipsa*..., which means "... plaster from the face itself ..." and later, ... *in eam formam gypsi infusa* ..., "... and poured plaster in the form ..."

We know from the finds of Egyptian casts, some of which we saw earlier (fig. 4), that this invention originated even further back in time, so Pliny is of course not correct when he attributes the invention to Lysistratus. For the Romans, however, this was a minor detail. When they suddenly found themselves in the middle of a world filled with Greek art and artists, the need almost automatically arose for a mythology on the origin of the visual arts and its various subdisciplines, of which working with plaster was one. The Roman interaction with Egyptian culture was characterised more by a distant fascination and exoticism, and probably nobody had a clear idea about the extent to which the Egyptians had in fact been the prime movers in many technological aspects of the ancient world, which was not insignificant. Certainly, when it came to art, some inventions were attributed to the Egyptians,[17] others clearly not.

Pliny writes in Latin, and the word he uses (NH 35.153) for plaster, *gypsum*, is the same as the Greek *gypsos*, clearly a loan word from Greek into Latin. Pliny provides us with an example of the word's usage for an object made from the material, the *gypso e facie*, as well as the word used for the material, *gypsi infusa*. So here, we see the use of the word 'plaster' in exactly the same way as today, which strictly speaking implies a 'cast'. The passage in Pliny (35.153) describes how Lysistratus invented the casting of statues. By *effigies* he means 'precise three-dimensional depictions (of something)', and this something is a *signum*, one of the Latin words for statue. *Exprimere* means to press or press out.[18]

An act of copying in this way, as described in Pliny, is probably what is also referred to by Plutarch in his *On the Cleverness of Animals* (*De sollertia animalium* = Moralia 984b) written in the second century AD. In an event which likely took place around 300 BC, envoys of the Egyptian king Ptolemy the First were aided by a dolphin to find their way, and as a sign of gratitude they were to remove a certain statue from their starting point, Sinope on the Black Sea coast, but to leave another in its place after having taken a copy of it.

The Plutarch quote (Mor. 984b) reads:[19] "Whence it came about that when they had offered thanksgiving for their safe landing, they came to see that of the two statues they should take away the one depicting Pluto but should merely take an impress [ἀπομάξασται - apomáxastai] of that of Persephone and leave it behind."

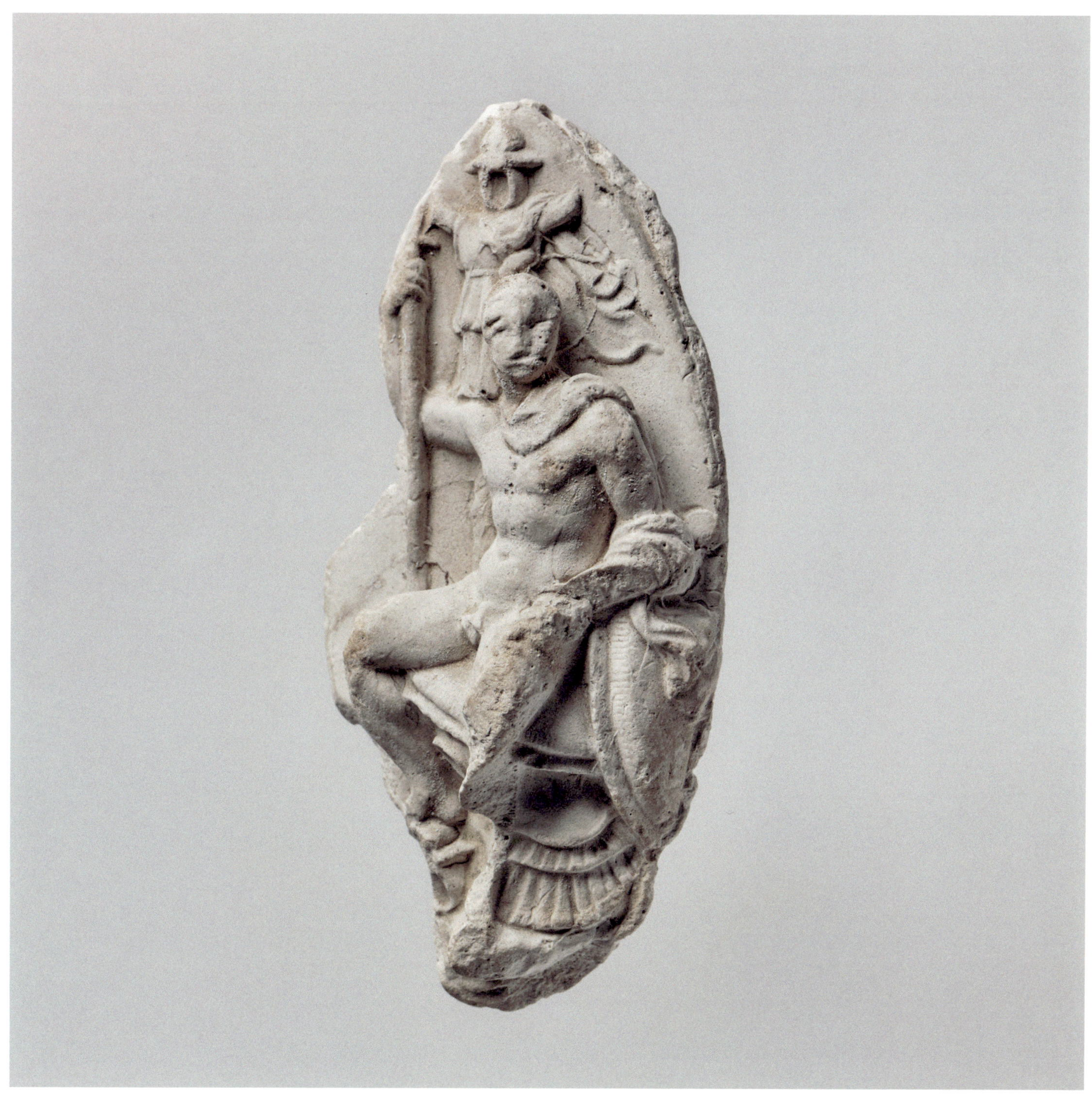

Fig. 6 | previous page

Face of *Aristogeiton*, the elder of the *Tyrant Slayers*
Fragment of head from plaster cast of the statue of Aristogeiton,
from Baia near Naples, Italy

A cast of the mould has been fitted into the cast of Roman marble head,
which is a copy of the original Greek bronze (made via a cast)

Fig. 7a

Nose piece from a harness (prometopídion), front side
Seated warrior before a trophy, third–second centuries BC
Princeton University Art Collection

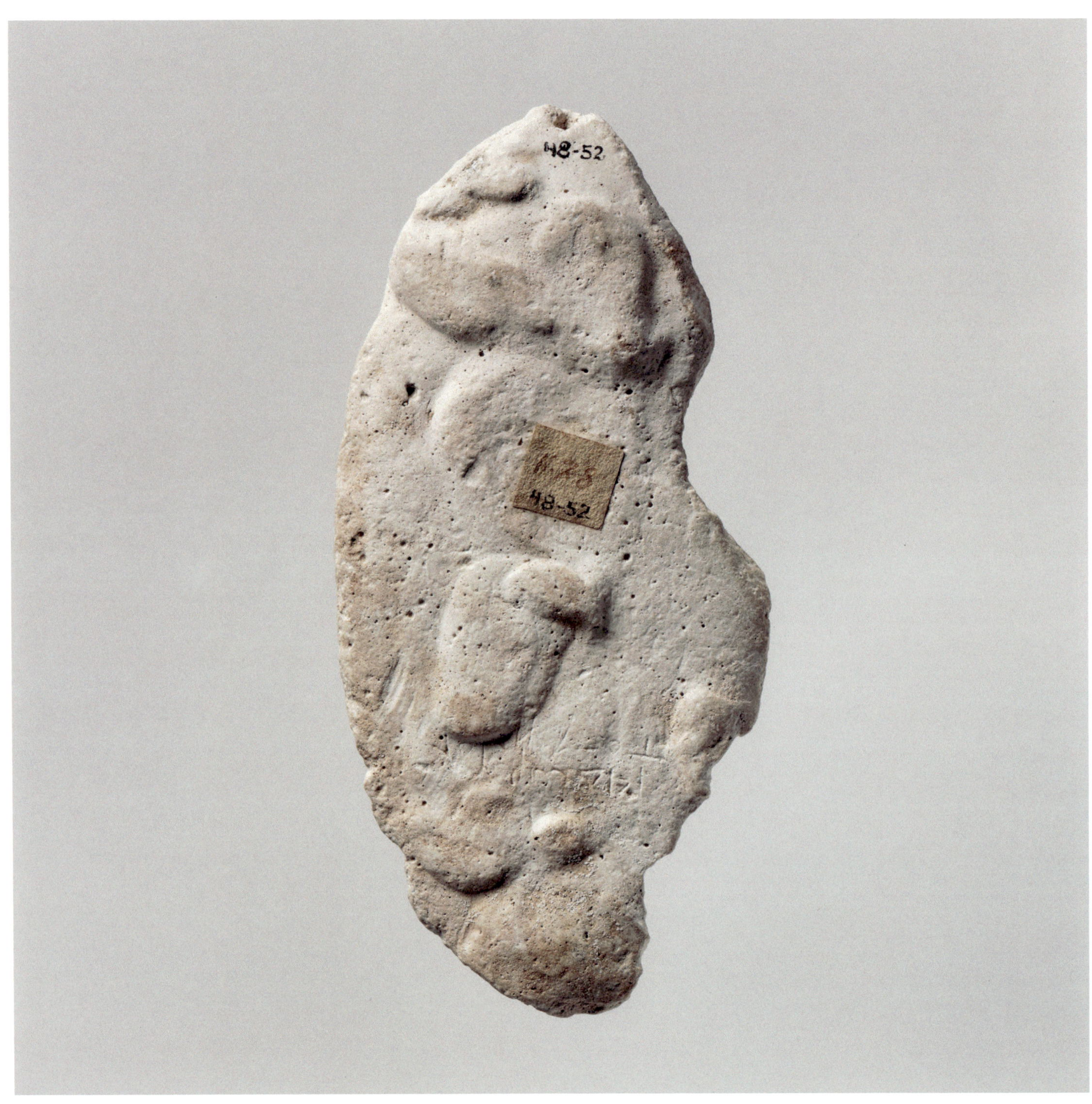

Fig. 7b

Nose piece from a harness (back side of fig. 7a)
with incised inscription

Fig. 8 | next page

Head from the Portrait Statue of Chrysippos
Head of the Stoic School in Athens
Roman first century AD, marble copy of an ancient Greek
third-century BC bronze portrait
Ny Carlsberg Glyptotek, Copenhagen

Plutarch writes in Greek and does not speak of *gypsos*. He uses the verb *apomásso* (in the medial form aorist infinitive, *apomáxastai*), which exactly means to model a statue, when the verb is used in the medial form. Now, *model* could mean that the envoys of Ptolemy *modelled* a copy by hand in clay of the statue of Persephone instead of casting it. This interpretation, that they modelled a copy, does not really make sense, however, since doing so would have been very time-consuming, and moreover, the modelled figure would have had to be cast in plaster afterwards anyway. It therefore follows that the correct reading of the passage must be that the envoys made a plaster cast of the statue of Persephone.

That *apomásso* in fact means, or could mean 'to make a mould in plaster' can be inferred from another Greek text, written somewhat later than Plutarch, in the first half of the third century AD. This concerns a certain Philostratus writing about the life of the famous Apollonius of Tyana. Here Apollonius is having an imagined discussion with a group of men about the looks of certain statues of the gods. One of them says to Apollonius:

"Your artists, then, like Phidias," said the other, "and like Praxiteles, went up, I suppose to heaven and took a copy [ἀπομαξάμενοι - *apomaxámenoi*] of the forms of the gods, and then reproduced these by their art or was there any other influence which presided over and guided their moulding [πλάττειν - *pláttein*]?"[20]

We notice, again, the use of *apomaxámenoi* (from *apomásso*) and we have a new verb *plásso* here in the infinitive *pláttein* which means 'to put in form'.

Another interesting text which gives us useful information is both amusing and unusual. This is a dialogue authored by Lucian of Samosata, in southern Turkey close to the border to Syria, dated between 120–200 AD. In the dialogue, the Greek god Zeus is in discussion with the hero Heracles, and Zeus makes the following comment of a statue located in the Athenian marketplace:

"Oh yes, it is your brother, Hermes, the one of the public square, beside the painted porch. At any rate he is all covered with pitch from the casts taken [ἐκματτόμενος – *ekmatómenos*] every day by the statue-makers."[21]

Important here is *ekmatómenos*, which is a participle form of *ekmásso*, which is similar to *apomásso*.

We can learn much about the technique and use of plaster casts by reading ancient Greek and Roman texts. However, there are challenges when relying on such texts, which are often notoriously ambiguous in their meaning.

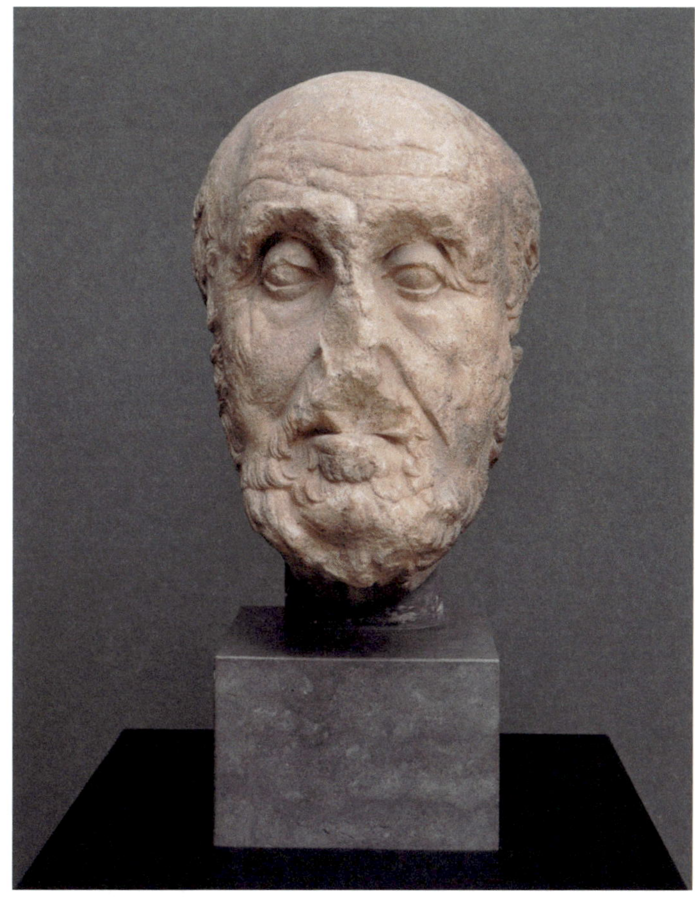

This we shall see in the next example, which we find among the lines authored by the learned Greek-speaking, second-century AD traveller Pausanias. Pausanias wrote what is usually referred to as the only preserved travel guide of the ancient Greek world, a description of some of the most important regions, written for tourists from the Roman elite – and other Greek-speaking citizens of the world at the time. Pausanias provides rich descriptions of a number of cities and sanctuaries, and of their monuments, while many of the events and circumstances he relates are anecdotal and were recorded many centuries after they happened. Nonetheless, much of what can be found in his writings is credible, and often Pausanias is our only source of certain information on a statue or a building from the ancient Greek world. In the passage here, Pausanias is on his way to the ancient Greek city state Thespiai in Boiotia (probably to visit the important sanctuary in the Valley of the Muses at Mount Helikon in its territory). He describes the harbour town Creusis and says:

"Creusis, the harbour of Thespiai, has nothing to show publicly, but at the home of a private person, I found an image of Dionysos made of gypsum, and adorned with painting."[22]

The important words in Greek are *agalma en Dionysou gypsou pepoeimenon* (ἄγαλμα ἦν Διονύσου γύψου πεποιημένον). We learn that the *agalma*, the statue of Dionysos, is made of gypsum, not *how* it was made. Strictly speaking it could have been modelled or carved from gypsum, rather than cast.

The latter is of course the more likely since stone and clay were the preferred materials for carving and modelling. We cannot, however, be sure solely on the basis of the text itself.

We possess examples from the Roman Latin textual universe where the reading is still not clear, but the reasons for interpreting them in a certain direction are even stronger. One such example can be found in the lines of the Roman satirical poet Juvenal, who, in his second book of satires, makes fun of middle-class Romans:

"I would fain flee Sarmatia and the frozen Sea when people who ape the Curii and live like Bacchanals dare talk about morals. In the first place, they are unlearned persons, though you may find their houses crammed with plaster casts of Chrysippus [*gypso Chrysippi*]; for their greatest hero is the man who has bought a likeness of Aristotle or Pittacus, or bids his shelves preserve an original portrait of Cleanthes."[23]

The middle-class Romans are ridiculed and derided for their ignorance. That they filled their houses with plaster busts of the Greek stoic philosopher Chrysippus (279–206 BC) is viewed as an attempt at feigning learnedness, and the term *gypso Chrysippi* is almost certainly discrediting. Had Juvenal simply said *imago* (or *signum*) *Chrysippi,* meaning an image or portrait of Chrysippus, it would have been implicit that the piece in question was made of bronze or perhaps rather marble. Explicitly referring to the fact that the portraits in the homes of certain ambitious citizens of Rome were made of plaster can only be assumed to have had a negative intent.

The translation of Juvenal can perhaps be challenged, as poetry is not always easily transformed into completely clear and unambiguous prose. The word "bust", for example, is not in the text, but it is known that busts were extremely popular among Romans, whereas the ancient Greeks preferred full-length portraits.[24] *Gypso Chrysippi* must therefore mean not simply a plaster (of whatever fabrication) of the ancient Greek philosopher Chrysippus, but a *plaster cast* of a head or bust of him. Here we assume that Juvenal was referring to "busts" as this was the preferred medium among Romans for sculptural portraits in the private sphere. Heads were not really used or exhibited alone without either the upper part of the body, as in a bust, or the entire body.[25] Interestingly, a reading of Juvenal suggests that a number of households in Rome (and beyond) possessed plaster casts of portrait busts of philosophers as well as other categories of important people, such as poets, politicians and generals, exhibited as part of the interior paraphernalia. However, as far as I am aware, we have found no such plaster busts. The fragile nature and low value of plaster means that many or most of them must have been lost even before the end of antiquity, while any that did survive are likely to have been destroyed in the subsequent centuries.[26] The ancient plaster casts that have come down to us are typically death masks or heads/busts with inserted death masks, produced for the purpose of making proper sculptural portraits of the deceased in other materials.[27]

A number of marble heads and busts of the Greek philosopher Chrysippus have been preserved, including one in the Ny Carlsberg Glyptotek in Copenhagen (fig. 8). They all look pretty much the same, as do most of the other portraits of Greek personalities in the Roman collections of imperial times. Recognition was important to the Romans, and it would be wrong to imagine that plaster heads of Chrysippus in private Roman contexts were not exactly like this one, only in plaster (gypsum) instead of marble. It would not have made any sense for the owner to have a plaster version that was not as immediately recognisable as one in marble.

The use of plaster casts as substitutes for sculptures in other media is not something unique to the nineteenth century. The Romans apparently also pursued this practice. There can be no doubt that Romans assembled collections of plaster casts, given that sculptors' workshops kept such ensembles as a kind of "catalogue" from which clients could choose which piece(s) they wanted to order in stone or metal. We do not know, however, if collections as we know them today, such as the nineteenth-century collection of the Museum of Fine Arts, Budapest, already existed in the world of the Romans two thousand years ago. The south Italian collection that is known from its famous fragments definitely existed, probably in Baia in imperial times. This was most likely a sculptor's showroom, rather than a museum for sculptural learning, although as the evidence stands, we cannot be completely certain.

Notes

1 See Szőcs 2021A.

2 For the story of the Danish Royal Cast Collection since its installation in the West Indian Warehouse in 1985, see Bencard et al. 2005, and the homepage of the Friends of the Royal Cast Collection (www.gipsen.dk [in Danish]; last accessed 25 October 2022).

3 Cf. Penny 1993, 196–97.

4 On the apparent lack of veritable collections of casts in antiquity, beyond those of workshops, see Frederiksen 2010, 35. Cf. e.g., Marchand 2010, 49–79.

5 Arnold 1996, 46–47, figs. 43, 45.

6 Landwehr 1985 and Frederiksen 2010, both with references to earlier literature.

7 For a general treatment of plaster casts used in toreutics, discussed around the significant finds of casts and likely workshop at Memphis in Egypt, see e.g., the comprehensive study by Reinsberg 1980. See also Frederiksen 2010, 22–23.

8 There is no complete agreement among scholars concerning how, and indeed if specific capitals, columns or other larger parts of certain buildings were usually copied as cast, or whether copying and inspiration were implemented with the use of other means.

9 Hansen and Nielsen 2004, 54.

10 Kleiner 1992, 29.

11 Ibid., 27–29. For a comprehensive treatment of the topic, see Pape 1975.

12 The production of plaster casts from ancient sculpture in Europe since the Enlightenment is not precisely the same as the Roman reproduction of ancient Greek sculpture. The Romans made plaster casts of the Greek statues primarily to make new Roman sculptures in marble, based on those Greek prototypes.

13 Cf. Boardman 1994, 286–88.

14 Theoph. *Peri Lithon,* transl.: "Gypsum is produced in Great quantities in the island of Cyprus, where it lies open, and easy to be discovered, and come at, the workmen having but very little earth to take away before they get it. In Phoenicia and Syria they also have gypsum, which they make by burning certain Stones." Greek text: ἡ δὲ γύψος γίνεται πλείστη μὲν ἐν Κύπρῳ καὶ περιφανεστάτη. Μικρὸν γὰρ ἀφαιροῦσι τῆς γῆς ὀρύττοντες. ἐν Φοινίκῃ δὲ καὶ ἐν Συρίᾳ καίοντες τοὺς λίθους ποιοῦσιν.

15 "Hominis autem imaginem gypso e facie ipsa primus omnium expressit ceraque in eam formam gypsi infusa emendare instisuit Lysistratus Sicyonius, frater Lysippi, de quo diximus." Transl. H. Rackham in the Loeb edition.

16 "... idem et de signis effigies exprimere invenit, crevitque res in tantum, ut nulla signa statuave sine argilla fierint. quo apparet antiquiorem hanc fuisse scientiam quam fundendi acris." Transl. H. Rackham in the Loeb edition.

17 Diodorus Siculus 1.98.5-9.

18 For these three words, see Liddell, Scott, and Jones 1958.[9]

19 "ὅθεν ἀναβατήρια θύσαντες, ἔγνωσαν ὅτι δεῖ δυεῖν ἀγαλμάτων τὸ μὲν τοῦ πλούτονος ἀνελέσται καὶ κομίζειν, τὸ δὲ τῆς Κόρης ἀπομάξασται καὶ καταλιπεῖν" (Plut. Mor. 984b).

20 Vita apollonii 6.19: οἱ Φειδίαι δὲʼ εἶπε:ʹκαὶ οἱ Πραξιτέλεις μῶν ἀνελθόντες ἐς οὐρανὸν καὶ ἀπομαξάμενοι τὰ τῶν θεῶν εἴδη τέχνην αὐτὰ ἐποιοῦντο, ἢ ἕτερόν τι ἦν, ὃ ἐφίστη αὐτοὺς τῷ πλάττειν. Philostratus, transl. Conybeare in the Loeb edition.

21 Loukianos, translated by the author. Zeus Tragoedus 33: "μᾶλλον δὲ ὁ σός, ὦ Ἑρμῆ, ἀδελφός ἐστιν, ὁ ἀγοραῖος, ὁ παρὰ τὴν Ποικίλην πίττης γοῦν ἀναπέπλησται ὀσημέραι ἐκματτόμενος ὑπὸ τῶν ἀνδριαντοποιῶν." Translated by Harmon in the Loeb: "oh yes, it is your brother, Hermes, the one of the public square, beside the painted porch. At any rate he is all covered with pitch from the casts taken every day by the workers in bronze for the sculptors." Harmon's translation differs on one essential issue: he apparently introduces "workers in bronze" because he believes that the forms made must be such for bronze casting. This does not really make sense, and the precise meaning of the text is "... forms being made by the sculptors". This must mean forms in which to reproduce the statues in plaster; there is no other meaningful explanation.

22 Paus. Perieg. 9.32.1: "τοῖς δὲ ἐν Κρεύσιδι, ἐπινείῳ τῷ Θεσπιέων, οἰκοῦσιν ἐν κοινῷ μέν ἐστιν οὐδέν, ἐν ἰδιώτου δὲ ἀνδρὸς ἄγαλμα ἦν Διονύσου γύψου πεποιημένον καὶ ἐπικεκοσμημένον γραφῇ."

23 Juv. Sat. 2.1–7: "Ultra Sauromatas fugere hinc libet et glacialem Occeanum, quotiens aliquid de moribus audent qui Curios simulant et Bacchanalia vivunt. Indocti primum, quamquam plena omnia gypso Chrysippi invenias; nam perfectissimus horum, si quis Aristotelen similem vel Pittacon emit et iubet archetypos pluteum servare Cleanthas." Translated by Ramsay 1930.

24 Kleiner 1992, 24; Richter and Smith 1984, 15.

25 The many ancient heads we see in museums today are simply broken from their busts or statues and would have made a strange impression to an ancient Roman eye, as indeed would the lack of polychromy on the sculptures.

26 A few plaster casts preserved to our time may constitute such ancient Roman portrait busts, see e.g., the fine bust from Alexandria in Egypt, Frederiksen 2010, 18–19, with fig. 1. 6 and 26–27, no. 3a. Ancient plaster casts have been found all over the Ancient World of the Mediterranean, but as they are very fragile, we should not be surprised to find an entire plaster bust in ancient Roman Egypt. The desert climate preserved much fragile material, which originally would have been everywhere, such as papyrus, cloth and other organically based human products, but which has disappeared almost entirely except for in the Egyptian context, with its stabile, dry climate since antiquity.

27 See Frederiksen 2010, 18–20.

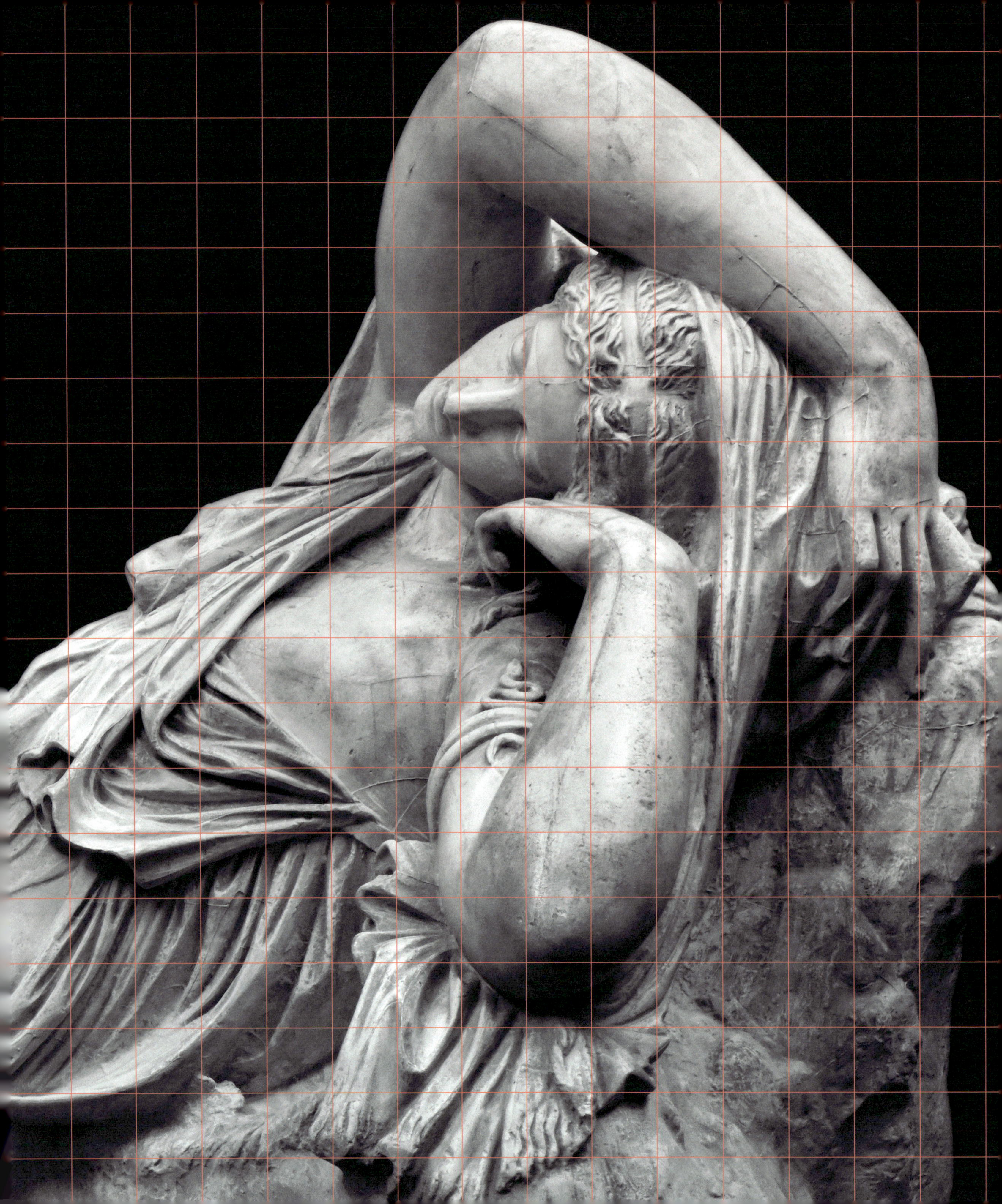

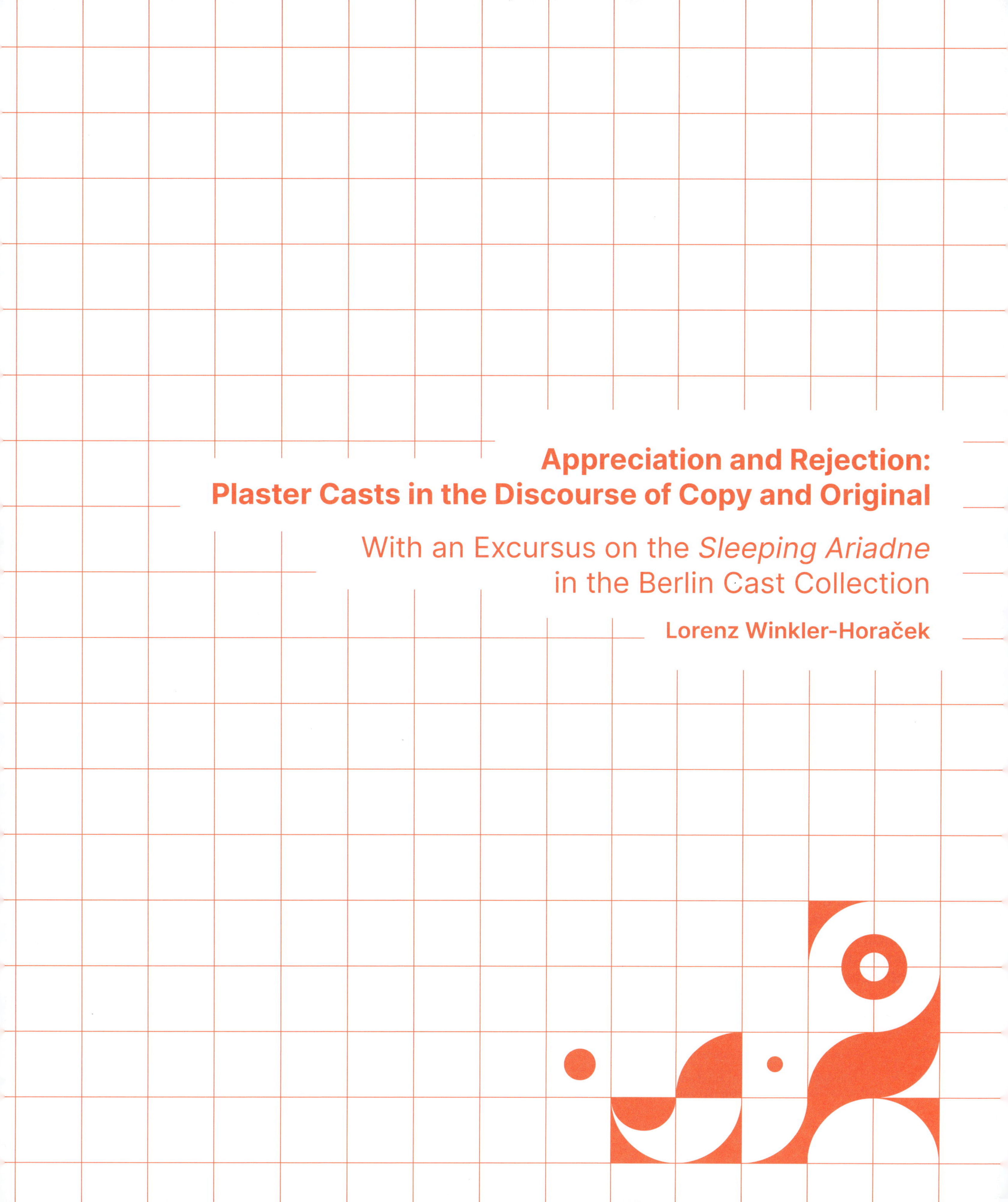

Appreciation and Rejection: Plaster Casts in the Discourse of Copy and Original

With an Excursus on the *Sleeping Ariadne* in the Berlin Cast Collection

Lorenz Winkler-Horaček

Appreciation and Rejection: Plaster Casts in the Discourse of Copy and Original

With an Excursus on the *Sleeping Ariadne* in the Berlin Cast Collection

Lorenz Winkler-Horaček

At the Budapest conference in May 2022, attendees were introduced to the plaster cast collection of the Museum of Fine Arts, Budapest. Their re-exhibition in the renewed Star Fortress in Komárom impressed with its curated display of excellently restored casts in well-lit rooms. The chronologically arranged sculptures could be regarded from new perspectives resulting from the different viewing angles afforded by openings in the casemates of the fortress.

This new presentation of the casts was honoured by the 2021 volume *Rebirth of a Collection*.[1] The term "rebirth" says a lot about the history of the collection in its own right – one which is shared with many other plaster cast collections in Europe and worldwide: a period of veneration and extensive purchasing of casts in the nineteenth and twentieth centuries, which was later followed by a phase of neglect and partial destruction that has in the past few decades been redeemed by a newfound appreciation for these objects.

When we work with casts today and call attention to their renewed popularity, we should also simultaneously consider their history. It is precisely because we value them now that we should engage with their rejection as it prevailed to some extent in the twentieth century. This is connected to the question: Where do we stand today? In the following lines, the shift in the appreciation – and, above all, the rejection – of casts will be summarised using the Berlin collection, among others, as an example. This is part of a larger project.[2] As a clear plea for the casts, the common separation of "original" and "copy" will subsequently be questioned by examining the statue of the *Sleeping Ariadne* as a case study.

By way of introduction, it is worth drawing a certain parallel between the cast collections in Berlin and Budapest. This is one that exists with numerous other collections and therefore only appears here as a representative example. When Ferenc Pulszky, director of the Hungarian National Museum beginning in 1869, first assembled an extensive cast collection, he was acting in accordance with a widespread idea of the time: a museum should provide a comprehensive representation of the art of humanity.[3] Pulszky drew inspiration from the British Museum, but lacking original artworks of his own, he could only implement this idea with the help of plaster casts. A similar starting point had also existed in Berlin a few years earlier.

The Cast Surpasses the Original?

Even though the Berlin Cast Collection had been founded as early as 1696, it – like many other collections – reached its apogee over the course of the nineteenth century. According to the eighteenth- and early nineteenth-century perception of art, pure white plaster casts were considered as valuable as (or more valuable than) the originals.[4] In the later course of the nineteenth century, the value of the casts increasingly lay in their potential for didactic completeness. Ignaz Maria von Olfers, director general of the Königliche Museen (Royal Museums) in Berlin since 1839, particularly encouraged the creation of a large plaster cast collection, "which would present outstanding sculptural achievements across all periods and countries as comprehensively as possible".[5] Ernst Curtius, a professor of classical archaeology and the head of the Antiquarium in Berlin, emphasised in an 1870 paper on the history and purpose of art museums that it was only possible to compensate for the haphazard nature of museum holdings through the use of plaster casts.[6] Although this attitude was prevalent in many countries, it held a special significance for Berlin: the city lacked the original artworks that would allow it to compete on the international stage with museums in Paris or London. In Berlin, the claim to a comprehensive world museum could only be fulfilled through casts. Consequently, the "Neues Museum" (New Museum) was opened in the city centre in the 1850s and was primarily intended to house plaster casts.[7]

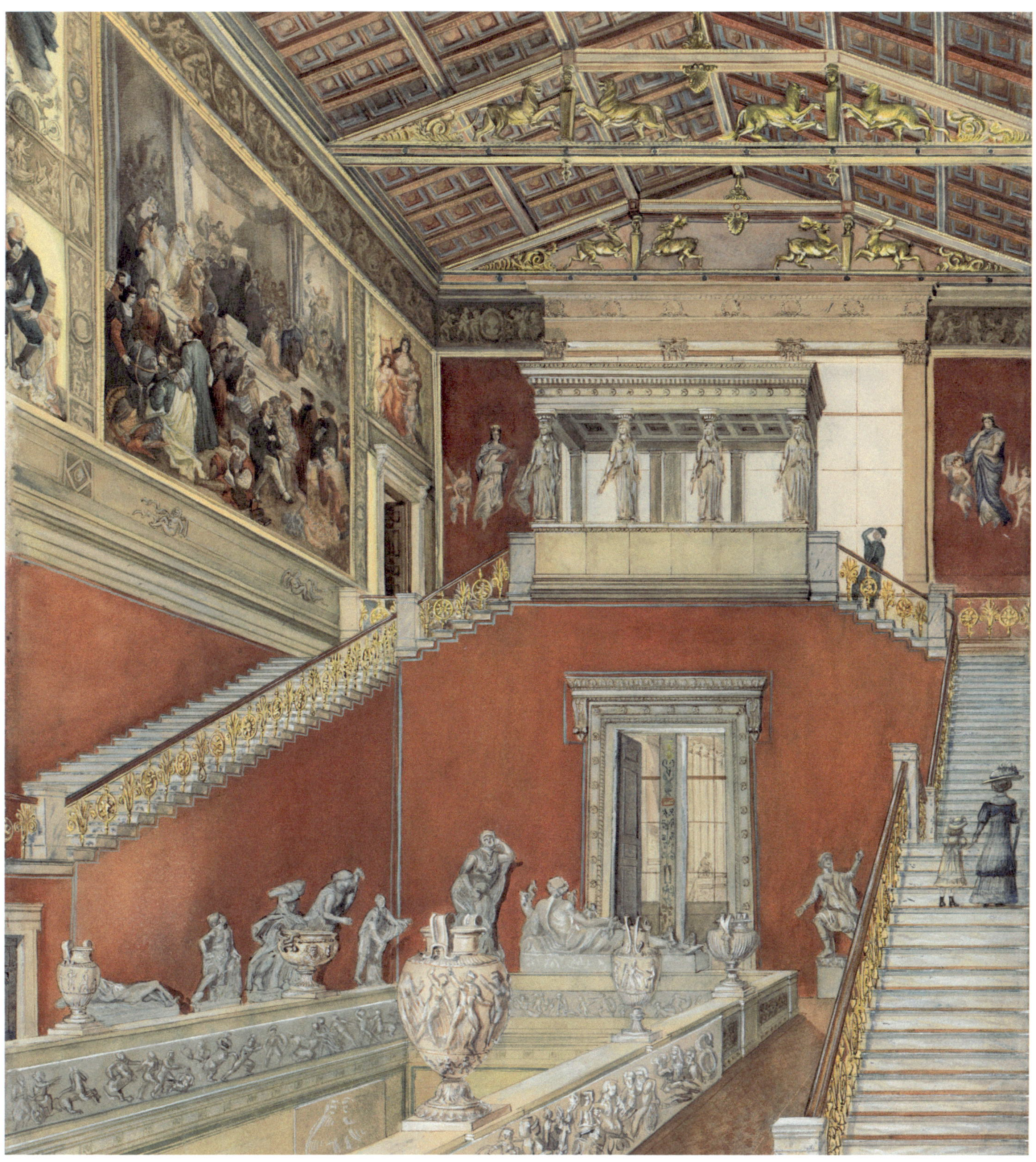

Fig. 1

Staircase of the Neues Museum in Berlin with part of the cast collection
Watercolour by H. Schultz-Voelcker, 1902

In 1871, Karl Bötticher, director of the Berlin Sculpture Collection, was still advocating this idea of an extensive education in "plaster". He commented that:

"[a] complete collection of gypsum casts of sculptural works of classical art epochs, arranged according to a scientific system in a lucid and instructive way, is far more useful for an understanding of art and for general scholarly instruction than a collection of valuable original works."[8]

The pursuit of the greatest possible completeness in the medium of casts even took precedence over the possession of less significant original works. Each individual artwork was itself secondary to the pedagogical and didactic aspiration of providing a comprehensive overview.

The Neues Museum in Berlin was one of the most eminent historicist museum constructions in Germany. Its rooms were designed in accordance with the exhibited objects themselves, staging them in the decorative systems of Greek, Roman, or Egyptian styles. A visitor to the museum ascended the staircase "out from the darkness of early history on the ground floor to the bright summit of Greek classical art"[9] (fig. 1), as was programmatically manifested in the casts of Greek and Roman sculptures according to the architect Friedrich August Stüler. As such, Greco-Roman culture was elevated to a position of paramount importance. Along with the works of classical antiquity, there was a medieval hall and a so-called modern hall on the first floor to complete the tour, both exclusively equipped with casts. In contrast, the casts of Egyptian and Near Eastern sculptures were displayed together with original pieces.

In the late nineteenth century, numerous original ancient works of art made their way to Berlin, particularly through the large-scale excavations conducted by the German Empire. The most spectacular finds were undoubtedly those from Pergamon, for which a dedicated museum was built in 1901 and 1930. With these new acquisitions and the development of Berlin as a museum hub that could (and wanted to) compete with other global cities as far as original works were concerned, the relevance of plaster casts diminished. Due to space constraints, casts were increasingly removed from museums. The most significant relocation phase occurred between 1917 and 1921, when the casts of sculptures from classical antiquity were transferred to the Friedrich-Wilhelms-Universität of Berlin. Although they were generously showcased in the university's main building on Unter den Linden, they had thus been removed from the centre of Berlin's museum landscape.[10]

Such relocations were not uncommon in these years and later – they affected many cast collections worldwide. For instance, in 1919, casts were moved from the collection of the Grand Duke of Schwerin to the University of Rostock; in 1934, the British Museum gave about 150 casts to University College London;[11] and in Boston, casts were banned from the Museum of Fine Arts,[12] with some of them ending up in Japan.[13] Many other examples could be cited here.

These displacements were essentially driven by two significant cultural-historical paradigm shifts: the partially radical anti-classicism of the artistic avant-garde, coupled with a struggle against classical ideals of education and academic traditions on the one hand, and a radical rejection of copies as a medium of mediation on the other.

Overcoming Academic Traditions

Until the end of the nineteenth century, traditions in art academies were characterised by the belief in the exemplary nature and canon of antiquity, but now the opposite was true. Impressionism had profoundly challenged this traditional understanding of art, and the artistic avant-garde of the early twentieth century pushed this attitude forward. In a 1935 interview, Pablo Picasso expressed this viewpoint:

"Academic training in beauty is a sham. We have been deceived, but so well deceived that we can scarcely get back even a shadow of the truth. The beauties of the Parthenon, Venuses, Nymphs, Narcissuses, are so many lies. Art is not the application of a canon of beauty but what the instinct and the brain can conceive beyond any canon."[14]

The Italian Filippo Tommaso Marinetti articulated this mindset most ruthlessly. In his *Manifeste du Futurisme*, published in the Parisian *Figaro* on 20 February 1909, he described the beauty of a roaring race car, which he held in higher esteem than the Nike of Samothrace: "We declare that the splendour of the world has been enriched by a new beauty: the beauty of speed. A racing automobile ... a roaring motor car which seems to run on machine-gun fire, is more beautiful than the *Nike of Samothrace*." He then explicitly calls for iconoclasm and a storming of museums and libraries. Italy should be freed from its archaeologists, travel guides, antiquarians, and, above all, from the "innumerable museums which cover it with innumerable cemeteries".[15] This radical stance was, however, an exception and should not be considered representative.

The departure from the idealism of antiquity was noticeable in many respects. Even in the study of art history, antiquity was only considered one epoch among many, and supra-temporal standards of beauty were no longer recognised. Yet, no other medium had been so representative of the old academic conception of art and the veneration of a "timeless" ideal as plaster casts. Now, however, they became the epitome of uselessness and "outdatedness", especially in art academies.[16]

It is astounding that the ancient original works were hardly subjected to this loss of prestige. On the contrary, they not only continued to be highly valued, but large museum buildings were now exclusively reserved for them. New museums were even constructed: in Berlin, for example, the above-mentioned Pergamon Museum with its various antiquities departments was opened as late as 1930.

The Cult of the Original Versus Copy or "Living Art Instead of Plaster!"

The battle against classical educational ideals and academic traditions was waged vicariously through the plaster casts, strongly fuelled by a second development: the increasing rejection of the casts as copies.

The possibilities for technical reproduction in the early twentieth century led to a re-evaluation of the relationship between "original" and "copy". The now limitless ability to reproduce objects through photography, facsimiles, casts, or other media led to fatigue towards the various forms of copies while simultaneously emphasising the "uniqueness" of the original. As such, the boundless veneration of a single original work replaced the didactic concept of casts. The viewer of the artwork was meant to have an emotional experience, engaging with the not-always-visible power of the piece; an encounter that could only be provided by the original.

Initially, a certain level of respect was retained for white plaster casts, so as to not entirely renounce their didactic potential. Though the casts were still utilised at universities, this needed to be done with caution. The German art historian Heinz Köhn emphasised in 1931 that the use of reproductions in art historical and archaeological institutes at universities was hardly superfluous, but he still explicitly warned against "all too much".[17] Another art historian, Julius Baum, also advocated academic plaster cast collections but stressed that "... every representative of the discipline of art history who conducts his research on plaster casts and similar materials renounces all artistic appreciation of the matter at the outset". He added: "Artistic enjoyment ... should not be impaired by plaster cast collections ..."[18]

The documented rejection of casts found in numerous sources could easily lead to a call for their destruction. On 9 November 1931, the Berlin newspaper *Deutsche Allgemeine Zeitung* called for parts of the Berlin casts to be thrown into the River Spree under the headline "Lebendige Kunst statt Gips!" (Living art instead of plaster!). The author, Bruno E. Werner, was by no means opposed to the traditions of art themselves. On the contrary, he offered nothing but praise for a small portrait exhibition in the Kaiser-Friedrich-Museum (today's Bode Museum). It was only that the rooms were inadequate to showcase the works. He set out on the search for more suitable premises for such exhibitions and found them in the northern wing of the Pergamon Museum (then the Deutsches Museum). However, casts after works of the Middle Ages were on display in that space. Werner was appalled and spoke of the "cadaverous atmosphere of that grey exhibition hall". One had the impression of "stepping into the lifeless casting plant of a modern industrial factory". He goes on to say:

"The museum's plaster figure hall, where these sculptures are presented to pitiable schoolchildren as life-size casts, has the inevitable effect that this grey, lifeless mass inserts itself like a thick barrier between the viewer and his own experience."

The casts were loaded with ideology and became the antithesis of immediate access to art. Finally, Werner suggested:

"The plaster casts can be distributed among the art history departments of the Prussian universities where they will do the least damage, that is if one decides not to engage in an act of Caesarian magnitude and dump every one of them into the [River] Spree."[19]

An explicit call for iconoclasm? At first, it was only a war of words.

Iconoclasm and Neglect

Classical modernism called for the overthrow of plaster casts in words only. Their physical destruction occurred mostly during the post-war modern era.

The large Berlin collection of casts modelled after ancient sculptures survived World War II, only to be dismantled in the winter of 1950–1951 due to a lack of space. The rest of the cast collection at the Technische Hochschule in Berlin was allegedly smashed during a raucous student party in the early 1960s. Casts based on Egyptian, Near Eastern, and medieval through modern models gradually disappeared in Berlin over the course of the twentieth century, with only a few exceptions.[20]

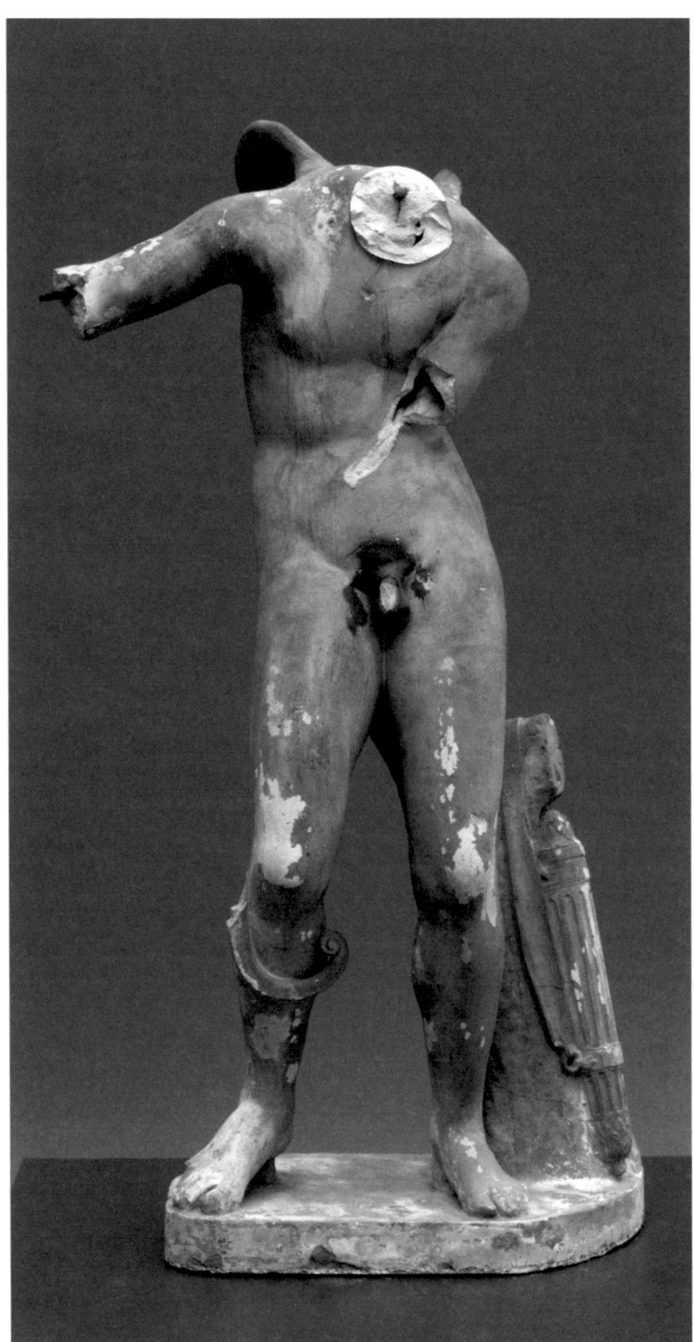

Fig. 2

Eros Stringing his Bow
Cast from the old Berlin collection
with traces of targeted and intentional destruction

The destruction of plaster cast collections was hardly unique to Berlin. Throughout Europe and the rest of the world, they were attacked or disappeared quietly, either in full or partially. Their dismantling at art academies was particularly programmatic. During the student revolts of 1968–1969, for example, the last remnants of the famous Mannheimer Antikensaal (Mannheim Gallery of Antiquities) – housed in Munich since the early nineteenth century – were used to construct an "art barricade" at the Munich Academy of Fine Arts.[21] The premises of the École Nationale Supérieure des Beaux-Arts in Paris became the logistical centre of the student movement of 1968, and some of the casts there were systematically smashed.[22] Similar acts of destruction occurred worldwide – in the United States, Latin America, and almost every country in Central and Western Europe. Destroying plaster casts was a symbolic act in the fight against the old and the outdated (fig. 2).

However, these iconoclastic acts of devastation were the exception. The majority of casts simply disappeared for rather mundane reasons: lack of space, deposition, or constant relocation and subsequent neglect. This indifference was fuelled by the same rejection as direct demolition. The casts had become outdated and therefore obsolete. Since plaster is more susceptible to damage from dirt, water, or impact than harder materials like stone, these forms of destruction often had more fundamental effects than simply smashing individual casts.

A New Beginning

Since the late twentieth century, plaster casts have experienced a renaissance. Old collections have been dusted off, restored, and put to new use, while new collections are being established. The Budapest cast collection is a good example of this revival. But also, the Berlin cast collection (Abguss Sammlung Antiker Plastik Berlin) was re-founded at the Freie Universität Berlin in the 1970s and opened as a museum in 1988; it now comprises 2,100 objects.

Through the process of rejection, it seems that plaster casts have been "purified" in many places. The educational ideals that have been associated with them have been so thoroughly deconstructed that people no longer have any "fear" of them. This allows them to be seen as they truly are: reliable copies that are suitable tools for research and teaching. In the field of archaeology, they function as important scientific aids. Separated originals can be brought together through casts, and the statues' contexts can be reconstructed on site while the original works are scattered throughout the world's many museums. It is possible to experiment with the colouration of ancient sculptures, and detailed scientific observations can be made. At the same time, plaster cast collections have also become archives of knowledge in their own right. The originals for some casts have been lost or destroyed. Other casts present an older state of the original work which is no longer preserved today.[23]

Against this background arises the question: Is the common demarcation between "original" and "copy", which has dominated the discourse of the past century, at all meaningful or relevant? This question is not insignificant, as it defines the value of the objects. But is the relationship between original and copy not also much more complex with regard to casts? We investigated this issue at the Berlin cast collection as part of a student project.

A Copy of What? A Cast of the *Sleeping Ariadne* in Berlin

The starting point of this project was the transport of a cast of the *Sleeping Ariadne* from a depot of the Staatliche Museen zu Berlin to the cast collection of the Freie Universität. This was a cast from the nineteenth century that had previously been located at the university of Jena and was transferred to the then East Berlin museums in the 1980s (fig. 3). At the depot, a tag with the note "Madrid" hung at the foot of the piece. Thus, one could assume that this was a cast of the *Sleeping Ariadne* that was modelled after the Roman sculpture found today in the Museo del Prado in Madrid.[24] However, a quick examination revealed that this could not have been the case since the statue in Madrid exhibits clear differences in the drapery of the garment (fig. 5). Additionally, the two other famous large-scale statues of the *Sleeping Ariadne* from the Roman Imperial period also proved to be too different to have served as the reference for the cast in Berlin. The position of the head of the Ariadne in Florence is different, and the Ariadne in the Vatican reclines in a much more upright position, facing the viewer more directly. This results in an entirely different impression of the statue (fig. 4).[25]

The solution was found quite quickly: the Berlin cast could be traced to the bronze statue by Francesco Primaticcio in Fontainebleau (fig. 6). However, this only shifted the problem because this statue was also a cast of the Ariadne in the Vatican, which Primaticcio had manufactured in the 1540s on behalf of King Francis I of France.[26]

Two questions arose regarding the Berlin cast. First, how could its dissimilarity to the Vatican statue be explained when it is a cast of a cast (Fontainebleau)? Second, was the designation of "Madrid" on the Berlin piece an insignificant or random error? The latter could have been

disregarded if not for the fact that it also appeared in the Berlin inventory lists and sales catalogues of the nineteenth century. Upon closer inspection, it became clear that this "mistake" was also related to the confusion resulting from the differences between the casts and the Vatican original. To further heighten and then resolve this confusion, we must shift our attention to nineteenth-century Berlin.

Berlin Confusion

A cast of the *Sleeping Ariadne* arrived in Berlin from Paris between 1858 and 1860. That it was a cast of Primaticcio's *Ariadne* from Fontainebleau should be considered as certain. Its transfer to Berlin was likely facilitated by German-born French architect Jakob Ignaz Hittorf. Soon after its arrival at the Berliner Gipsformerei (plaster cast workshop), the cast was reworked into a mould model by being divided into several parts and coated in shellac. This process aimed to facilitate further re-casting (fig. 7). Subsequently, negative moulds (*Gipsstückformen*, plaster piece moulds) were taken from this model, allowing the workshop to create its own casts.[27]

Starting in 1871, the Berliner Gipsformerei offered this cast for sale, as evident from the workshop's catalogues. However, the knowledge of the model's origin from Fontainebleau appears to have been lost because the 1871 sales catalogue indicates that the original of the statue is from "Rome, Vatican".[28] This information is still provided by the 1880 edition, but it was crossed out by hand and replaced with the designation "Madrid, Mus." (fig. 8). Even in the later catalogues from 1882, 1893, and 1906, we repeatedly read "Madrid" as the origin of the original. How did this change come about?

One possible explanation can be found in the statue's inclusion in the Neues Museum, which was opened in 1856. In the 1885 catalogue by Carl Friedrichs and Paul Wolters that documents the plaster casts of ancient sculptures in the Königliche Museen of Berlin, two large-scale statues of the *Sleeping Ariadne* are listed: the "marble statue, formerly in the Odescalchi Museum in Rome, now in Madrid" and the "marble statue, located in the Vatican since Julius II".[29] In the first edition by Carl Friedrichs from 1868, only one of the Ariadne statues was described – the one from the Vatican, on display in the *Niobidensaal* (Niobid Hall).[30] It is reasonable to assume that this Ariadne was already a cast of the sculpture from Fontainebleau made from the Berliner Gipsformerei's own moulds. When another cast of the *Sleeping Ariadne*, presumably obtained directly from the Vatican, arrived in Berlin during the 1870s as part of an expanded acquisition policy, only the differences were acknowledged. The "old" statue from Fontainebleau was

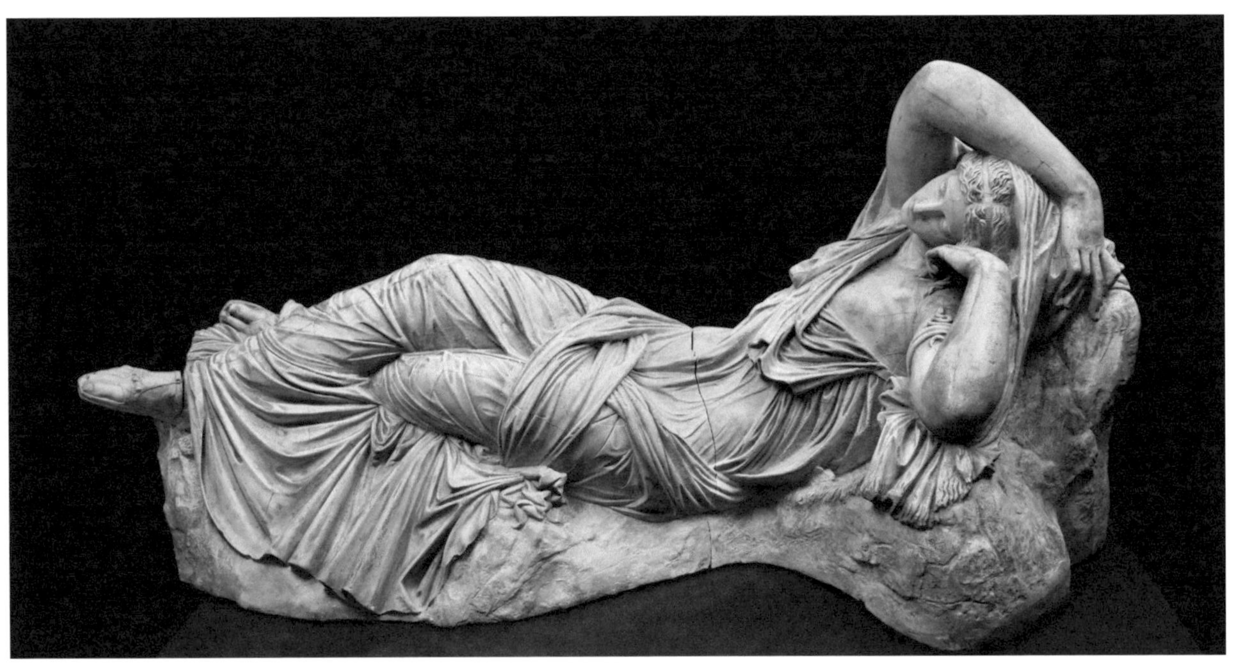

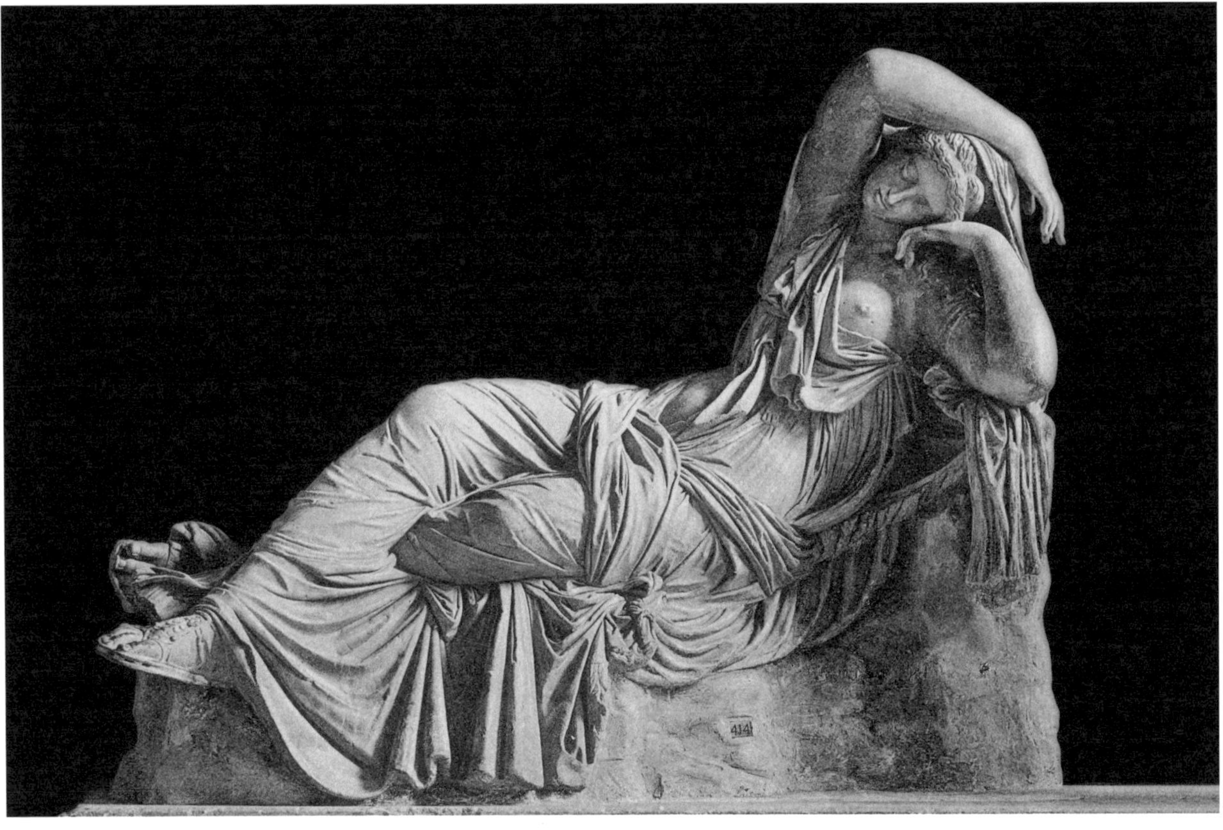

Fig. 3 | above

Cast of the *Sleeping Ariadne* in Berlin

Fig. 4

Roman statue of the *Sleeping Ariadne*
in the Museo Pio-Clementino,
Galleria delle Statue, Vatican

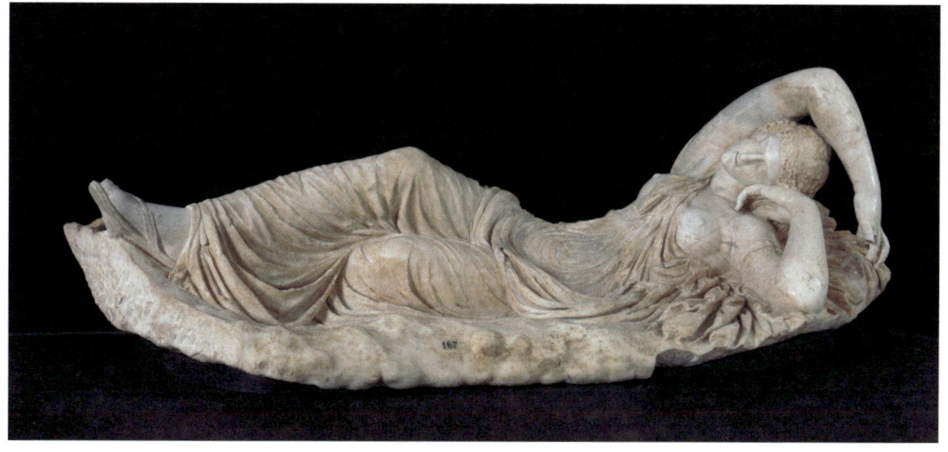

Fig. 5

Roman statue of the *Sleeping Ariadne*
in the Museo del Prado, Madrid

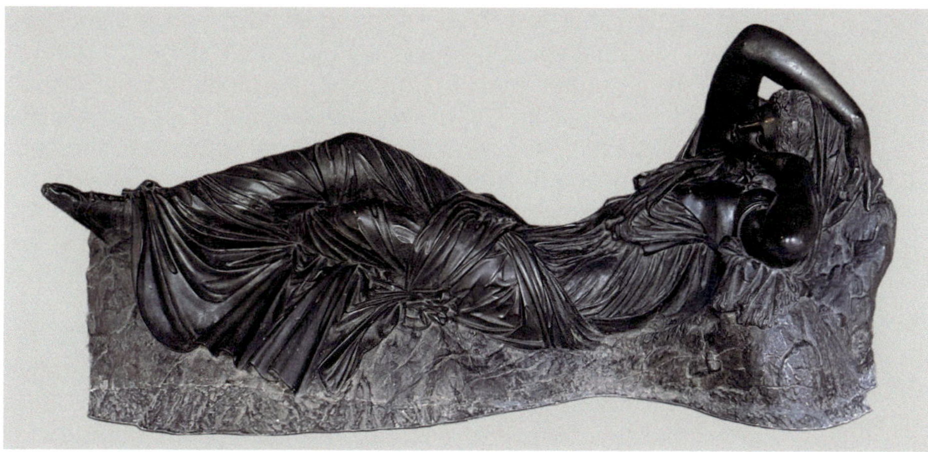

Fig. 6

Bronze statue of Francesco Primaticcio's
Sleeping Ariadne in Fontainebleau

Fig. 7

The so-called master model
of the *Sleeping Ariadne* in the
Gipsformerei of the Staatliche Museen zu Berlin,
between 1858 and 1871

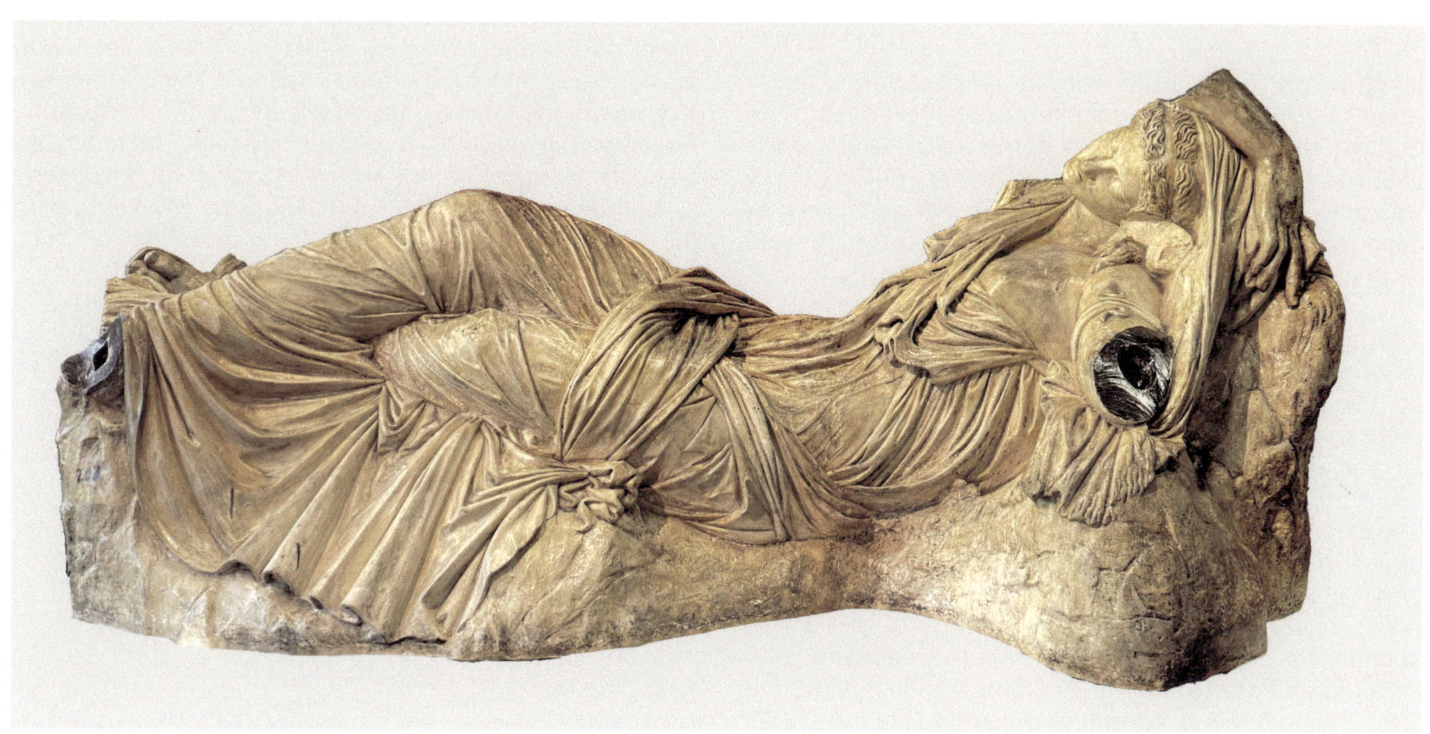

No.	Gegenstand.	Material des Originals.	Aufbewahrungs-Ort des Originals.	Höhe in Metern.	Breite in Metern.	Preis. *M.* | *₰*
85	Artemis	Bronze.	Kassel.	0,10	—	1 | —
86	Hermes	desgl.	desgl.	0,13	--	2 | —
87	Archaischer Herakles	desgl.	desgl.	0,10	—	2 | —
88	Geflügelte weibliche Figur	desgl.	desgl.	0,15	—	2 | 50
89	Desgl.	desgl.	desgl.	0,11	—	2 | —
90	Jünglind, ein Idol und eine Maske haltend.	desgl.	desgl.	0,11	—	2 | 50
91	Nackte männliche Figur, alterthümlich.	desgl.	desgl.	0,11	—	1 | 50
92	Torso einer kleinen Wiederholung des Herakles Farnese. (G. No. 681 A.)	Marmor.	Karlsruhe.	0,23	—	3 | —
93	Weibliche Gewandfigur, sitzend. (G. No. 1005.)	Terracotta.	desgl.	0,16	—	2 | 50
94	Weibliche Gewandfigur, stehend. (G. No. 1010.)	desgl.	München. Antiq.	0,31	—	3 | —
95	Isis Felicitas	Bronze.	Schwerin.	0,16	—	2 | —
96	Venustorso (vergl. Fried. No. 597. — G. No 1078.)	Marmor.	angebl. Wien.	0,52	—	15 | —
97	Torso eines stehenden Hermaphroditen. (G. No 323. A.)	desgl.	Miramare.	0,59	—	15 | —
98	Demeter von Knidos. (Newton, Pl. 55.)	desgl.	London.	1,57	0,84	140 | —
99	Diadumenos Farnese. (Müller. I, 31, 136.)	desgl.	desgl.	1,57	—	120 | —
100	Männliches Sitzbild aus Milet, von Chares dem Apollon geweiht. (Overb. I², 95.)	desgl.	desgl.	1,49	0,86	140 | —
101	Der Borghesische Fechter. (Müller-W. I, 48, 216.)	desgl.	Paris.	1,54	—	120 | —
102	Kauernder Perser, aus dem Weihgeschenk des Attalos. (Mitth. I, T. 7. — Vergl. No. 118, 119 und 120.)	desgl.	Aix.	0,64	—	36 | —
103	Aphrodite vom Kapitol. (Müller-W. II, 26, 278.)	desgl.	Rom, Cap.	1,88	—	120 | —
104	Dioskur, mit Pferd. Kolossalstatue angebl. von Phidias. (Clarac, 812 A, 2043.)	desgl.	Rom, Monte Cavallo.	5,56	—	5000 | —
105	Desgl., angebl. von Praxiteles. (eb. daselbst.)	desgl.	desgl.	5,51	—	5000 | —
106	Schlafende Ariadne. (Müller. II, 35, 418.)	desgl.	~~Rom, Vat.~~ *madrid, Mus.*	1,14	—	150 | —

declared as the "Madrid Ariadne" because the knowledge of the Renaissance sculpture had been lost. The Gipsformerei's catalogues were corrected by hand and the cast was henceforth referred to as the Madrid Ariadne. It was only in the 1928 catalogue that the designation was changed, and the statue was once again offered for sale as the "Sleeping Ariadne, Rome, Vatican".[31]

The fact that the statues from the Gipsformerei were labelled with changing designations is supported not only by the sales catalogues themselves. Evidence of this can also be found on the surviving negative moulds, as well as on one of the earliest so-called form models.

The inventory number "I A 88" is still legible on the casing of one of the negative moulds. This was later crossed out and replaced with the new number "I B 106", which itself was subsequently changed to "206" (fig. 9). This corresponds precisely to the changing inventory numbers in the catalogues from 1871 (I A 88 = Rome Ariadne), 1880 (I B 106 = Rome Ariadne, corrected by hand to Madrid), 1882,

1893, and 1906 (206 = Madrid Ariadne, then Rome Ariadne post-1928). In the catalogue from 1871, in addition to the number 88, the number 206 was also later added by hand; this is the exact number found on the form model. The trail of inventory numbers confirms the connection and reveals that the surviving negative moulds date back to before 1871.

We can assume that the cast of the Ariadne from Fontainebleau made its way from Berlin into numerous academic collections under the name "Madrid Ariadne". Tracing this exact distribution is part of ongoing research. It is certain, however, that a cast was sold to Jena. It came to the university there in the nineteenth century and returned to Berlin in the 1980s, where it serves as the starting point of our project (fig. 3). This piece still exhibits the casting seams that result from pouring into a mould with multiple individual sections. Not only do the old negative moulds from the Berliner Gipsformerei, exemplified by a section of the foot (fig. 10), fit precisely onto the piece today, but the casting seams also precisely correspond to the sectioned mould. Therefore, the cast is directly derived from the old mould that is still preserved today. The tag on the foot of the sculpture with the note "Madrid" is, therefore, the designation of the piece at the time of its acquisition.

Orders also came from the Metropolitan Museum of Art in New York and numerous other collections. A "Tentative List" by the Metropolitan Museum from 1891 indicates that two casts of the *Sleeping Ariadne* were intended for purchase: one in Madrid and the other in the Vatican.[32] The Madrid statue was to be acquired in Berlin. The inventory book from 1908 confirms this purchase and references the Friedrichs-Wolters catalogue of Berlin casts with the number 1573 for the Madrid Ariadne.[33] This refers to the aforementioned cast of the Ariadne from Fontainebleau. However, this matter becomes increasingly complicated because the cast from the New York collection is currently on permanent loan in Munich.[34] According to a stamp on the cast, it is not from Berlin at all but from France. Thus, this requires further research.

Fig. 8

Extract from the sales catalogue of the Berlin Gipsformerei of 1880 with handwritten corrections to the statue of Ariadne (no. 106)

Fig. 9 | next page at upper left

Mould of the arm of Ariadne and the various inventory numbers in the Berlin Gipsformerei

Fig. 10 | next page at upper right

Adaptation of the nineteenth-century piece mould to the cast in Berlin

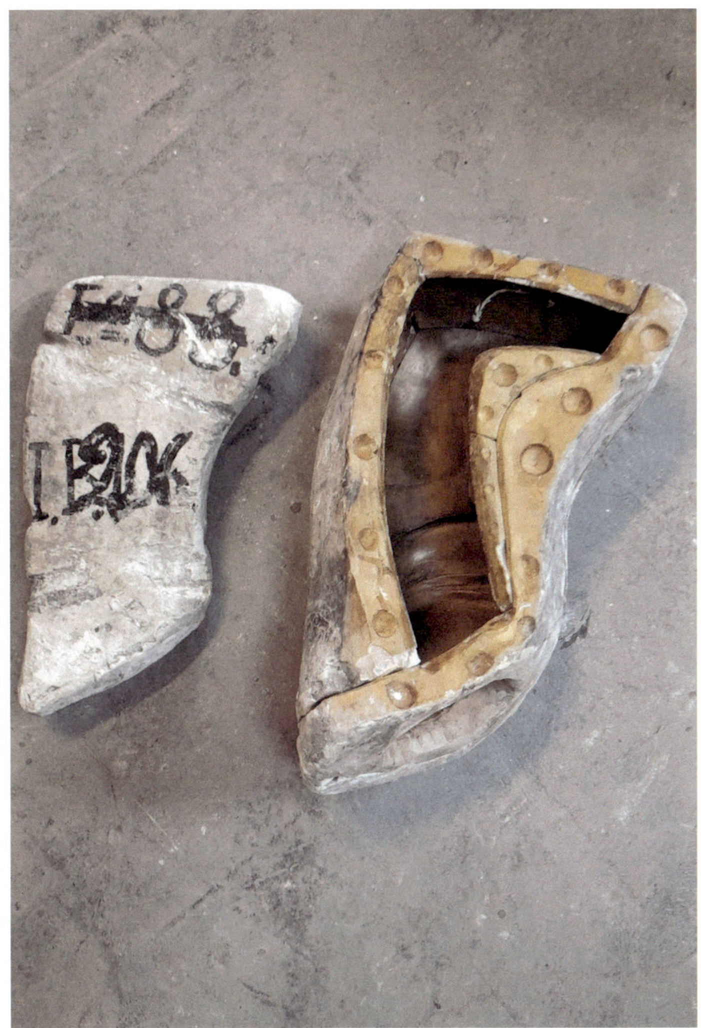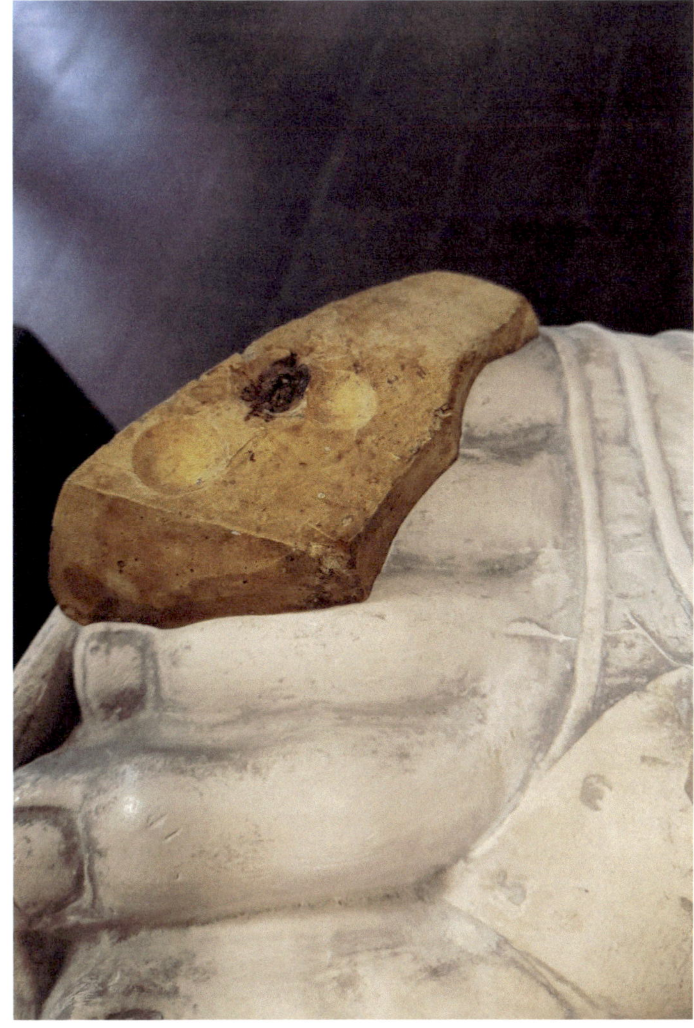

The *Ariadne* in Fontainebleau: Copy and Original?

But what was actually sold there? For even the Ariadne in Fontainebleau cannot be definitively categorised.

When the French king commissioned Primaticcio to make casts of Rome's most famous statues in 1540, this included not only the *Sleeping Ariadne* but also the *Laocoön,* the *Apollo Belvedere,* and many others. Since these statues were supposed to present Fontainebleau as a new Rome,[35] authenticity was at the heart of the matter.

Yet, how can we explain the differences between the bronze in Fontainebleau and the Roman marble statue in the Vatican? Researchers have posited numerous hypotheses. One is that changes in the posture of the statue may have been made during the casting process, whether intentional or not.[36] Another possibility arises.

In the years 1772 and 1773, a substantial restoration of the statue in the Vatican took place. Among these alterations were the removal of old additions and the replacement of certain elements, including the right hand and, notably, the rock on which Ariadne is positioned – which consequently affected the overall posture of the statue.[37] The new rock and thus the statue's pedestal may not have corresponded to the original ancient arrangement.[38] The reasons for these new modifications and the resulting change in Ariadne's posture may be linked to its new display context. Since the late eighteenth century, it has stood – with a brief interruption following Napoleon's theft – in the Galleria delle Statue of the Museo Pio Clementino in the Vatican.[39] Positioned above a sarcophagus, it serves as the northwestern termination and thus the focal point of the long room in which it is displayed. By adopting a more viewer-oriented positioning on the rock and a rotation of the figure towards the viewer, the statue could have a more pronounced impact when placed above the sarcophagus. The upright positioning of the figure is therefore a likely consequence of the statue's restoration and its intended effect in its new exhibition space. But some changes could also be older and go back to a restoration by Danielle di Volterra in the middle of the 16th century. After this restauration, a cast was brought to Spain, which shows Ariadne in another slightly different pose.[40]

Whether the bronze in Fontainebleau reflects the condition of the marble statue in the Vatican during the sixteenth century or whether Primaticcio himself chose this form of the pedestal has been interpreted differently in research.[41] However, there is a consensus that the flatter depiction of Ariadne on the rock in Fontainebleau provides a much more reliable impression of the ancient statue than the current upright version in the Vatican. If one compares the piece in the Vatican with the Roman sculptures in Florence and Madrid, which themselves are all copies (Rome, Florence) or variants (Madrid) of a lost Greek original from the second century BC,[42] it is the only one where Ariadne is positioned as such. The examples in Florence and Madrid, on the other hand, have a similar posture to the one from Fontainebleau. This also holds true for another Roman sculpture of the *Sleeping Ariadne*, which was only discovered in the necropolis of Perge in 2000.[43] Here, too, she is reclining in a flatter position but otherwise largely follows the Vatican sculpture. It can therefore be concluded that the Ariadne in Fontainebleau, as it was rendered in the sixteenth century, is much more analogous to the ancient statue than the one currently on display in the Vatican.[44]

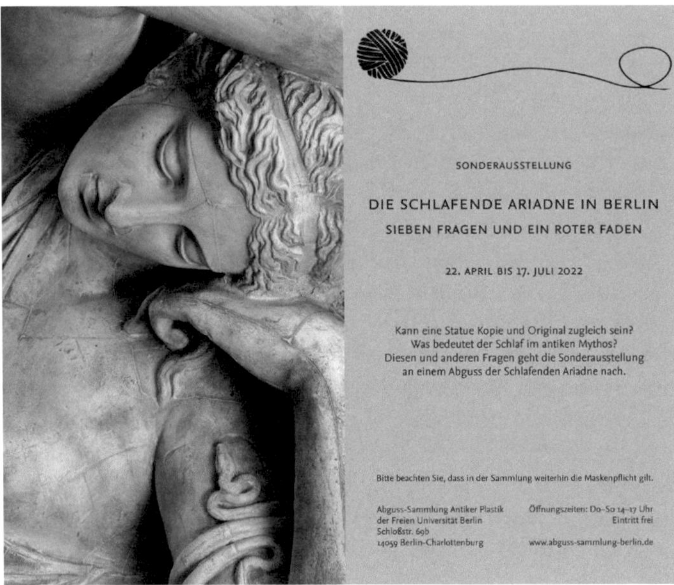

Fig. 11

Flyer for the 2022 exhibition in Berlin

Cast – Copy – Original:
A Confusing Game

The *Sleeping Ariadne* in Berlin is therefore a cast of a Renaissance bronze that is currently located in Fontainebleau. This Renaissance statue is original because of its uniqueness and is simultaneously a cast of a Roman marble sculpture in the Vatican whose appearance has been altered through later restorations. The piece in the Vatican is also original (for the cast), but, at the same time, it is a copy of a Greek statue that no longer exists. The *original* Greek sculpture has disappeared and can only be reconstructed through the various Roman "copies". The Berlin/Fontainebleau cast is of particular importance for accessing the Greek original.

The casts made from the Berlin model (new silicone negative moulds were later created from it) can also be regarded as both original and copy. The American artist Jeff Koons has adorned this very Ariadne from the Berliner Gipsformerei with a blue ball and declared it to be an original work of art. Sold under the name *Gazing Ball (Ariadne)*, it has fetched art market prices.[45]

Against the backdrop of this case study, the discussion about the value of copy and original, of aura and authenticity – as it was conducted in the twentieth century and still to some extent today – seems almost absurd. Who determines what is an original? At what point is a cast also an original, and until when is it only a negligible copy? Fundamentally, the relationship between original and copy needs to be entirely rethought – and with it, the value of casts.

The case study of Ariadne was the subject of a student exhibition project in Berlin. Under the title *The Sleeping Ariadne in Berlin: Seven Questions and a Red Thread*, the students presented different aspects of the statue in a straightforward manner for a wider audience (fig. 11) – ranging from the myth behind the sculpture, the significance of sleep, the comparison with the Roman "originals", and, finally, to the journey of Ariadne via Rome and Fontainebleau to Berlin. This project, implemented cost-effectively in the context of teaching, is just one of many exhibitions of this kind in various cast collections, each one serving an important purpose.[46]

Against the background of the fundamental questioning and rejection of casts in the twentieth century, it is important to understand their value as carriers and mediators of knowledge. It is equally important to work with the casts, to use them – in whatever way. Above all, they should not remain static and unused.

Notes

1 Szőcs 2021A.

2 Alexandridis and Winkler-Horaček 2022.

3 Szőcs 2021A, 96–97.

4 Winkler-Horaček 2022B, 528–29.

5 Quoted and translated after: *Königlichen Museen* 1880, 122.

6 Curtius 1870, 25–26; Winkler-Horaček 2022B, 531–33.

7 Platz-Horster 2012.

8 Quoted and translated after: Platz-Horster 2012, 62–63.

9 After: Scholl 2009, 128.

10 Summarised in Winkler-Horaček 2022A.

11 Payne 2022, 212.

12 Dyson 2010, 573.

13 Araki 2022, 83–84.

14 Zervos 1946, 273.

15 After: Marinetti 1909. For the English version see: https://www.societyforasianart.org/sites/ default/files/ manifesto_futurista.pdf (last accessed 1 June 2023).

16 Winkler-Horaček 2022B, 542–43.

17 Köhn 1931, 57.

18 Quoted and translated after: Baum 1931, 143.

19 Deutsche Allgemeine Zeitung (9 September 1931). Full German text in Winkler-Horaček 2022B, 574–77.

20 Winkler-Horaček 2022A.

21 Grasskamp 2002, 91 with note 32.

22 Pinatel 2022, 425–30.

23 A comprehensive compilation of casts after lost or damaged originals, as well as casts with historical additions, can be found in the exhibition catalogue Bonn 2000.

24 Wolf 2002, 93–100; Schröder 2004, 396–401, no. 187.

25 On the statues in Rome and Florence: Wolf 2002, 65–93; Valeri 2019; https://www.engramma.it/eOS/index.php?id_articolo=3572 (last accessed 1 June 2023); for this and the following in particular: Stähli 2001.

26 Pressouyre 1969, 223–39, 231; Haskell and Penny 1988, 2–6.

27 Here, I would like to thank Thomas Schelper of the Gipsformerei der Staatlichen Museen zu Berlin for his invaluable advice and for providing me with access to its historical catalogues.

28 *Verzeichnis der Abgüsse* 1871, 66.

29 After: Friedrichs and Wolters 1885, 628–30.

30 Friedrichs 1868, 367–69, no. 634.

31 *Abbildungen der Gipsabgüsse* 1928, pl. 12, no. 206.

32 *Tentative List of Objects...* 1891, 30.

33 *Catalogue of the Collection of Casts...* 1908, 126, no. 836.

34 https://www.abgussmuseum.de/de/mediaguide/schlafende-ariadne (last accessed 1 June 2023).

35 Haskell and Penny 1988, 4–5. Bensoussan 2009; Bensoussan 2015.

36 Haskell and Penny 1988, 186; Wolf 2002, 275–76; Bensoussan 2009, 215–25.

37 Valeri 2019.

38 Stähli 2001, 382–83. Cf. Valeri 2019.

39 Valeri 2019.

40 https://www.academiacolecciones.com/vaciados/inventario.php?id=V-011 (last accessed 1 September 2023).

41 Cf. Stähli 2001, 386; Wolf 2002, 274. Bensoussan 2009, 215-25.

42 On other replicas, see Stähli 2001, 383 and Wolf 2002, 65–108.

43 Zanker 2012, 173, fig. 7; Valeri 2019, fig. 12.

44 The associated different effect on the viewer has been emphasised by Stähli 2001, 387–97.

45 http://www.jeffkoons.com/artwork/gazing-ball-sculptures/gazing-ball-ariadne (last accessed 1 June 2023).

46 https://abguss-sammlung-berlin.de/veranstaltungsarchiv/2022-2/ (last accessed 1 June 2023).

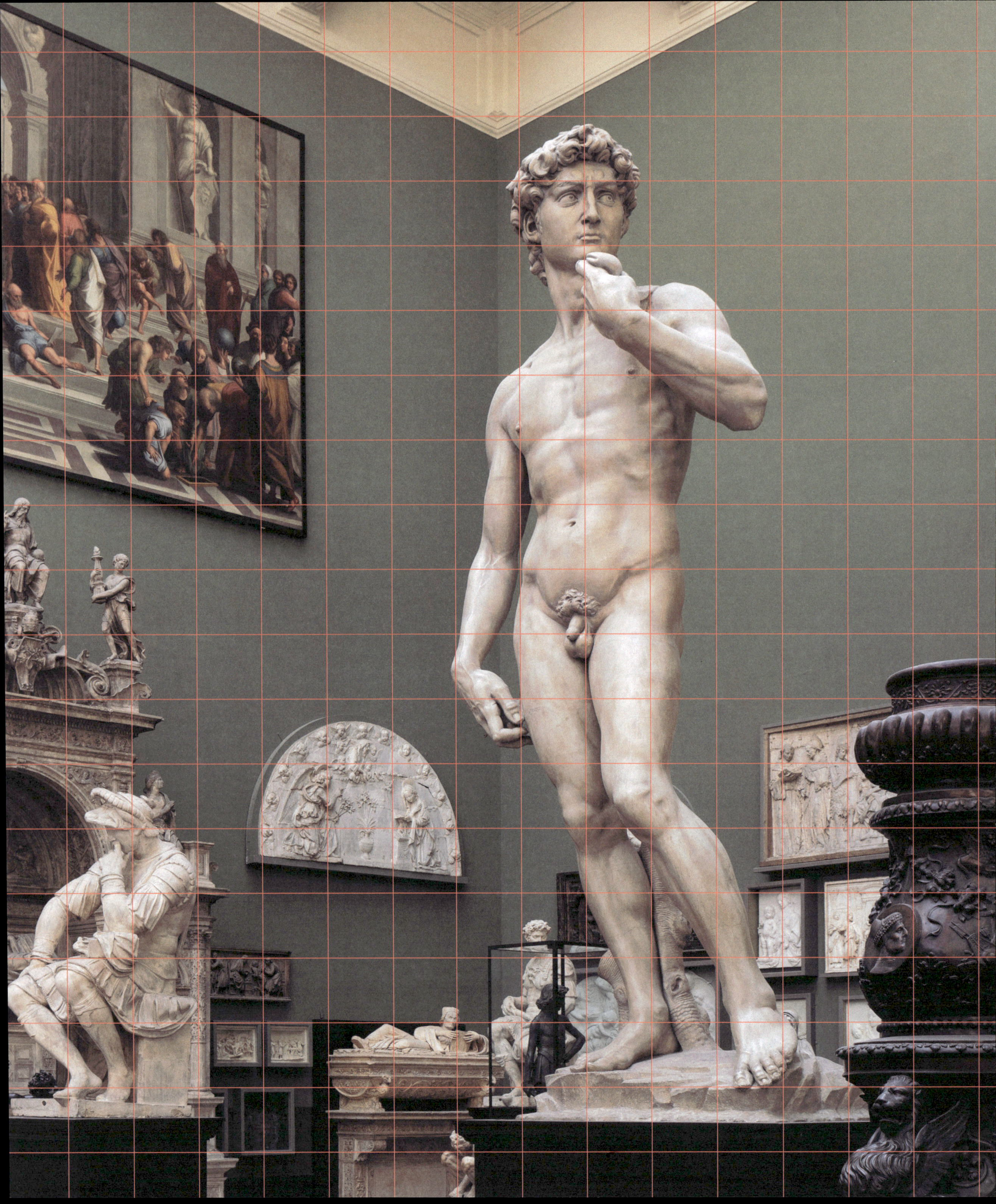

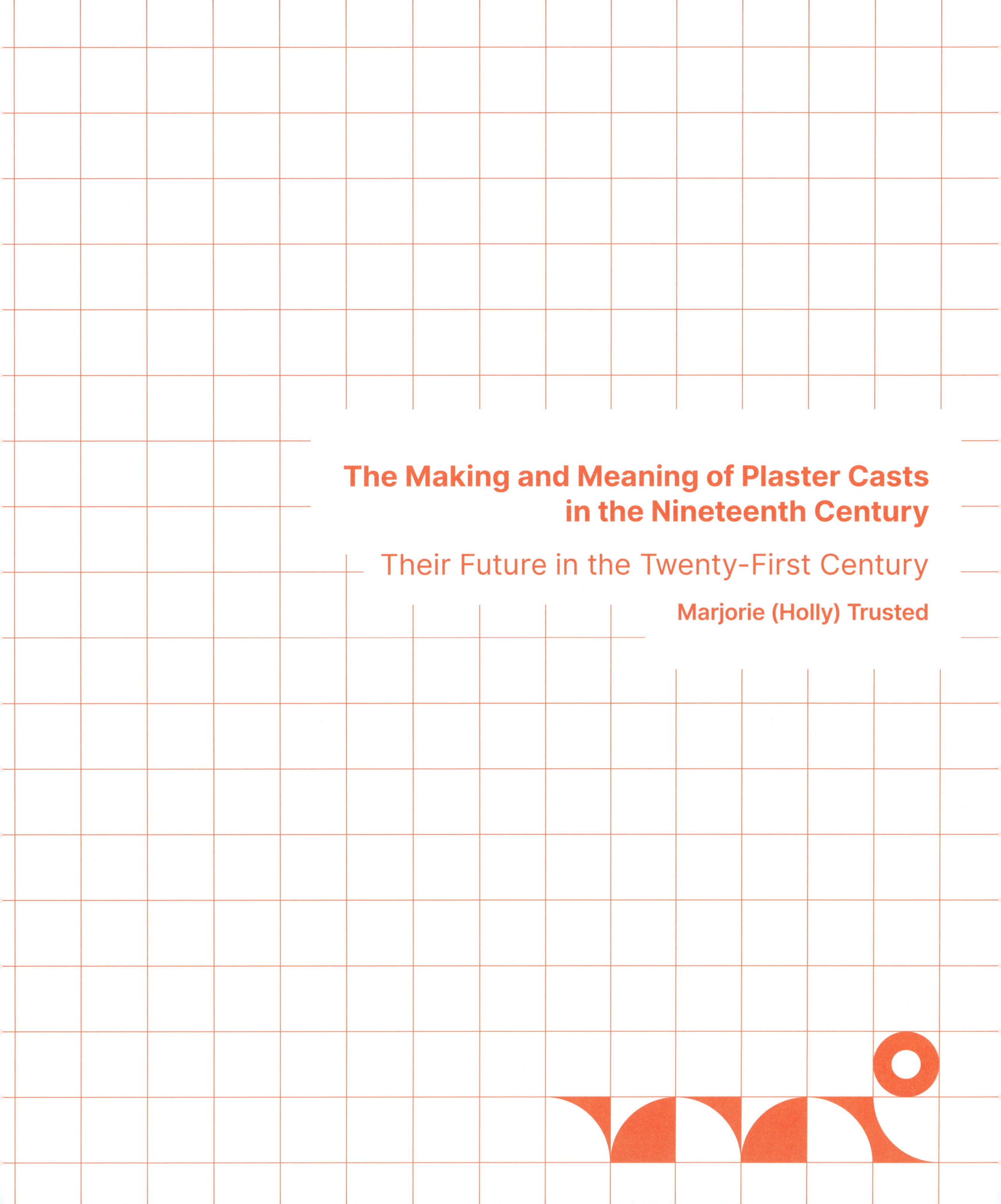

The Making and Meaning of Plaster Casts in the Nineteenth Century

Their Future in the Twenty-First Century

Marjorie (Holly) Trusted

The Making and Meaning of Plaster Casts in the Nineteenth Century

Their Future in the Twenty-First Century*

Marjorie (Holly) Trusted

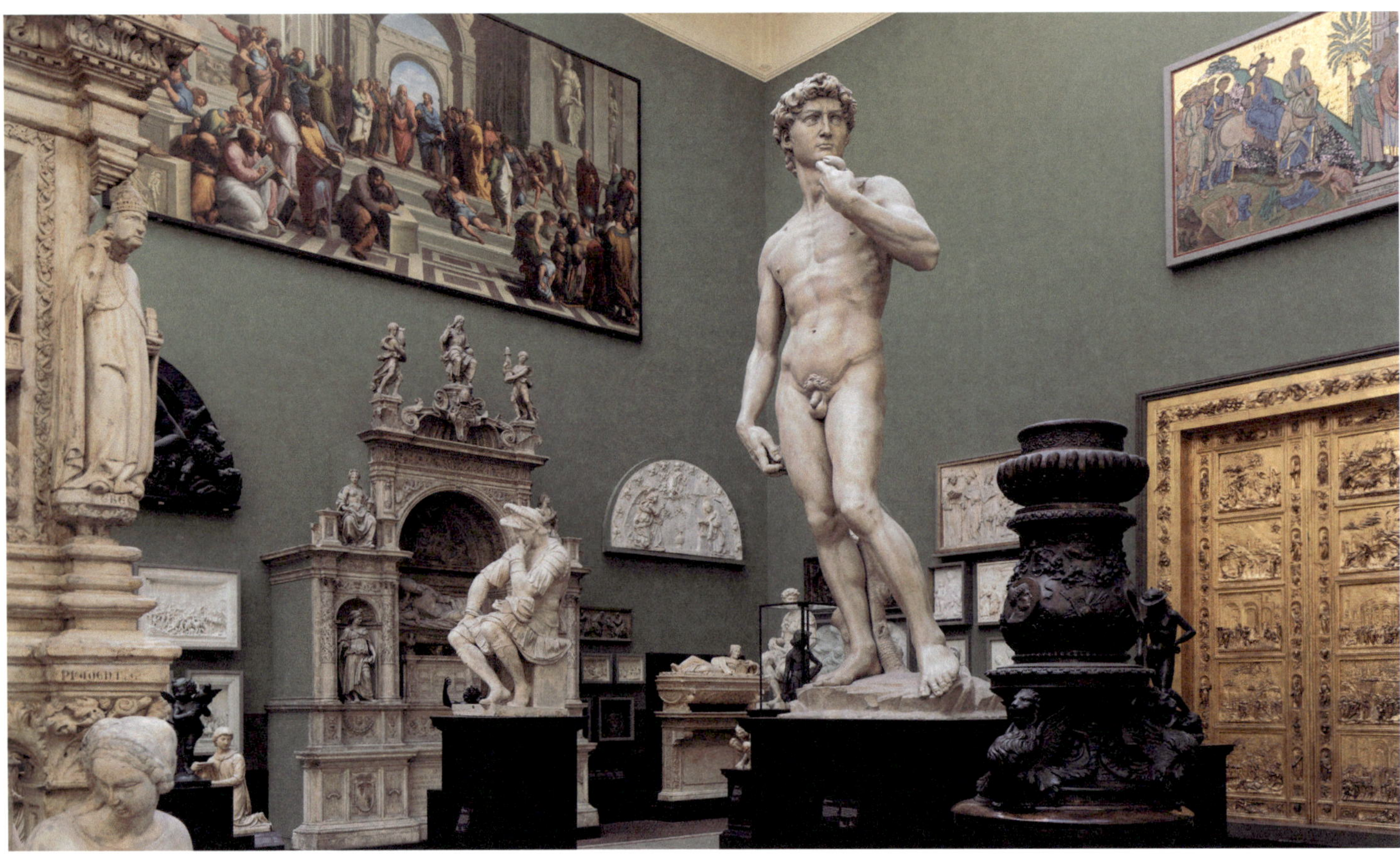

Fig. 1

View of the Weston Gallery, the Italian Cast Court
at the Victoria and Albert Museum, London

Soon after the Cast Courts (then the Architectural Courts) opened at South Kensington in London in October 1873, a contemporary noted with awe, "There are some impressions that can scarcely be effaced. Innumerable 'things of beauty' may be seen in the course of a lifetime … There are some experiences … however … which … are so striking, it may be unique … and the impression they make is indelible … the remembrance of the first visit to these new halls [the Architectural Courts] [is] amongst the impressions likely to remain."[1] In other words, this visitor – as well as countless others since then – experienced unique feelings of awe when they first saw the magnificent Cast Courts in what is now the Victoria and Albert Museum. That emotional response is still felt by many today when they enter these galleries (figs. 1–2). These feelings epitomise the excitement a work of art can give us. But how should curators present the

casts today? Can these galleries give us a glimpse of the Victorian age, a theatrical sensation, and yet, at the same time, evoke the original Renaissance and medieval objects which inspired these great Cast Courts? I believe we should and can convey the drama, the Victorian thrill, whilst simultaneously imparting scholarly information on the prototypes which inspired our casts. I am going to discuss three main topics in this essay, all of which relate to how we address the great historic spaces housing the casts; the layout of the casts within those spaces; and finally, how we convey information about the casts.

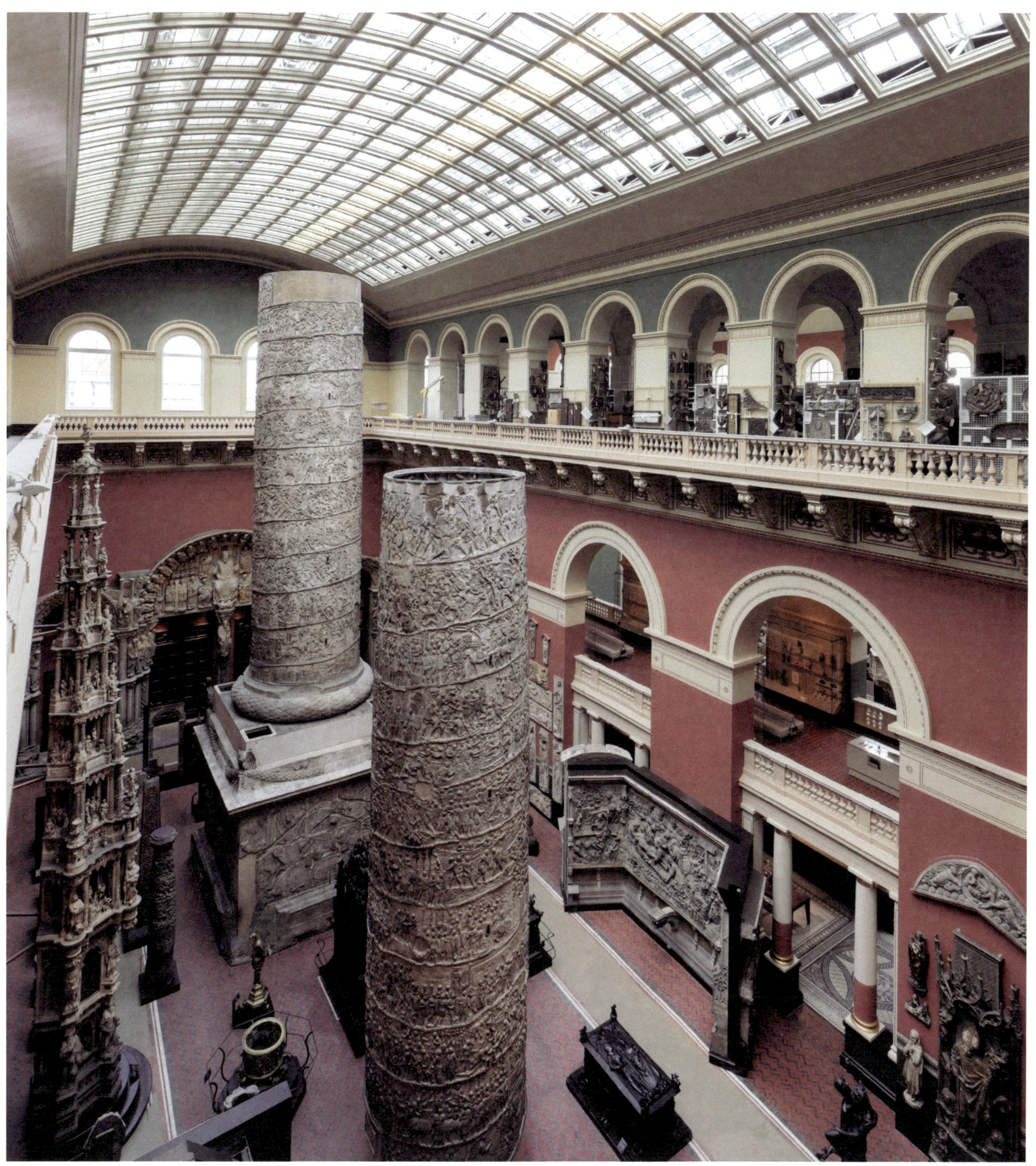

Fig. 2

View of the Ruddock Family Gallery,
the Northern European and Trajan's Column Cast Court
at the Victoria and Albert Museum, London

History of the Spaces

The chief topic is the appearance past and present of the spaces themselves, and they indeed are the reason the cast collection survives at the Victoria and Albert Museum, while other collections of reproductions in museums elsewhere have been dispersed, or even destroyed. The South Kensington galleries have only ever functioned as areas where mainly casts have been shown since they first opened in the 1870s. It is impossible to divorce their history from what curators are trying to do today. And moreover, I believe we should always nurture visitors' awe-struck reactions to art, in whatever era we live and work as curators.

Over 140 years ago, on Thursday 10 July 1873, the great Architectural Courts (now called the Cast Courts) opened at the South Kensington Museum, today the Victoria and Albert Museum (V&A). The first Director of the Museum, Henry Cole (1808–1882) noted in his diary, "New Architectural Court opening in Evening. Generally much approved."[2] This laconic entry underplays the impact of the Courts at the time, as can be seen from the quotation above.

Without question the Cast Courts epitomised the aims of the South Kensington Museum as envisaged by Henry Cole: not only breathtaking, but educational in the broadest sense, and encyclopaedic in their scope, giving the public a taste of the great monuments of Europe and indeed monuments from India, whether through plaster reproductions, electrotypes, photographs, brass rubbings, drawings or paper mosaics. In the days before cheap international travel, and before the era of the well-illustrated art book, such reproductions were fundamental for those who wished to see or learn about great works of art elsewhere. But how do Victorian notions of education and culture chime in with our perceptions of presenting objects and information to visitors today?

This essay will explore how the recent renovations in the Cast Courts at the V&A have had to tread a delicate line between preserving, if not re-creating, the Victorian splendour of the Cast Courts, and moving forward to the twenty-first century, giving visitors information which is both comprehensible and enjoyable. The very architecture of the space dictates the ways in which we present the simulacra, and the spaces themselves are an indelible part of the visitors' experience.

Three spaces will be discussed: the Italian Cast Court, now known as the Weston Gallery (fig. 1), the second Cast Court, now known as the Ruddock Family Cast Court, previously called Trajan's Column Cast Court (fig. 2), and the gallery between them (fig. 5). *Trajan's Column* was

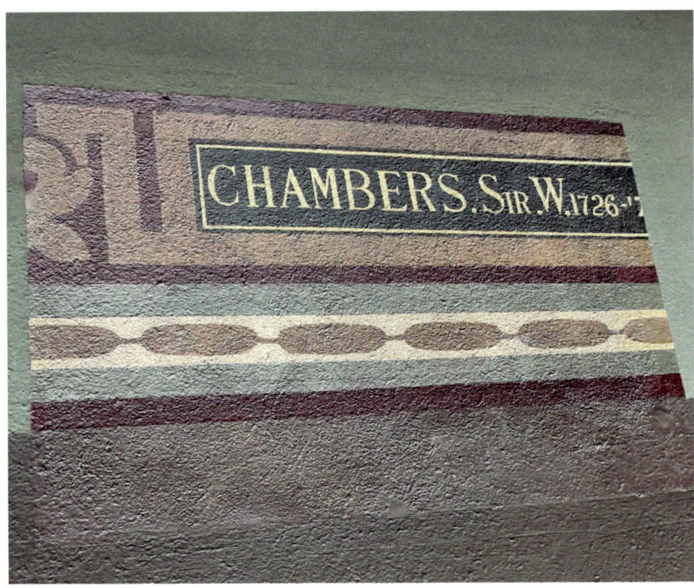

Fig. 3

Remains of the original painted inscription on the wall recording the architect Sir William Chambers in the Weston Gallery, the Italian Cast Court at the Victoria and Albert Museum, London

seen as an anomaly in the collection in the twentieth century because it is antique. Why include an ancient Roman monument in a gallery devoted to medieval and Renaissance items? However, its paradoxical status has endured, not least because the inscription at its base has been recognised as a fundamental calligraphic type, and because now this cast (made by the French in the 1860s) is in far better condition than the original in Rome. The paradoxes of the Cast Courts are, in actuality, part of the reason they are so beloved by visitors: they seem to overpower rational museological justifications.

Since 1873, when both Cast Courts were first unveiled at the V&A, they have been continuously admired and loved. The renovations of these spaces were completed by 2018. Between the Cast Courts is a didactic gallery showing the history and process of the making of plaster casts and electrotypes, as well as groupings of architectural casts.

The Italian Cast Court:
The Weston Gallery

The Italian Cast Court was renovated from 2010 to 2014, having last been refurbished in 1981 (fig. 1). After the great razzmatazz of the opening in 1873, the fortunes of the Cast Courts had waxed and waned over the decades. At the beginning, many objects were housed there, jostling for attention, including not only reproductions but also "real" objects, such as the great rood loft from 's-Hertogenbosch in the Netherlands, now in the Medieval and Renaissance Galleries at the V&A. During the recent renovation programme, many people asked if we were restoring the Courts to their original appearance in the 1870s. The enormous and indeed sometimes confusing range of material displayed there in the Victorian era was one reason we decided not to do that. Indeed, that is one question: should original works of art be displayed alongside reproductions? In general, we thought not, although one important exception to this rule is arguably the painting by Anton Raphael Mengs (1728–1779) after Raphael's fresco, *The School of Athens* of 1509–1511 in the Vatican. This is an eighteenth-century copy, made for the Duke of Northumberland in 1749 by a known painter, illustrating the taste for painted reproductions of great works of art in the Georgian period, well before the Victorian era. It is also, of course, a painting, unlike the other three-dimensional objects on display in the Cast Court. It has been treated as a special anomaly, which in fact works, partly because it introduces the idea of colour. Of course, many of our casts were painted to imitate the colours of the originals. For instance, the copies of the polychromed limewood sculptures by Tilman Riemenschneider (ca. 1460–1531), but also the marbles by Michelangelo or bronzes by Donatello were suggested through the use of monochrome painted surfaces, rather than leaving bare white plaster.

But clarity of display and the comprehensible presentation of information was always an issue, and caused the museum problems as the nineteenth century wore on. In contrast to the initial enthusiasm of the 1870s to the great spectacle of the Courts, in 1882, a contemporary commentator noted in a letter to *The Times* "the most extraordinary jumble of works" at South Kensington, particularly in comparison with the displays of casts at the Kaiser-Friedrich-Museum (now Bode Museum) in Berlin.[3] The displays in Berlin were to be praised once more a few years later by a curator and future director of South Kensington, Arthur Banks Skinner (1861–1911), in 1887. He noted the "Collection of Renaissance Italian casts in the Royal Museum, Berlin, gathered together by Mr. W. Bode [Wilhelm Bode] ... is one of the most interesting collections,

which I visited in Germany. The casts are very carefully arranged ... The order is as far as possible chronological."[4] The casts in London were perceived as confusing and lacking in rigour, in contrast to the better-ordered galleries on the Continent.

However, the apparent "jumble" of the 1870s, to which the museum did not want to return in 2014, was compounded by the fact that we could not in effect go back to any notional original display. The arrangements at South Kensington changed constantly, every few years, from the start, because new objects were continually entering the galleries, while others were dispatched elsewhere. The museum continued acquiring plaster casts up to the end of the nineteenth century and beyond, and these new acquisitions needed to be accommodated in the Cast Courts. Conversely, the Indian plaster casts, acquired shortly before the Courts opened in the 1870s, were de-accessioned in the early twentieth century, and were sent to the Imperial Institute (now Imperial College, London University). Again, South Kensington was unusual, and I think perhaps unique, in juxtaposing reproductions of European and Asian art within the same gallery. A contemporary commentator noted that it "is wonderful indeed that it should be left to this age and to England to appreciate the romance of the East ...".[5]

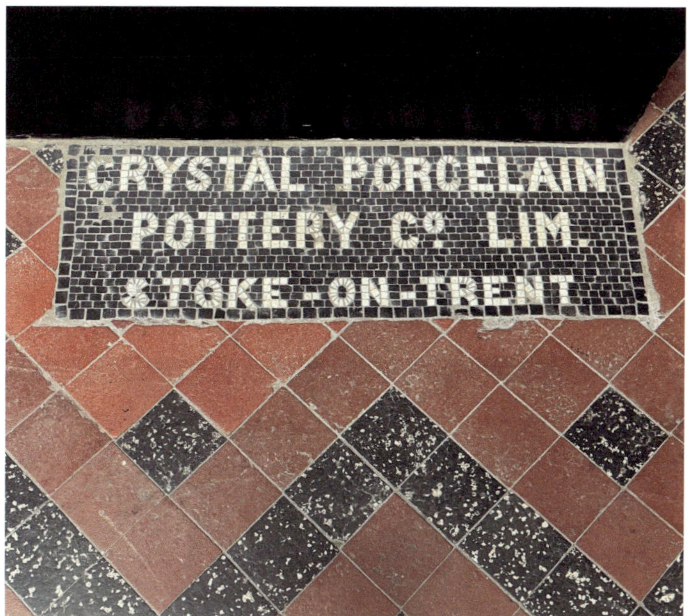

Fig. 4

The floor tiles in the Weston Gallery, the Italian Cast Court at the Victoria and Albert Museum, London

But not only the displays, the colour scheme of the Cast Courts changed constantly too. In the twentieth century the once brilliant Victorian polychromy on the walls, with their friezes of gilded cartouches giving names of famous artists and artistic cities of the past "from Ahmedabad to Zurich",[6] was dulled down to neutral, modernist colours, literally grey, with no gilding or inscriptions, the cartouches having been obliterated. The inscriptions recording the British eighteenth-century architect Sir William Chambers (1723–1796) and a Spanish artist only survived because they were hidden behind casts. We have now revealed and restored the Chambers inscription as a lone surviving fragment of the original rich mural decoration (fig. 3). However, we were not able to restore all the gilded cartouches on the walls for two reasons: most importantly, because they did not survive and no photographic or other records had been kept. The actual names were lost and would have had to be recreated through surmise. Secondly, these decorative friezes ran around the walls at different levels, meaning that the installation of casts on the walls would have been difficult, and would certainly have interrupted the friezes.

When the last restoration programme was carried out in the early 1980s, the walls were painted a sienna yellow, since there were insufficient funds to restore them to their original colours. However, in the 2014 restoration, the original mossy green colour of the walls below, with maroon purple above in the clerestory, was carefully restored. Not only were the right hues chosen, but the texture of the paint was researched too. These colours reflect the distemper finish given to the walls, a soft powdery surface, very different from the previous eggshell emulsion with its satiny sheen.

The Floors

The floors of both Courts were covered in black linoleum at some point in the twentieth century, concealing the original tiles (fig. 4). These tiles were made by the Crystal Porcelain Company, a ceramic company in Stoke-on-Trent, Staffordshire, and revealing them made an enormous difference to the sense of light and colour in the gallery. This ceramic company specialised in hard porcelain tiles and plaques.[7] However, even the story of the tiles changed as time went on. Three large areas of tiles, about a metre square, were installed probably in the late nineteenth century. Previously, coloured glass panels had been fitted into the floor, through which the crypt beneath the gallery could be viewed. Whether for safety or aesthetic reasons, these were sadly removed and subsequently vanished.[8]

Originally running around the circumference of the gallery was an elaborate heating and ventilation system covered in brass grilles. These were removed when the heating system of the museum was renovated in the early twentieth century, and again no longer remain. We therefore filled this through with a filler coloured to tone in with the wall colours.

The Lighting

The glass roof and electric lighting system had to be overhauled. For that reason, scaffolding was erected throughout the gallery. The new lighting system is a softer version of the electric lights installed during the 1980s and 1990s. Daylight plays a vital part, and most of the time, the public is unaware of the source of light; it simply pervades the ambient space. The scaffolding enabled conservators to reach casts otherwise too high for cleaning, such as Lorenzo Ghiberti's *Gates of Paradise*.

The Layout

The layout of the plaster casts and electrotypes was re-done, but again constantly bearing in mind the interplay between the wish to retain a sense of the authentic Victorian interior, alongside a desire to show these works in ways that allow today's visitors to understand them. We did not want a modern display.

When the renovation on the Cast Courts commenced, focus groups of members of the public were convened, and people were asked what they most liked and what they most disliked about the Cast Courts as they then were, before the renovations. Everyone liked most the sense of drama and surprise in the Cast Courts, the feeling of the unexpected, and extraordinarily apparent juxtapositions of monuments which are, in reality, hundreds of miles apart. When asked what they least liked, people said they disliked the sense of confusion, of not knowing how to navigate the spaces. In other words, what they most liked and what they most disliked was the same thing. We therefore wanted to hold on to the theatrical, extraordinary impact the Cast Courts have, whilst at the same time helping people understand the groupings and conveying helpful information about these works. One of the most dramatic ways in which we did this was to move Michelangelo's *David* from one side of the gallery to the other. This sculpture now has a commanding presence at the south end of the gallery, and is grouped with other casts after Michelangelo. The great electrotype copy by Giovanni Franchi of Ghiberti's *Gates of Paradise* from the Florentine Baptistry was also moved to be positioned behind the *David*, conveying a sense of the history of Florentine Renaissance sculpture.

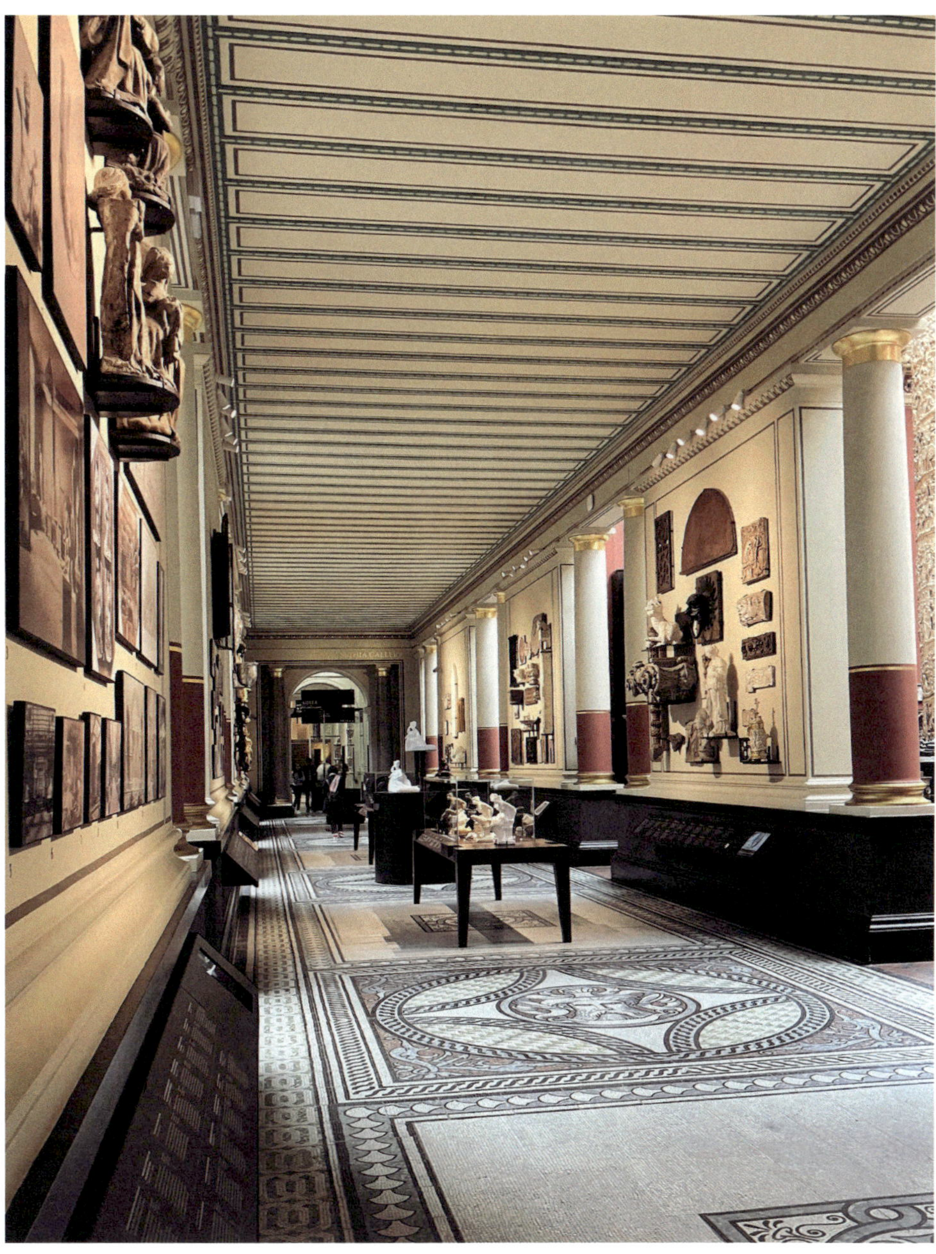

Fig. 5

The central corridor
between the two Cast Courts
at the Victoria and Albert Museum, London

Conservation and Research

Conservation was a fundamental aspect of the renovations. All the casts were cleaned, though it was important not to overclean them. The surfaces of many of the plasters are coloured to resemble the original material, whether marble or painted terracotta, and these surfaces clearly had to be retained. During this work, research by the conservators took place, and they uncovered many interesting aspects of the production of the casts and their surface treatments.

Labels

One aspect of these great Courts is that some visitors do not immediately realise these astounding objects are reproductions. People have been overheard to say they did not realise Michelangelo's *David* was in London, rather than in Florence. Of course, it does not help that two marble copies of the *David* are also in Florence, while the original is in the Galleria dell'Accademia. In fact, the V&A's plaster version was made in the 1850s, when the Florentines were making moulds of the original marble figure in order to

151

produce the marble copies. When the Italian government presented the plaster version to Queen Victoria in 1857, she immediately gave it to the South Kensington Museum, recognising she had no space suitable for it. When it was first shown in the museum it had to be displayed in parts. A plaster fig leaf was made for the figure at the same time, ostensibly so that it could be attached to cover his genitals if royal ladies visited the museum. It was last used on the occasion of a visit from Queen Mary in the 1930s.

We wanted the labels to indicate both the importance of the original work, and to some extent the story of the actual nineteenth-century cast since these plasters and electrotypes now have their own validity as objects from the early history of the museum and Victorian attitudes to art. This encompasses such concepts as the idea of the canon of art: specific works perceived as fundamental to the study of art history, such as Brunelleschi's and Ghiberti's competition reliefs for the Baptistry doors in Florence in the early quattrocento. But the casts can also illustrate how nineteenth-century decorative forms were influenced by Italian Renaissance architecture and sculpture, for example, the plaster copy of a capital from Moissac of ca. 1100 could be said to have influenced Gothic revival architecture in Britain. It is additionally fascinating to see how certain works, compelling and imposing as they are, such as Jacopo della Quercia's San Petronio doorway in Bologna, have not entered the canon in the same way. Other works in the Italian Cast Court are still seen as fundamental, and are constantly being drawn or studied, notably works by Donatello and Michelangelo, or the Pisano pulpits.

The wording of the labels is therefore in two halves: first information is given about the original work, and often how it relates to nineteenth-century perceptions. Then further "tombstone" information is presented about how and when it was cast, as well as the name of the artist who made the cast. Many of these plaster cast makers were Italian practitioners living in London, though some were based in Florence or Milan. It was a thriving industry. Visitors say they prefer reading traditional printed labels to seeing digital information on their mobile phones or on a screen in the gallery. Oddly enough, even younger visitors explicitly say they prefer traditional formats over digitised screen information. The format and history of the Cast Court seem to predicate this printed form, rather than electronic data. It is clear and accessible, and does not need any further technical equipment or understanding.

Some of the V&A casts depict objects which were subsequently damaged, such as Francesco Laurana's *Bust of a Woman*, perhaps Ippolita Sforza, the wife of Alfonso II of Naples (inv. no. 1889-94). The original marble bust was damaged during World War II and only survives in fragmentary form in the Bode Museum in Berlin. The plaster cast was purchased from the Kaiser-Friedrich-Museum (now the Bode Museum) in Berlin in 1889, and so the cast is apparently the only surviving three-dimensional record of the complete marble bust, although evidently damaged fragments also survive in Russia. This information, too, is now included on the relevant label.

Techniques of Plaster Casting and Electrotypes

One of the fundamental aspects of the Courts is the explanation of techniques. Moulds, newly-cast plasters, and surface finishes are shown in freestanding cases in the middle of the corridor between the two Cast Courts (fig. 5). The display also demonstrates how electrotypes are made, and discusses the whole notion of reproduction in the nineteenth century.

The Ruddock Family Cast Court

The other great Cast Court housing *Trajan's Column* was the next major phase of our project (fig. 2). Once again, the original wall colours were restored, the floor tiles revealed, and the lighting and labelling improved. The biggest change effected was to allow visitors to enter one half of *Trajan's Column* (the original column in Rome dating from the second century AD; the plaster cast dating from the 1870s), and experience the extraordinary brick interior, redolent of history both ancient and Victorian (fig. 6).

Above all, the Cast Courts remain an overwhelming, glorious aspect of the V&A, both Victorian and Renaissance, both nineteenth-century and medieval, all at the same time, and showing through our museum displays ways in which we can celebrate great monumental art, as well as our own history as an institution, reflecting the ideals of education and inspiration to artists, students, children and all visitors who come to South Kensington.

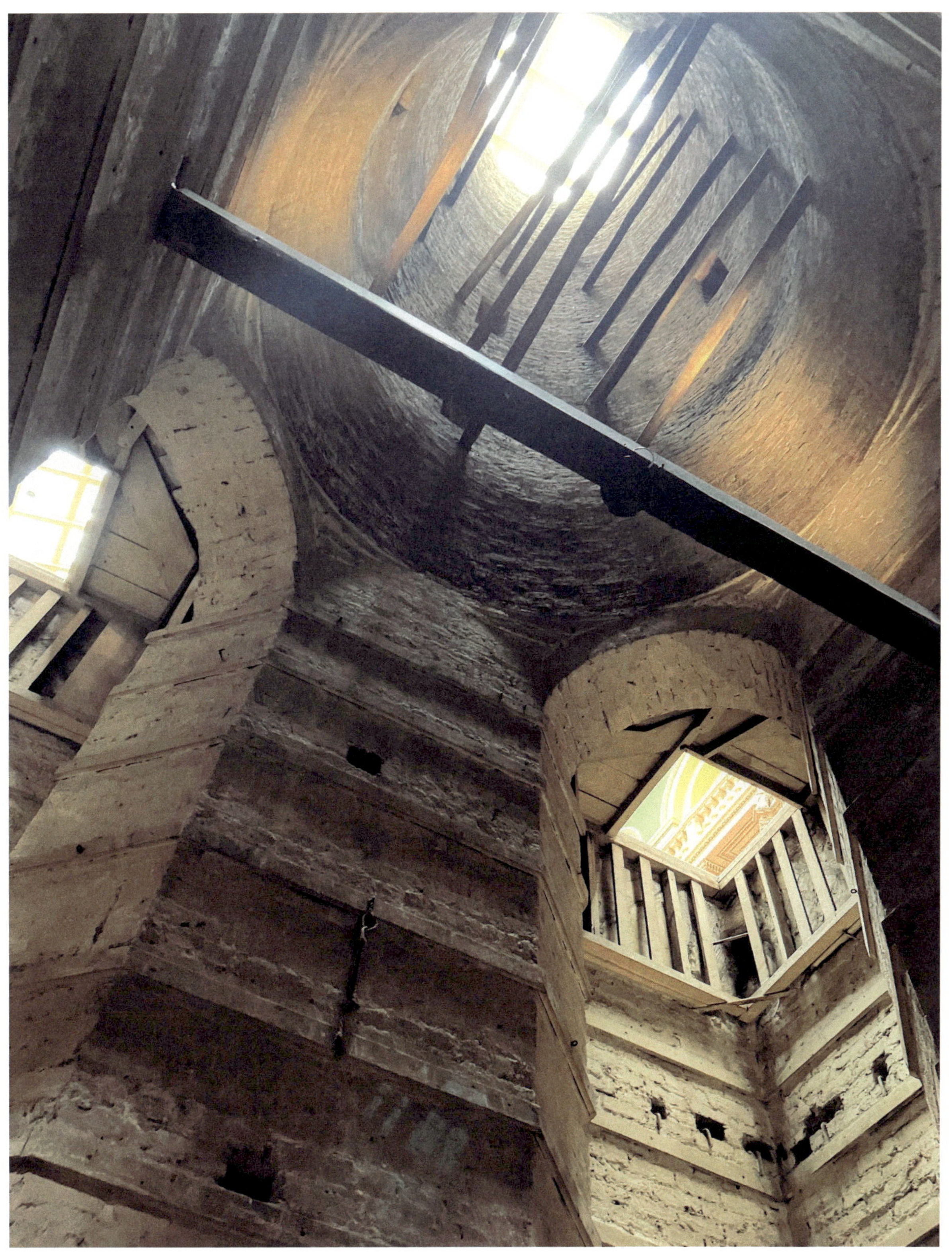

Fig. 6

The interior of the plaster cast of *Trajan's Column*
at the Victoria and Albert Museum, London

Notes

* I am most grateful to Miriam Szőcs and Márton Tóth for inviting me to the conference on plaster casts held in Budapest in 2022.
This essay is based on the lecture I gave on that occasion, and partly derives from a paper I had given in 2011 at the Bode Museum in Berlin.

1 Anonymous article in *The Builder,* 4 October 1873, 789.

2 Henry Cole Diaries (typed transcript held at the National Art Library, Victoria and Albert Museum), 10 July 1873.

3 See Trusted 2012, 364.

4 Arthur Banks Skinner, *Report,* 17 November 1887.

5 Mitter and Clunas 1997, 225.

6 *Building News* 1873.

7 Jewitt [1878] 1972, 36.

8 *Building News* 1873.

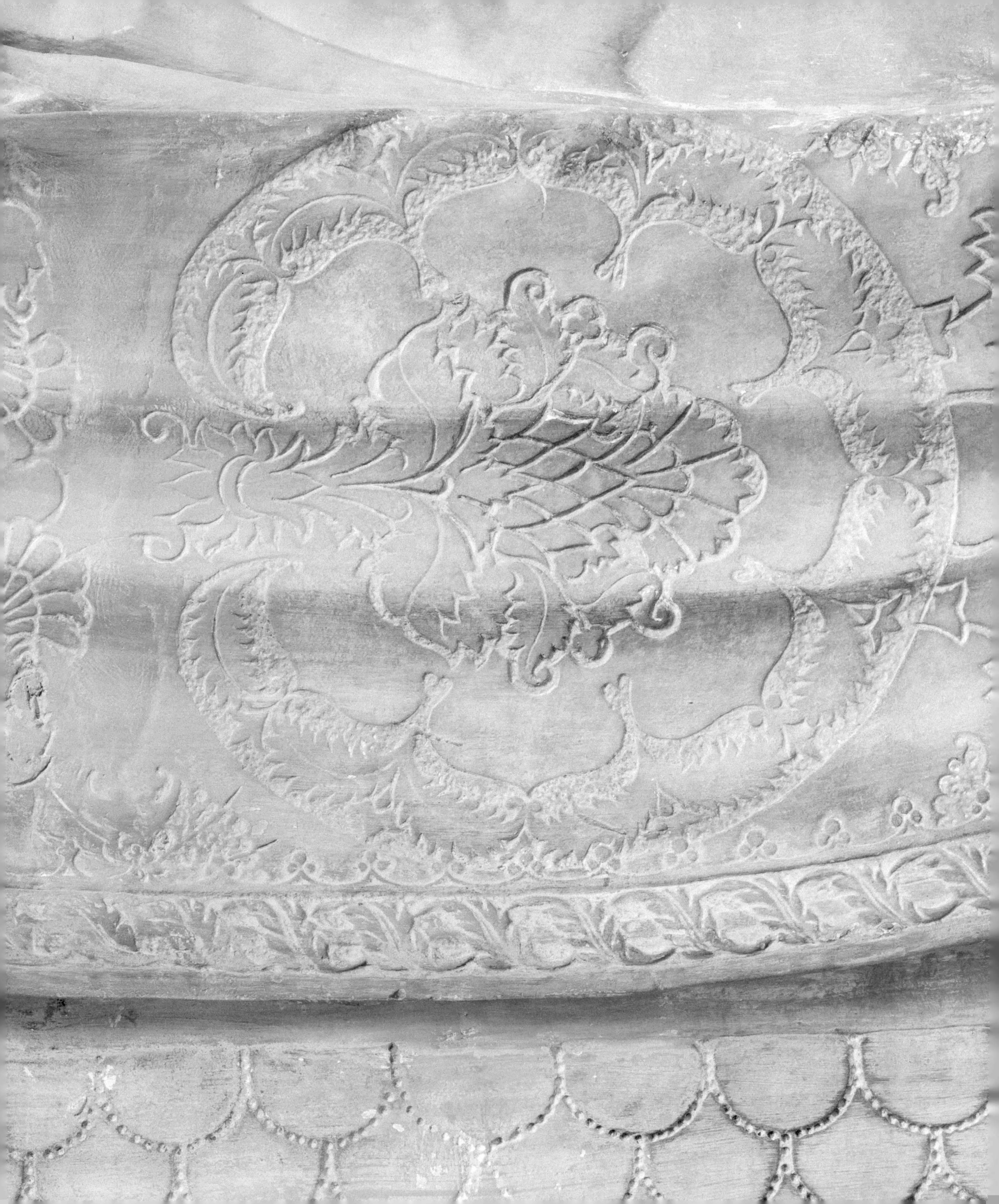

About the Authors

Géza Andó started working on the plaster cast collection in 1993 as a member of the Collection of Classical Antiquities of the Museum of Fine Arts, Budapest. He has worked on the rehabilitation of the collection since 2000. He participated to all major surveys of the plaster cast collection of the Museum of Fine Arts, Budapest in 1993, 2000, and 2013. He was curator of the Classical Antiquities section of the museum's plaster cast exhibition in the Star Fortress, Komárom, and of the visible storage at the National Museum Conservation and Storage Centre in Budapest.

Flavia Berizzi is a restorer of cultural heritage, specialising in plaster casts, with particular expertise in new technologies and digital bi- and three-dimensional documentation systems applied to the protection and enhancement of cultural heritage. She studied at the Brera Academy of Fine Arts in Milan and the Sapienza University in Rome, and her research focuses on ancient moulding methods and the reconstruction of the activities of formatori workshops operating in the Lombard area in the nineteenth century. Since 2015, she has been an external teacher for the conservation project of the plaster cast collection of the Liceo Artistico di Brera (Brera Art School) and is currently in charge of the restoration of monumental plaster casts, moulded in 1883 by the Milanese master Carlo Campi, at the Federal Polytechnic in Zürich. She collaborates with the Academy and Pinacoteca di Brera in the conservation and digitisation of historical collections, in particular, the relocation of over 300 classical, medieval, and Renaissance plaster casts into a new storage, and also the 3D photogrammetric survey campaign of the founding nucleus of the didactic gipsoteca.

Rune Frederiksen (†2023) studied classical archaeology in Copenhagen and Rome earning a PhD from the Copenhagen Polis Center (2004). Between 2003–2004, he was employed by the Ny Carlsberg Glyptotek and taught at the University of Copenhagen, and between 2004–2007, he held a research fellowship at Oxford connected to the University collection of plaster casts of ancient sculpture. From 2008 to 2015, he was based in Athens, from 2010 as the director of the Danish Institute at Athens, and from 2016, he was employed by the Ny Carlsberg Glyptotek as Head of Collections and Research. Rune has participated in and led a number of excavations around the Mediterranean and curated exhibitions in Denmark, England, Greece and Portugal.

Eszter Hajós-Baku is an expert in the preservation of built heritage. She graduated from Pázmány Péter Catholic University as an art historian in 2009, and received her PhD in 2018 at the Faculty of Architecture, Department for History of Architecture and Monuments at the Budapest University of Technology and Economics. Her main research fieldis sacred architecture in the interwar period, especially in Hungary, with a special focus on foreign parallels and the connection between architecture, liturgy, and structure. She has coordinated several research projects, mostly focusing on sacral architecture between the world wars in Hungary. She has a special interest in historical plaster casts. She is also a recipient of the three-year research scholarship from the Hungarian Academy of Arts Research Institute of Art Theory and Methodology.

Jean-Marc Hofman has been deputy curator of the cast gallery at the Cité de l'Architecture & du Patrimoine in Paris since 2004. He has published articles on the genesis of the museum's collections, as well as on the individual and professional trajectory of cast makers and their workshops in Paris. He has curated about twenty exhibitions on archaeology, arts, and historical monuments.

Júlia Katona is an art historian, researcher, and curator. She studied art history at Eötvös Loránd University in Budapest and obtained her PhD in 2017. Currently, she is working as the secretary for scientific research at the Museum of Applied Arts, Budapest and is head of collection and curator at the Schola Graphidis Art Collection of the Hungarian University of Fine Arts – High School of Visual Arts, Budapest. In 2017 she was invited by the Institut national d'histoire de l'art (Paris) as a researcher with her project, *The Corpus of Pattern Books and Ornamental Prints Published in the 19th–20th Centuries in Europe*. Her fields of interest span across research (ornamental art, theory of ornament, pattern books, rare book collections, plaster cast collections, history of architecture in the nineteenth–twentieth centuries, history of art education, Hungarian art), and museum studies (museum informatics, integrated collection management systems, digitisation, process management).

Eckart Marchand has been Assistant Archivist at the Warburg Institute in London since 2008. From 2014 to 2023, he was also a member of the International Research Group *Bilderfahrzeuge: Iconology and the Legacy of Aby Warburg*. He has worked extensively on plaster and plaster casts, studying their functions both as copies of well-known originals and as models in sculptors' workshops. Together with Rune Frederiksen, he was editor of *Plaster Casts: Making, Collecting and Displaying from Classical Antiquity to the Present* (2010). More recently, he edited and contributed to a special issue on the topic for *Sculpture Journal* (no. 3, 2019), a periodical of which he is also co-editor.

Eszter Süvegh studied Classical and Roman provincial archaeology at Eötvös Loránd University in Budapest and is currently working on her PhD thesis on grotesque depictions in ancient Greek art, particularly in Hellenistic coroplasty. As an employee of the Collection of Classical Antiquities of the Museum of Fine Arts, Budapest, she joined the ancient Greek and Roman plaster casts project in 2018, working on the preparation of the exhibition and of the visible storage organised from the collection until 2021. She has also gained experience in museum education at the Museum of Fine Arts, Budapest and at the King Saint Stephen Museum, Székesfehérvár.

Miriam Szőcs is head of the Department of Sculptures at the Museum of Fine Arts, Budapest. She specialises in Renaissance and baroque bronzes. Her field of research also include the study of the oeuvre of the eighteenth-century German-Austrian sculptor Franz Xaver Messerschmidt. She was the curator of the new permanent exhibition of sculptures at the Museum of Fine Arts that opened in 2013. Between 2013 and 2021, she worked on the project of the refurbishment of the plaster cast collection of the Museum of Fine Arts, being the chief curator of the plaster cast exhibition at the Star Fortress in Komárom.

Beáta Szűts graduated from Pázmány Péter Catholic University with a major in art history in 2016. She began working in the Department of Graphics, Form, and Design at the Budapest University of Technology and Economics in 2013. She participates in all aspects of scientific and academic life in the department, including the organisation of conferences and exhibitions. Since 2016, she has been in charge of the management and study of the collections of historical plaster casts, historical textbooks, and drawings. She started the course Preservation of Built Heritage and Monument Protection Specialist (part-time education) in 2020.

Holly Trusted FSA (formerly known as Marjorie Trusted) was senior curator of sculpture at the Victoria and Albert Museum, London, from 1990 until 2018, and was the lead curator for the Cast Courts at the V&A. She has lectured and published widely on sculpture, and is co-founder and co-chair of the Public Statues and Sculpture Association, as well as the founding editor of the *Sculpture Journal*. A senior research fellow at Durham University and honorary senior research fellow at the University of Glasgow, her book on baroque sculpture in Germany and Central Europe appeared at the end of 2022. Her catalogue of the Spanish sculpture at Bishop Auckland is due to be published in late 2024.

Lorenz Winkler-Horaček is the curator of the Cast Collection (Abguss-Sammlung Antiker Plastik) at the Freie Universität Berlin, where he is also a professor of classical archaeology. He received his doctorate from the University of Heidelberg in 1991, and worked for fourteen years at the University of Rostock. He habilitated in 2004 and moved to the Freie Universität, Berlin in 2007. His field of research is heavily image-based and covers both the Greek and Roman periods. Additionally, he focuses on the history of casts. He has curated exhibitions on archaeological themes at the Berlin Cast Collection and has organised numerous events with contemporary artists.

Bibliography

A Budapesti Áll. Felső Ipariskolával… 1904

A Budapesti Áll. Felső Ipariskolával kapcsolatos gipszminta-öntőműhelyben készülő minta- és szobormásolatok árjegyzéke [Price list of the copies of sculptures and models made in the Plaster Casting Workshop of the Budapest National Higher School of Industry]. Budapest: Hornyánszky, 1904.

Abbildungen der Gipsabgüsse 1928

Abbildungen der in der Gipsformerei der Staatlichen Museen käuflichen Gipsabgüsse. Vol. 2. Berlin: Staatliche Museen zu Berlin, 1928.

Alexandridis 2022

Alexandridis, Annetta. "'Classical' Plaster Casts in Enlightenment and Colonialist Discourses on Race." In Alexandridis and Winkler-Horaček 2022, 493–526.

Alexandridis and Winkler-Horaček 2022

Destroy the Copy – Plaster Cast Collections in the 19th - 20th Centuries: Demolition, Defacement, Disposal in Europe and Beyond. Edited by Annetta Alexandridis and Lorenz Winkler-Horaček. Berlin–Boston: De Gruyter, 2022.

Andó and Baku 2016

Andó, Géza, and Eszter Baku. "'Ne bántsd a gipszet!' A Szépművészeti Múzeum szobrászattörténeti gipszmásolat-gyűjteményének felmérése és katalogizálása" ["Don't hurt the cast!" The survey and cataloguing of the historical plaster cast collection of sculptures of the Museum of Fine Arts, Budapest]. *Ars Hungarica* 42, no. 2 (2016): 127–38 [English summary on 138].

Andó 2021

Andó, Géza. "The Greek and Roman Cast Collection of the Museum of Fine Arts, Budapest." In Szőcs 2021A, 90–129.

Araki 2022

Araki, Shinya. "Embrace the Copy: Plaster Casts and Modernity in Art Education in Japan." In Alexandridis and Winkler-Horaček 2022, 77–101.

Armuth and Lőrinczi 2013

A történeti Műegyetem – The Historic Campus. Edited by Miklós Armuth and Zsuzsa Lőrinczi. Budapest: BME, 2013.

Az Erdélyi Múzeum-Egylet Évkönyvei 1860–1873

Az Erdélyi Múzeum-Egylet Évkönyvei [Yearbooks of the Transylvanian Museum Association]. Edited by Sámuel Brassai. Kolozsvár, 1860–1873.

Az Erdélyi Múzeum-Egylet Szabályai 1859

Az Erdélyi Múzeum-Egylet Szabályai [Rules of the Transylvanian Museum Association]. Kolozsvár: Evangélikus Református Főtanoda Nyomdája, 1859.

Bacher 1956

Bacher, Béla. "A Szépművészeti Múzeum története" [The history of the Museum of Fine Arts]. In *A Szépművészeti Múzeum. 1906–1956*, edited by Gábor Ö. Pogány and Béla Bacher, 5–48. Budapest: Képzőművészeti Alap Kiadóvállalata, 1956.

Báez Macías 2019

Báez Macías, Eduardo. *Historia de la Escuela Nacional de Bellas Artes (Antigua Academia de San Carlos) 1781– 1910.* Mexico: Universidad Nacional Autónoma de México, 2019.

Bakó 1993

Bakó, Zsuzsanna Ildikó. *Gerecze Péter fényképhagyatéka* [Péter Gerecze's bequest of photographs]. Budapest: Országos Műemlékvédelmi Hivatal, 1993.

Balogh 1954

Balogh, Jolán. "La Collection des Sculptures Anciennes Étrangères." *Bulletin du Musée Hongrois des Beaux-Arts* 4 (1954): 58–62.

Banner 1963

Banner, János. "Emlékezés Pósta Bélára, születése századéves fordulóján" [Commemoration of Béla Pósta, on the centenary of his birth]. *Dissertationes Archaeologicae* (Régészeti Dolgozatok) 5, 17–28. Budapest, 1963.

Bardon 1952

Bardon, Alfréd. "Rajzoktatás az építőművészeti nevelés szolgálatában" [Drawing classes in the service of the education of the art of architecture]. *Magyar Építőművészet*, nos. 5–6 (1952): 232–47.

Barros Grez 1869

Barros Grez, Daniel. "De la formación de galerías de bellas artes i de un museo de industria i de costumbres nacionales." *Revista Las Bellas Artes* 14, no. 1 (5 July 1869): 111–12.

Bauer 2012

Bauer, Johannes. "Gipsabgüsse zwischen Museum, Kunst und Wissenschaft. Wiener Abguss-Sammlungen im späten 19. Jahrhundert." In *Gipsabgüsse und antike Skulpturen. Präsentation und Kontext*, edited by Charlotte Schreiter, 273–90. Berlin: Reimer, 2012.

Baum 1931

Baum, Julius. "Gipsabgüsse." *Museumskunde. Neue Folge* III, no. 4 (1931): 141–43.

Beltrami 1910

Beltrami, Luca (under pseudonym "Polifilo"). *Il Museo Campi Carlo, Milano*. Milan: Tip. E. Berardi e C., 1910.

Bencard et al. 2005

Afstøbningssamlingen. Død eller Levende? Edited by Ernst Jonas Bencard et al. Copenhagen: Afstøbningssamlingens Venne, 2005.

Bensoussan 2009

Bensoussan, Nicole. *Casting a Second Rome: Primaticcio's Bronze Copies and the Fontainebleau Project*. Dissertation, Yale University, 2009.

Bensoussan 2015

Bensoussan, Nicole. "From the French Galerie to the Italian Garden. Sixteenth-Century Displays of Primaticcio's Bronzes at Fontainebleau." *Journal of the History of Collections* 27, no. 2 (2015): 175–98.

Berizzi 2020/2021A

Berizzi, Flavia. *Il Museo Campi Carlo in Brera: nascita, sviluppo ed eredità di una gipsoteca cittadina*. Master's thesis, vol. 2, Brera Academy of Fine Arts, a.y. 2020/2021.

Berizzi 2020/2021B

Berizzi, Flavia. *Idrogeli e fluidi nanostrutturati nel restauro di manufatti in gesso: l'intervento sul calco del Monumento a Giacomo Stefano Brivio in Brera formato da Carlo Campi*. Master's thesis, vol. 1, Brera Academy of Fine Arts, a.y. 2020/2021.

Berlin 2019A

Nah am Leben: 200 Jahre Gipsformerei. Edited by Veronika Tocha. Exhibition catalogue. Staatliche Museen zu Berlin, James-Simon-Galerie, 2019–2020. Berlin: Staatliche Museen zu Berlin; Munich – London – New York: Prestel Verlag, 2019.

Berlin 2019B

Near Life. The Gipsformerei. 200 Years of Casting Plaster. Edited by Veronika Tocha. Exhibition catalogue. Staatliche Museen zu Berlin, James-Simon-Galerie, 2019–2020. Berlin: Staatliche Museen zu Berlin; Munich – London – New York: Prestel Verlag, 2019.

Bernardini and Mastrorocco 1985

Bernardini, Luisella, and Mila Mastrorocco. "Per una storia della Gipsoteca." In *Donatello e il primo Rinascimento nei calchi della Gipsoteca*. Edited by Luisella Bernardini, Annarita Caputo Calloud, and Mila Mastrorocco. Exhibition catalogue. Istituto Statale d'Arte, Florence, 1985–1986. Florence: SPES, 1985.

Boardman 1994

Boardman, John. *The Diffusion of Classical Art in Antiquity*. London: Thomas & Hudson, 1994.

Bognár and Rózsavölgyi 2016

Bognár, Zsófia, and Andrea Rózsavölgyi. "The Collection of Medieval and Renaissance Plaster Casts of the Budapest Museum of Fine Arts." *Hungarian Review* VII, no. 2 (2016): 93–107.

Boime 1964

Boime, Albert. "Le Musée des Copies." *Gazette des Beaux-Arts* (October 1964): 237–47.

Bonn 2000

Gips nicht mehr. Abgüsse als letzte Zeugen antiker Kunst. Edited by Johannes Bauer and Wilfred Geominy. Exhibition catalogue. Akademisches Kunstmuseum, Bonn. Bonn: Köllen Druck, 2000.

Building News 1873

"The New Court, South Kensington." *Building News*, 23 April 1873, 469.

Bulletin of the Art Institute of Chicago 1908

Bulletin of the Art Institute of Chicago 2, no. 1 (July 1908).

Buranelli 2006

Buranelli, Francesco. "La scoperta del Laocoonte e il Cortile delle Statue in Vaticano." In Rome 2006, 49–60.

Burg 2010

Burg, Tobias. "Building a Small Albertinum in Moscow: the Correspondence between Georg Treu and Ivan Tsvetaev." In Frederiksen and Marchand 2010, 539–55.

Butterfield 1997

Butterfield, Andrew. *The Sculptures of Andrea del Verrocchio*. London – New Haven: Yale University Press, 1997.

Cambareri 2011

Cambareri, Marietta. "Italian Renaissance Sculpture at the Museum of Fine Arts, Boston: the Early Years." In *Sculpture and the Museum*, edited by Christopher R. Marshall, 95–114. Farnham: Ashgate, 2011.

Cardoso Denis 2000

Cardoso Denis, Rafael. "Academicism, Imperialism and National Identity: The Case of Brazil's Academia Imperial de Belas Artes." In *Art and the Academy in the Nineteenth Century*, edited by Rafael Cardoso Denis and Colin Trodd, 53–67. Manchester: Manchester University Press, 2000.

Catalogo dei monumenti… 1883

Catalogo dei monumenti, statue, bassorilievi, ornamenti, ecc., in gesso di varie epoche formanti la storia dell'arte che si trovano presso Edoardo del fu Pietro Pierotti, formatore delle R. Accademie, Milano, via Macello n.1. Milan: Simonetti & C., 1883.

Catalogo dei monumenti… 1906

Catalogo dei monumenti, statue, bassorilievi e ornamenti in gesso di varie epoche che si trovano presso Pietro Pierotti, formatore delle R. Gallerie. Milan: Tip. Ghezzi, 1906.

Catalogo riproduzioni in gesso… 1906

Catalogo riproduzioni in gesso di opere d'arte: Scultura, Bassorilievo, Architettura. Dal Vero. Campi Carlo, Milano, via Moscova n. 64. Fornitore Regie Accademie. Scuole. Musei. Milan: Tip. Matelli, 1906.

Catalogue of the Collection of Casts… 1908

The Metropolitan Museum of Art. Catalogue of the Collection of Casts. New York: The Metropolitan Museum of Art, 1908.

Curtius 1870

Curtius, Ernst. *Kunstmuseen. Ihre Geschichte und ihre Bestimmung. Mit besonderer Rücksicht auf das königliche Museum zu Berlin. Vortrag, gehalten im wissenschaftlichen Vereine am 26. Februar.* Berlin, 1870.

Csorba 1971

Csorba, Csaba. "Pósta Béla kolozsvári régészeti iskolája és a 'Dolgozatok'" [Béla Pósta's Kolozsvár School of Archeology and the journal "Dolgozatok"]. In *A Debreceni Déri Múzeum Évkönyve 1969–1970*, 117–46. Debrecen, 1971.

Delamotte 1855

Delamotte, Philip Henry. *Photographic Views of the Progress of the Crystal Palace Sydenham.* London: Crystal Palace Company, 1855.

Dyson 2010

Dyson, Stephen L. "Cast Collecting in the United States." In Frederiksen and Marchand 2010, 557–75.

Échanges internationaux… 1885

Échanges internationaux de reproductions artistiques. Conférence de Bruxelles (16, 17, 18 et 19 septembre 1885). Bruxelles, 1885.

Egyed 2006

Egyed, Ákos. "Az Erdélyi Múzeum-Egyesület megalakulásának előzményei" [The antecedents of the establishment of the Transylvanian Museum Association]. In *A Csíki Székely Múzeum Évkönyve*, vol. 1 (2005), 233–41.

Egyed and Kovács 2009

Okmány- és irománytár az Erdélyi Múzeum-Egyesület történetéhez I (1841–1859) [Records and handwritten document archive for the history of the Transylvanian Museum Association]. Edited by Ákos Egyed and Eszter Kovács. Kolozsvár: EME, 2009.

Elek 1923

Elek, Artúr. "A Szépművészeti Múzeum antik gipszgyűjteménye" [The Museum of Fine Arts's plaster collection of classical antiquities]. *Nyugat*, no. 16 (1923): 597–600.

English patents… 1856

English patents of Inventions, Specification, 1856, no. 2494.

Építő Ipar 1901

Épitő Ipar 25, no. 1253 (2), (13 January 1901): 6.

Erdey 1908

Erdey, Aladár. "A gipsz-muzeumról" [About the plaster cast museum]. *Budapesti Szemle* 134, no. 378 (1908): 451.

Falser 2019

Falser, Michael. *Angkor Wat. A Transcultural History of Heritage.* 2 vols. Berlin: De Gruyter, 2019.

Farkas 1913

Farkas, Zoltán. "A Szépművészeti Múzeum szobortermei" [The sculpture galleries of the Museum of Fine Arts]. *Vasárnapi Újság* 60, no. 20 (1913): 394–95.

Fehér 2010–2012

Fehér, Ildikó. "Károly Pulszky and the Florentine Acquisitions for the Szépművészeti Múzeum in Budapest Between 1893 and 1895." *Mitteilungen des Kunsthistorischen Institutes in Florenz* 54, no. 2 (2010–2012): 319–64.

First Report... 1882

First Report of the Curator of Ancient Monuments in India for the Year 1881–1882. Simla: Government Central Branch Press, 1882.

Frederiksen 2010

Frederiksen, Rune. "Plaster Casts in Antiquity." In Frederiksen and Marchand 2010, 13–33.

Frederiksen and Marchand 2010

Plaster Casts: Making, Collecting and Displaying from Classical Antiquity to the Present. Edited by Rune Frederiksen and Eckart Marchand. Berlin – New York: De Gruyter, 2010.

Frederiksen and Smith 2013

Frederiksen, Rune, and R. R. R. Smith. *The Cast Gallery of the Ashmolean Museum. Catalogue of Plaster Casts of Greek and Roman Sculpture.* Oxford: Ashmolean Museum, 2013.

Friedrichs 1868

Friedrichs, Carl. *Die Gipsabgüsse antiker Bildwerke in historischer Folge erklärt.* Berlin, 1868.

Friedrichs and Wolters 1885

Friedrichs, Carl, and Paul Wolters. *Königliche Museen zu Berlin. Die Gipsabgüsse antiker Bildwerke in historischer Folge erklärt.* Berlin: W. Spemann, 1885.

Frischer 2009

Frischer, Bernard. "Laocoon. An Annotated Chronology of the 'Laocoon' Statue Group." In *Digital Sculpture Project*, University of Virginia. http://www.digitalsculpture.org/laocoon/chronology/ (accessed: 13 December 2022).

Fuentes Rojas 2010

Fuentes Rojas, Elizabeth. "Art and Pedagogy in the Plaster Cast Collection of the Academia de San Carlos." In Frederiksen and Marchand 2010, 229–47.

Gaal 2001

Gaal, György. *Egyetem a Farkas utcában.
A kolozsvári Ferenc József Tudományegyetem előzményei,
korszakai és vonzatai* [University in Farkas Street.
The antecedents, eras and implications of the Franz Joseph
University of Kolozsvár]. Kolozsvár: Erdélyi Magyar
Műszaki Tudományos Társaság, 2001.

Gallardo Saint-Jean 2015A

*Museo de Copias: El principio imitativo
como proyecto modernizador. Chile, Siglos XIX y XX*.
Edited by Ximena Gallardo Saint-Jean. Santiago de Chile:
Ediciones Universidad Alberto Hurtado, 2015.

Gallardo Saint-Jean 2015B

Gallardo Saint-Jean, Ximena. "Introducción:
El Museo de Copias en Chile. Prácticas Artísticas
y Académicas en el Tránsito del siglo XIX al
XX." In Gallardo Saint-Jean 2015A, 9–52.

Garcia-Ventura and Vidal 2020

Garcia-Ventura, Agnès, and Jordi Vidal.
"International Networks and the Shaping of Nineteenth-Century
Spanish Collections: A Glance at the Correspondence of
Juan Facundo Riaño." *Journal of the History of Collections* 32,
no. 3 (2020): 481–90.

Gerber 1910

*Reproduktionen klassischer Bildwerke aus der Kunstanstalt
August Gerber, Köln am Rhein*. August Gerber Kunstanstalt
für klassische Bildwerke. Cologne, 1910.

Gipsoteca Vallardi n. d.

*Gipsoteca Vallardi (già Museo Campi). Catalogo
illustrato riproducente in 96 tavole la ricca raccolta
di circa seimila calchi in gesso tratti dai più notevoli
capolavori di architettura e scultura dall'epoca
egiziana alla moderna e da elementi anatomici
e naturali*. Milan: A. Vallardi, n. d.

Gipsoteca Vallardi 1930

*Gipsoteca Vallardi, già Museo Campi. Raccolta
di 6000 calchi in gesso*. Edited by Alfonso
Du Bois. Milan: A. Vallardi, 1930.

Grasskamp 2002

Grasskamp, Walter. *Ist die Moderne eine Epoche?
Kunst als Modell*. Munich: Beck, 2002.

Hajós-Baku and Szűts 2021

Hajós-Baku, Eszter, and Beáta Szűts. "Drawings, Ornaments,
and Historical Plaster Casts: The Reform of Drawing Education
in the Technical University of Budapest."
Symmetry: Culture and Science 32, no. 3 (2021): 431–49.

Hajós-Baku and Szűts 2022

Hajós-Baku, Eszter, and Beáta Szűts. "Historical Plaster Casts
in Architecture Education. History of the Plaster Cast
Collection of the BME Faculty of Architecture from the
Beginnings to 1930s." *RIHA Journal,* 2022 [under publication].

Hansen and Nielsen 2004

Hansen, Mogens Herman, and Thomas Heine Nielsen.
*An Inventory of Archaic and Classical Poleis:
An Investigation Conducted by the Copenhagen
Polis Centre for the Danish National Research
Foundation*. Oxford: University Press, 2004.

Haskell and Penny 1988

Haskell, Francis, and Nicholas Penny. *Taste and the Antique.
The Lure of Classical Sculpture 1500–1900*[3].
New Haven – London: Yale University Press, 1988.

Hecht 2019

Hecht, Romy. "Visions of an Unrealized Park: Chile's Cerro
San Cristóbal, 1915–1927." *Studies in the History of Gardens
& Designed Landscapes* 39, no. 3 (2019): 213–33.

Hekler 1924

Hekler, Antal. "Az antik gipszgyűjtemény rendezése / Die Neuordnung der Sammlung von antiken Gipsabgüssen." In *Az Országos Magyar Szépművészeti Múzeum Évkönyvei / Jahrbücher des Museums der Bildenden Künste in Budapest III,* 1921–1923 (1924). Budapest: Országos Magyar Szépművészeti Múzeum kiadása; Franklin-Társulat Nyomdája, 1924, 102–7, 129.

Helleland 2005

Helleland, Allis. "Afstøbningssamlingen 1995–2002, Erfaringer & Status." In Bencard et al. 2005, 27–33.

Hofman 2010

Hofman, Jean-Marc. "The Cast Collection of the Musée des Monuments. 'A Panegyric of the French Heritage'." In Frederiksen and Marchand 2010, 11–15.

Hofman 2016

Hofman, Jean-Marc. "Éphémères musées d'archéologie médiévale. La collection de moulages de l'humble M. Malzieux." *In Situ*, no. 28 (2016). https://doi.rg/10.4000/insitu.12648.

Hofman and Lancestremère 2013

Hofman, Jean-Marc, and Christine Lancestremère. "Aux sources du musée de Sculpture Comparée." *Dans l'intimité de l'atelier. Geoffroy-Dechaume (1816–1892), sculpteur romantique*. Exhibition catalogue. Cité de l'architecture et du patrimoine, Paris, edited by Carole Lenfant and Laurence de Finance, 207–13. Paris: Honoré Clair, 2013.

Holm 2022

Holm, Henrik. "The (Mis)Performance of Cast Collections." In Alexandridis and Winkler-Horaček 2022, 25–50.

Jewitt [1878] 1972

Jewitt's Ceramic Art of Great Britain 1800–1900. Revised by Geoffrey A. Godden. London: Barrie & Jenkins, [1878] 1972.

Kabdebo 1979

Kabdebo, Thomas. *Diplomat in Exile. Francis Pulszky's Political Activities in England, 1849–1860*. East European Monographs, 56. New York: Columbia University Press 1979.

Katona 2016

Katona, Júlia. "Gipszminták a rajzoktatásban. A Budapest Székesfővárosi Iparrajziskola egykori gipszgyűjteménye" [Plaster casts in the teaching of drawing. The former plaster casts collection of the Budapest Metropolitan Industrial Drawing School]. *Ars Hungarica* 42, no. 2 (2016): 157–67 [English summary on 168].

Katona 2018

Katona, Júlia. "Képek, előképek, koncepció. A Szépművészeti Múzeum Román Csarnokának falfestése és épületszobrászati kialakítása" [Images, prototypes, concept. Sculptural decoration of the Museum of Fine Arts's Romanesque Hall]. In Szőcs 2018A, 62–101.

Keller 2022

Keller, Natalia. "The Rise and Fall of the Museo de Copias: On the History of the Collection of Sculpture Replicas in the National Museum of Fine Arts in Santiago de Chile." In Alexandridis and Winkler-Horaček 2022, 51–76.

Kleiner 1992

Kleiner, Diana E. E. *Roman Sculpture*. New Haven: Yale University Press, 1992.

Knoll and Elsner 1994

Knoll, Kordelia, and Gudrun Elsner. *Das Albertinum vor 100 Jahren – die Skulpturensammlung Georg Treus. Erinnerung an die Eröffnung der Sammlung der Originalbildwerke am 22. Dezember 1894*. Exhbition catalogue. Dresden, 1994–1995. Dresden: Staatliche Kunstsammlungen Dresden, 1994.

Köhn 1931

Köhn, Heinz. "Original und Faksimile." *Museumskunde. Neue Folge* III, no. 2 (1931): 53–58.

Königlichen Museen 1880

Zur Geschichte der königlichen Museen in Berlin. Festschrift zur Feier ihres fünfzigjährigen Bestehens am 3. August 1880. Berlin: Königliche Museen, 1880.

Landwehr 1985

Landwehr, Christa. *Die antiken Gipsabgüsse aus Baiae: griechische Bronzestatuen in Abgüssen römischer Zeit*. Berlin: Gebr. Mann Verlag, 1985.

Le Journal du Cher 1842

Le Journal du Cher, no. 128 (25 October 1842): n. p.

Lebrun 1838

Lebrun. *Nouveau manuel du mouleur, ou L'art de mouler en plâtre, carton, carton-pierre, carton-cuir, cire, plomb, argile, bois, écaille, corne, etc., etc*. Manuels-Roret. Paris: Librairie encyclopédique de Roret: 1838.

Lending 2017

Lending, Mari. *Plaster Monuments. Architecture and the Power of Reproduction*. Princeton–Oxford: Princeton University Press, 2017.

Liddell, Scott, and Jones 1958[9]

Liddell, Henry George, and Robert Scott. *A Greek-English Lexicon*. Revised by Henry Stuart Jones. Oxford: Clarendon Press, 1958[9].

Liverani 2006

Liverani, Paolo. "Braccio Pollak." In Rome 2006, 192 (no. 90).

Lodi 2008

Lodi, Letizia. "Il Museo e il ruolo di Luca Beltrami: l'allestimento del 1911–1912." In *La Certosa di Pavia e il suo museo. Ultimi restauri e nuovi studi*, edited by Beatrice Bentivoglio Ravasio, Letizia Lodi, and Mari Mapelli, 391–417. Milan, 2008.

Lützow 1885

Lützow, Carl von. "Ein neues plastisches Museum für Wien." *Mittheilungen des k. k. Östereichischen Museums für Kunst und Industrie*, no. 20 (1885): 473–80, 501–6.

Mackenna Subercaseaux 1901

Mackenna Subercaseaux, Alberto. "Una obra necessaria." *La Libertad Electoral* 15, no. 4382 (19 February 1901): 1–2.

Mackenna Subercaseaux 1915

Mackenna Subercaseaux, Alberto. "El origen del 'Museo de Copias': Conferencia en el ateneo de Santiago el Lúnes 22 Mayo 189[9]." In Idem, *Luchas por el Arte*, 3–14. Santiago-Valparíso: Soc. Imprenta-Litografia "Barcelona", 1915.

Magi 1960

Magi, Filippo. *Il ripristino del Laocoonte. Atti della Pontifica Accademia Romana di Archeologia, Memorie* III.9.1. Vatican City, 1960.

Malosetti Costa 2001

Malosetti Costa, Laura. *Los primeros modernos: arte y sociedad en Buenos Aires a fines del siglo XIX*. Buenos Aires: Fondo de Cultura Económica, 2001.

Marchand 2010

Marchand, Eckart. "Plaster and Plaster Casts in Renaissance Italy." In Frederiksen and Marchand 2010, 49–79.

Marinetti 1909

Marinetti, F. T. "Le Futurisme." Cover of *Le Figaro*, 20 February 1909.

Márki 1922

Márki, Sándor. *A Magyar Királyi Ferenc József Tudományegyetem története 1872–1922* [The history of the Royal Hungarian Franz Joseph University 1872–1922]. Szeged: Szeged Városi Nyomda és Könyvkiadó Rt., 1922.

McClellan 1999

McClellan, Andrew. *Inventing the Louvre: Art, Politics, and the Origins of the Modern Museum in Eighteenth-Century Paris*. Berkeley, CA: University of California Press, 1999.

McKee 1964

McKee, J. H. "George Ade Reports The World's Fair (1893 at Chicago)." *Nieman Reports* XVIII, no. 3 (1964): 18–22.

Messermann 1845

Messermann, Jacques Olivier Marie de. *Cheminée de la salle d'audience des magistrats du Franc de Bruges*. Bruges: Vandecasteele-Werbrouck, 1845.

Meyer and Savoy 2014

The Museum Is Open. Towards a Transnational History of Museums 1750–1940. Edited by Andrea Meyer and Benedicte Savoy. Berlin–Boston: Walter de Gruyter GmbH, 2014.

Millar 1897

Millar, William. *Plastering, Plain and Decorative*. London: Batsford, 1897.

Mitter and Clunas 1997

Mitter, Partha, and Craig Clunas. "The Empire of Things: Engagement with the Orient." In *A Grand Design: The Art of the Victoria and Albert Museum*. Exhibition catalogue. Victoria and Albert Museum, London and Baltimore Museum of Art, edited by Malcolm Baker and Brenda Richardson, 221–29. New York: Harry N. Abrahams; Baltimore: The Baltimore Museum of Art 1997.

Nagy 2006

Nagy, Árpád Miklós. "'Classica Hungarica' – die Entstehung der Antikensammlung im Budapester Museum der Bildenden Künste." In *The Nineteenth-Century Process of "Musealization" in Hungary and Europe*, edited by Ernő Marosi and Gábor Klaniczay, 213–31. Budapest: Collegium Budapest, 2006.

Nagy 2013

Nagy, Árpád Miklós. *Classica Hungarica. A Szépművészeti Múzeum Antik Gyűjteményének első évszázada 1908–2008* [The first century of the Collection of Classical Antiquities of the Museum of Fine Arts, 1908–2008]. MúzeumCafé Könyvek 2. Edited by Orsolya Radványi. Budapest, 2013.

Nécrologie [Alexandre Desachy] 1886

"Nécrologie [Alexandre Desachy]." *La Chronique des Arts et de la Curiosité*, no. 37 (27 November 1886): 293–94.

Newmann 1888

Newmann, Francis William. *Reminescences of Two Exiles (Kossuth and Pulszky) and Two Wars (Crimean and Franco–Austrian)*. London: Kegan Paul, Trench & Co. 1888.

Nichols 2015

Nichols, Kate. *Greece and Rome at the Crystal Palace: Classical Sculpture and Modern Britain, 1854–1936*. Oxford Scholarship Online: April 2015.

Notes, circulaires et rapports… 1862

Note, circulaires et rapports sur le service de la conservation des monuments historiques. Paris, 1862.

Pape 1975

Pape, Magrit. *Griechische Kunstwerke aus Kriegsbeute und ihre öffentliche Aufstellung in Rom: von der Eroberung von Surakus bis in augusteische Zeit*. Hamburg, 1975.

Paris 2009

Brueghel, Memling, Van Eyck… La collection Bruckenthal. Edited by Jan De Maere and Nicolas Sainte Fare Garnot. Exhibition catalogue. Musée Jacquemart–André, Paris. Bruxelles: Fonds Mercator, 2009.

Payne 2022

Payne, Emma. "From Pillar to Post: Classical Casts at the British Museum." In Alexandridis and Winkler-Horaček 2022, 201–20.

Penny 1993

Penny, Nicholas. *The Materials of Sculpture*. New Haven – London: Yale University Press, 1993.

Peregriny 1915

Peregriny, János. *Az Országos Magyar Szépművészeti Múzeum állagai, III. rész, 3. füzet. Új szerzemények. Plastikai művek*. [Collections of the National Hungarian Museum of Fine Arts, part III, booklet 3. New acquisitions. Sculptural works]. Budapest: Athenaeum Irodalmi és Nyomdai Részvénytársulat 1915.

Petrovics 1926

A közép- és renaissancekori gipszgyűjtemény [The medieval and Renaissance plaster collection]. Catalogue by Zoltán Oroszlán and Andor Pigler. Introduction by Elek Petrovics. Budapest: Szépművészeti Múzeum, 1926.

Pinatel 2022

Pinatel, Christiane. "Destruction of Plaster Casts in Workshops and Collections of Important French Institutions in the 19th and 20th Centuries." In Alexandridis and Winkler-Horaček 2022, 407–34.

Platz-Horster 2011

Platz-Horster, Gertrud. "'…der eigentliche Mittelpunkt aller Sammlungen…': Die Gipssammlung im Neuen Museum, 1855–1916." In *Museale Spezialisierung und Nationalisierung ab 1830. Das Neue Museum in Berlin im internationalen Kontext*, edited by Ellinoor Bergvelt, Debora J. Meijers, Lieske Tibbe, and Elsa van Wezel, 191–205. Berliner Schriften zur Museumsforschung, Bd. 29. Berlin, 2011.

Platz-Horster 2012

Platz-Horster, Gertrud. "Die Gipssammlung im Neuen Museum – Ausstattung und Aufstellung." In *… von gestern bis morgen … Zur Geschichte der Berliner Gipsabguss-Sammlung(en)*, edited by Nele Schröder and Lorenz Winkler-Horaček, 57–68. Rahden/Westf.: Verlag Marie Leidorf, 2012.

Pollak 1905

Pollak, Ludwig. "Der rechte Arm des Laokoon", *Römische Mitteilungen* no. 20 (1905): 277–282.

Pontarmé 1901

Pontarmé. "Les doyens au travail." *Le Petit Parisien* 26, no. 9168 (4 December 1901): 1–2.

Pressouyre 1969

Pressouyre, Sylvia. "Les fontes de Primatice à Fontainebleau." *Bulletin Monumental* 127, no. 3 (1969): 223–39.

Pulszky 1852

Pulszky, Francis. "I. On the Progress and Decay of Art; and on the Arrangement of a National Museum." *The Museum of Classical Antiquities. A Quarterly Journal of Ancient Art* 2, no. 5 (March 1852): 1–15.

Pulszky 1875

Pulszky, Ferenc. "A muzeumokról" [About museums]. *Budapesti Szemle*, no. 16 (1875): 241–57. Republished in *Vasárnapi Ujság* vol. 22, no. 28 (11 July 1875): 439; vol.22, no. 29 (18 July 1875): 454–55; vol. 22, no. 30 (25July 1875): 470–71; vol. 22, no. 31 (1 August 1875): 486.

Raabe Cercone 2012

Raabe Cercone, Laura. "Los antiguos yesos de bellas artes." *Kanina, Rev. Artes y Letras, Univer. Costa Rica*, no. 36 (2012): 95–98.

Radványi 2006

Radványi, Orsolya. *Térey Gábor 1864–1927. Egy konzervatív újító* [Gábor Térey 1864–1927. A conservative innovator]. Budapest: Szépművészeti Múzeum, 2006.

Ramsay 1930

Ramsay, G. G. *Juvenal and Persius: with an English Translation by G.G. Ramsay.* London – New York, 1930.

Raumschüssel 1994

Raumschüssel, Ingeborg. "Zur Rekonstruktion des Laokoon durch Georg Treu." In Knoll and Elsner 1994, 277–80.

Rebaudo 2007

Rebaudo, Ludovico. *Il braccio mancante. I restauri del Laoconte (1506–1957).* Trieste: Editreg, 2007.

Regolamento… 1904

Regolamento per l'esecuzione della Legge 12 Giugno 1902, N. 185 sulla conservazione dei monumenti e degli oggetti di antichità ed arte e della Legge 27 Giugno 1903, n. 242 sull'esportazione degli oggetti di antichità ed arte. Rome, 1904

Reinsberg 1980

Reinsberg, Carola. *Studien zur hellenistischen Toreutik: die antiken Gipsabgüsse aus Memphis.* Hildesheim: Gerstenberg, 1980.

Revista Pluma y Lápiz 1901

"El Museo de Copias o la Odio-Sea de Alberto Mac-Kenna." *Revista Pluma y Lápiz* 1, no. 43 (18 September 1901): 20–21.

Reynolds-Kaye 2019

Reynolds-Kaye, Jennifer. "Circulating Casts of the Coatlicue: Mariana Castillo Deball's Unearthing of the Aztec Earth Goddess's History of Reproduction and Display." *Sculpture Journal* 28, no. 3 (2019): 365–80.

Richter and Smith 1984

Richter, Gisela Marie Augusta. *The Portraits of the Greeks.* Abridged and revised by R. R. R. Smith. Oxford: Phaidon Press, 1984.

Rodríguez Castresana 2017

Rodríguez Castresana, Elisa. "Le Musée européen des copies de Charles Blanc comme 'pendant' du Louvre – Charles Blanc's Musée européen des copies as a 'pendant' to the Louvre." *Les Cahiers de l'École du Louvre*, no. 11 (2017): 1–13.

Rome 2006

Laocoonte. Alle origini dei Musei Vaticani. Exhibition catalogue. Musei Vaticani, Rome, 2006–2017. Edited by Francesco Buranelli, Paolo Liverani, and Arnold Nesselrath. Rome: "L'Erma" di Bretschneider, 2006.

Rózsavölgyi 2021

Rózsavölgyi, Andrea. "The Meeting of Past and Present: The Museum of Fine Arts Plaster Cast Collection of Medieval and Renaissance Sculpture." In Szőcs 2021A, 130–57.

Salamon 2016

Salamon, Gáspár. "Az anyagszerűség és a gipsz konfliktusa Maróti Géza oktatási programjaiban" [Truth to materials and plaster in the educational programmes of Géza Maróti]. *Ars Hungarica* 42, no. 2 (2016): 183–93 [English summary on 193].

Scholl 2009

Scholl, Andreas. "Gradus ad Parnassum. Die Erechtheion-Zitate im Treppenhaus und Ihre Bedeutung." In *Neues Museum. Architektur Sammlung. Geschichte*, edited by Elke Blauert and Astrid Bähr, 122–31. Berlin: Staatliche Museen, 2009.

Schreiter 2014

Schreiter, Charlotte. "Competition, Exchange, Comparison: Nineteenth-Century Cast Museums in Transnational Perspective." In *The Museum is Open: Towards a Transnational History of Museums, 1750–1940*, edited by Andrea Meyer and Bénédicte Savoy, 31–43. Berlin and Boston: De Gruyter, 2014.

Schröder 2004

Schröder, Stephan F. *Katalog der antiken Skulpturen des Museo del Prado in Madrid II. Idealplastik.* Mainz: Zabern, 2004.

Schröder and Winkler-Horaček 2012

...von gestren bis morgen... Zur Geschichte der Berliner Gipsabguss-Sammlung(en). Edited by Nele Schröder and Lorenz Winkler Horaček. Rahden/Westf.: Verlag Marie Leidorf GmbH, 2012.

Sipos 2009

Az Erdélyi Múzeum-Egyesület gyűjteményei [The collections of the Transylvanian Museum Association]. Edited by Gábor Sipos. Kolozsvár: Erdélyi Múzeum-Egyesület, 2009.

Stähli 2001

Stähli, Adrian. "Vom Auge des Betrachters entkleidet. Inszenierung des Themas und Konstruktion des Betrachters in der hellenistischen Plastik: Die 'Schlafende Ariadne' im Vatikan." In *Zona Archeologica. Festschrift für Hans Peter Isler zum 60. Geburtstag*, 381–97. Bonn: Habelt, 2001.

Stiassny 1910

Stiassny, Robert. "Vom Gipsmuseum der Wiener Kunstakademie." *Museumskunde*, no. 6 (1910): 1–17.

Süvegh 2021

Süvegh, Eszter. "Laocoön Group." In Szőcs 2021A, 242–43, cat. no. 10.

Szabó 1942

Szabó, T. Attila. *Az Erdélyi Múzeum-Egyesület története és feladatai* [The history and duties of the Transylvanian Museum Association]. Kolozsvár, 1942.

Szakács 2005

Szakács, Béla Zsolt. "Másolás és újraalkotás: a pécsi altemplomi lejáratok domborművei" [Copying and redesigning: reliefs of the entrance-stairs of the crypt in Pécs]. *Ars Hungarica* 33, no. 1 (2005): 241–56.

Szalay 1888

A Magyar Nemzeti Múzeum épülete. A Vallás- és Közokt. m. kir. Minister megbizásából összeállította Szalay Imre osztálytanácsos. A fényképeket és fény-nyomatokat készitette Weinwurm Antal [The building of the Hungarian National Museum. Compiled by department advisor Imre Szalay on behalf of the Hungarian Royal Minister of Religion and Public Education. The photographs and heliogravures were made by Antal Weinwurm]. Budapest: M. Kir. Egyetemi Könyvnyomda, 1888.

Szentesi 2005

Szentesi, Edit. "Az epreskerti szobrászműtermek Parthenón-fríze" [The Parthenon Frieze from the studios in Epreskert]. *Ars Hungarica* 33 (2005): 383–404.

Szentesi 2006A

Szentesi, Edit. "Abgusssammlungen im Ungarischen Nationalmuseum im letzten Drittel des 19. Jahrhunderts: Ist die Geschichte der griechischen oder der ungarischen Skulptur, die praesentiert werden soll?" In *The Nineteenth-Century Process of "Musealization" in Hungary and Europe*, edited by Ernő Marosi, Gábor Klaniczay and Ottó Gecser (Collegium Budapest Workshop Series, 17), 335–55. Budapest: Collegium Budapest, 2006.

Szentesi 2006B

Szentesi, Edit. "Szobrászattörténeti másolatgyűjtemények a Magyar Nemzeti Múzeumban a 19. század utolsó harmadában. I. Pulszky Ferenc görög szobrászattörténeti másolatgyűjteménye" [Art historical plaster cast collections in the Hungarian National Museum in the last third of the 19th century. Part I. Ferenc Pulszky's Greek plaster cast collection]. *Művészettörténeti Értesítő* 55, no. 1 (2006): 1–94.

Szentesi 2006C

Szentesi, Edit. "Görög szobrászattörténeti másolatgyűjtemény a Magyar Nemzeti Múzeumban a 19. század harmadik harmadában" [Plaster cast collection of Greek sculpture in the Hungarian National Museum in the last third of the 19th century]. *Ókor* 5, no. 1 (2006): 20–26.

Szilágyi 1997

Szilágyi, János György. "'Ismerem helyemet' (a másik Pulszky-életrajz). A Fejérváry–Pulszky-gyűjtemény ókori anyaga. Források az antik tárgyak gyűjteményének történetéhez" ["I know my place" (the other Pulszky biography). Ancient material from the Fejérváry–Pulszky collection. Resources for the history of antique collections]. In *Pulszky Ferenc (1814–1897) emlékére*. Exhibition catalogue. Edited by Ernő Marosi et al., 24–36. Budapest: MTA Művészeti Gyűjtemény, 1997.

Szilágyi 2007

Szilágyi, János György. „Pulszky Ferenc (1814–1897). Ulixes Pannoniaban." In *"Emberek és nem frakkok."* *A magyar művészettörténet-írás nagy alakjai*, I. Edited by Markója Csilla and Bardoly István. (*Enigma* no. 47) Budapest: Meridián, 2006. 91–110.

Szőcs 2016

Szőcs, Miriam. "A freibergi Aranykapu gipszmásolat-beépítésének története a Román Csarnokban" [The installation of the Golden Gate of Freiberg's plaster cast in the Romanesque Hall]. *Ars Hungarica* 42, no. 2 (2016): 139–47.

Szőcs 2018A

Újranyitás hetven év után. A Szépművészeti Múzeum Román Csarnokának története [Re-opening after seventy years. The history of the Romanesque Hall of the Museum of Fine Arts]. Edited by Miriam Szőcs. Budapest: Szépművészeti Múzeum, 2018.

Szőcs 2018B

Szőcs, Miriam. "A freibergi Aranykapu másolata a Román Csarnokban" [The copy of Golden Gate of Freiberg in the Romanesque Hall]. In Szőcs 2018A, 128–51.

Szőcs 2021A

Rebirth of a Collection: The Plaster Casts of the Museum of Fine Arts, Budapest in the Renewed Star Fortress in Komárom. Edited by Miriam Szőcs. Budapest: Museum of Fine Arts, 2021.

Szőcs 2021B

Szőcs, Miriam. "Restoration of a Collection. The Museum of Fine Arts' Medieval and Renaissance Plaster Cast Collection after World War II." In Szőcs 2021A, 158–83.

Tali 2021

Tali, Margaret. "Tisztázatlan múltak bizonytalan jövői: a Tehnica Schweiz 'Kék terem' / Uncertain Futures in Unsettled Pasts: Tehnica Schweiz's 'The Blue Room'." In *A kék terem: A projektje / The Blue Room: A Project by Tehnica Schweiz / Gergely László and Péter Rákosi*, edited by Eszter Lázár and Tehnica Schweiz, 19–31. Berlin–Budapest: Archive Books 2021.

Tar 2007

Tar, Ibolya. "A klasszika filológus Csengery János" [The classical philologist János Csengery]. *Magyar Pedagógia* 107, no. 1 (2007): 49–55.

Tentative List of Objects... 1891

Metropolitan Museum of Art. Tentative List of Objects Desirable for a Collection of Casts Sculptural and Architectural intended to illustrate the History of Plastic Art. New York, 1891.

The Art Institute of Chicago... 1904

The Art Institute of Chicago. Twenty-fifth Annual Report, June 1903–1904. Chicago, 1904.

The Art Institute of Chicago... 1954–1955

The Art Institute of Chicago. Quarterly Annual Reports. Chicago, 1954–1955.

Tóth F. 2007

Tóth, Ferenc. "Pulszky Károly tragédiája új dokumentumok tükrében" [The tragedy of Károly Pulszky in the light of new documents], *Művészettörténeti Értesítő* 56, no. 2 (2007): 233–58.

Tóth F. 2012

Tóth, Ferenc. *Donátorok és képtárépítők. A Szépművészeti Múzeum modern külföldi gyűjteményének kialakulása* [Donators and creators of galleries. The creation of the Modern International Collection of the Museum of Fine Arts]. Budapest: Szépművészeti Múzeum, 2012.

Tóth F. 2016

Tóth, Ferenc. "International Exhibitions of the National Hungarian Fine Arts Society." In *The First Golden Age. Painting in the Austro–Hungarian Monarchy and the Műcsarnok*. Exhibititon catalogue, Műcsarnok, Budapest, 2016, edited by András Bán, 196–209. Budapest: Műcsarnok, 2016.

Tóth S. 2010

Tóth, Sándor. *Román kori kőfaragványok a Magyar Nemzeti Galéria Régi Magyar Gyűjteményében* [Romanesque stone carvings in the Old Hungarian Collection of the Hungarian National Gallery]. Budapest: Magyar Nemzeti Galéria, 2010.

Trusted 2006

Trusted, Marjorie. "In all Cases of Difference Adopt Signor Riaño's View: Collecting Spanish Decorative Arts at South Kensington in the Late Nineteenth Century." *Journal of the History of Collections* 18, no. 2 (2006): 225–36.

Trusted 2012

Trusted, Marjorie. "Reproduction as Spectacle, Education and Inspiration. The Cast Courts at the Victoria and Albert Museum: Past, Present and Future." In *Gipsabgüsse und antike Skulpturen. Präsentation und Kontext*, edited by Charlotte Schreiter, 355–72. Berlin, 2012.

Turco 1961

Turco, T. *Il Gesso. Lavorazione Trasformazione Impieghi*. Milan: Hoepli, 1961.

Vaisse 1976

Vaisse, Pierre. "Charles Blanc und das 'Musée des Copies'." *Zeitschrift für Kunstgeschichte*, no. 39 (1976): 54–66.

Valeri 2019

Valeri, Claudia. "L'Arianna addormentata dei Musei Vaticani, già Cleopatra in Belvedere." *La Rivista di Engramma* 163 (March 2019), 12–33.

Vedovello 1992

Vedovello, Giovanna Giacomelli. "I Gessi." In *Il Museo della Certosa di Pavia. Catalogo generale*, edited by Barbara Fabjan and Pietro C. Marani, 127–45. Florence: Cantini, 1992.

Verzeichnis der Abgüsse 1871

Verzeichnis der im Königlichen Museum zu Berlin käuflichen Gyps-Abgüsse. Berlin, 1871.

Vidéky 1897

Vidéky, János. *A Fővárosi Községi Iparrajziskola tudósítványa az 1896–1897. tanév* végén [Report of the Budapest Metropolitan Industrial Drawing School at the end of school year 1897–1897]. Budapest: Pesti Könyvnyomda-Részvény-Társaság, 1897.

Vincze 2014

Vincze, Zoltán. *A kolozsvári régészeti iskola a Pósta Béla-korszakban (1899–1919)* [The Archaeological School in Kolozsvár in the era of Béla Pósta (1899–1919)]. Kolozsvár: Erdélyi Múzeum-Egyesület, 2014.

Wagstaffe Yapp 1853

Wagstaffe Yapp, George. *Art Education at Home and Abroad. The British Museum, the National Gallery, and the Proposed Industrial University*. London: Chapman & Hall, 1853.

Wallach 1998

Wallach, Allan. "The American Cast Museum: An Episode in the History of the Institutional Definition of Art." In *Exhibiting Contradiction: Essays on the Art Museum in the United States*, edited by Allan Wallach, 38–56. Boston: University of Massachusetts Press, 1998.

Wilson 2010

Wilson, David M. "A Hungarian in London: Pulszky's 1851 Lecture." *Journal of the History of Collections* 22, no. 2 (2010): 271–78.

Winkler-Horaček 2022A

Winkler-Horaček, Lorenz. "The Fate of the Berlin Plaster Cast Collections: From Veneration to Destruction, Defacement, and Disposal." In Alexandridis and Winkler-Horaček 2022, 349–74.

Winkler-Horaček 2022B

Winkler-Horaček, Lorenz. "Destroy the Copy? Destroy the Copy! A History of (Non-)appreciation." In Alexandridis and Winkler-Horaček 2022, 527–77.

Wlassics 1900

Wlassics, Gyula. *A Vallás- és Közoktatásügyi M. Kir. Minister jelentése a Szépművészeti Muzeum ügyében* [Report of the Royal Minister for Religion and Public Education concerning the Museum of Fine Arts]. Budapest: Pesti Könyvnyomda-Részvény-Társaság, 1900.

Wolf 2002

Wolf, Claudia Marie. *Die schlafende Ariadne im Vatikan. Ein hellenistischer Statuentypus und seine Rezeption*. Hamburg: Kovač, 2002.

World's Columbian Exposition... 1893

World's Columbian Exposition. Official Publication. Revised Department of Fine Arts. Chicago: W. B. Conkey Company, 1893.

Zahle 2010

Zahle, Jan. "Lacoön in Scandinavia. Uses and Workshops 1578 onwards." In Frederiksen and Marchand 2010, 143–61.

Zanker 2012

Zanker, Paul. "Reading Images Without Texts on Roman Sarcophagi." *RES: Anthropology and Aesthetics* 61–62 (Spring–Autumn 2012): 167–77.

Zervos 1946

Zervos, Christian. "Statement by Picasso: 1935." In *Picasso: Fifty Years of His Art,* edited by Alfred H. Barr, Jr., 272–74. New York: The Metropolitan Museum of Art, 1946.

Abbreviations

Archives MFAB: Central Archives of the Museum of Fine Arts, Budapest
BME: Budapest University of Technology and Economics
BME-OMIKK: Budapest University of Technology and Economics – National Technical Information Centre and Library
MAK: Museum für angewandte Kunst, Vienna
MFAB: Museum of Fine Arts, Budapest
MNM ÉRT: Hungarian National Museum, Department of Coins and Antiquities
NMCSC: National Museum Conservation and Storage Centre, Budapest

Illustration Credits

Page 2, 4, 105, and 155: Cast of Desiderio Settignano's *Tomb of Carlo Marsuppini* (details)

Page 6: Cast of Andrea del Verrocchio's *Equestrian Statue of Bartolomeo Colleoni* (detail)

Page 8: Cast of Benedetto da Maiano's *Portrait of Matthias Corvinus* (detail)

Page 57: Cast of Giovanni Antonio Amadeo's *Tomb of Medea Colleoni* (detail)

Page 73: Cast of Claus Sluter's *Well of Moses* (detail)

All the above mentioned artworks are part of the plaster cast collection of the Museum of Fine Arts, Budapest and are exhibited in the Star Fortress, Komárom. Photos: Gellért Áment and Áron Harasztos

Eckart Marchand

"The best laid schemes ...": The Politics of the Universal Museum and the Vicissitudes of their Plaster Cast Collections at the Turn of the Twentieth Century (pages 12–25)

Fig. 1: Wiener Photographen-Association (Verlag), Wien Museum, inv. 75608/7. Photo: György (Johann Justus Georg) Klösz (Kloess)
Fig. 2: MTVA. Photo: Zoltán Máthé
Fig. 3: The Metropolitan Museum of Art, New York
Fig. 4: Wikimedia Commons. Photo: Hermann Wendler, 2010
Fig. 5: Library and Archive of the Hungarian Academy of Sciences. Photo: Ede Ellinger
Fig. 6: Museum of Fine Arts, Budapest
Fig. 7: Enterreno, Chile

Miriam Szőcs

The *Colleoni Monument* and the *Medici Tombs*: Monumental Renaissance Casts in the Museum of Fine Arts in Budapest (pages 26–39)

Fig. 1: Museum of Fine Arts, Budapest
Fig. 2: Museum of Fine Arts, Budapest
Fig. 3: Museum of Fine Arts, Budapest
Fig. 4: MTVA Sajtó- és Fotóarchívum [Media and Photo Archive]
Fig. 5: MTVA Sajtó- és Fotóarchívum [Media and Photo Archive]
Fig. 6: Museum of Fine Arts, Budapest
Fig. 7: Museum of Fine Arts, Budapest
Fig. 8: Museum of Fine Arts, Budapest
Fig. 9: Museum of Fine Arts, Budapest
Fig. 10: Museum of Fine Arts, Budapest
Fig. 11: Museum of Fine Arts, Budapest. Photo: Gellért Áment, 2021

Flavia Berizzi

From Northern Italy to Hungary: Medieval and Renaissance Monumental Casts from the Museo Campi Carlo in Milan to the Museum of Fine Arts in Budapest (pages 40–57)

Fig. 1: Superintendence of Archaeology, Fine Arts and Landscape for the metropolitan city of Milan. Source: *Riproduzione d'oggetti d'arte Campi Carlo,* Milano [Illustrated album 1884–1887]
Fig. 2: (1) Superintendence of Archaeology, Fine Arts and Landscape for the metropolitan city of Milan; (2 and 6) New Library, State Archive of Turin; (3 and 4) Kunstbibliothek, Staatliche Museen, Berlin; (5) Cantonal Library of Bellinzona; (7) Victoria and Albert Museum Archive, London; (8 and 9) State Archive of Canton Ticino, Bellinzona
Fig. 3: State Archive of Canton Ticino, Bellinzona Source: *Riproduzione d'oggetti d'arte Campi Carlo,* Milano [Illustrated album 1898–1900]
Fig. 4: Beltrami 1910
Fig. 5: Beltrami 1910
Fig. 6: Beltrami 1910
Fig. 7: Museum of Fine Arts, Budapest
Fig. 8: National Széchényi Library, Budapest. Source: *Vasárnapi Ujság* 67, no. 23 (1920): 265.
Fig. 9: *Gipsoteca Vallardi* n. d.
Fig. 10: Museum of Fine Arts, Budapest

Jean-Marc Hofman

Generation and Regeneration of the Cast Collections of the Musée de Sculpture Comparée, Paris (pages 58–73)

Fig. 1: © Cité de l'architecture et du patrimoine / MMF
Fig. 2: Victoria and Albert Museum, London
Fig. 3: © Cité de l'architecture et du patrimoine / MMF
Fig. 4: Victoria and Albert Museum, London
Fig. 5: © Cité de l'architecture et du patrimoine / MMF
Fig. 6: London Metropolitan Archives (City of London)
Fig. 7: London Metropolitan Archives (City of London)
Fig. 8: © Cité de l'architecture et du patrimoine / MMF
Fig. 9: The New York Public Library
Fig. 10: The Metropolitan Museum of Art, New York
Fig. 11: The Art Institute of Chicago
Fig. 12: The Art Institute of Chicago
Fig. 13: The Art Institute of Chicago / Art Resource, NY / Scala, Florence
Fig. 14: The Art Institute of Chicago / Art Resource, NY / Scala, Florence
Fig. 15: Library of Congress, Prints and Photographs Division, Washington, D.C.

Géza Andó and Eszter Süvegh

The Ways of the Casts: Plaster Casts of Antiquities in Budapest and Kolozsvár (today Cluj-Napoca, Romania) (pages 74–87)

Fig. 1: Inv. 54.312, Hungarian National Museum, Budapest
Fig. 2: National Archives of Hungary, Budapest Source: Szalay 1888, plate II
Fig. 3: Arcanum. Source: *Magyar Salon*, vol. 8 (1887–1888/I): 465.
Fig. 4: Inv. no. 32913, Museum of Fine Arts, Budapest
Fig. 5: Photo: Melinda Mihály, 2021
Fig. 6: Photo: László Mátyus, 2021
Fig. 7: Museum of Fine Arts, Budapest
Fig. 8: Museum of Fine Arts, Budapest
Fig. 9: Source: Raumschüssel 1994, fig. 2.

Eszter Hajós-Baku and Beáta Szűts

A Brief History of the Plaster Cast Collection
of the Department of Graphics, Form, and Design
at the Budapest University of Technology and Economics (pages 88–105)

Fig. 1:   Photo: Beáta Szűts
Fig. 2:   BME, Archive of the Department of Graphics, Form, and Design,
          inv. 300.061. Photo: Eszter Hajós-Baku
Fig. 3:   BME, Department of Graphics, Form, and Design,
          inv. 200.006. Photo: István Frigyes Váli
Fig. 4:   BME, Department of Graphics, Form, and Design,
          inv. 200.248. Photo: Beáta Szűts
Fig. 5:   BME, Department of Graphics, Form, and Design,
          inv. 200.228. Photo: Beáta Szűts
Fig. 6:   BME, Department of Graphics, Form, and Design,
          inv. 200.079. Photo: István Frigyes Váli
Fig. 7:   BME, Department of Graphics, Form, and Design,
          inv. 200.115/1. Photo: István Frigyes Váli
Fig. 8:   BME, Department of Graphics, Form, and Design,
          inv. 200.156. Photo: István Frigyes Váli
Fig. 9:   BME, Department of Graphics, Form, and Design,
          inv. 200.215. Photo: István Frigyes Váli
Fig.10:   BME, Department of Graphics, Form, and Design,
          inv. 200.081. Photo: István Frigyes

Júlia Katona

Nineteenth-Century Constructions and Monument Reconstruction
in Hungary in the Context of Educational Plaster Cast Collections:
A Case Study with Special Focus on the Romanesque Hall
of the Museum of Fine Arts, Budapest (pages 106–17)

Fig. 1:   Museum of Fine Arts, Budapest. Photo: Gellért Áment, 2018
Fig. 2:   Museum of Fine Arts, Budapest. Photo: Gellért Áment, 2018
Fig. 3:   Museum of Fine Arts, Budapest. Photo: Gellért Áment, 2018
Fig. 4:   Diocese of Pécs, Christian Heritage Research Institute
Fig. 5:   Museum of Fine Arts, Budapest. Photo: Gellért Áment, 2018
Fig. 6:   Hungarian University of Fine Arts, Library,
          Archive and Art Collection, Budapest
Fig. 7:   Hungarian University of Fine Arts, Library,
          Archive and Art Collection, Budapest
Fig. 8:   Hungarian University of Fine Arts, Library,
          Archive and Art Collection, Budapest
Fig. 9:   Inv. 2015.600.057, Schola Graphidis Art Collection, Budapest
Fig. 10: Hungarian University of Fine Arts, Library,
          Archive and Art Collection, Budapest
Fig. 11: Hungarian University of Fine Arts, Library,
          Archive and Art Collection, Budapest

Rune Frederiksen

The Role of Ancient Plaster Casts in Ancient Art:
The Written Evidence (pages 118–29)

Fig. 1:   Photo: T. Antonov
Fig. 2:   Photo: Jonas Heide Smith
Fig. 3:   Photo: Friends of the Royal Cast Collection, Copenhagen
Fig. 4:   Inv. 21355, Staatliche Museen zu Berlin, Ägyptisches
          Museum und Papyrussammlung, photo: Sandra Steiß
Fig. 5:   Inv. 6009 and 6010. Photo: Profimedia.hu / Alamy
Fig. 6:   Source: Landwehr 1985, Plate 5a
Fig. 7a: Inv. y1948-52, Princeton University Art Collection
Fig. 7b: Inv. y1948-52, Princeton University Art Collection
Fig. 8:   Inv. 2575. Photo: Rune Frederiksen

Lorenz Winkler-Horaček

Appreciation and Rejection: Plaster Casts in the Discourse
of Copy and Original. With an Excursus on the *Sleeping
Ariadne* in the Berlin Cast Collection (pages 130–43)

Fig. 1:   Staatliche Museen zu Berlin,
          Kupferstichkabinett. Photo: J. P. Anders
Fig. 2:   Abguss-Sammlung Antiker Plastik Berlin. Photo: Antonia Weiße
Fig. 3:   Abguss-Sammlung Antiker Plastik Berlin. Photo: Hans R. Goette
Fig. 4:   Walther Amelung, *Die Sculpturen des Vaticanischen
          Museums* II (Berlin: Reimer 1908), Plate 57
Fig. 5:   Museo Nacional del Prado, Madrid
Fig. 6:   Photo and editing: Lorenz Winkler-Horaček
Fig. 7:   Photo and editing: Lorenz Winkler-Horaček
Fig. 8:   Note and scan: Thomas Schelper
Fig. 9:   Photo: Thomas Schelper
Fig. 10: Photo: Thomas Schelper and Lorenz Winkler-Horaček
Fig. 11: Abguss-Sammlung Antiker Plastik Berlin

Marjorie (Holly) Trusted

The Making and Meaning of Plaster Casts
in the Nineteenth Century: Their Future in the
Twenty-First Century (pages 144–55)

Fig. 1:   Victoria and Albert Museum, London
Fig. 2:   Victoria and Albert Museum, London
Fig. 3:   Photo: Marjorie (Holly) Trusted
Fig. 4:   Photo: Marjorie (Holly) Trusted
Fig. 5:   Photo: Marjorie (Holly) Trusted
Fig. 6:   Photo: Marjorie (Holly) Trusted

Index of Names

A

Akhenaten 122
Alfonso II of Naples 152
Amadeo, Giovanni Antonio 51
Apollonius 127
Aristogeiton 122, 125
Aristotle 123, 128
Arrondelle, Auguste Alexandre 65
Arrondelle, Eugène Denis 64–66, 72
Aurelius, Marcus 20, 23

B

Balduccio, Giovanni di 51
Ballu, Roger 70
Banks Skinner, Arthur 149, 154
Barros Grez, Daniel 21–22, 24
Barsugli, Giuseppe 61
Baudot, Anatole de 72
Baum, Julius 135, 143
Beatty, John W. 70
Beltrami, Luca 46–48, 52, 54
Blackstone, Timothy Beach 72
Blanc, Charles 17, 19, 21–23
Bode, Wilhelm von 20, 149
Bötticher, Karl 134
Brucciani, Domenico 64, 81
Brukenthal, Samuel 86
Brunelleschi, Filippo 152
Burckhardt, Jacob 29
Burns, Robert 23
Busti, Agostino [Bambaia] 48

C

Campi, Carlo 42, 44–48, 50–52,
54–55, 96–97, 156
Campi, Emma 46, 51
Campione, Giovanni da 48
Carnegie, Andrew 70
Cazzaniga, Tommaso 51
Chambers, Sir William 148, 150
Chennevières-Pointel,
Charles-Philippe de 19
Chrysippos 126
Cleanthes 128
Cole, Henry Hardy 66, 68, 148, 154
Colleoni, Bartolomeo 19–20, 28–30,
33–39, 45, 50, 52, 55
Colleoni, Medea 45, 48, 50, 54, 56

Cornacchini, Agostino 84
Csengeri, János 78, 80–81, 86
Curtius, Ernst 132, 143

D

Daniele da Volterra 142
Davioud, Gabriel Jean Antoine 52
Delamotte, Philip Henry 66, 72
Desachy, Alexandre 64–66, 72
Desachy, Joséphine Théodorine 72
Donatello 28, 68, 95–96, 98–99, 149, 152
Dürer, Albrecht 17

E

Elek, Artúr 24
Este, Beatrice de 46, 48, 56

F

Feigenspan, Christian 38
Fellner, Sándor 114
Foix, Gaston de 48, 56
Franchi, Giovanni 150
Francis I, King of France 137
Franz Joseph, Emperor of Austria
and King of Hungary 23, 78, 80, 87
Friedrichs, Carl 137, 140, 143

G

Garnier, Charles 52
Gerber, August 31–32, 38–39, 84, 87, 95–96
Gerecze, Péter 111
Ghiberti, Lorenzo 29, 36, 150, 152
Giorgione 17
Girardon, François 84

H

Hampel, József 19, 81
Harsdorph, Caspar Frederik 121
Hauszmann, Alajos 99, 101, 103–4
Hekler, Antal 39, 78, 82–83, 87
Herzog, Fülöp 30, 109, 117
Hittorf, Jakob Ignaz 137

I

Isidoros 123
Ives, Halsey Cooley 69

J

Jacquet, François Henri 65, 72
Jones, Owen 64–66
Juhbál, Károly 100
Juvenal 128

K

Kammerer, Ernő 20, 31, 35, 38, 46–48,
50, 52, 56, 78, 81
Karácson, Mihály 100
Kelety, Gusztáv 93
Knoedler, Roland F. 70
Koons, Jeff 142
Köhn, Heinz 135, 143

L

Langer, Ignácz 109–12, 114, 116–17
Laurana, Francesco 152
Layard, Austen Henry 14, 23
Lelli, Giuseppe 45, 56
Lelli, Oronzio 45, 56
Longo, Giuseppe 35
Louis-Philippe I., King of the French 65
Lucian of Samosata 127
Lux, Kálmán 33–36, 39, 86
Lysippus 124
Lysistratus of Sicyon 124, 129
Lützow, Carl von 19–24
Lützow, Heinrich Graf von 35

M

Mackenna Subercaseaux, Alberto
21–22, 24–25
Maffioli, Alberto 51
Maiano, Benedetto da 29–30, 38
Malpieri, Cesare 54
Malpieri, Leopoldo 54
Malzieux, Auguste 61–62
Mambretti, Giovanni 51
Marinetti, Filippo Tommaso 134, 143
Maróti, Géza 97, 103
Martinelli, Felice Napoleone 77, 86–87
Mary of Teck, Queen of United Kingdom 152
Massey Rhind, John 38
Medici, Giuliano de', Duke of Nemours
28–32, 35–39
Medici, Lorenzo de', Duke of Urbino
28–32, 35–39
Melocco, Miklós 37

Mengs, Anton Raphael 149
Mersseman, Jacques Olivier Marie de 65
Michelangelo (Michelangelo Buonarroti) 28–32, 35–39, 84, 86, 98–99, 149–50, 152
Mikó, Imre 87
Módy, Péter 103
Montorsoli, Giovanni Angelo 82, 84
Moretti, Gaetano 50
Moro, Ludovico il 46, 48, 56

N

Ney, Ede 109

O

Olfers, Ignaz Maria von 132
Ongaro, Massimilano 50

P

Pausanias 127
Phidias 127
Philostratus 127, 129
Picasso, Pablo 134, 173
Pierotti, Edorardo 45–48, 51–52, 161
Pierotti, Pietro 45–48, 51–52, 161
Pisano, Nicola 152
Pittacus 128–29
Pliny the Elder 123–24
Plutarch 124, 127
Pollak, Ludwig 84, 87, 165, 167
Pósta, Béla 81, 159, 161, 172
Pouzadoux, Edouard Charles 70, 72
Pouzadoux, Jean 68
Praxiteles 127
Primaticcio, Francesco 137, 139, 141–42, 139, 159
Proust, Antonin 69
Ptolemy I, King of Egypt 124, 127
Pulszky, Ferenc 17–25, 28, 76–77, 80–81, 86–87, 132, 164, 166, 168, 170, 173
Pulszky, Károly 19, 162, 171

Q

Quercia, Jacopo della 152

R

Raphael 17, 20, 149
Rauscher, Lajos 35, 94, 99
Reichenberger, József 86
Riaño, Juan Facundo 14, 23, 163, 172
Riccio, Andrea 50
Riemenschneider, Tilman 149
Robbia, Andrea della 97
Robbia, Luca della 98
Romani, Leonino 48

S

Sauvageot, Louis 72
Schickedanz, Albert 30, 109, 117
Schroth, Alexander 116
Schroth, Moriz 116
Schulek, Frigyes 114
Scott, George Gilbert 62
Settignano, Desiderio da 98
Sforza, Ippolita 152
Sironi, Silvio 47–50, 52
Somssich, József 35
Stoczek, József 100
Stoß, Veit 96
Stüler, Friedrich August 134
Subercaseaux Vicuña, Ramòn 25
Szalay, Imre 28, 170, 175
Szandház, Károly 100

T

Térey, Gábor 20, 23–24, 29–30, 33, 36, 38, 45, 48, 168
Theophrastus 123
Thiers, Adophe 17, 19
Thomas II, Count of Savoy 48, 56
Thutmose 121
Timmons, Edward J. Finley 70
Trajan 147–48, 152–53
Trefort, Ágost 28
Treu, Georg 84, 160, 165, 168

U

Uhrl, Ferenc 100

V

Van Dyck, Anthony 17
Velázquez, Diego 17
Velten, Ernest Albert 64
Verrocchio, Andrea del 28, 50, 68, 98–99, 160
Victoria, Queen of the United Kingdom of Great Britain and Ireland 152
Vincze, Zoltán 81, 87, 172
Viollet-le-Duc, Eugène Emmanuel 52, 60–63, 66, 68, 70, 72, 114

W

Werner, Bruno E. 135
Wlassics, Gyula 19–20, 23–24, 28–29, 38–39, 173
Wolters, Paul 137, 140, 143, 162

Z

Zala, György 97

Front and back cover:
Cast of Nicola Pisano's *Pulpit*
from the Siena Cathedral (detail)

Inside of the front cover:
Cast of *A Statue of an Unknown Ruler*
(original: 230–150 BC) during the installation in the
Star Fortress in Komárom

Inside of the back cover:
Cast of Andrea del Verrocchio's
Equestrian Statue of Bartolomeo Colleoni
during the installation in the Star Fortress in Komárom

Page 179:
Cast of Andrea del Verrocchio's
Equestrian Statue of Bartolomeo Colleoni (detail of the pedestal)

All the above mentioned artworks are part of the plaster cast collection
of the Museum of Fine Arts, Budapest and are exhibited in the
Star Fortress, Komárom. Photos: Gellért Áment and Áron Harasztos

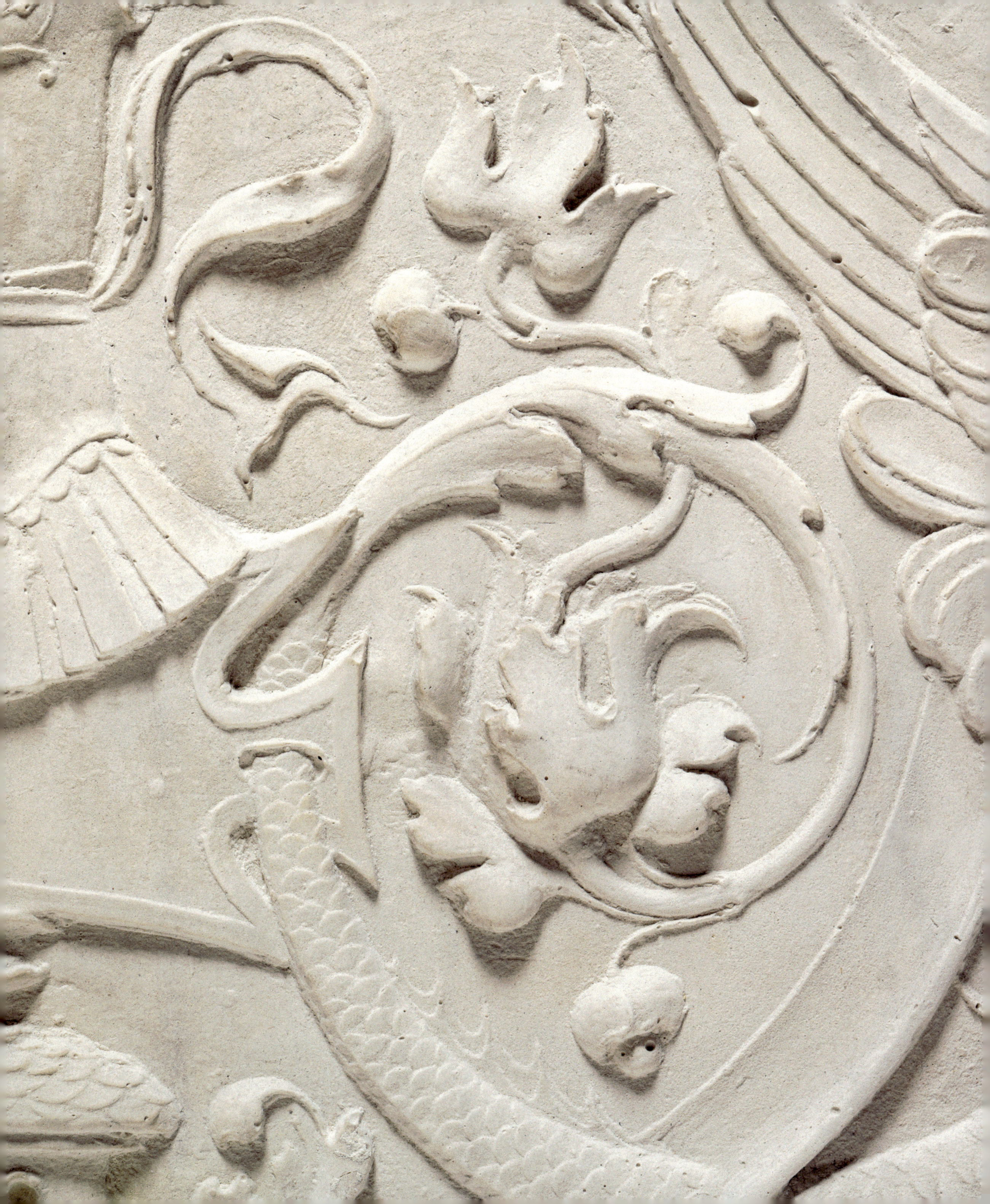

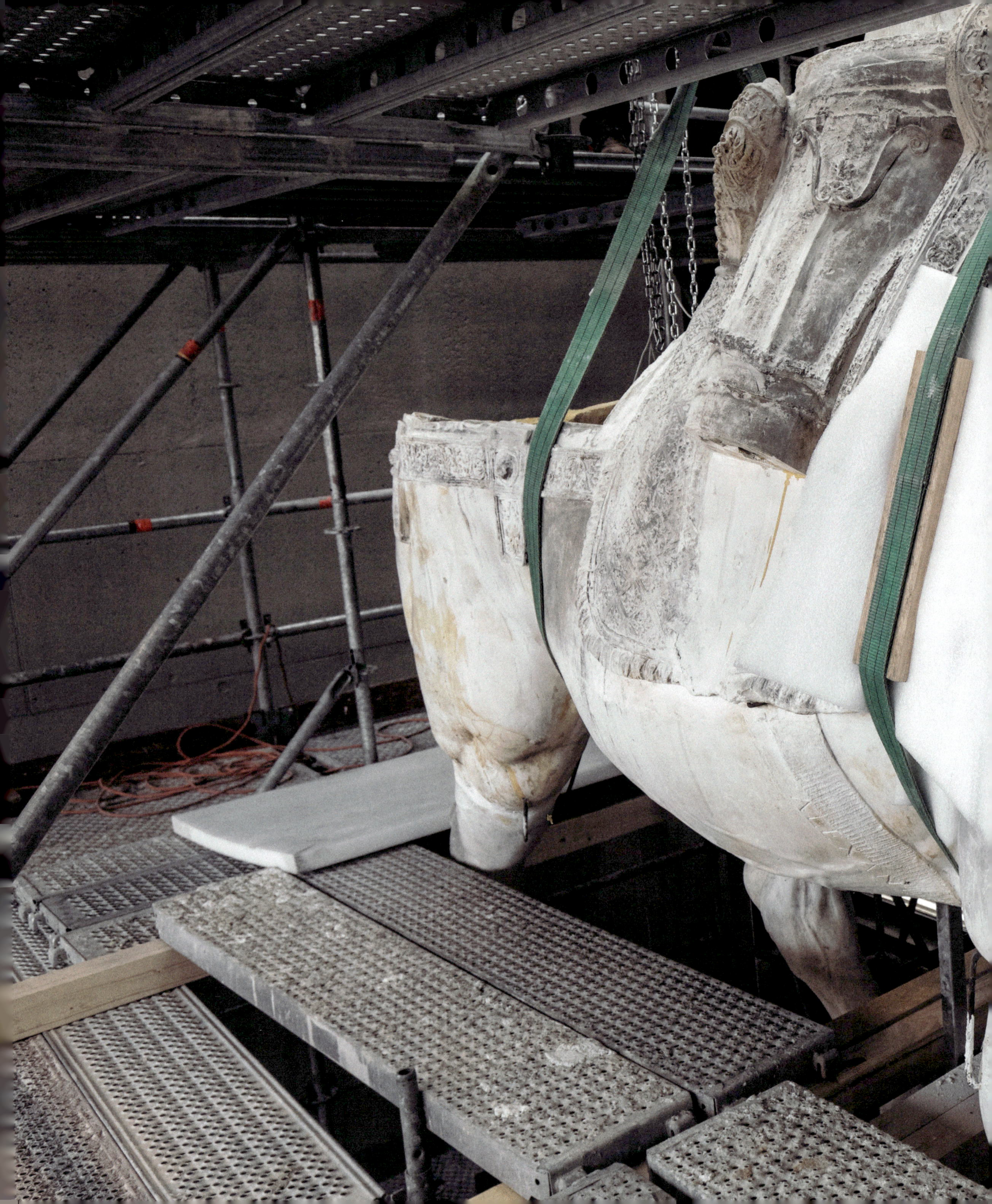